MARRIAGES
Northampton County, Virginia
1660-1854

Third Revised Edition

Abstracted and Compiled by
Jean M. Mihalyka

HERITAGE BOOKS
2008

HERITAGE BOOKS
AN IMPRINT OF HERITAGE BOOKS, INC.

Books, CDs, and more—Worldwide

For our listing of thousands of titles see our website
at
www.HeritageBooks.com

Published 2008 by
HERITAGE BOOKS, INC.
Publishing Division
100 Railroad Ave. #104
Westminster, Maryland 21157

Copyright © 1991, 1995, 2000 Jean M. Mihalyka

Other books by the author:

Graven Stones: Inscriptions from Lower Accomack County, Virginia, Including Liberty and Parksley Cemeteries. Third Edition
Jean Merritt Mihalyka and Faye Downing Wilson

All rights reserved. No part of this book may be reproduced or transmitted in any form or by any means, electronic or mechanical, including photocopying, recording or by any information storage and retrieval system without written permission from the author, except for the inclusion of brief quotations in a review.

International Standard Book Number: 978-0-7884-1506-7

TABLE OF CONTENTS

	Page
Acknowledgements	v
Preface	vii
Illustrative Documents	xiii
Abbreviations	xxi
Explanation of Entries	xxiii
MARRIAGES	1
Ministers	129
Clerks of Court	131
Free Negro Surnames	133
Statistics	135
References	137
INDEX	139

ACKNOWLEDGEMENTS

Grateful appreciation is expressed to the Clerk of the Northampton County, Virginia Circuit Court, Clyde E. Gibb and to his Deputies, Estelle Murphy and Mary Linda Elliott. They have provided access to the numerous records used, many of which were not on the open shelves. Their help and cooperation was always given unstintingly.

The compiler feels especially fortunate to have been able to call upon a host of research scholars for advice and information; to each she is ever indebted. To Brooks Miles Barnes, Librarian, Eastern Shore Public Library, whose knowledge of and willingness to share the resources of the Eastern Shore of Virginia Room is unparalleled. To Gail S. Terry, historian and archivist, whose instruction as to the handling and preservation of documents made it possible to handle and store the many fragile papers utilizing safe, state-of-the-art methods. To John M. Hemphill, II, historian, whose knowledge of colonial Virginia, especially its courts, provided answers to some of the questions which arose during this project. I am further indebted to John and Gail and Miles Barnes for reading sections of this compilation. John Frederick Dorman, F.A.S.G., historian and genealogist, also graciously agreed to read and review the final draft and for this the undersigned is most appreciative. To John B. Bell, Clarence E. Doughty, David Scott, Ruth E. Williams and E. Spencer Wise, genealogical scholars who so willingly searched their voluminous research files in order to provide data to clarify names, dates and confused entries. To Baxley T. Tankard, attorney, who searched the collection of very old volumes in his law library for needed references. To Kirk Mariner, an authority on the Shore's religious history who identified the denomination to which many of the ministers belonged. To Nora Miller Turman, the acknowledged doyenne of Eastern Shore genealogists, who always allowed me to reach into her storehouse of data for that one elusive fact and who continually encouraged me in this endeavor. To Lila H. Schmidt whose flawless typing expedited the realization of this project. Lastly but not least, to my husband, Dr. Eugene E. Mihalyka who tolerated months of a cluttered library, late meals and frequent disruptions to the usual routine.

Jean M. Mihalyka
"Cherry-Core"
Cheriton, Virginia 23316

September, 1990

PREFACE

Since its publication in 1929, *The Marriage License Bonds of Northampton County, Virginia From 1706 to 1854*, Listed and Indexed by Stratton Nottingham, has been the standard source for Northampton County marriages. Data for this splendid reference was taken from the original bonds which were required prior to 1850. These documents are in the Northampton County Clerk's Office. In compiling his book, Nottingham abstracted some marriages, for which he found no bonds from the collection of ministers' returns (1791-1854) also in the Clerk's Office. But there are minister returns for nearly two thirds of the marriage bonds which Nottingham omitted from his compilation. They are a valuable resource. Each gives the exact marriage date, the minister's name, an indication of the possible religious persuasion of the couple and often some details not shown on the bond. Unfortunately the manuscript returns have been used only rarely by the average researcher. While the bond shows that a marriage was seriously intended, the minister's return is proof that the marriage did take place.[1]

The initial intention for this compilation was to add to the bond entry any pertinent data found on the minister's return when one exists. However, good research technique dictated that before adding the data, the bond entry should be checked against the original document.[2] When various errors and omissions became apparent, it seemed appropriate to review all of the Nottingham entries. Every effort was made during this process to record all witnesses and to abstract all genealogical data from the age certification and consent papers attached to many of the original bonds. The undertaking has evolved into a thorough revision of the 1929 bond listings. This is to detract in no way from the value of Stratton Nottingham's *The Marriage License Bonds of Northampton County* which has been of such immense help to researchers for so many years.

With this new direction in mind it was further decided to include marriage data from other available sources and to make the entries as complete as possible. The General Assembly directed as early as 1631/1632 that "ministers or churchwardens of every parish at midsomer quarter cort on the first day of June make yearlie theire presentments with a register of all burials, christenings and marriages..."[3] It was not until 1659/1660 that the law required "in the month of March in every yeare a true certificate unto the clerke of every county on the intent the same may there remaine on record for ever."[4] Unfortunately only two such lists, both from the 1660's, were recorded in the Order Book.[5] This general lack of compliance with the earlier laws was addressed by Governor Lord Howard of Effingham, who, in a lengthy and detailed Proclamation in July, 1686 did "Strictly charge and Require the Vestry of every Respective Parish which hath hitherto neglected or Omitted the providing such a necessary Booke as a Register forthwith to provide a Register, wherein to Register and Incert all marriages, Births and Burials which happen within the precincts of their parish ... and Annually on the sixth day of Aprill General Court to Returne an account thereof to the Secretaryes Office ..." His Proclamation further directed that fines be laid so that "this most necessary and usefull Law may be noe Longer Neglected, nor Omitted ..."[6] No such Registers are known to exist today. Only some few licenses issued and recorded by the clerks during the 1720's through the 1740's remain. They, of course, and the above noted 1660's lists, have been included in this compilation.[7]

Only scattered lists submitted by the ministers in the 18th century have survived for the years prior to the disestablishment of the Church of England. Most probably the clerks recorded ministers' returns in an earlier register similar to that which does exist, dated 1791-1854, and which has been used in this study. Even the number of marriage bonds which exist for the pre-Revolutionary War years is distressingly small. Those which do exist for the first half of the 18th century number less than two or three per year. It must be understood that marriage banns could be published in church as an alternative to posting a bond but if so the ministers should have submitted their returns to the court. It appears that a good many documents simply have not survived.

A brief overview of the marriage laws in Virginia may be helpful to clarify the relationship between banns, bonds and licenses.[8] An act of the Grand Assembly in James City in September, 1632, was a "revisal and cleerer explanation of former acts" and stipulated that "noe mynister shall celebrate matrymony betweene any persons without a facultie or lycense graented by the Governor except the banes of matrymony have beene first published three severall Sondayes or holidayes in the tyme of divine service in the parish churches where the sayd persons dwell accordinge to the Booke of Common Prayer ..."[9] Later in the century, the clerk of court instead of the Governor was authorized to issue the licenses.

At the October, 1705, session of the General Assembly, "An Act Concerning Marriages" was enacted which required "That all licenses for marriage shall be issued by the clerk of the court of the county where the feme shall have her usual residence and by him only ... he shall take bond to our sovereign lady the Queen ..., with good surety in the penalty of fifty pounds current money in Virginia, under condition, that there is no lawful cause to obstruct the marriage, for which the license shall be desired; and each clerk failing herein, shall forfeit and pay fifty pounds current money of Virginia: And if either of the persons ... shall be under the age of one and twenty years, and not theretofore married, the consent of the parent or guardian of every such person ... shall be personally given before the said clerk, or signified under the hand and seal[10] of the said parent or guardian, and attested by two witnesses: All which being done, the clerk shall write the license, and shall certify specially the said bond ..."[11] The Act prescribed a penalty of 500 pounds current money and imprisonment, without bail, for one year for any minister in breech of the marriage law. Regulations were stated for the publication of banns, penalties on females between 12 and 16 years for marrying without consent, penalties on ministers for marrying servants without leave of owner and for free persons marrying with a servant. A fee schedule was included for the dues for marriage licenses: to the governor, to the clerk of the county court, to the minister and to the reader of banns. In addition, the clerk of each court was ordered to annually send to the governor an account of the marriage licenses issued and the dues collected. There was no requirement that a duplicate list be filed in the county.

The marriage act of 1705 was detailed and specific. During the next century and a half, minor modifications were made but the 1705 legislation remained essentially as written. At the beginning of the Revolutionary War, the law was adjusted so that the marriage bond was made to the Governor of Virginia rather than to the British sovereign. A year before the war ended, the Assembly passed significant legislation which permitted licenses to solemnize marriages to be granted to ministers other than those of the established church. A limit of four ministers from a sect, acting only in their county was imposed.[12] The Act was broadened in 1784 so that upon presentation of proper credentials, taking the Oath of Allegiance to the Commonwealth and posting a bond of 500 pounds current money, with good security, any minister of dissenting denominations could perform marriages anywhere in Virginia.[13] One of these bonds dated 1785 exists for Elijah Baker, a Baptist, to "Perform agreeable to the late Marriage Act entitled An Act to Regulate the Solemnization of Marriages."[14] His returns to the clerk are the only ones which exist from 1786-90. Coventon Simkins, a Methodist, submitted one list in 1790 and for the next five years his and Baker's were the only lists returned to the clerk. If others were submitted they have not been located in the clerk's office.

In 1848 a basic change was made in the marriage law by eliminating publishing banns as an alternative to obtaining a license. The clerk of the court in which the female usually resided was charged with issuing the license.[15] The Code[16] in 1849 does not mention the requirement of a bond; simply a license secured from the clerk in the bride's place of residence, consent of parent or guardian for any applicant under 21 years of age and the license to be registered in a book kept by the clerk. The last bond given in Northampton County was in March, 1850. The register to accompany the new procedure was not started in the County until 1854. Fortunately the new licenses issued between 1850 - 1854 do survive, and these have been included in this compilation.

As well as combining information from bonds, licenses and minister's returns, marriage references unrecorded by clerk or minister have also been abstracted from entries made in family Bibles. Such entries are especially valuable sources for ages, complete names of parents, family relationships and where marriages took place. They serve as well to verify other records.

Several remarks may be in order concerning various considerations involved in the preparation of this compilation. Whenever possible names have been spelled as the individual signed on the marriage bond or other documents. The clerk's spelling has to be used, of course, when a person made his or her mark. In the text, the various spellings of a surname have been grouped together using the most usual spelling with the others cross referenced. (i.e., Read, Reed, Reid).

In many cases before issuing a bond the clerk required proof that the bride and groom to-be were over 21 years of age. The designation used on entries such as "John Jones as to Ann's age" indicates that John Jones appeared before the clerk and certified that Ann, the bride to-be, was "upwards of 21 years of age". If the entry shows "John Jones as to ages", the indication is that John Jones certified that both bride and groom to-be were "upwards of 21 years of age." If under 21 years old, consent of a parent or guardian was required. Said person had to testify before the clerk or send a written note consenting to the proposed marriage. Much useful information has been abstracted from such communications attached to the bonds.

When doing research it is often helpful to know the name of the person who served as security for the bond of 50 pounds in current money, as well as the names of witnesses. In most instances these individuals were parents, other relatives or close friends. These have been routinely recorded.

It is observed that during the 18th century, the bond was not obtained always at the Clerk's Office but upon numerous occasions at his home where the clerk's wife or another relative would serve as witness. (i.e., Hillary Stringer/wife Elishe; Griffin Stith/wife Mary; Godfrey Pole/son George).[17] A holiday did not appear to hinder obtaining a bond and license nor having a marriage performed.[18] Although much less celebrated than now, Christmas was nevertheless a holiday. However, more than one bond and minister's return is dated the 25th day of December.

Data supplied by the compiler from her personal research and review of the marriage materials used in preparing this project has been included within brackets. Most cite the reference and all can be verified.

Considering the number of surviving records pertaining to marriages in Northampton County (over 5300 references in all) there are surprisingly few instances where bond, return and/or Bible record do not agree. When the problem does exist, the error probably lies with the minister, who often compiled his list at the end of the year before submission to the Clerk. Unless he recorded at the time of the ceremony, his recall could have been faulty. On the other hand, the clerk recorded the information when the bond was obtained. Some clerks were less attentive to details than others. For instance, one clerk in the 1820's too often neglected to enter the year, filling in only the day and month. He failed, as well, to ask for proof of ages. Most clerks, but unfortunately not all, often included such details as widow, deceased, parents, witnesses and other identifying facts. However, by comparing all of the marriage documents available, a fairly good record usually can be obtained. For instance, the clerk on an 1802 bond for George Abdell put the surety's name in place of the bride's. An attached note from Moses Roberts gave consent for his daughter; thus the bride was a Roberts. Fortunately the minister recorded the bride as "Peggy" with all other details agreeing. An 1816 bond did not show the bride's name at all; the return of the minister supplied it; a Bible record gave her parents' names.

The thrust of this endeavor has been to bring together data from the available sources in order to present the most correct and complete record for each marriage entry. It is hoped that a comprehensive compilation of the existing Northampton County marriages from 1660/1661-1854 has resulted. If this volume proves to be a useful tool for the individual doing research in Northampton County, Virginia, the compiler will be gratified.

Jean M. Mihalyka

NOTES

1. For a more detailed discussion of the minister's returns see the Commentary in "Minister's Marriage Returns, Northampton County, Va. 1791-1854." Before restoration and rebinding, the undersigned prepared a Commentary and Index for the volume which is now in the Northampton County Clerk's Office, Eastville, Virginia.

2. The individual bonds, originally folded and tied in bundles have now been put in order by year and alphabetized. Each document has been laid flat, put between acid-free papers, laid in acid-free folders, placed in archival storage boxes and microfilmed because of their fragile condition. Copies of these original bonds and attachments taken from the microfilm have been bound in volumes which are now available on open shelves in the Clerk's Office for use by the researcher.

3. Hening, William Waller, editor. *The Statues at Large; Being a Collection of all the Laws of Virginia ... 1619-1792.* New York, 1969 Reprint. Vol 1, p 155.

4. Ibid. Vol 6, p 542.

5. Not all of the laws of the General Assembly are recorded in Hening's Statues. A subsequent law could have eliminated the requirement that the clerk keep a record of vital statistics. The law in 1705 which required the bond, did not require entering such lists in the Order Book.

6. Billings, Warren M. *The Papers of Francis Howard, Baron Howard of Effingham.* Richmond, 1989. pp 261-263.

7. "Northampton County, Virginia Order Book" IX, pp 92; 113-114.

8. See also Turman, Nora M. *St. James Church and St. George Parish, 1763-1990.* Onancock, Virginia, 1990. pp 51-54.

9. Hening, Op cit. Vol. 1, p 181.

10. *The Acts of the General Assembly of Virginia.* Richmond, 1845. p 59. Although considered a very important part of the consent form, the requirement of the seal was eliminated by the Assembly in February, 1845.

11. Hening, Op cit. Vol 3, pp 441-445.

12. Ibid. Vol 10, p 363 (October, 1780).

13. Ibid. Vol 11, p 363.

14. See the 1785 bond for Elijah Baker in the section following the Footnotes.

15. *The Code of Virginia.* Richmond, 1847-1848. p. 165.

16. Ibid. pp 469-471.

17. See Marriage Bond for Waterfield Dunton and Susanna Waterfield, 1756, in the section following the Footnotes. Griffin Stith, Clerk of Court, and Mary, his wife, witnessed the bond. This suggests that the bond was obtained at the Clerk's home; not at his office.

18. Hening, *Op cit.* Vol 1, p 181. The Act in 1632 by the Grand Assembly directed that "noe mynister ... shall ioyne any person ... in marriage at any unseasonable tymes but onlie betweene the hours of eight and twelve in the forenoon."

ILLUSTRATIVE DOCUMENTS

The following documents are representative of those housed in the Clerk's Office in Northampton County and used in this study. With but a few exceptions they were stored in several ancient document boxes; very large tin ones, black with nice bold striping. The papers were folded to about 2 1/2" in width and about 6"-8" in length. A close inspection of the following xeroxed copies will reveal the original fold lines. They were bundled according to date and tied with pink cotton tape or occasionally with string. As cited in the Footnotes, modern preservation technique now has been used to store these very fragile documents.

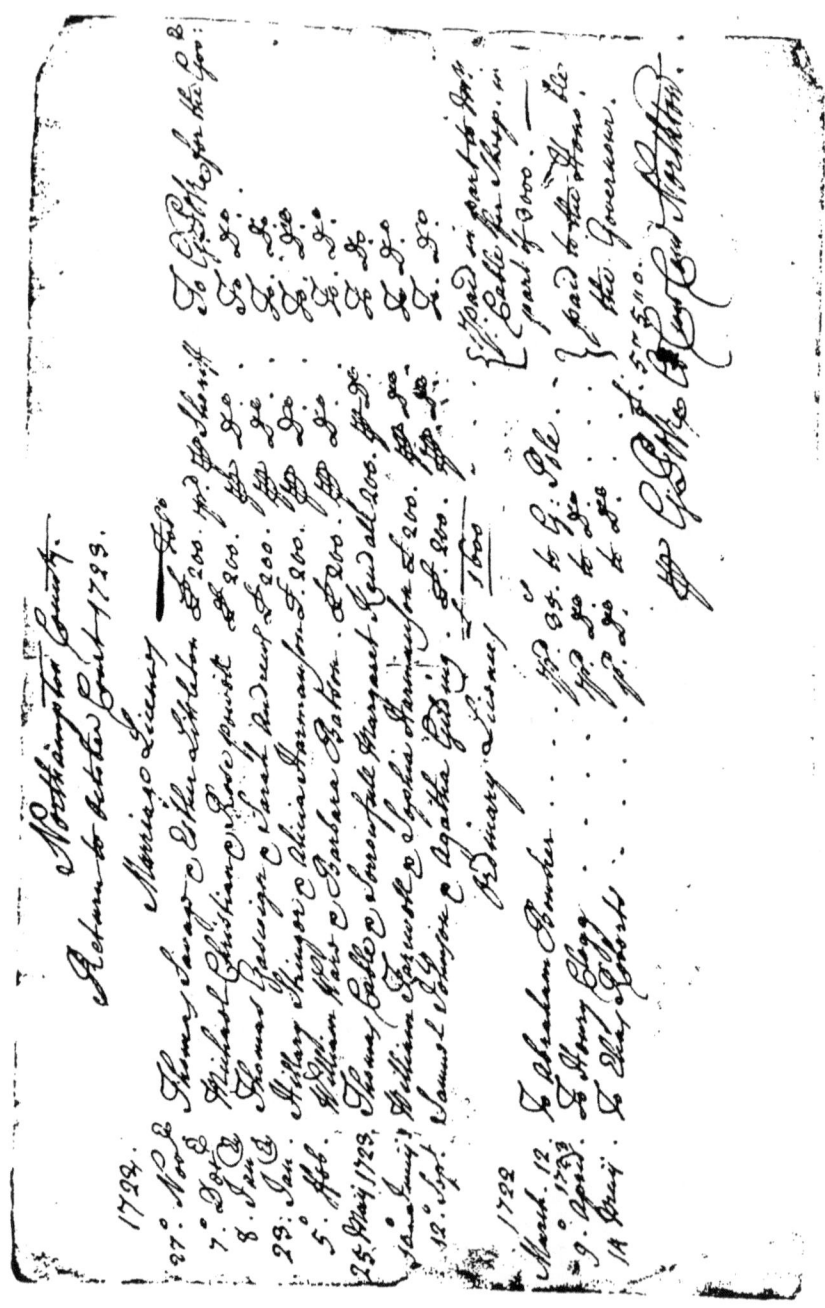

List of licenses submitted by Godfrey Pole, Clerk to the October Court, 1723. Only Marriages and Ordinary licenses are given in the above document, but quite often the return also included Fines, Deodards & Forfeitures and Passes Granted. Unfortunately very few of these returns exist.

Know all men by these presents that We Elijah Baker, John Pigg, Robert Bell & M.K. Gatjegen all of Northampton County Residents, Are Held & firmly Bound unto The Governor or Chief Magistrate of This Commonwealth, Patrick Henry Esq. & his Successors in the Just & full Sum of Five Hundred pounds Current money to be paid unto The s.d Governor or his Successors, to which Payment well and truly To be made, We bind Our Selves, Our heirs, Ex.ors & Admors jointly, by these Presents, Sealed with Our Seals & dated this ____ day of ____ One Thousand Seven hundred & Eighty five.

The Condition of the above Obligation is such that if the above Bound Elijah Baker should Truly & Faithfully Perform his Trust Agreeable to the Late Marriage Act Entitled, an Act to Regulate the Solemnization of Marriages, that then the above Obligation to be Void Else to remain in Full force & Virtue.

Signed & Acknowledged }
in Presence of }

Acknowledged in Court
Test. Jno. K. K.

Elijah Baker (Seal)

John Pigg (Seal)

Nath. Gatjegen (Seal)

Robert Bell (Seal)

This 1785 bond allowed Elijah Baker, a Baptist minister (i.e., of a dissenting denomination) to perform marriages anywhere in Virginia. Note "the Just & full Sum of Five Hundred Pounds Current money to be Paid unto ..." Governor Patrick Henry, Esq. Note also the number of individuals who signed as security on this bond.

A List of Marriges Solemnised by Thomas A. Elliott
In Northampton County from December 1, 1810
to December 1, 1811

Mr. Wm. K. Finney to Miss Rosanna Johnson — Dec 19
Mr. John Robins to Miss Jane Core — Dec 20
Mr. Shadrick Mears to Miss Jemima Westcoat October 10th 1811

Given under my hand as Minister
This 1st of December 1811

Thos. A. Elliott

At a Court held for Northampton County the 9th December 1811.
This List of Marriages was returned by Thos. A. Elliott
Minister of the Methodist Church and ordered to be
registered.
Teste. Thos. L. Savage ck.

A minister's return submitted to the clerk to be recorded in the official Register of Ministers' Returns.

Know all men by these Presents that We Waterfield Dunton and Isaac Dunton of the County of Northampton, are held and firmly Bound unto our Sovereign Lord King George the second, in the Sum of fifty Pounds Current money of Virginia, to be paid unto our said Lord the King his Heirs & Successors; To the which payment well and Truly to be made, We Bind our Selves & Each of us, our & Each of our Heirs Executors & Administrators jointly and Severally firmly By these Presents; Sealed with our Seals & Dated the Seventeenth Day of May 1756

The Condition of the above obligation is such that Whereas there is a marriage Suddenly intended to be Solemnized, between the above Bound Waterfield Dunton and Susanna Waterfield daughter of Jacob Waterfield of the said County — If therefore there be no Lawful Cause to Obstruct the said Marriage then this obligation to be void or else to Remain in full force

Sealed & Delivered
in the Presence of

Mary Smith   Waterfield his Dunton
Griffin Smith   mark

Isaac Dunton

This rather early marriage bond was signed in the presence of both the clerk and his wife, indicating that it was probably obtained at his home, rather than at the Clerk's Office. Attached to the bond is an appealing permission note. It is written in fine penmanship by one of the witnesses and signed by the intended bride's father who shows his romantic side by placing a nicely drawn heart after his name.

May yᵉ 16. 1756

Sʳ these lines are to acquaint You that I am willing and Agreeable that You should Grant Waterfield Dunton and my Daughter Susannah Watafield Licence and in so Doing You'l Oblige Yours to Command as Witness my hand and Seal

Testᵉ By the Day and Date above Written

Henry Bryant
Richeard smith

Jacob Waterfield

Know all Men by these Presents, That we Fuckle Matthews & John Johnson are held and firmly bound unto James Pleasants jr Esquire, Governor or Chief Magistrate of the Commonwealth of Virginia, in the just and full sum of one hundred and fifty dollars, to which payment, well and truly to be made, to the said Governor and his successors for the use of the Commonwealth, we bind ourselves, and each of us, our and each of our Heirs, Executors and Administrators, jointly and severally, firmly by these Presents. Sealed with our Seals, and dated this 28th day of June one thousand eight hundred and twenty four

THE CONDITION of the above obligation is such, That whereas there is a Marriage shortly intended to be had and solemnized between the above bound Fuckle Matthews & Betsey Johnson Now therefore, if there be no lawful cause to obstruct said Marriage, then the above obligation to be void, otherwise to remain in full force and virtue.

Signed, Sealed, and delivered
in the presence of

Fuckle X Matthews [SEAL]
        his mark
John X Johnson [SEAL]
     his mark

Thomas G. Broughton, Printer, Norfolk. Va.

Northampton County Court Clerks Office
I John Johnson do hereby certify that my sister Betsey Johnson within named is considerably upwards of twenty one years of age, she being older than myself, who am more than twenty one — Given under my hand this 28th day of June 1824.
Test   John X Johnson
  U. I. Winson   his mark
Sworn to before me
       U. I. Winson C&C

A printed form is used for this later marriage bond rather than on one copied from a guide book by the clerk. (See the Dunton - Waterfield Bond on the preceding page). The included age certification gives more than the required data. Similar useful genealogical information is found on the numerous attachments to many of the marriage bonds.

NORTHAMPTON COUNTY, to wit:

THIS day *William White Senr.* made oath before me as Clerk of the Court of Hustings for the said county that *Beverwell Bailey* above named is of the full age of twenty one years and a resident of said county. Given under my hand this 22d day of *November 1814.*

C. B. *[signature]*

(illustration caption)
One of several forms used for the certification of age of persons applying for a marriage bond. Some forms read "upwards of twenty one years of age".

ABBREVIATIONS

To conserve space, various abbreviations have been used throughout the entries.

& - and
Acc - Accomack County
as to age - indicates the individual is 21 years of age or older
app't - appointed
b - born
bet - between
br/o - brother of
BRec - Bible Record
CN - Church Neck
Co - County
Col - Colonel
con - consent (of a parent/guardian for an individual under 21 years of age)
con/o - consent of
cou/o - cousin of
CtRec - Court Record
d - died
dau - daughter
d/o - daughter of
dec'd - deceased
Esq - Esquire
FN - Free Negro(s)
f/o - father of
gdn - guardian
gdn/o - guardian of
Gent - Gentleman
grd/o - grandaughter of
HunParReg - Hungars Parish Register
inv - inventory
Jr - Junior
lic - license
Lyt - Lieutenant
m - married
MBay - Magothy Bay
MBk - Minute Book
Md - Maryland
MinRet - Minister's Return
m/o - mother of
months: Jan, Feb, Mar, Apr, May, Jun, Jul, Aug, Sep, Oct, Nov, Dec.
Names:
    Alexr   -   Alexander
    Art   -   Arthur

Benja	-	Benjamin
Chas	-	Charles
Cath	-	Catherine
Dan'l	-	Daniel
Edw'd	-	Edward
Geo	-	George
Jas	-	James
Jno	-	John
Marg't	-	Margaret
Matt	-	Matthew
Nath'l	-	Nathaniel
Rich'd	-	Richard
Sam'l	-	Samuel
Sol	-	Solomon
Thos	-	Thomas
Wm	-	William
Zob	-	Zorobabel

SMITH James of John = James Smith, son of John. If there were several James Smiths living at the same time, the individual always signed as above to identify himself. Also frequently used was the geographical location or occupation; i.e. John Wilkins OP (Old Plantation Creek); John Wilkins, blacksmith.

North - Northampton County
OBk - Order Book
Occ - Occohonnock Neck (or Creek)
OP - Old Plantation (Creek)
orp - orphan
orp/o - orphan of
perm - permission
sec - security (If no security appears on an entry, there is no bond; therefore the data was abstracted from a Court Record, Minister's Return, or a license issued before 1705 or after March, 1850.)
s/o - son of
secs - securities
sis/o - sister of
sl/o - slave of
Sr - Senior
test - testified
Va - Virginia
WBk - Will book
Whl - Whitelaw's Virginia Eastern Shore
wid - widow
wid/o - widow of
widr - widower
wit - witness
wits - witnesses
w/o - wife of
wrd - ward
wrd/o - ward of
y - year(s)
ø - Original bond missing since recorded by S. Nottingham in 1929

EXPLANATION OF ENTRIES

SAMPLE ENTRY:
JONES Jno of Rob't to Mary Smith 19 Jul 1800; wid/o Jas Smith & d/o Thos White dec'd & wife Ann con; Henry Lake sec & as to ages; Geo Green wit; m Jul 1800 by E Baker; (m 22 Jul 1800. see BRec V2:71)

EXPLANATION:
John Jones, son of Robert Jones bond for marriage to Mary Smith issued on 19 July 1800. Mary is the widow of James Smith and the daughter of Thomas White, deceased, and his wife, Ann, who gives consent to the intended marriage. Henry Lake has made security for the bond to the Clerk of the Court. He has also testified that both John and Mary are 21 years of age or older. George Green is a witness to the correctness of the data given. The couple was married by Minister E. Baker in July, 1800. The actual date in July - the 22nd - is found in a family Bible record, volume 2, page 71 of the series in the Northampton County Clerk's Office in Eastville, Virginia.

A

ABBOTT Zephaniah T to Margaret Howell 20 Mar 1804; Wm Howell sec; m bet 1 Jan - 10 Sep 1804 by C Fisher.

ABDALE, ABDEEL, ABDELL, ABDIL, ABDILL.

ABDEEL Abel to Nancy Dixon 17 Jun 1779; d/o Tilney Dixon dec'd; Luke Heath sec.

ABDELL Abel to Rachell Johnson 14 Sep 1807; Wm D James sec.

ABDELL Ezekiel to Sarah Dalby 16 Sep 1779; d/o Waterfield Dalby dec'd; Ezekiel s/o Abel Abdell con; Wm Abdeel sec.

ABDILL George to Peggy Roberts 20 Apr 1802; d/o Moses Roberts who gives her age as 22y on 24 Jun (1801); John Harrison sec; Solomon Richardson wit; m (1802) by I Bratten.

ABDELL George D to Miss Mary F Hallett 1 Feb 1853; (George of Acc Co); con/o Wm T Fitchett gdn/o Mary; Jas G Floyd wit; m 2 Feb 1853 by P Warren.

ABDEEL Hancock to Keziah Dalby 7 Mar 1780; Henry Warren sec.

ABDEEL Henry to Sarah Tankard 26 Apr 1781; wid/o John Tankard; Wm Belote sec.

ABDIL Henry to Hetty Stott 1 Oct 1796; Thos Dowty sec; m (1796) by J Elliot.

ABDEEL John to Elizabeth Kelly 29 Dec 1791; Severn Abdeel sec; m 29 Dec 1791 by C Simkins.

ABDILL Preeson to Polly Kee (Key) 30 Jul 1795; Nicholas Bloxom sec; m 1795 by J Elliot.

ABDELL Preson to Nancy Lewis 25 Mar 1840; John B Wescoat sec & as to Nancy's age; Wm T Nottingham, wit.

ABDELL Shepherd to Margaret Kendall 15 Oct 1811; John Jacob sec; m (1811) by J Elliott.

ABDIL Thomas to (Peggy Mathews) 9 Aug 1794; Wm Garris sec; m Aug 1794 by C Simkins (MinRet shows bride's name which was omitted on bond).

ABDEEL William to Levicy Gooday 11 Apr 1786; Moses Roberts sec.

ABDALE William to Amy Pettitt 25 Apr 1794; Wm Chance sec; m Apr 1794 by C Simkins.

ABDELL William H to Miss Elizabeth Barcraft 28 Mar 1848; d/o Wm Barcraft dec'd; John Belote sec & as to ages; Sylvestor Kelly wit.

ABDIL, ABDILL See ABDALE

ACTHISON Samuel to Esther Respess 16 Aug 1771; d/o John Respess; John Lewis Fulwell sec.

ADAIR George H to Frances E Kellam 18 May 1852; wid/o Francis Kellam; m 18 May 1852 by J Allen.

ADAMS John to Sarah Kendall 21 Feb 1816; C B Upshur sec.

ADDISON Arther to Tabitha Joyne 22 May 1756; d/o Edmund Joyne, Mariner con; Stratton Cobb sec; Thos Joyne & Edward Isdell wits.

ADDISON Arthur to Esther Oag 8 Mar 1786; Severn Kellum sec.

ADDISON Arthur to Elizabeth Cook 10 Apr 1787; Henry Harmanson sec; m (1787) by E Baker.

ADDISON Arthur to Rosey James 3 Feb 1812; Andrew James sec; m 5 Feb 1812 by Thos Davis.

ADDISON Edward W to Miss Elizabeth West 11 Oct 1826; Charles West sec; m 26 Oct 1826 by S S Gunter.

ADDISON John to Peggy White 27 Dec 1802; Wm P Harmanson sec; m (1802) by I Bratten. see BRec V8:8.

ADDISON John to Miss Ann E Kellam 30 Nov 1842; d/o Col Thomas H Kellam dec'd; Kendall F Addison sec & as to ages; m 2 Dec 1842 by G C Wescoat.

ADDISON Kendall to Palmer Rodgers 26 Jun 1787; Wm Satchell Jr sec.

ADDISON Dr Kendall F to Miss Arinthia S Wilkins 12 May 1851; d/o Wm E Wilkins; Leonard T Wilkins as to Arinthia's age; m 14 May 1851 by P Warren.

1

ADDISON Thomas to Margaret Waltham 14 Oct 1775; wid; Edw'd Turner sec.

ADDISON Thomas Jr to Peggy Savage 11 Jan 1780; d/o Nath'l Savage dec'd; John Turner sec.

ADDISON Thomas E to Rosey W Savage 23 Nov 1816; Wm Savage sec; m 28 Nov 1816 by C Bonewell.

AIMES See AMES

ALLEN Thomas to Elizabeth Massey 11 Dec 1789; Thomas of Baltimore; d/o Anne Massey con & gives Elizabeth's age as 18y; John O'Hara of Philadelphia sec; D Rowand wit.

AMES, AIMES.

AMES James to Rachel Johnson 26 Mar 1811; Leavin Beach sec states both are 23y & Rachel is sis/o his wife, Sally.

AMES John G to Ann Hunt 16 Jan 1809; Amos Underhill Jr sec; m (1809) by J Elliott.

AMES Levin S to Margaret Brittingham 22 May 1838; d/o Elijah Brittingham Sr sec; m 23 May 1838 by P Williams.

AMES Mark to Peggy Pool, FN 30 Sep 1840; Benjamin J Dalby sec; m 1 Oct 1840 by S T Ames.

AMES Nelson to his ward Peggy Brickhouse, FN 9 Jun 1851; Mary Ames as to Nelson's age; F Anderson wit; m 9 Jun 1851 by P Warren.

AMES Richard to Nancy Milby 4 Mar 1805; John P Johnson sec.

AMES Shadrack to Matilda Christian 28 Feb 1775; wid; Adiel Milby sec; Drury Stith & Wm Waltham wits.

AMES Shadrack T to Sarah S Gardiner 4 Aug 1830; d/o Walter C Gardiner dec'd; Jno Simkins sec; Jno A Ames as to Shadrack's age; Benja J Dolby as to Sarah's age; m 4 Aug 1830 by E Stevenson.

AMES Teackle to Margaret Belote 10 Jan 1831; Margaret wrd/o Alexander W Ward sec & as to Teackle's age; m 10 Jan 1831 by G Wescoat.

AMES Thomas to Sally Christian 21 May 1800; John P Johnson sec; m May 1800 by C Simkins.

AMES Thomas to Leanne Long 11 Mar 1822; John N Brickhouse sec; Wm A Christian as to Leanne's age; m 13 Mar 1822 by C Bonewell.

AMES Thomas to Miss Mary Clark 12 Dec 1842; d/o Wm Clark dec'd; Alexander W Ward sec & as to ages; m 13 Dec 1842 by G C Wescoat.

AIMES William to Patsey Booll 20 Dec 1796; Richard Coleburn sec; m (1796) by J Elliot.

AMES William C L to Miss Sally A Henderson 13 Jun 1848; d/o John T Henderson; Wm B Savage sec & as to Sally's age; Jesse N Jarvis wit; m 17 Jun 1848 by M Oldham.

ANDERSON Edward W to Miss Sarah A H Young 25 Apr 1837; d/o George H Young dec'd; Wm W Oliver as to Sarah's age; Wm B Anderson sec; m 26 Apr 1837 by W B Snead.

ANDERSON Matthew to Rosey Collins 8 Apr 1794; John Graves Sr sec; m (1794) by E Baker.

ANDREWS Isaac to Tamar A Savage 14 Jun 1824; d/o William Savage Sr sec; m bet 15 Jun - 22 Dec 1824 by G C Wescoat.

ANDREWS Isaac to Miss Joanna Heath 5 Mar 1827; d/o Seth D Heath dec'd; Jno R Fisher sec & as to Joanna's age; Geo T Yerby and Rich'd Mapp wits; m 1827 by G C Wescoat.

ANDREWS Isaac to Mrs Juliet J Parker 9 Jun 1842; (wid/o Wm A Parker); Alexander W F Mears sec; m 10 Jun 1842 by G C Wescoat. see BRec V2:41-2.

ANDREWS Jacob to Margaret Joyne 19 Aug 1752; spinster; Jacob of Acc Co; Wm Joyne of Acc Co sec; Jno Wise Jr wit.

ANDREWS Jacob to Catharine

Harmon 2 May 1808; Wm James sec; m (1808) by I Bratten.

ANDREWS Major to Hannah Bell Powell 30 Jan 1774; Hannah orp/o George Powell; Nathaniel Powell sec; Richards Dunton wit.

ANDREWS Major to Nancy Custis 24 Jun 1795; John Boggs sec.

ANDREWS Major to Patsey Cox 16 Oct 1804; George Belote Jr sec.

ANDREWS Robert to Betsey Stratton 11 Dec 1788; Robert of Acc Co; d/o Benjamin Stratton dec'd, sis/o Wm Stratton con; Thos Parker of Acc Co sec.

ANDREWS Sheperd to Nancy Dowty 27 Dec 1819; d/o Zob Dowty con; Thos Johnson Jr sec; Wm P Copes and Wm Dowty wits.

ANDREWS Southey to Adah Carpenter 18 Jan 1819; d/o John Carpenter con; John Dowty sec; Sam'l Kellam & Thos Henderson wits.

ANDREWS William to Bridget Heath 20 Apr 1781; d/o William Heath dec'd; John Dolby Jr sec.

ANDREWS William to Sarah Hunt 23 Jul 1787; John Wheeler sec.

ANDREWS William to Sally Waterfield 20 Jun 1791; John Wheelor sec.

ANDREWS William to Adah Dennis 14 Aug 1792; John Dolby sec; m (1792) by E Baker.

ANDREWS William to Drusilla Floyd 19 Mar 1808; Nath'l Widgeon sec; m (1808) by J Elliott.

ANDREWS William W to Margaret Dowty 17 Oct 1831; Margaret wrd/o John Adams sec; Westerhouse Widgeon as to Wm's age; m 24 Oct 1831 by P Williams.

ANDREWS William W to Polly S Parsons 8 Dec 1838; d/o Wm Parsons Sr dec'd; Custis F Williams sec; Littleton Townsend as to ages; m 11 Dec 1838 by P Williams.

ARBUCKLE William to Athaliah Hall 20 May 1765; William of Acc Co; d/o John Hall sec; con/o James Arbuckle for William.

ARMISTEAD Ellison to Susanna Christian 5 Apr 1780; d/o Michael Christian; Griffin Stith Jr sec. see BRec V7:151.

ARMISTEAD Francis to Sarah Smith 29 Oct 1715; Francis of Gloster Co; Richard Nottingham sec; Benja Nottingham wit.

ASHBY James to Elizabeth S Johnson 10 Mar 1851; wid/o George F Johnson; S S Nottingham wit; m 12 Mar 1851 by M Oldham.

ASHBY William to Margaret A T Turner 10 Jun 1846; d/o Teagle J Turner con; Joshua B Turner sec; Joshua G Stewart wit; m 25 Jun 1846 by M Oldham.

ASHLY (ASHBY) Washpon to Ann Smith 8 Oct 1838; Ann wrd/o George Smith sec; Wm Lewis as to Washpon's age; James Young wit; m 17 Oct 1838 by L Dix.

AVERY Isaac to Esther Preeson 4 May 1768; (wid/o Thos Preeson); Wm Kendall sec.

AVERY Isaac to Margaret Stringer 7 Jun 1785; d/o Hillary Stringer; Geo Fisher sec.

AVERY Isaac W to Sally T Savage 14 Dec 1821; wid/o George Savage; Peter S Bowdoin sec; m 15 Dec 1821 by C Bonewell.

AYRES See also EYRE.

AYRES Edmund to Cassa Johnson 8 Mar 1800; William Johnson sec; m 1800 by J Elliott.

AYRES Richard J to Leah W Johnson 20 Dec 1827; d/o John Johnson dec'd; Wm P Johnson sec & as to ages; m 1827 by G C Wescoat.

AYRES Thomas to Miss Ann Taylor 29 Sep 1846; John S Turpin sec & as to Ann's age; m 29 Sep 1846 by P Warren.

B

BACHURST James to Bridgit Stott 2 Dec 1782; Wm Stott sec.

BADDAM Jno to Barbary Hudson 29 Aug 1660. Bk IX:92.

BADGER Ezekiel to Mary Dunton 22 May 1798; Michael Dunton sec.

BADGER Nathaniel to Mary Robins; s/o Nath'l & Joyce Badger; d/o Thos & Lettice Robins; (m 18 Dec 1806. see BRec V6:114).

BADGER Nathaniel to Sally Martin 11 Apr 1832; s/o Nath'l & Mary Badger. see BRec V6:114.

BADGER Nathaniel to Margaret S Kellam 20 Dec 1832; s/o Nath'l & Mary Badger. see BRec V6:114.

BADGER Thomas Wyatt to Sally Dixon 10 Oct 1808; (s/o Nath'l & Joyce Badger); (d/o John & Bridget Dixon); Harrison Thomas sec; m (1808) by I Bratten (at Red Bank Ch). see BRec V6:114.

BADGER Thomas Wyatt to Margaret Churn 28 Dec 1818; d/o Severn & Tamor Churn; Benjamin F Dunton sec; m 30 Dec 1818 by G Bonewell.

BAGWELL George T to Elizabeth M Johnson 19 Dec 1848; con/o Egbert G Bayly, gdn/o Elizabeth; John W F Gunter sec; m 20 Dec 1848 by M Oldham.

BAGWELL Hely D to Eliz A Mears 14 Dec 1835; s/o Hely & Ann Bagwell; wid/o Rev Wm Mears & d/o Sam'l Ashby; Leonard B Nottingham sec; m 21 Jan 1836 by J Lewis. see BRec V4:11.

BAGWELL Heley P to Sarah Ann Edmunds 24 Oct 1843; s/o Heley D & E P Bagwell; d/o Thos & Ann Edmunds; m by Rev Geo C Wescott. see BRec V4:12.

BAILEY See BAYLY

BAIN William to Judith Stevenson 31 Aug 1785; Robert Hewitt sec.

BAIN William to Susanna (Sukey) Dunton 16 Jul 1793; Thomas Dunton sec; m 16 Jul 1793 by C Simkins.

BAIN William to Betsey Robins 8 Jun 1797; Coventon Simkins sec; m Jun 1797 by C Simkins.

BAKER Elijah to Anne Widgeon 5 Nov 1787; wid/o Thos Widgeon; John Dennis sec; m (1787) E Baker's Ret.

BAKER Savage to Edith Heath 11 Dec 1837; wid/o Augustus C E Heath; Thomas E Brickhouse sec; Obed Goffigon as to Savage's age; m 11 Dec 1837 by P Williams.

BAKER Savage to Lavinia Williams 8 May 1843; d/o Peter Williams con & sec; m 9 May 1843 by J D Curtis.

BAKER Thomas to Betsey Bingham 5 Dec 1805; Nathan Drighouse sec (FN); m (1805) by J Elliott.

BAKER Thomas to Mary Bevans 29 Jan 1825; d/o John Bevans sec (FN).

BAKER Timothy to Jane Wilkins 27 Nov 1766; d/o John Wilkins Sr Gent; Edmund Glanville sec.

BALL David B to Sally Parsons 5 Jan 1842; d/o Marriott Parsons dec'd; John Ball as to David's age; James Warren as to Sally's age; Leonard B Nottingham sec; m 5 Jan 1842 by P Warren.

BALL John to Margaret Warrington 5 Apr 1830; d/o George Warrington con; Smith Nottingham sec; Jno Ker, L B & Wm Nottingham, & Jno Carson wits; m 7 Apr 1830 by G Wescoat.

BALL Luther to Esther Wheeler 26 Dec 1826; Thomas Duncan as to Luther's age; John Bishop sec & as to Esther's age; Arthur Rooks wit; m 28 Dec 1826 by P Williams Jr.

BAPTIST Edward to Maria S Satchell 14 Mar 1820; John Simkins sec.

BARCRAFT, BARCROFT, BEAR-CRAFT

BARCRAFT James to Sally Floyd 10 May 1813; Edmund Fletcher sec; m (1813) by I Bratten.

BARCROFT John T to Arinthia J Harman 10 Jul 1850; d/o Kely Harman dec'd; John H Rayfield as to ages; C F Anderson wit; m 10 Jul 1850 by M Oldham.

BARCRAFT William to Elizabeth Speakman 19 Feb 1781; d/o Thos Speakman; Stuart

Saunders sec.
BARLOW Thomas to Jane Mapp 6 Feb 1765; wid/o (Robins Mapp); Samuel Holbrook sec.
BARLOW Thomas to Anne Stott 9 May 1775; orp/o (Jonathan Stott); John Burton sec.
BARLOW Thomas to Elizabeth Rascoe 26 Sep (no year - in 1780-1782 bundle); Griffin Stith Jr sec.
BARNES James to Salley Pake (Peck) 25 Aug 1790; d/o Elisabeth Pake con; Benja Griffith sec; m (1790) by E Baker.
BARNES John Jr to Elizabeth Jacob 6 Dec 1775; d/o Esau Jacob dec'd; Thorowgood Smith sec.
BARNES Nicholas to Sara Sarrell 14 Dec 1661. Bk IX:115.
BARRETT, BARROTT
BARROTT John W to Isetta Rooks 11 Oct 1842; d/o Wm Rooks Sr dec'd & Sally Rooks con; William Lewis sec & as to John's age; Bennet Stott wit; m 12 Oct 1842 by G C Wescoat.
BARRETT John William to Miss Mary Nottingham 31 Dec 1845; d/o Thomas W Nottingham; William P Nottingham wit; m 31 Dec 1845 by P. Williams.
BATSON Ralph to Sarah Moor 6 Dec 1749; wid/o Levi d/o John & Elizabeth Waterson. CR PK 40 Jan 1753 "Pigot vs Elliott."
BAYLY, BAILEY
BAILEY Edmund to Rachel Upshur 14 Sep 1790; James Upshur sec.
BAYLY Edmund W to Miss Sally Ker 25 May 1847; Wm J Bowdoin as to Edmund's age; Leonard B Nottingham sec & gdn/o Sally; m 25 May 1847 by J Ufford.
BAILEY Edward to Nancy Pitts 21 Sep 1802; d/o Hezekiah Pitts con; Major S Pitts sec.
BAYLY Edward L to Miss Pamela E J Powell 13 Nov 1834; Pamela wrd/o Miers W Fisher sec; Thomas B Custis as to Edward's age; m 19 Nov 1834 by L Dix.
BAYLY John H to Margaret S Wilson 4 Sep 1816; d/o Wm W Wilson con; Edw'd H C Wilson sec; Go Hanby Jr wit; m 7 Nov 1816 by R Symes.
BAYLY Peter to Sukey Bevans; d/o Samuel Bevans, sec FN 22 Nov 1825.
BAYLY Richard Drummond to Sarah Downing Upshur 9 Dec 1801; d/o John & Margaret Upshur. see BRec V7:158.
BAYLY Rodney N to Miss Sally A S Brickhouse 18 Dec 1838; d/o George Brickhouse; Edmund W Underhill sec & as to ages; m 28 Dec 1838 by G C Wescoat.
BAYLY (Col)* Thomas M to Mrs Jane O Addison 4 Oct 1826; Richard D Bayly sec; m 21 Dec 1826 by S S Gunter. * Whl:815.
BEACH, BEECH
BEECH James to Esther Hall 9 Dec 1811; John Scott Sr sec; E Hall wit; m (1811) by J Elliott.
BEACH James to Betsey Dann 4 Jul 1829; d/o Silas Dann dec'd; Robert A Joynes sec & as to Betsey's age; m 6 Jul 1829 by G Wescoat.
BEACH James to Elizabeth Robins 17 Dec 1844; wid/o John Robins; John M Henderson sec; m 17 Dec 1844 by G C Wescoat.
BEACH Levin to Sally Johnson 11 Apr 1808; Silas Dan sec.
BEECH Reuben to Mary Wilkins 6 Jan 1779; d/o Patrick Wilkins dec'd; Wm Waterfield sec.
BEACH William T to Miss Margaret S Churn 7 Jun 1848; d/o William Churn; Arthur E Roberts sec & as to Margaret's age; m 7 Jun 1848 by M Oldham.
BEAVANS, BEAVENS, BEVANS, BEVENS, BIVENS, BIVINS.
BEAVANS Hezikiah to Mary Morris 31 Jul 1798; Revel Morris sec (FN); m (1798) by J Elliott.
BEAVANS John to Mary Ann Carter (FN) 2 Jan 1822; Mac Collins sec; m 3 Jan 1822 by C Bonewell.
BEAVANS Moses to Nancy West 1807; by J Elliott.
BIVENS Moses to Damaris

Matthews (FN) 5 Feb 1850; s/o Esther Bivens, d/o Mary Matthews, John S Turpin all secs; m 7 Feb 1850 by M Oldham.

BEAVENS Peter to Louisa Toyer 11 Mar 1823; d/o George Toyer sec (FN).

BEVANS Revel to Rachel Bevans 6 Aug 1817; John Bevans sec; m 7 Aug 1817 by C Bonewell.

BEVANS Sam to Molly Press 19 Aug 1797; Abraham Lang sec (FN); m Aug 1797 by C Simkins.

BEVANS Samuel Jr to Matilda Stephens 10 Mar 1841; d/o Adah Read sec FN; John Kendall sec & as to Samuel's age.

BEVANS Samuel S to Mary Collins FN 28 Dec 1829; Samuel Bevans sec; Wm West FN as to Mary's age; m 30 Dec 1829 by P Williams.

BEAVANS Sol to Esther Casey 24 Sep 1796; Edmund Press sec (FN); m Sep 1796 by C Simkins.

BEVANS Thomas to Nancy Jeffery 19 Sep 1827; wid/o Littleton Jeffery (FN); John Bevans f/o Thomas sec.

BEAZLEY Ephraim H to Miss Sally J Warren 19 Feb 1849; orp/o John Warren Sr; con Patrick Warren Jr former gdn/o Sally; Rev Peter Williams sec & gdn chosen by Sally in 1829; John Birch as to Ephraim's age; Wm E Waddy wit; m 20 Jan 1849 (min mistake probably 20 Feb 1849) by P Williams.

BECKET Abraham to Sarah Thompson 26 Oct 1797; Jacob Thompson sec (FN); m (1797) by J Elliott.

BECKET Arthur to Ann ___ 14 Jan 1839; Ann sl/o Matthew Floyd who gives permission & states Ann is of age; Alfred Parker & Sarah Becket secs; m 16 Jan 1839 by S T Ames.

BECKET Isaac to Betsey Bevans 28 Dec 1816; Saul Becket (FN) sec.

BECKET Joshua to Sally Stevens 21 May 1803; Jacob Thompson sec (FN); m (1803) by I Bratten.

BECKET Peter to Ann Read FN 21 Nov 1851; Betsy Read as to Ann's age; Wm J Nottingham wit; m 22 Nov 1851 by H Dalby.

BECKET Smith to Fanny Collins FN 12 Mar 1839; Sarah Becket as to ages; Smith S Nottingham sec; m 16 Mar 1839 by S T Ames.

BECKET Solomon to Adah Liverpool 7 Jul 1801; Josiah Liverpool sec (FN); m Jul 1801 by C Simkins (MinRet gives "Sarah" Liverpool).

BECKET Solomon to Abigail Stevens 19 Feb 1803; Jacob Thompson sec (FN); m (1803) by J Elliott.

BEDELL James to Caroline Evans 16 Jun 1835; d/o Nancy Evans con; Wm Snead sec & as to James' age; Wm Miles & Wm Wilson wits; m 18 Jun 1835 by P Williams.

BELL Anthony to Tabitha Harman 14 Sep 1807; Thos N Widgeon sec; m (1807) by I Bratten.

BELL Baly (Bayly) to Miss Mary C Dunton 11 May 1840; Sam'l W Dunton as to Mary's age; Joseph E Bell sec & as to Baly's age; m 14 May 1840 by G C Wescoat. see BRec V2:128; V8:113.

BELL Edmund to Polly Hanby 27 Dec 1802; d/o Joseph Hanby con; Wm Parkerson sec; m (1802) by C Fisher.

BELL Ezekiel to Anne Carpenter 3 May 1748; wid/o (Stephen Carpenter); Philip Jacob sec.

BELL George to Susey Bell 19 Dec 1795; Anthony Bell sec; m 1795 by I Bratten.

BELL George to Elizabeth Scott 23 Jul 1808; Wm Bell sec; m (1808) by I Bratten.

BELL George to Margaret W Colonna 25 Jan 1832; d/o Major Collonna dec'd; Lorenzo D Mears sec & as to ages; m 25 Jan 1832 by G Wescoat.

BELL George Jr to Elizabeth P Badger 5 Feb 1833; d/o Thomas W Badger sec & as to George's age; m 9 Feb 1833 by G Wescoat.

BELL Jeptha to (Miss) Louisa Bell 11 Jan 1830; d/o Jesse Bell sec & as to Jeptha's age; m 12 Jan 1830 by G Wescoat.

BELL Jesse to Nancy Richardson 13 Dec 1811; d/o Kendall Richardson con; James Tatum sec & states Nancy's age as 23y; Wm Richardson wit.

BELL Jesse to Mary Tatum 3 May 1828; d/o James Tatum sec; Geo Richardson wit; m 3 May 1828 by G C Wescoat.

BELL John to Sally Tylor 12 Mar 1804; John H Harmanson sec; m (1804) by I Bratten.

BELL John F to Miss Margaret Jane Nelson 9 Dec 1845; Jane wrd/o Hezekiah Dalby con; Benjamin J Dalby sec; John T Collins wit; m 17 Dec 1845 by P Warren Jr.

BELL Joseph E to Miss Rosey Clegg 10 Nov 1834; Rosey wrd/o Edmund Watson sec; John G Minson as to Joseph's age; m 10 Nov 1834 by L Dix.

BELL Nathaniel to Elizabeth Turpin 20 Dec 1786; Elizabeth cou/o Thos Upshur con; Thomas Upshur Jr sec.

BELL Robert to Abagail Grice 12 Nov 1771; d/o Thomas Grice sec.

BELL Robert to Mary Jarvis 17 Jun 1772; d/o William Jarvis sec.

BELL Robert to his ward Maria Isdell 11 Feb 1828; orp/o Matthew Isdell; Hez P Wescoat sec; Richard Bell as to Rob't's age; L B Nottingham & Jno S Dix wits; m 1828 by G C Wescoat.

BELL Savage to Elizabeth Spires; m Nov 1822 by L Dix.

BELL Smith to Peggy Wescoat 10 Mar 1828; s/o Edmund Bell; d/o Edmund Wescoat; Edm'd Bell & Edm'd Wescoat secs; m 1828 by G C Wescoat. see BRec V2:14.

BELL Thomas to Sarah Gascoyne 28 Sep 1780; d/o (Henry Gascoyne Sr dec'd); Robert Bell sec.

BELL Thomas to Tinney Chance 18 Nov 1797; d/o William Chance con; Southy Webb sec; m (1797) by I Bratten.

BELL William Jr to Esther Scott 4 Sep 1797; Rickard Dunton Jr sec; m (1797) by I Bratten.

BELOAT, BELOTE.

øBELOTE, Abbot to Betsey Abdell 8 Jul 1822; wid; David Ewing sec; m 11 Jul 1822 by L Dix.

BELOTE Abel to Susan West 24 Nov 1818; Caleb B Upshur sec; m 26 Nov 1818 by C Bonewell.

BELOTE Benjamin to Miss Elizabeth Joynes 13 Jan 1834; d/o Robert A Joynes sec; m 16 Jan 1834 by L Dix.

BELOTE Edward to Mary Nottingham 25 Nov 1760; d/o Jacob Nottingham dec'd; Adderson Nottingham sec.

BELOTE George to Molly Westcoat 24 May 1798; Wm Parramore sec; m 1798 by J Elliot.

BELOTE George T to Margaret Ross 12 Jan 1830; d/o Ann Ross; Teackle J Turner sec & as to Ann's age; m 13 Jan 1830 by G Wescoat.

BELOTE George T to Rosaline Costin 24 Dec 1838; Rosaline wrd/o Miers W Fisher sec; m 2 Jan 1839 by P Williams.

BELOTE Hezekiah to Nancy Eshon 4 Jun 1817; Sam'l S West sec; Nath'l West con for Nancy; Patrick Rooks wit; m 5 Jun 1817 by C Bonewell.

BELOTE Hezekiah to Susan Kendall 26 Nov 1828; wid/o John W Kendall; Thomas Smith Jr sec.

BELOTE Hezekiah to Lucretia Harmanson 1 Jan 1833; d/o Henry Harmanson dec'd; Seldon Ridley sec; John M Savage as to Lucretia's age.

BELOTE Hezekiah to Betsy Taylor 18 Oct 1837; wid/o John Taylor; Smith Belote sec; m 19 Oct 1837 by L Dix.

BELOTE Hezekiah to Margaret Ann Bool 16 Apr 1845; wid/o Edward Bool; Wm J Fitchett sec; m 16 Apr 1845 by J Ufford.

BELOTE John to Frances Fitchett (alias Frances Williams) 22 May 1832; d/o Rob't F Williams dec'd; Azariah Williams sec & as to ages; m 25 May 1832 by P Williams.

BELOTE John to Ann Darby 14 May 1834; d/o Shadrack Darby dec'd; Hezekiah P James sec & as to ages; m 18 May 1834 by G Wescoat.

BELOTE John to Miss Maria C Savage 24 Dec 1849; d/o William F Savage dec'd; Joseph E Bell wit; Peter B Savage sec & as to Maria's age; m 25 Dec 1849 by P Warren.

BELOTE Jonas to Susanna Holt 21 May 1791; wid/o Stuart Holt; Geo Moore sec.

BELOTE Kendall to Sukey Widgeon 31 Jul 1793; John Widgeon sec; m Aug 1793 by C Simkins.

BELOTE Kendall to Sukey Lingo 10 Dec 1832; Sukey wrd/o Thomas Smith Jr sec & as to Kendall's age.

BELOTE Laban to Esther Dolby 20 Dec 1793; d/o John Dolby Sr con; Reubin Westerhouse sec; m Dec 179(4?) by C Simkins.

BELOTE Laban Jr to Susan Dolby 11 Dec 1833; d/o James Dolby con; John Ewell sec & as to Laban's age; Rich'd Young wit.

BELOTE Perry L to Peggy Smith 16 Dec 1806; s/o Noah Belote con; d/o Wm Smith con; Arthur Cobb sec.

BELOTE Robert to Elizabeth Richardson 14 Jul 1828; Elizabeth wrd/o Wm Roberts sec & as to Robert's age; m 16 Jul 1828 by G Wescoat.

BELOTE Smith to Margaret A J Gunter 20 Apr 1836; d/o Rev Stephen S Gunter dec'd; Thomas Smith Jr sec & as to ages; m 21 Apr 1836 by W B Snead.

BELOTE Smith to Catharine P Gunter 20 May 1843; (d/o Rev S S Gunter dec'd) Smith Belote gdn/o Catharine sec; John S Gayle states that Catharine is upwards of 14y; m 21 May 1843 by P Warren Jr.

BELOAT Walter to Nancy Westcot 13 Sep 1802; George Beloat Jr sec; m (1802) by J Elliott.

BELOTE Walter to Esther Warren 10 Dec 1834; d/o Seth Warren dec'd; Hezekiah Dalby sec & as to Esther's age; Susan Belote as to Walter's age; m 10 Dec 1834 by L Dix.

BELOTE William to Sarah Tankard 16 Apr 1779; d/o John Tankard dec'd; Thos Parramore sec.

BENNETT Covey Jr to Miss Mary A Gildon 18 Jun 1849; s/o Covey Bennett; d/o Mrs Elizabeth R (Gildon) Fartherly con; Geo Waterfield sec & as to Covey Jr's age; m 20 Jun 1849 by M Oldham.

BENSON Azariah to Sarah Cutler 15 Dec 1796; Michael Dunton sec; m 19 Dec 1796 by C Simkins.

BENSON Edmund to Rachael Richardson 3 Jul 1815; Daniel Luke sec; m (1815) by C Bonewell.

BENSON James to Betsey Benston (Benson) 21 May 1804; Wm Only sec; m (1804) by I Bratten.

BENSON James to Elizabeth Dowty 16 Jun 1828; wid/o Wm Dowty; Thos W Badger sec; Ann Edmonds as to James' age; m 20 Jun 1828 by G Wescoat.

BENSON James to Sally Roberts 27 Mar 1841; d/o Teackle Roberts dec'd; Wm J Fitchett sec & as to Sally's age; Geo T Yerby wit; m 29 Mar 1841 by G C Wescoat.

BENSON James H to Elizabeth Stott 21 Dec 1802; Laban Stott sec; m (1802) by C Fisher.

BENSON Nathaniel to Polly Willis 11 Jun 1823; Polly b 22 Jan 1799 d/o Josiah Willis; m Jun 1823 by L Dix.

BENSON Patrick to Elizabeth Kelly 29 Jan 1816; George Parkinson sec; m bet 1 Jan - 12 Feb (1816) by C Bonewell.

BENSON Samuel to Nancy Savage 11 Sep 1812; Samuel of Acc Co; Joshua Garrison sec; m (1812) by I Bratten.

BENTHALL Caleb to Elizabeth Stripe 21 May 1799; d/o Moses Stripe; John Nelson sec.

BENTHALL Daniel to Adah Warren 19 Feb 1785; Nath'l Goffigon sec.

BENTHALL Daniel to Betsey Moore 4 Jul 1791; d/o Isaac Moore dec'd; Geo Moore sec; m (1791) by E Baker.

BENTHALL John to Elizabeth Goffigon 8 Jan 1753; wid/o (Thos Goffigon)*; John Flood sec; Geo Kendall wit. * Whl:104.

BENTHALL Nathaniel to Elizabeth Nottingham 2 Apr 1793; d/o Richard Nottingham sec; m Apr 1793 by C Simkins.

BENTHALL Nathaniel to Peggy O'dear 24 Mar 1796; Richard Evans sec; m (1796) by I Bratten.

BERRY John H to Miss Louisa Y West 9 Aug 1841; John wrd/o Thomas B Williams sec; d/o Nathaniel West sec.

BEVANS See BEAVANS.

BIGGS Christofer to Jenny S Trower 12 Sep 1803; con Jno Elliott gdn/o Christofer; Elizabeth Trower Jenny's mother/gdn con; Wm Knight sec; John Brickhouse Jr wit; m bet Mar 1803 - Feb 1804 by J Elliott.

BIGGS Christopher to Tinny Speakman 11 Mar 1829; d/o Thomas Speakman sec.

BIGGS James to Nicey Courser 13 Sep 1796; Henry Wilkins sec; m 1796 by E Baker.

BIGGS John to Tabitha Goffigon 31 May 1773; wid/o (Peter Goffigon)*; Wm Biggs sec. *North Co OB 30:337.

BIGGS John to Catherine Floyd 16 Dec 1817; d/o James Floyd con; Sam'l G Floyd sec; Major Floyd wit; m 18 Dec 1817 by C Bonewell.

BIGGS, Thomas to Ann Warren 9 Dec 1794; Wm Scott Sr sec; m (1794) by E Baker.

BIGGS William to Elishe Smaw 9 Mar 1769; d/o John Smaw; James Biggs sec.

BINGHAM Henry to Ritter Collins 13 Jun 1794; Ralph Collins sec (FN).

BINGHAM Littleton to Rosey Becket 18 Sep 1804; Moses Bingham sec (FN); m (1804) by I Bratten.

BINGHAM Moses to Esther Collins (FN) 24 Nov 1819; d/o Rafe Collins who states her age as 25 yrs on 23 Nov 1819; Caleb Downing Jr sec; Henry G Dunton wit.

BIRD John to Peggy Meholloms 26 Nov 1792; orp d/o Elisebeth Perkeson con; Peter Dowty sec; Selbey & Betsy Hickman wits; m Nov 1792 by C Simkins.

BIRD Thomas to Catherine West 13 May 1825; George Gray sec & as to ages; m 1825 by G C Wescoat.

BIRD Thomas to Mahala Fletcher 10 Sep 1831; James R B Martin sec & as to ages; m (1?) Sep 1831 by G Wescoat.

BISHOP George to Mrs Polly Bird 13 Feb 1837; Wm F Bishop sec; m 15 Feb 1837 by W B Snead.

BISHOP Lyt Henry to Ann Bowen 12 May 1661. Bk IX:104.

BISHOP John to Anne Dixon 4 Oct 1775; orp/o Wm Dixon dec'd; Ralph Dixon sec.

BISHOP John to Rachell Wilson 13 May 1809; Wm Kendall sec; m (1809) by J Elliott.

BISHOP John to Miss Gracy Fitchett 1 Sep 1845; James S Wilson sec; m 3 Sep 1845 by G G Exall.

BISHOP William to Nancy Freshwater 23 May 1790; by C Simkins.

BISHOP William to Lurana Mehollomes 16 Jan 1828; d/o Thomas Mehollomes sec & as to Wm's age; m 1828 by G C Wescoat.

BISHOP William Jr to Elizabeth Graves 29 Jan 1765; d/o Wm Graves; George Graves, sec.

BIVINS See BEAVANS.

BLACKWELL John to Margaret Jarvis 9 Oct 1789; d/o Wm Jarvis con; John Williams sec; m (1789) by E Baker.
BLAIR John to Sarah Mapp 18 May 1768; d/o Samuel Mapp dec'd; John Mapp sec.
BLAIR John to Mary Darby 22 Jan 1772; d/o Benjamin Darby dec'd; John Mapp sec.
BLAKE Joshua to Esther Warren 18 Mar 1775; d/o Devorix Warren dec'd; Major Brickhouse sec; Devorax Godwin wit.
BLOXOM Nicholas to Peggy Abell (Abdell?) 2 May 1793; Wm Garris sec; m (1793) by E Baker.
BLOXOM Samuel to Lucretia Willis 3 Aug 1824; Lucretia wrd/o Keley Stott sec.
BLOXOM William to Kesiah Core 25 Jun 1788; wid/o Charles Core; Kendall Addison sec; Benja Stratton wit.
BLOXOM William to Mary Johnson 3 Aug 1790; wid/o Robinson Johnson; Wm Wescoat sec.
BLOXOM William to Elizabeth Pettit 9 Sep 1816; Christopher Gayle sec; Bowdoin Abdell as to Elizabeth's age; m 9 Sep 1816 by C Bonewell.
BOGGS George to Margaret Stringer 11 Feb 1795; (wid/o Hillary Stringer); Thos Dunton sec; m Feb 1795 by C Simkins.
BOISNARD Dr Edward R to Anne Holland 4 Feb 1818; (d/o Nath'l & Susanna B Holland*); Nath'l Holland sec. * see BRec V5:180.
BOISNARD John to Esther Robins 17 Feb 1789; John of Acc Co; d/o Edward Robins Esq dec'd; John Robins sec.
BOISNARD John to Nancy Kendall 8 Aug 1798; Joseph Moore sec.
øBOLLING Robert to Mary Burton 3 Jun 1763; Robert of Buckingham Co; d/o Wm Burton Gent con; Wm Waters of City of Williamsburg sec.
BONNELL Cap't Amos to Miss Tabitha J Thompson 17 Dec 1845; d/o Mrs Elizabeth Collins con; James M Bool sec & as to Amos' age; L B Nottingham & Wm Thompson wits; m 17 Dec 1845 by G C Wescoat.
BONWELL, BONAWELL, BONAWILL, BONIWELL.
BONWELL Arthur to Susanna Toleman 16 Jan 1794; Wm Tolman sec; m Jan 1794 by C Simkins.
BONWELL Rev'd Charles to Nancy Scott 6 Jan 1816 by J Burton.
BONWELL Charles S to Lucy Jane Smith 11 Dec 1843; d/o John Smith (alias John C Smith) con; Alex W F Mears sec; Louis D Heath & Jno Adams wits; m 13 Dec 1843 by P Warren Jr.
BONWELL James to Mary Robins 21 May 1783; James of Acc Co; (d/o Arthur Robins Jr & Tillar, his wife); Arthur Robins Jr sec.
BOOLE, BOOL See also BULL.
BOOL David N to Sally Bell 23 Nov 1840; d/o Edmund Bell dec'd; Jacob Spady sec & as to ages; m 24 Nov 1840 by G C Wescoat.
BOOL Edward to Margaret Ann Ward 13 Nov 1832; (d/o Tully S Ward dec'd) & wrd/o Wm Wyatt Jr sec; m 13 Nov 1832 by G Wescoat.
BOOL Ezekil to Mahala Stott 15 May 1819; d/o Labon Stott Sr con; Spencer Bool sec; Geo D White & Luther Stott wits; (m 27 May 1819. see BRec V1:22).
BOOL George to Mary Thompson 1798; by J Elliott.
BOOL George N to Ann Spady 9 Apr 1827; John Roberts sec & as to George N's age; Angelo A Townsend as to Ann's age; Severn E Parker & Isaac Andrews wits.
BOOL James M to Miss Elizabeth Rayfield 26 Feb 1852; Wm M Dunton as to Elizabeth's age; m 9 Mar 1852 by M B Newell.
BOOL John to Priscillah Addison 11 Jun 1776; d/o Thos Addison con; Hez Pitts sec; Jno Waltham &

Jno Turner wits.

BOOL Jonathan to Peggy Bool 8 Jun 1801; Teackle Turner sec; m (1801) by J Elliott.

BOOL Jonathon to Sally Dunton 22 Oct 1818; Samuel S West sec.

BOOLL Major to Patience Turner 28 Feb 1781; wid/o John Turner; Richard Booll sec; Elisha Abdeel wit.

BOOL Major to Eliza Roberts 3 Aug 1831; d/o Elizabeth Roberts & wid/o Francis Roberts; James Pratt sec; Elizabeth Roberts as to Eliza's age; m 3 Aug 1831 by G Wescoat.

BOOL Michael to Adeline Dunton 13 Jul 1840; d/o Rickard Dunton; David Bool as to Michael's age; Jacob Spady as to Adeline's age; Richard Miles sec; Geo P Scarburgh wit; m 16 Jul 1840 by W A Dix.

BOOL Nicholas to Elizabeth Nottingham 18 Aug 1802; Edmund Bell sec; m (1802) by I Bratten.

BOOL Richard to Margaret Addison 31 May 1787; Jonathan Stott sec.

BOOL Spencer to Charlotte Stott 5 Jun 1821; Thomas B Snead sec & as to Charlotte's age; m 25 Jul 1821 by C Bonewell. see BRec V1:22.

BOOLL See BOOLE

BOOTH John to Esther Cowdry 30 Apr 1792; d/o Wm Cowdry con; Jas Johnson sec; Sarah Godmin (Godwin?) wit; m Apr 1792 by C Simkins.

BOOTH William to Elizabeth Floyd (alias Elizabeth Roberts) 10 Dec 1821; Stephen Wilkinson sec & as to "Betsey's" age; s/o Easter Booth gives his age as 24y Feb next the 30 day 1822; Custis Kellum & Sam'l Dennis wits; m 20 Dec 1821 by C Bonewell.

BORROWS See BURRIS.

BOSMAN William to Elizabeth Mattocks 15 Feb 1660/1. Bk IX:92.

BOSS Nathaniel G to Mary A Powell Sep 1851; P Williams wit. Holmes Presb Ch Rec:12.

BOSWELL Abraham to Elishe Jacob 15 Mar 1763; d/o Esau Jacob sec.

BOSWELL Abraham to Mary Dixon 19 Aug 1774; wid; Jacob Moor sec.

BOSWELL James to Margaret Jacob 31 Dec 1770; James of Gloucester Co; Edmund Glanville sec.

BOW Moses to Margaret Savage 23 Sep 1710; he mariner; d/o Capt Thomas Savage; Hillary Stringer & Thomas Savage secs; Rob't Howson wit.

BOWDOIN John to Grace Stringer 10 Jan 1754; spinster; Littleton Eyre sec.

BOWDOIN Peter to Susanna Preeson 13 May 1733; d/o Thos & Elizabeth Preeson; Custis Kendall sec; John Custis & Mary Godwin wits.

BOWDOIN Peter to Lear Teackle 1 Aug 1801; John Robins sec.

BOWDOIN Peter S to Susan M Jacob 17 Oct 1818; Peter Bowdoin sec; (m 21 Oct 1818. see BRec V1:49).

BOWDOIN Preeson to Sarah Eyre 19 Feb 1759; d/o Littleton Eyre Esq con; Severn Eyre sec; Joachim Michael wit.

BOWDOIN Severn E to Laura A Upshur 21 Apr 1834; d/o Ann B Upshur sec.

BOYD Alexander to Sally Goffinson 24 Jan 1780; d/o Peter Goffigon dec'd; con Tabitha Biggs m/o Sally; Wm Stoakley sec.

BOYLE Charles D to Charlotte Jenkins 9 Aug 1847; wid/o George Jenkins; Jackson B Powell sec.

BOZMAN John S to Miss Margaret Elizabeth Kelly 14 Aug 1849; d/o Jesse Kelly dec'd; Joseph J Pearson sec & as to ages; Alfred Parker wit; m 15 Aug 1849 by P Warren.

BRADFORD Abel to Susan Gildon 29 Nov 1836; d/o John Gildon con; Teackle J Turner sec; George Gildon wit; m 1 Dec 1836 by W B Snead.

BRADFORD Abel to Miss Tamarzene White 23 Jul 1850; d/o Teackle S White dec'd; Wm Bradford as to Abel's age; Wm Hanby as to Tamarzene's age; Wm J Nottingham wit; m 25 Jul 1850 by P Warren.

BRADFORD Brown to Peggy Johnson 14 Mar 1788; d/o Obedience Johnson; Nath'l Darby sec.

BRADFORD Charles to Nancy Abdeel 7 Mar 1788; Rob't Rogers sec; m (1788) by E Baker.

BRADFORD Esrail to Sally Waltham 3 Jun 1795; Coventon Simkins sec; m Jun 1795 by C Simkins.

BRADFORD Ezra to Ann Smith 29 Dec 1784; George Pitts sec.

BRADFORD George to Elizabeth Boswell 31 Jan 1797; Rich'd Nottingham sec; m (1797) by J Elliott.

BRADFORD George to Sarah Willis 5 Apr 1822; Johannis Johnson sec & as to Sarah's age; m (23 Mar ?) 1822 by C Bonewell.

BRADFORD George to Mrs Nancy Dennis 19 May 1827; James Charnock sec; m 1827 by G C Wescoat.

BRADFORD George to Miss Betsy Kilman 20 Jun 1837; Wm Savage Sr sec & as to Betsy's age; Smith S Nottingham wit; m 22 Jun 1837 by G Wescoat.

BRADFORD Rev George to Mrs Elizabeth M Christian 30 Mar 1842; Patrick Warren Jr sec; m 7 Apr 1842 by P Warren.

BRADFORD John to Miss Esther P Ridley 28 Dec 1846; d/o Wm W Ridley sec & as to ages; J P Wescoat wit; m 30 Dec 1846 by M Oldham.

BRADFORD John Brown to Peggy Addison 3 Jul 1810; Thomas Addison sec; m (1810) by C Bonewell.

øBRADFORD Nathaniel G to Esther Ridley 12 Apr 1847; wid/o Wm P Ridley; John W Leatherbury sec; m 14 Apr 1847 by M Oldham.

BRADFORD William to Mary Williams 12 Jun 1837; William wrd/o Newton Harrison sec; wid/o John Williams; Wm W Wilson sec; Edmund Godwin wit; m 15 Jun 1837 by P Williams.

BRATTEN Isaac to Nancy Nottingham 27 Dec 1788; d/o Jacob Nottingham; John Nottingham sec; m (1788) by E Baker.

BRIAN See BRYAN.

BRICKHOUSE Albert S to Margaret S Mears 15 Nov 1836; d/o Thomas C Mears sec; Smith L Brickhouse as to Alfred's age; m 16 Nov 1836 by W B Snead.

BRICKHOUSE Charles O P to Peggy J Cutler 17 Sep 1852; s/o Elam L & Elizabeth Brickhous; m in Snow Hill, MD. see BRec V7:145.

BRICKHOUSE Elam L to Elizabeth P Fitchett 4 Sep 1828; Elam wrd/o Thomas S Brickhouse sec; d/o Charles Fitchett dec'd; Thos Fitchett as to Elizabeth's age; m 4 Sep 1828 by P Williams. see BRec V7:145.

BRICKHOUSE George to Hanna Luddington 4 Nov 1661. BK IX:114.

BRICKHOUSE George to Mary Belote 21 Nov 1781; d/o Edward Belote dec'd; Rich'd Nottingham sec.

BRICKHOUSE George Jr to Ann Sanford 20 Dec 1815; d/o James Sanford con; Wm White Jr sec; m (1815) by I Bratten.

BRICKHOUSE George to Sally B Nelson 23 Jun 1840; wid/o Charles Nelson; Louis P Rogers sec.

BRICKHOUSE John Jr to Susanna Nottingham 19 Feb 1785; d/o Thos Nottingham Sr; Robert Brickhouse sec.

BRICKHOUSE John to Polly Taylor

12 Dec 1825; John s/o George; wid/o Bartholomew Taylor; Edward R Turner sec; m 1825 by G C Wescoat.

BRICKHOUSE John N Jr to Catherine C Ames 22 Nov 1817; d/o Thomas Ames con; Thos S Brickhouse sec; Wm A Christian wit; m 26 Nov 1817 by C Bonewell.

BRICKHOUSE Robert to Sarah Nottingham 11 Mar 1783; Jno Williams sec.

BRICKHOUSE Smith to Peggy G Dunton 23 Mar 1808; Elias Dunton sec; Arthur R Savage con to Peggy; Thos Seaton wit; m (1808) by I Bratten.

BRICKHOUSE Smith to Miss Susanna G Dunton 19 Aug 1824; Henry G Dunton sec & as to ages; Benja F Dunton wit; m 19 Aug 1824 by C Bonewell.

BRICKHOUSE Smith L to Elizabeth W Nottingham 7 Apr 1834; d/o Major Smith Nottingham; Smith Nottingham sec; Jno N Brickhouse sec & as to Smith L's age; m 9 Apr 1834 by W B Snead.

BRICKHOUSE Theophilus H to Eliz S Brickhouse 7 Mar 1846; d/o Thomas S Brickhouse; Southey S Wilkins sec & as to ages; m 7 Mar 1846 by P Warren.

BRICKHOUSE Thomas E to Elizabeth N Luker 21 Dec 1835; wid/o John W Luker; James Saunders sec; Jno N Brickhouse as to Thomas' age; m 22 Dec 1835 by L Dix.

BRICKHOUSE Thomas S to Nancy Waterfield 29 Nov 1803; s/o John Brickhouse Jr con; Nancy wrd/o Richard Waterfield con; John Stratton sec; m (1803) by J Elliott.

BRITTINGHAM Elijah Jr to Miss Virginia S Nottingham 31 Dec 1840; d/o Sally R Nottingham sec; (Tubman?) L Moore wit.

BRITTINGHAM George W to Emily Jacob 22 Dec 1836; wid/o John C Jacob; George F Wilkins sec; m 22 Dec 1836 by W B Snead.

BRODWATER William to Ann Hall 11 Jan 1828; he Wm orp/o Robert P, wrd/o Obed Adams con; d/o Robert Hall dec'd; Shepherd A Joynes sec & as to Ann's age (Wm's gdn choice 31 Dec 1827 in Acc Co); m 1828 by G C Wescoat.

BROWN Allen to Nancy Smith 6 Apr 1808; Thomas Dillon sec; m (1808) by I Bratten.

BROWN Allen to Nancy Dowty 10 Jul 1816; Mat H Dunton sec.

BROWN Allen to Jenny (Jane) Davis 11 Mar 1822; wid; Charles Dillion sec; m 18 Mar 1822 by L Dix.

BROWN Allen to Rachel Williams 8 Jan 1838; wid/o Thomas Williams; John Segar sec; m 10 Jan 1838 by P Williams.

BROWN Charles T to Margaret Ames 17 Jul 1844; d/o Mrs Rachel Ames con; Smith Richardson sec & as to Charles' age; m 17 Jul 1844 by G C Wescoat.

BROWN Nathaniel to Nanny Dillion 9 Feb 1778; wid; Wm Saunders sec.

BRUFF John W to Miss Sarah J W Floyd 22 Feb 1843; John b 7 Apr 1818 s/o Joseph Bruff, Bayside, Talbot Co, MD; Sarah d/o Elijah Floyd dec'd; James R Garrison sec & as to Sarah's age; Louis P Regus wit.

BRYAN Henry to Nancey Holland 28 Mar 1764; Daniel Eshon sec. see BRec V5:180.

BRIAN Henry to Nancy Dunton 14 Dec 1818; Wm Dunton sec.

BRYAN Nath'l to Esther Mapp 20 Dec 1797; Nath'l Holland sec.

BUCKLAND Richard to Charity Coulston 26 Nov 1660. Bk IX:92.

BULL James to Mary Mears 24 Dec 1821; d/o William Mears (Mearse) con; Robert Sanford sec; Wm Mears as to James' age; Reubin Mears wit; m 26 Dec 1821 by C Bonewell.

BULL John to Sarah Ann Wingate

24 Dec 1838; Wm S Floyd sec & gdn/o Sarah.

BULL Richard to Keziah Bool 10 Dec 1783; Geo Ashby sec.

BULLOCK Thomas to Athaliah Underhill 11 Oct 1774; Thos Underhill sec.

BULLOCK Thomas to Mary Meholloms 12 Jan 1778; wid; Thos Cowdry sec.

BULLOCK Thomas to Nancy Wingate 30 May 1798; Wm B Wilson sec.

BUNDICK John S to Ann Custis West 19 Nov 1811; John of Acc Co; Charles West sec. see BRec V1:21.

BUNTING George to Elizabeth Johnson 6 Aug 1770; George of Acc Co; d/o Moses Johnson dec'd; Moses Johnson sec.

BUNTING Holloway to Priscilla Turner 21 May 1787; d/o John Furbush Turner con; Thos Clark sec.

BUNTING Holloway to Sally White 10 Jul 1797; Arthur Savage sec; m (1797) by J Elliot.

BUNTING James to Sally Harman 28 Dec 1816; Reuben Gooday sec; m 1 Jan 1817 by C Bonewell.

BUNTING James to Margaret Dunton 28 Dec 1840; d/o John Dunton dec'd; James & Thomas Dalby secs; James Dalby as to ages; Wm T Nottingham wit.

BUNTING John S to Dreusilla Jacob 8 Dec 1828; Nath'l Winder sec; Jno W Leatherbury gdn/o John S sec; Jno Gildon as to Dreusilla's age; Geo Wescoat & Chas Wilson wits; m 10 Dec 1828 by G Wescoat.

BUNTING John S to (Miss) Rachel Abdell 12 Jul 1830; d/o Abel Abdell dec'd & wrd/o Alexander W Ward sec; m 13 Jul 1830 by G Wescoat.

BUNTING Jonathan to Nancy White 9 Dec 1791; d/o Obedience White dec'd; Holloway Bunting sec; m Dec 1791 by C Simkins.

BUNTING Levin to Anne Bunting 13 Dec 1771; d/o Solomon Bunting sec.

BUNTING Samuel to Margaret Savage 9 Dec 1822; d/o Wm Savage Jr con; Benjamin N Scott sec.

BUNTING Shephard to Mary Denis 9 Sep 1812; d/o Sukey Denis con; Nath'l West sec; Andrew James & Lucy Denis wits; m (1812) by I Bratten.

BUNTING Solomon to Polly Pitts 30 May 1776; wid; Geo Bonnewill sec.

BUNTING William to Anne B Poulson 10 Dec 1821; Anne wrd/o Robert Ashby sec.

BURGESS Nathaniel to Anne Goffigon 14 Jan 1772; Nathaniel of Norfolk Co; d/o Peter Goffigon dec'd; Jno Nottingham sec.

BURRIS, BURRUS, BORROWS.

BURRUS Anthony to Mary Bell 12 Feb 1790; wid/o Robert Bell; Thos Jarvis sec; m (1790) by E Baker.

BURRIS Nathaniel to Frances D Goffigon 13 Jan 1817; d/o John Goffigon; Jno Goffigon sec; m (Jan 1817) by R Windsor; (m 16 Jan 1817. see BRec V1:107; V2:5).

BURRIS Nathaniel to Mary Ann Scott 5 Jan 1835; wid/o Benja N Scott; Nath'l L Goffigon sec; m 9 Jan 1835 by L Dix.

BURRIS Nathaniel G to Miss Mary Ann Powell 3 Nov 1851; Mary gdn/o Daniel Fitchett Esq con; Southey Goffigon & Wm S Burris & Andrew J Nottingham wits; m 6 Nov 1851 by P Williams. see BRec V1:107.

BORROWS Thomas to Sally Richardson 16 Nov 1807; Levi Richardson sec; m (1807) by I Bratten.

BURROWS See BURRIS.

BURTON John to Bridget Dalby 21 Jan (undated - in 1772 bundle; bef 1773 see North Co DB21:75); d/o Thomas Dalby Gent;

Edmund Glanville sec.
BURTON John to Ann Simkins 20 Feb 1800; Coventon Simkins sec; m Feb 1800 by C Simkins.
BURTON Peter to Betsy Drighouse 13 Oct 1829; d/o Nathan Drighouse (FN) sec ; m 15 Oct 1829 by P Williams.
BURTON William Jr to Elizabeth Eyre 25 Dec 1721. Geo Harmanson & Zerub Preeson secs; John West wit; Clerk directs the license to minister Thomas Dole (Dell).
BUTLER Thomas to Frances Costin 19 Feb 1778; Abraham Costin sec.
BUXTON Thomas to Maria Parvin 3 Jun 1818; Zacheus Parvin sec; m 3 Jun 1818 by C Bonewell.
BYRD See also BIRD.
BYRD William to Polly Richardson 12 Nov 1821; Thomas Mehollomes sec; m 12 Nov 1821 by C Bonewell.

C

CABLE Thomas to Sorrowful Margaret Kendall 25 May 1723; wid/o Wm Kendall; Gawton Hunt & Edw'd Carter secs; lic 25 May 1723. CTRet Oct 1723.
CAMALL James to Katherine Larre 26 May 1661. Bk IX:114.
CAMPBELL Nicholas to Anne Pigot 21 Dec 1779; d/o Salem Pigot dec'd; John Dolby sec.
CAMPBELL Simon to Joannah Roberts 17 May 1736; wid/o Elias Roberts; Geo Holt sec; lic 17 May 1736. CTRet Oct 1736.
CAMPBELL William J to Mary A H Brittingham 26 Mar 1828; d/o Elijah Brittingham sec; m 27 Mar 1828 by P Williams.
CAMPBELL William J to Elizabeth W Young 24 Aug 1840; widr; spinster d/o John Young dec'd; Wm W Cutler sec & late gdn/o Elizabeth & as to her age; Rich'd Mapp wit; m 24 Aug 1840 by S T Ames.
CAMPBELL William T to Miss Eleanore S Floyd 27 Feb 1831; d/o Mrs Lavenia A Floyd con; Joseph E Bell as to William's age; Wm T Duncan wit; m 27 Feb 1851 by P Warren.
CAPLE John to Anne Phaben 20 Dec 1788; d/o Paul Phaben dec'd; Wm Phaben sec; m (1788) by E Baker.
CAPLE William to Anne Luke (undated in 1787 bundle); John Roberts sec.
CAPLE William to Esther Odear 14 Aug 1787; s/o Major Caple con; d/o Wm Odear con; John Groves sec.
CARMINE See also COMINES.
CARMINE Elijah to Camilla White 28 Jun 1798; John White sec.
CARMINE James to Elishe Trower 14 May 1808; Henry Fitchew sec.
CARMINE John to Polly Abdill 25 May 1801; John Nottingham Sr sec; m 1801 by I Bratten.
CARMINE William to Nancy Beloat 13 Mar 1797; Ezra Bradford sec; m (1799) by C Simkins.
CARMINE William to Elizabeth Abdell 30 Dec 1826; Geo C Wescoat sec & as to Elizabeth's age; m 1826 by G C Wescoat.
CARMINE William T to Lavenia Rayfield 8 Jan 1845; d/o Harrison T Rayfield dec'd; Joshua G Stewart sec & as to ages; Wm P Nottingham wit; m 8 Jan 1845 by G C Wescoat.
CARPENTER Aden to Elizabeth Dunton 23 Jan 1849; d/o Rickards Dunton con; Wm T Nottingham sec; Thos Dalby as to Aden's age; Wm A Williams & Robins Mapp & James S Ball wits; m 24 Jan 1849 by P Warren.
CARPENTER Charles Jr to Elizabeth Mathews 15 Apr 1758; d/o John Custis Mathews sec; Jno Bowdoin wit.
CARPENTER Charles to Bridget Matthews 8 Nov 1768; wid; Hezekiah Brickhouse sec.
CARPENTER Charles to Susanna

Waltham 18 Sep 1782; John Carpenter sec.

CARPENTER James to Nelly Fletcher 15 Dec 1824; d/o Jas Fletcher of Hog Island, VA con; Ely Dowty & Samuel Fletcher wits; Shepperd B Floyd sec.

CARPENTER James S to Anne Dennis 1 Oct 1834; d/o Archibald Dennis; James Isdell sec & as to Anne's age; m 3 Oct 1834 by L Dix.

CARPENTER Jas S to Adeline Bool 22 Nov 1843; wid/o Michael Bool; Michael Dennis sec; m 23 Nov 1843 by P Warren Jr.

CARPENTER John to Lucy Gault 22 Sep 1787; d/o Dicky Gault; Wm Jacob sec.

CARPENTER John to Adah Floyd 14 Nov 1796; Wm Roberts Jr sec; Mathew Floyad con; m (1796) by J Elliot; m 17 Nov 1796 Brec V 11: 111.

CARPENTER John Jr to Fanny Scott 11 Mar 1799; d/o John Scott con; John Carpenter Sr sec; m 18 Mar 1799 by C Simkins.

CARPENTER John to Peggy Floyd 10 Apr 1809; John Floyd sec.

CARPENTER John B to Mary Harrison 1 Jan 1830; d/o Abel Harrison of Hog Island, VA con; James S Carpenter sec; Samuel Fletcher & Ely Dowty wits; Jas S Harrison as to John B's age; m 11 Jan 1830 by G Wescoat.

CARPENTER John B to Miss Sally Fletcher 18 Jan 1849; d/o Wm Fletcher; James S Carpenter sec & as to Sally's age; Wm M Dunton wit; m 18 Jan 1849 by P Warren.

CARPENTER John B to Miss Mary Martin 2 Dec 1852; widr; m 2 Dec 1852 by P Warren.

CARPENTER John C to Eliza Clay 12 Jun 1826; ELiza wrd/o Peter Williams Jr sec; m 15 Jun 1826 by P Williams Jr.

CARPENTER John P to Miss Mary Harrison 12 Sep 1853; Jno S Robins as to ages; Jas S Carpenter wit; m 12 Sep 1853 by P Warren.

CARPENTER Lewis to Miss Ann Ward 18 Nov 1851; d/o Mrs Susan Ward con; Samuel B Ward wit; John H Rayfield & Smith N Brickhouse as to Lewis' age; m 19 Nov 1851 by P Warren.

CARPENTER Samuel G to Elizabeth W Nelson 9 Jan 1826; Sally T Nelson gdn/o Elizabeth con; William Goffigon sec; Ves Ellis wit; m Jan 1826 by L Dix.

CARPENTER William to Tabitha Goffigon 28 May 1781; d/o Peter Goffigon dec'd & d/o Tabitha Biggs con, also Alex Boyd con; Michael Dunton sec.

CARTER Benjamin to Betsey Drighouse 26 Nov 1823; Betsey wrd/o the said Benjamin Carter; Charles Pool sec (FN).

CARTER Edward to Mary Mapp 13 Jan 1725; Ether Mapp & Jno Mapp secs; Wm Eyre wit.

CARTER James Jr to Adah Collins Jr 13 Oct 1818; Jacob Wooser sec; m 15 Oct 1818 by C Bonewell.

CARTER Major to Juliet Ann Scisco (FN) 20 Dec 1824; Peter Thompson sec & as to Juliet Ann's age; m bet 15 Jun - 22 Dec 1824 by G C Wescoat.

CARTER Thomas to Sophia Jeffries 7 Dec 1803; Peter Toyer sec (FN); m (1803) by J Elliott.

CARVEY Richard to Sarah Walter 1 Oct 1722; wid; John West & Sorrowful Margaret Kendall secs; Thos Dell (minister) asks clerk to grant Richard a license and place fee to Dell's account.

CARY Obed to Esther Nottingham 16 Dec 1783; Seth Powell sec.

CARY William to Esther Matthews 8 Mar 1768; d/o John Custis Matthews; Arthur Simpkins sec.

CASEY John to Ann Willis 8 Jan 1820*; Marriott Willis sec; Isaiah W Baker wit; m 11 Jan 1821* by C Bonewell. *discrepancy

CASEY John T to Miss Malinda

O'dear 25 Nov 1850; d/o William O'dear dec'd; m 27 Nov 1850 by P Warren.

CHANDLER Lucius Henry to Miss Susan Ann Kendall 9 Dec 1833; John Goffigon Sr sec; Temple N Robins as to Susan's age; John Barnard as to Lucius Henry's age; m 10 Dec 1833 by P Williams.

CHARNICK John to Polly Roberts 23 Dec 1833; John Speakman sec & as to ages; m 25 Dec 1833 by L Dix.

CHARNICK John to Miss Fanny Rippin* 27 Dec 1837; d/o* Thomas Speakman (dec'd); James Willis sec; m 28 Dec 1837 by L Dix. *discrepancy

CHARNICK John T to Harriet Williams 11 Jan 1845; d/o Peter Williams Sr dec'd; Benjamin Nottingham sec & as to ages; m 18 Jan 1845 by G G Exall.

CHARNICK William H to Mrs Mary P Ames 22 Jan 1849; d/o William Clark; Covington Bennett sec & as to Mary's age; Jno R Birch & Rich'd H Read wits; m 24 Jan 1849 by M Oldham.

CHARNOCK Abel to Peggy Collins 14 Mar 1803; Emanuel Hosier sec; m bet 1 Jan - 13 Apr 1803 by I Bratten.

CHARNOCK Eli (Elias) to Jenny Dennis 12 May 1817; John Ross sec; m 14 May 1817 by C Bonewell.

CHARNOCK George to Margaret S Bonewell 31 Mar 1834; d/o John K Bonewell sec; Southy Rew as to George's age.

CHARNOCK James to Sally Robinson 16 Jan 1832; Samuel Watson sec & as to ages.

CHARNOCK John T to Leah Spady 19 Jan 1850; wid/o John Spady of John dec'd; Major Richardson sec; George O'dear as to John's age; Jas H White wit.

CHASE William to Sarah Hewitt 16 Dec 1660. BK IX:92

CHRISTIAN James to Charlotte Bingham 18 Sep 1810; Benja Gardner sec.

CHRISTIAN Michael to Rose Powell d/o John & Sarah 7 Dec 1722; lic CT Ret Oct 1723. see BRec V7:151; CR PK 4 Feb 1722/3.

CHRISTIAN Michael to Patience Michael 30 Dec 1747; spinster & d/o Joachim Michael con; Geo Holt sec. see BRec V7:151.

CHRISTIAN Michael to Elizabeth Barlow 20 Feb 1770; Rob't Polk sec; Wm Benthall wit.

CHRISTIAN William to Kasiah Blair 7 Jun 1750; wid; John Flood sec; Mary Stith wit.

CHRISTIAN William to Matildah Johnson 6 Jan 1761; d/o Kelly Johnson dec'd & Kelly's wife Butifiler con; Obadiah Johnson sec.

CHRISTIAN William S to Miss Susan Wilkins 11 Jun 1845; William wrd/o M W Fisher & W B Upshur secs; d/o George F Wilkins sec; m 19 Jun 1845 by J Ufford. HunParReg:35.

CHURCH Littleton to Louisa Thompson FN 20 Jul 1826; Wm Thompson & Wm Church secs & as to ages; m 20 Jul 1826 by S S Gunter.

CHURCH Peter to Eliza Collins FN 24 Dec 1828; d/o Ritta Collins FN & as to Eliza's age; George Upshur FN sec & as to Peter's age.

CHURCH Solomon to Arinthia Stevens FN 15 Jan 1850; d/o Lilly Tomson con; Horace Stevens as to Solomon's age; Tully R Wise sec; m 22 Jan 1850 by P Warren.

CHURCH Toney to Anne Johnson FN 3 Jan 1834; Robert J Bingham FN sec & as to ages.

CHURCH Tony to Elizabeth Floyd 14 Dec 1840; d/o Sally Floyd FN sec; Littleton Church sec.

CHURN George E to Miss Rosey Scott 30 Dec 1849; s/o Thomas Churn dec'd; d/o Ann Carpenter dec'd; James Dennis sec; Edw'd R Waddy as to ages; m 31 Dec

1849 by P Warren.
CHURN Severn to Tamar Melholloms 13 Jan 1791; Archibald Dowty sec; Geo Brickhouse gives Tamar's age as 21y the 2 Jan 1791; m (1791) by E Baker.
CHURN Thomas to (Miss) Catharine Fletcher 13 Dec 1830; d/o Wm Fletcher dec'd; Thos W Badger sec; Wm W Churn as to Catharine's age; m 15 Dec 1830 by G Wescoat.
CHURN William to Dimarara Roberts 19 Jan 1826; Geo C Wescoat gdn/o William sec; Joshua K Roberts gdn/o Dimarara sec; m 1826 by G C Wescoat.
CHURN William W to Sally Powell 11 Jan 1831; wid/o James Powell; Wm Church sec & as to William W's age; m 11 Jan 1831 by G Wescoat.
CLARK Thomas to Elizabeth Warren 23 Mar 1787; Wm Godwin sec.
CLARK Thomas to Adah Ward 8 Dec 1806; James Ward sec; m (1806) by I Bratten.
CLARK William to Polly Parker 28 Sep 1810; Polly wrd/o Hezekiah Pitts con; Keley Stott sec; Edw'd Bailey & John Core wits; m (1810) by C Bonnewell.
CLAY James to Elizabeth Hickman 20 Aug 1816; Thomas Powell sec; m 25 Aug 1816 by R Windsor.
CLAY Thomas to Sally Freshwater 2 Nov 1796; d/o Wm Freshwater con; Peter Bowdoin sec; m 1796 by E Baker.
CLAY William to Nancy Fitchett 8 Jan 1782; d/o Joshua Fitchett dec'd; John Wheeler Jr sec.
CLEGG Hillary to Mary Elligood 14 Dec 1786; John Tyson sec; m (1786) by E Baker.
CLEGG Hillary to Peggy Knight 29 Nov 1788; d/o Wm Knight dec'd; Westerhouse Widgen sec.
CLEGG Isaac to Peggy Major 25 Feb 1756; d/o Wm Major (dec'd ? - bond damaged); Patrick Harmanson sec; Wm Wilson wit.
CLEGG Isaac to Esther Jacob 17 Jun 1763; wid/o (Abraham Jacob); John Waterfield sec.
CLEGG Isaac Jr to Agnes Piper 2 Dec 1783; d/o Josiah Piper con & gives Agnes' age as 17y last April; John Dalby (CN) sec.
CLEGG Isaiah to Anne Belote 8 May 1764; wid; Benja Dixson sec.
CLEGG James E to Miss Elizabeth W Mears 30 Oct 1843; d/o Wm Mears sec & as to James' age; Jno T Wilkins wit; m 1 Nov 1843 by P Warren Jr.
CLEGG Major to Patience Benthall 9 Oct 1794; Peter Clegg sec.
CLEGG Major to Nancy Mehollomes 18 Jan 1800; Johannes Johnson sec; m (1800) by J Elliott.
CLEGG Peter to Rosanna Milby 2 Jul 1784; Rosanna orp; Thos Waterfield sec; Coventon Simkins con for the marriage.
CLEGG Peter M to Lovely Watson 31 Jul 1810; d/o Edmund Watson con; John S Heath sec; m (1810) by J Elliott.
CLEGG Robert to Elizabeth Scott 21 Dec 1784; wid/o Wm Scott; Arthur Evans sec; WB 27:70 DB 23:37,205.
CLEGG Robert to Polly Bloxom 24 Dec 1798; Stuart Sanders sec; m (1798) by J Elliot.
CLEGG William to Susanna Dixon 20 Nov 1779; d/o John Dixon dec'd; John Widgeon Sr sec.
CLEGG William m Sally Stoyte 1811 by J Elliott.
CLEGG William to Miss Elizabeth Spady Speakman 23 Dec 1845; d/o Wm S Speakman sec & as to William's age; Calvin L Warren wit; m 25 Dec 1845 by P Williams.
CLOWES Peter to (Miss) Margaret F Mears 13 Dec 1830; d/o Richard Mears dec'd; Thos P Wise sec & as to ages; m 14 Dec 1830 by G Wescoat.
COBB Arthur to Peggy Edmunds 1 Dec 1803; Dickie Dunton sec; m

(1803) by C Fisher.

COBB Nathan F to Esther Fletcher 13 Sep 1842; wid/o Charles Fletcher; Wm W Andrews sec; m 27 Sep 1842 at Sandshoal by G L Lunsden.

COBB Nathan F Jr to Miss Sally Dowty 2 Dec 1848; John H Powell gdn/o Sally con; John W Dowty sec; Edw'd R Waddey as to Nathan's age; m 3 Dec 1848 by P Warren.

COBB Southy to Anne Pratt 29 Aug 1787; Wm Rippin sec.

COBB William H to Betsey Peake 17 Jan 1822; s/o Southey Cobb con; Salley Pratt & Siller (?) Peak as to Betsey's age; John Bull sec; m 17 Jan 1822 by C Bonewell.

COE Timothy to Eliza Teague 29 Sep 1660. Bk IX:92.

COEDY Robert m Mary Gale 1 Dec 1821 by L Dix.

COLEBURN John F to Miss Eliza C Wiliams 14 Feb 1848; d/o Rev Peter Williams sec; Wm W Creekmore as to John's age; Luther Nottingham wit; m 15 Feb 1848 by B H Johnson.

COLEBURN Richard to Peggy Booll 20 Dec 1796; Wm Aimes sec; m (1796) by J Elliot.

COLEBURN Thomas A to Maria S Holland 20 Mar 1834; d/o Nathl Holland sec. see BRec V5:180.

COLLINS Caleb to Sabra Stephens FN 9 Jun 1851; d/o Adah Stephens con; Severn Collins as to Caleb's age; m 9 Jun 1851 by M Oldham.

COLLINS Henry to Susan Pool 12 Feb 1827; s/o Ralph Collins; d/o Charles Pool sec.

COLLINS Jacob to Susan Weicks FN 3 Sep 1851; s/o Margaret Collins; d/o Jenny Weicks now Jenny Collins; John Collins as to ages; m 4 Sep 1851 by M Oldham.

COLLINS James to Betsey Stevens FN 23 Dec 1822; d/o Littleton Stevens who gives her age as 22y; Jacob Collins sec; m 23 Dec 1822 by S Wilmer.

COLLINS James to Eliza Wilkerson 22 May 1837; Wm D Mitchell as to Eliza's age; James Wilkins sec & as to James' age.

COLLINS James to Miss Margaret Weicks FN 27 Dec 1851; Gabe Weicks wit; Edm'd Press & Thos J Nottingham as to James' age; m 28 Dec 1851 by H Dalby.

COLLINS John to Anne Clegg 21 Nov 1786; Hillary Clegg sec.

COLLINS John to Nanny Sabers 11 Aug 1790; Peter Warren sec; m (1790) by C Simkins (MinRet reads "Nancy Sobers").

COLLINS John to Grace Costin 12 Sep 1796; John Trower sec; m 1796 by E Baker.

COLLINS John to Betsey Jeffries 3 Feb 1803; Samuel Beavans sec (FN); m (1803) by J Elliott.

COLLINS John to Nancy Pratt 7 Oct 1813; Nath'l Bishop sec; m (1813) by J Elliott.

COLLINS John to Comfort Beavans 19 Feb 1823; Mac Collins sec (FN).

COLLINS (Short) John to Adah Bevans FN 30 Oct 1830; d/o Molly Bevans; Nath'l J Winder sec; Molly Bevans as to Adah's age; m 2/3 Nov 1830 by Sorin.

COLLINS John to Betty Jenney Brickhouse 29 Dec 1830; s/o Betty Collins; d/o Esther Brickhouse FN; Wm Stevens sec (notation states "see Fr Negro's Register No. 143"); Adah Perkins as to ages; m 30 Dec 1830 to G Wescoat.

COLLINS John to Mary Juliet Scott 4 Jun 1834; d/o John Scott dec'd & wife Salley Scott con; Obediah Scott sec & as to John's age; Daniel Scott & Thomas Jarvis wits; m 5 Jun 1834 by P Williams.

COLLINS John to Mary Jane Upshur FN 6 Mar 1851; d/o Susan Upshur con; A J Nottingham & Sam'l Scherer wits; m 12 Mar 1851 by M

Oldham.

COLLINS Joseph to Betsey Anderson 31 Jan 1799; John Collins sec; m 1 Feb 1799 by A Foster.

COLLINS Leonard to Emeline Howell FN 17 Feb 1841; d/o Mary Howell sec FN; Jno Kendall sec & as to Leonard's age.

COLLINS Lighty (Lite) to Lear Drighouse (FN) 3 Jan 1795; Thos Lewis sec; m Jan 1795 by C Simkins.

COLLINS Mac to Betsey Shepherd 27 Nov 1809; Abraham Lang sec (FN); m (1809) by J Elliott.

COLLINS Nathaniel to Salley Wilson 6 Oct 1807; d/o Stoakly Wilson con; Anthony Bell sec; m (1807) by J Elliott.

COLLINS Nathaniel to Molly Sample FN 16 Aug 1810; Isaiah Carter sec; Thos Simkins as to Nath'l being a free man; m (1810) by J Elliott.

COLLINS Nathaniel to Molly Widgeon 24 Mar 1812; Westerhouse Widgeon sec; m (1812) by J Elliott.

COLLINS Nathl to Margaret Collins FN 5 Dec 1849; Margaret wrd/o the said Nathaniell; Frederick Moses sec; Joseph E Bell wit; m 15 Dec 1849 by H Dalby.

COLLINS Patrick to Sukey Becket 14 Nov 1807; Wm Drigus sec (FN); m (1807) by J Elliott.

COLLINS Patrick to Comfort Francis 26 Dec 1829; d/o Wm Francis Jr sec; Jacob (Long Jake) Collins sec & as to Patrick's age FN; m 31 Dec 1829 by P Williams.

COLLINS Ralph to Tamar Bingham 20 Dec 1794 (FN); John Simkins sec; m Dec 1794 by C Simkins.

COLLINS Severn (alias Weeks) to Nancy Beavans 25 Mar 1823; d/o John; Mac Collins sec (FN).

COLLINS Severn to Margaret Collins 8 Aug 1850; s/o Eliza Collins; d/o Jenny Collins FN; m 10 Aug 1850 by M Oldham.

COLLINS Victor to Ann Maria Read 21 Dec 1839; d/o Adah Read (alias Adah Stephens) con; Smith S Nottingham sec; m 26 Dec 1839 by S T Ames.

COLLINS William to Susan Parsons 14 May 1827; Susan wrd/o Thomas Hallett sec.

COLLINS William to Betsy Thompson 11 Jun 1838; wid/o Wm Thompson; Samuel Bunting as to Wm's age; John S Bunting sec; m 13 Jun 1838 by G C Wescoat.

COLONNA Michael to Miss Eliz A Evans 16 Aug 1848; d/o Mrs Lucinda Evans; Thos H Bagwell & Obedience R Johnson as to ages; Samuel H Parsons sec; m 17 Aug 1848 by P Williams.

COLONA William P to Miss Sarah D Pitts 27 Feb 1826; George C Wescoat sec; m 1826 by G C Wescoat.

COMER Michael to Margt Griffeth 3 Jan 1778; Wm Rippin sec.

COMINES William to Elizabeth Garrett 13 Sep 1813; Harrison Nottingham sec; m (1813) by I Bratten.

COMMINES William to Peggy Wilson 4 Jan 1803; d/o Anne Wilson con; John Commines sec; m bet 1 Jan - 12 Apr 1803 by I Bratten.

COOKE Giles to Margaret Savage 3 Oct 1750; Giles of Gloucester Co; spinster & d/o Esther Savage who gives Marg't's age as 21y; Wm Tazewell Jr sec.

COOK John to Molly Graves 9 Dec 1799; Robertson Custis sec.

COPELAND William to (Mary Savage* - no name on Bond) 19 Sep 1721; Thos Savage Sr & Thos Savage Jr secs; Geo Harmanson wit. * see Wh1:221.

COPES James S to Miss Margaret S Saunders 1 Nov 1852; d/o Samuel Saunders; James Saunders as to James' age; m 3 Nov 1852 by P Warren.

COPES Leonard B to Elizabeth Bell 22 Nov 1848; d/o Polly Bell con; David Bool & Wm W Mehollomes wits; Lafayette Harmanson sec; m 23 Nov 1848 by P Warren.

COPES Levin to Polly Viccus 13 May 1811; Wm Downes sec; m (1811) by J Elliott.

COPES Thomas to Jenney Luke 12 Mar 1804; Zachariah Wise sec; m (1804) by I Bratten.

COPES Thomas to Fanny Warren 6 Jan 1815; John Upshur Jr sec; m (1815) by J Elliott.

COPES Thomas Jr to Sally Saunders 21 Jan 1817; James Floyd sec; m (1817) by R Windsor.

COPES Thomas Sr to Damia Hickman 17* May 1817*; Wm G Pitts sec; m 16* May 1817 by G Bonewell. *discrepancy

COPES Thomas to Miss Elizabeth W Cottingham 19 Dec 1853; d/o Henry Cottingham con & as to Thomas's age; C F Anderson wit.

CORE Caleb to Sarah Parramore 27 Sep 1793; Kendall Belote sec; m Sep 1793 by C Simkins.

CORE Caleb to Susey Hickman 28 Aug 1806; Richard Dunton sec; m (1806) by I Bratten.

CORE Charles to Betty Dolby 12 Jan 1768; Edmund Core sec.

CORE Edmund to Sarah Garris 25 Dec 1760; d/o Thomas Garris; John Downing sec.

CORE Eleazer to Keziah Rodgers 15 Jan 1783; Stuart Holt sec.

CORE John to Susanna Baker 20 Dec 1785; Wm Wilkins Sr sec.

CORE Posthumos to Susanna Henderson 12 Mar 1750; Jacob Henderson sec.

CORE William H to Margaret Wheeler 10 Dec 1832; d/o Thomas A Wheeler sec; Elijah Brittingham as to Wm H's age; m Dec 1832 by L Dix.

COSDY See COEDY.

COSTIN Abraham Jr to Peggy Costin 21 Jul 1798; d/o Francis Costin con & sec.

COSTIN Abraham to Mary Goffingon 7 Jan 1806; Thos Nottingham sec; m (1806) by J Elliott.

COSTIN Coventon to Mary Taylor 8 Jan 1827; Mary wrd/o Thos S Evans sec; Isaac S Evans as to Coventon's age; John Spady Sr wit.

COSTIN Elijah to Charlott Trower 6 Oct 1817; Laurance Enholm sec; m 9 Oct 1817 by S W Woolford.

COSTIN Elijah to Rosy S Spady 30 Oct 1830; wid/o Southy Spady; Silas Jefferson sec.

COSTIN Francis to Susanna Elliot 7 Dec 1764; d/o Thos Elliot sec.

COSTIN Francis to Mary Pratt 9 Oct 1820; Thos Moore sec; m 28 Dec 1820 by L Dix.

COSTIN Henry to Racheal Saunders 14 Feb 1782; d/o James Saunders dec'd & wife Tibitha con; Stuart Saunders & Elligood Ayres secs.

COSTIN Henry to Margaret Dumus 20 May 1817; Abram Costin sec; m 4 Jun 1817 by C Bonewell.

COSTIN Isaac to Nancy Nottingham 1 Jan 1819; d/o Wm Nottingham con; John Evans sec; John Graves & Rachel Joins wits; m 7 Jan 1819 by W Costin.

COSTIN Jacob to Sophia Savage 1 Feb 1733; James Forse sec.

COSTIN James H to Margaret Spady 10 Mar 1828; d/o Southy Spady; Silas Jefferson sec; Elijah Costin as to James' age; m Mar 1828 by L Dix.

COSTIN John to Elizabeth Fitchett 6 Aug 1793; d/o Joshua Fitchett con; Henry Giddens sec; m (1793) by E Baker.

COSTIN John to Nancy Evans 5 Sep 1800; John Evans sec; m Sep 1800 by C Simkins.

COSTIN John to Maria Ellis 23 Jul 1821; William Dixon sec & as to Maria's age.

COSTIN John W to Louisa Griffith 10 Dec 1810; d/o B Griffith con; Patrick Warren sec; Peter Williams Jr & John Griffith wits; m (1810) by J Elliott.

COSTIN Matthew to Mary Joynes 24 Nov 1791; wid; Wm Satchell Jr

COSTIN Patrick F to Anne Nottingham 9 Dec 1822; Anne wrd/o James Saunders sec; m 12 Dec 1822 by L Dix.
COSTIN Samuel to Elizabeth Griffith 13 Dec 1785; d/o ___ con; Thos Widgeon sec.
COSTIN Samuel to Polly Roberts 19 Jan 1796; Parker Willis sec.
COSTIN Samuel to Mary T Whitehead 10 Mar 1851; d/o Thomas Whitehead; Thos S Evans as to Samuel's age; Zerobabel Gibb as to Mary's age; Jas M Brickhouse wit.
COSTIN Seth to Priscila Elliott 16 Dec 1839; d/o Jerimiah Elliott; James Hampleton sec & as to ages; m 19 Dec 1839 by P Williams.
COSTIN Stephen to Peggy Kellam 12 Jun 1838; Victor A Nottingham sec; John Moore as to ages; m 14 Jun 1838 by P Williams.
COSTIN William to Anne Trower 23 Mar 1773; s/o Mathew Costin con - Mathew at first denied con; d/o Robert Trower dec'd; Wm Trower sec;
COSTIN William to Lucretia Dixon 12 Jan 1791; Griffin Stith sec; Elizabeth Dixon con for Lucretia; m (1791) by E Baker.
COSTIN William Jr to Elizabeth Thurston 6 Aug 1811; Peter Williams sec; m (1811) by I Bratten.
COSTIN William G to Elizabeth S Brickhouse 18 Dec 1833; d/o Smith Brickhouse dec'd; John N Brickhouse sec; Elam L Brickhouse as to Elizabeth's age; Benja J Dalby as to William's age; m 24 Dec 1833 by P Willams.
COSTIN William G to Ann S Dalby 25 Nov 1837; d/o Hezekiah Dalby sec; m 30 Nov 1837 by P Williams. see BRec V1:78.
COSTIN William T to Nancy Roberts 21 Nov 1838; d/o Thomas Roberts Sr; Thomas S Brickhouse sec; James Hampleton as to ages; m 27 Nov 1838 by P Williams.
COTTINGHAM Elisha D to Harriet S Nicholson 16 Apr 1844; wid/o Levin H Nicholson; Sylvestor Kelly sec; m 16 Apr 1844 by G G Exall.
COTTINGHAM Henry to Miss Elizabeth G Smith 8 Dec 1824; Elijah Brittingham sec & as to ages; m Dec 1824 by L Dix.
COTTINGHAM Henry to Elizabeth Wilkins 5 Dec 1827; d/o Benjamin Wilkins dec'd; Wm B Nottingham sec & as to ages; m Dec 1827 by L Dix.
COTTINGHAM Thomas to Ann Davis 27 Dec 1802; John Taylor sec; m (1802) by I Bratten.
COTTINGHAM William H to Mary Ann Casey 9 Jun 1851; s/o Henry Cottingham con & as to Mary Ann's age; d/o John Casey dec'd.

COTRAL, COTTRELL.
COTRAL James to Elizabeth Stephens FN 26 Jan 1848; d/o Susan Stephens sec; Jesse N Jarvis sec; m 28 Jan 1848 by H Dalby.
COTTREL John to Betsey Fletcher 22 May 1800; Thomas Fletcher sec; m 1800 by I Bratten.
COTTRELL John S to Miss Elizabeth Carpenter 1 Jan 1849; d/o John Carpenter Sr; James Dennis sec & as to Elizabeth's age; m 1 Jan 1849 by P Warren.
COWDRY Savage to Mary Barlow 15 Jun 1758; d/o Rev Henry Barlow con; Thos White sec; Sarah Seymour & Bridget Westerhouse wits.
COWDRY Thomas to Sarah Jacob 11 Nov 1769; d/o Esau Jacob; Edmund Glanville sec.
COWLES John to Rachel Stephens 1 Mar 1787; Rachel gives con for herself to marry; Wm Stith sec.
COX Moses to Jeaca Mills 24 Mar 1749; Moses of Norfolk Co; d/o Wm Mills con; John Flood sec;

Michael Nottingham & Wm Scott & Sarah Scott wits.
COX Samuel m Susanna Beloat (1798) by J Elliott.
COX Samuel to Nancy Whitehead 14 Nov 1820; Charles Bonwell sec; m 18 Nov 1820 by C Bonewell.
CRAIG, CRAIK.
CRAIK John to Rosey Cutler 9 Jan 1804; Wm Parkinson sec; m 1804 by C Fisher.
CRAIK William A to Ann W Gunter 12 Apr 1824; Thomas E Addison gdn/o William sec; S S Gunter gdn/o Ann sec; m 14 Apr 1824 by S S Gunter.
CROSWELL William to Elisha Strips 25 Nov 1786; Nath'l Eshon sec; m (1786) by E Baker.
CULLIN Samuel to Polly Rippin 10 Apr 1792; Southy Cobb sec; m Apr 1792 by C Simkins.
CULPEPPER Jesse to Edith S Brickhouse 10 Sep 1838; Elam L Brickhouse sec & gdn/o Edith; m 13 Sep 1838 by P Williams.
CUSTIS Henry to Betty Downing 29 Aug 1763; Henry of Acc Co; d/o Arthur Downing dec'd; John Downing Jr sec.
CUSTIS John to Anne Kendall 3 Mar 1732; Thos Cable sec; Peggy Kendall & Custis Kendall wits. Wm & Mary Q:264.
CUSTIS John W to Margaret W Addison 5 Jul 1826; d/o J Addison con; Jno R Wise sec; Jno W Leatherbury wit; m 12 Jul 1826 by S S Gunter.
CUSTIS Robinson to Mary Savage 6 Aug 1793; Thomas Dunton sec; m Aug 1793 by C Simkins.
CUSTIS Thomas to Anne Kendall 24 Jun 1717; Thomas of Acc Co; Sarah Custis of Northampton Co sec.
CUSTIS Thomas to Ann Parsons 21 May 1808; Wm White sec.
CUSTIS Thomas O to Betsy Powell 11 May 1846; wid/o Jesse Powell; Wm G Johnson sec; m 11 May 1846 by G C Wescoat.
CUSTIS Dr Thomas V to Miss Peggy Dixon 2 Jul 1803; d/o Samuel W Brown & wife con (to "our dau Peggy"); Coventon Simkins sec; con signed from "Golden Quarter."
CUSTIS William to Elizabeth Willett 20 Dec 1803; Robinson Custis sec; m (1803) by J Elliott.
CUSTIS William S (Jr?) to Eleanor D Wise 13 Dec 1832; Eleanor wrd/o John Addison con; Samuel L Floyd sec; Teackle W Jacob wit.
CUTLER Peter to Rosey Finney 1 Sep 1818;' James Johnson sec.
CUTLER Richard to Margaret Dann 21 Jan 1819; John Adams sec.
CUTLER Richard to Delitha A Wilkins 30 Apr 1831; Delitha wrd/o Delitha Wilkins con; John Wilkins Jr sec; John M Wilkins wit.

D

DALBY See DOLBY.
DANN Samuel to Mrs Naomi Wheeler 10 Dec 1838; Wm H Wescoat sec.
DAN Silas to Mary Sheerwood 10 Jul 1802; Michael Savage sec; l (1802) by I Bratten.
DARBY John to Esther Harmanson 31 Dec 1777; d/o Jno Harmanson Sr; Wm Harmanson sec.
DARBY Col John to Esther Christian 14 May 1782; Griffin Stith Jr sec; (m 15 May 1782. see BRec V7:151).
DARBY Walter W to Juliet Robins 2 Aug 1837; d/o Thomas Robins Sr dec'd; George Gray sec & as to ages; m 4 Aug 1837 by G Wescoat.
DASHIELL Col George to Elizabeth Fairfax 15 Oct 1740; George of Sommerset Co, MD; (wid/o Jas Fairfax); Thomas Preeson sec; CR PK 27 Jul 1741; PK 37 Oct 1750.
DASHIELL George to Rose Fisher 12 Aug 1760; d/o Maddox Fisher dec'd; John Dolby sec.
DAVIDSON Edward to Jenney McMeth 23 May 1801; John

Wescoat Jr sec; m (1801) by J Elliott.

DAVIS Levin to Susanna Westerhouse 31 Dec 1778; Geo Bonnewill sec.

DAVIS Robert to Sarah Andress 4 Aug 1786; d/o Andrew Andress con; Wm Waterfield sec; Manuel Hosir wit.

DAVIS Thomas to Jane Gothing 26 May 1661. Bk IX:114.

DAWSON Thomas to Louisa Costin 7 May 1816; Wm Jarvis Jr sec; m 9 May 1816 by G Bonewell.

DELASTATIOUS Ezekiel S to Frances Smith 12 Mar 1823; Frances wrd/o Silas Jefferson sec; m 12 Mar 1823 by C Bonewell.

DELASTATIOUS Thomas C to Elizabeth Trower 14 Sep 1848 by P Williams.

DELL Thomas to Mary Reeve 30 Nov 1723; Thos Clerke (cleric); Mary spinster; Peter Rasco & Henry Speakman secs; lic 30 Nov 1723. CT Ret Oct 1724.

DELPEACH James to Peggy Sampson 29 Sep 1743; wid; Jno Marshall sec; Jno Roberts wit.

DENNIS Arcibald to Sally Dennis 13 Oct 1804; John S Stott sec; m (1804) I Bratten.

DENNIS Archibald to Betsey Dennis (MinRet states Betsey "Benston") 29 Sep 1810; Arthur Cobb sec; m (1810) by C Bonewell.

DENNIS Archibald to Lucy Poulson 21 Jan 1812; John Wheelor sec who gives Lucy's age as 22y Christmas last; m bet 1 Jan - 14 Feb (1812) by I Bratten.

DENNIS Archibald to Leah Window 4 May 1813; Samuel Dalby sec; m (1813) by I Bratten.

DENNIS Archibald to Rachel Benson 3 Jul 1838; wid/o Edmund Benson; Montcalm Oldham sec; m 6 Jul 1838 by M Oldham.

DENNIS Denock to Elice Nehulian 31 Jul 1661. Bk IX:114.

DENNIS James to Miss Nancy Isdell 23 Dec 1846; d/o James Isdell dec'd; Thomas Dalby as to ages; James Dalby sec; L Harmanson wit; m 23 Dec 1846 by P Warren.

DENNIS John to Susanna Widgeon 15 Dec 1786; wid/o Levin Widgeon; Rob't Greenaway sec; m (1786) by E Baker.

DENNIS Joseph to Livinia Birch 24 Apr 1788; Thos Griffith sec; m (1788) by E Baker.

DENNIS Laban to Jenney Bunting 14 Jan 1811; Archibald Dennis sec; m bet 1 Jan - 8 Apr (1811) by J Elliott.

DENNIS Littleton to Elizabeth Upshur 3 Dec 1788; d/o John Upshur Gent; James Upshur sec.

DENNIS Major to Mary Robins 3 Aug 1802; Hezekiah Dennis sec; m (1802) by I Bratten.

DENNIS Major to Nancy Nottingham 1 May 1805; d/o Ann Nottingham gdn con; Johannes Johnson sec; John S Stott wit; m (1808) by I Bratten.

DENNIS Michael to Molly Jackson 12 Jan 1788; David Jones sec; m (1788) by E Baker.

DENNIS Michael to Ansley James 28 Feb 1805; John Nottingham sec; m (1805) by I Bratten.

DENNIS Michael to (Miss) Mary Dennis 28 Dec 1829; d/o Archibald Dennis sec; J W Leatherbury as to Michael's age; m 29 Dec 1829 by G Wescoat.

DENNIS Teackle to Patty Hale 20 Jan 1791; John Dolby sec; m (1791) by E Baker.

DENNIS William to Susanna Whitehead 29 Sep 1791; d/o Jno Whitehead dec'd; Jacob Moore sec; m (1791) by E Baker.

DENNIS William to Ann Caple 8 Jan 1800; Wm Wingate sec; m Jan 1800 by C Simkins (MinRet states "Peggy" Caple).

DENNIS William to Betsey Spady 13 Nov 1826; Shepherd Abdell sec & as to ages.

DENWOOD Levin to Isabell Stringer 12 Mar 1744; Levin of MD; Isabell spinster; John Kendall

sec; Littleton Eyre con for Isabell; Jno Cormick wit.
DICKERSON Peter to Mary Waterfield 20 Apr 1774; wid; Walter Hyslop sec.
DICKERSON Samuel to Adah Heath 24 Feb 1802; George Heath sec; m (1802) by I Bratten.
DILASTATIOUS, see DELASTATIOUS.
DILLON Charles to Lucey Moore 17 Jun 1802; Charles Fitchett sec; m Jun 1802 by C Simkins.
DILLON Charles to Elizabeth Stripe 22 Mar 1806; Daniel Eshon sec; m (1806) by J Elliott.
DILLON Thomas to Bridget Widgeon 3 Dec 1803; Chas Dillon sec; m (1803) by I Bratten.
DILLON William to Nancy Fisher 4 Jun 1798; Arthur Roberts sec; m 1798 by J Elliot.
DIX Isaac to Ann Jacob 12 Jan 1830; d/o John Jacob con; George F Outten sec; Wm Rooks Sr as to Isaac's age; m 13 Jan 1830 by P Williams.
DIX William A to Elizabeth S Scott 1 May 1838; s/o Levin Dix sec; d/o Wm W Scott sec; m 2 May 1838 by L Dix.
DIXON Benjamin to Eliz Nelson 5 May 1770; Thos Widgeon sec.
DIXON Benjamin to Fanny Fletcher 13 Jan 1806; Geo Abdell sec; m (1806) by J Elliott.
DIXON Chris to Sabra Simkins 22 Sep 1783; Wm Simkins Jr sec.
DIXON John to Bridget Thomas 11 Sep 1781; d/o John Thomas con; Isaac Bell sec.
DIXON John to Lucretia Costin 2 Aug 1786; Abraham Costin sec.
DIXON John to Nelley Costin 18 Jul 1791; d/o Abraham Costin con; Jacob Moore sec; Matthew Costin wit.
DIXON John W to Molly Lewis 13 May 1811; d/o Margaretta Lewis con; Wm Nottingham Jr sec; Sally Nottingham wit; m (1811) by J Elliott.
DIXON Thomas to Elizabeth Holmes 17 Aug 1790; wid; Azariah Williams sec; m 23 Aug 1790 by C Simkins.
DIXON Thomas Jr to Betsey Smith 23 Jun 1791; d/o Rich'd Smith as to ages; Thos Smith sec; m 26 Jun 1791 by C Simkins.
DIXON Thomas to Anne Nottingham 7 Mar 1793; Levin Mathews sec; m (1793) by E Baker.
DIXON William to Esther Kendall 29 Dec 1784; Teagle Jacob sec.
DIXON William to Betty Dunton 14 Mar 1787; wid/o Jacob Dunton; James Powell sec.
DIXON William to Ann D Garrison 2 Jun 1807; d/o Sarah Savage con; Jeptha Johnson sec; Arthur (J?) Savage wit; m (1807) by I Bratten.
DIXON William to Sukey Costin 10 Oct 1808; Wm Costin sec; m (1808) by J Elliott.
DIXON Capt William W to Mary P Fitchett 16 Jul 1831; wrd & d/o Martha Fitchett con; John Barnard sec; m Jul 1831 by L Dix; (m 21 Jul 1831. see BRec V10:8).
DIXON William W to Gracy Bishop 16 Jun 1851; wid/o John Bishop; Luther H Read wit; (m 17 Jun 1851. see BRec V1:27).
DOE Ralph to Mary Curtis 29 Oct 1660. Bk IX:92.
DOLBY, DALBY.
DOLBY Benjamin to Ann Ro (name appears to be possibly incomplete on bond) Feb 1705/1706; Richard Smith sec; John Custis & Mary Custis wits.
DOLBY Benjamin to Mary Core 19 Jul 1786; Wm Dolby sec.
DOLBY Benjamin to Sarah Bull 17 Dec 1789; John Satchell sec.
DALBY Benjamin J to Mary Ann Kendall 17 Jun 1830; d/o Dr John Kendall dec'd; Wm J Campbell sec; John Kendall as to Mary Ann's age. see BRec V9:81.
DALBY Branson W to Miss Margaret Ann Hall 18 Mar 1852; d/o Thomas Hall dec'd & wife Elisha

Hall as to Margaret Ann's age 21y on 6 Apr 1851; m 18 Mar 1852 by H Dalby.

DOLBY Henry to Rachel Andrews 7 Nov 1772; Wm Waltham sec.

DALBY Henry to Susanna Sturgis 9 May 1787; John Darby sec.

DALBY Hezekiah to Nancy Nottingham 20 Dec 1815; d/o Richard Nottingham con; Samuel R Collins sec; Harrison Nottingham wit; m (1815) by I Bratten; (m 28 Dec 1815. see BRec V1:78).

DOLBY Isaac to Peggy Mathews 14 Aug 1759; d/o John Custis Mathews con; John Dolby Jr sec; Custis Mathews & Rachall Stott wits.

DALBY Isaac to Catherine Dalby 25 May 1798; (wid/o Thomas Dalby Sr); Matthews Harmanson sec; m (1798) by I Bratten.

DOLBY Jacob to Abigail Bell 10 Nov 1789; Wm Roberts sec; m (1789) by E Baker.

DOLBY James to Anne Griffith 16 Nov 1789; Wm Dolby sec; m (1789) by E Baker.

DALBY James to Betsey Griffin 3 Aug 1805; Dickie Dunton sec; m (1805) by I Bratten.

DALBY James to Catharine Mears 9 Dec 1845; d/o John Mears dec'd; Thomas Dalby as to ages; James Dennis sec; m 10 Dec 1845 by P Warren Jr.

DALBY James to Miss Ann Elizabeth Williams 30 Nov 1848; d/o Christopher Williams dec'd; Thomas Kellam as to Ann's age; John E Winder sec & as to James' age; m 30 Nov 1848 by H Dalby.

DALBY James B to Elizabeth Leatherbury 28 Oct 1845; wid/o James M Leatherbury; Wm T Nottingham sec; Edw'd R Waddey as to James B's age; W T Fitchett wit; m 28 Oct 1845 by P Williams.

DALBY John Jr to Susanna Jacob 25 Feb 1769; d/o Isaac Jacob dec'd; John Burton sec; Rob't C Jacob con for Susanna.

DALBY John to Keziah Westerhouse 10 Oct 1769; Edm'd Glanville sec.

DOLBY John to Leah Dunton 1 Jan 1780; Michael Dunton sec.

DALBY John Jr to Elizabeth Barlow 9 Mar 1790; wid/o Thomas Barlow; John Dalby (CN) sec.

DALBY John Calvin to Mary A Saunders 21 Oct 1845. see BRec V5:22.

DOLBY Joseph to Jane Luke 19 May 1764; wid/o (Daniel Luke); John Dolby sec.

DALBY Littleton to Bridget Fisher 28 Aug 1794; Steward Pettit sec; m (1794) by E Baker).

DALBY Nathaniel to Miss Nancy Wilkins 14 Oct 1824; George F Outten sec & as to Nancy's age & that Nancy's father approves of the marriage; m Oct 1824 by L Dix; (m 14 Oct 1824. see BRec V5:21).

DALBY Nathaniel m (2) Ellin G Riley 22 Sep 1830; d/o Geo & Frances Riley. see BRec V5:21.

DALBY Samuel to Peggy Watch 9 Jun 1814; Timothy Outin sec; John Upshur Jr wit.

DALBY Severn to Sukey Spady 2 Aug 1821; wid/o Wm Spady; Thomas Dalby sec; m 4 Aug 1821 by C Bonewell.

DOLBY Spencer to Nancy Watson 4 Apr 1780; d/o Littleton Watson; Levin Parkerson sec.

DALBY Thomas Jr to Margaret Haze 19 Aug 1772; orp/o John Haze; Thos Dalby gdn/o Margaret con; Joseph Dalby sec.

DOLBY Thomas Esq to Catharine Harmanson 8 Oct 1789; d/o John Harmanson Esq dec'd; Wm Stith sec; m (1789) by E Baker.

DOLBY Thomas to Priscilla Rogers 8 Jun 1795; Wm Roberts Jr sec; m 1795 by I Bratten.

DALBY Thomas to Delitha Bunting 27 Dec 1837; James S Carpenter sec & as to ages; m 27 Dec 1837 by G Wescoat.

DALBY Thomas to Mary Robinson 23 Dec 1846; wid/o William Robinson; James Dalby as to Thomas' age; James Dennis sec; m 23 Dec 184 by P Warren.

DOLBY William to Sarah Eshon 12 Feb 1785; Obid Cary sec.

DALBY William to Martha Bool 29 Aug 1788; wid/o Nicholas Bool; Wm Bloxom sec.

DALBY William to Susanna Kendall 26 Dec 1805; Major Andrews sec; George Boggs gives William permission for license; m (1805) by J Elliott.

DOLBY William L to Sarah S Ames 14 Aug 1847; wid/o Shadrack T Ames; James B Dalby sec & as to William's age; m 16 Aug 1847 by C Hall.

DONNELL John to Anna Teackle Smith 10 Oct 1798; John of Baltimore; d/o Isaac Smith con sec.

DORMAN William to Peggy Dunton 24 Nov 1795; Thos Hall sec; m 1795 by I Bratten.

DORSEY Hill to Elizabeth B Jacob 13 Oct 1812; Hill of Anne Arundel Co, MD; (d/o Rob't & Elizabeth Jacob); John K Evans gdn con; Geo Parrott sec; Wm H Dorsey app't gdn to Hill on 11 Jul 1807 in AA Co con; Jonathon Harvey wit; (m 14 Oct 1812. see BRec V1:49).

DOUGHTY See also DOWTY.

DOUGHTY Archibald to Miss Mary Ann Kelly 16 Jul 1850; d/o Charles Kelly; David Bool wit; m 17 Jul 1850 by P Warren.

DOUGHTY Archabald to Mary ____ 16 Jul 1859. see BRec V3:136.

DOUGHTY James C to Margaret S Johnson 12 Dec 1842; d/o Thomas Johnson dec'd; Frances L Mears now w/o Thomas C Mears & m/o Margaret S con; Richard J Ayres sec; m 13 Dec 1842 by G C Wescoat.

DOUGHTY William J to Harriet Cotteril 20 Dec 1841; d/o Cap't John Cotteril dec'd; Major Dowty sec & as to ages; S S Nottingham wit; m 21 Dec 1841 by G C Wescoat.

DOWNES, DOWNS.

DOWNES Daniel to Charlotte Costin 10 Jan 1825; Christopher Fitchett sec & as to ages; m Jan 1825 by L Dix.

DOWNS Henry to Maria Costin 17 Nov 1830; wid/o John Costin; John M Savage sec; m Nov 1830 by L Dix.

DOWNES Nathaniel G to Miss Dianna Hallett 11 Nov 1844; James B Nottingham gdn/o Nathaniel sec; d/o Thomas Hallett; m 20 Nov 1844 by P Williams. see BRec V5:80.

DOWNES Robert to Mary Avory 31 Jan 1661/1662. Bk IX:114.

DOWNS Thomas to Anne Williams 7 Feb 1783; Joseph Warren sec.

DOWNS Thomas to Margaret Biggs 31 Oct 1809; Southey Goffigon sec; m (1809) by J Elliott.

DOWNS Thomas to Elizabeth Nottingham 5 Jun 1820; James Goffigon sec.

DOWNES Thomas A to Miss Arinthia S Spady 9 Dec 1850; Thomas F Spady gdn/o Arinthia con; N G Burris as to Thomas's age; m 18 Dec 1850 by P Williams.

DOWNS William to Elizabeth Warren 27 Dec 1798; Wm Wilkins sec; m (1798) by J Elliot.

DOWNS William to Esther Warren 2 Sep 1809; David Topping sec; m (1809) by J Elliott.

DOWNES William to Margaret Rippin 2 Jan 1837; d/o Thomas Rippin dec'd; Severn Wilkins sec & as to ages; m 12 Jan 1837 by L Dix.

DOWNING Arthur Sr to Zillah Turner 19 Feb 1785. see BRec V2:18.

DOWNING Caleb to Lucy Thompson 30 Jun 1821; d/o Isaac Thompson (FN); Isaac Becket sec & as to Lucy's age; W E Jacob

wit; m 1 Jul 1821 by C Bonewell.
DOWNING Edmund W P to Mary Bell 11 Dec 1809; James Sanford sec.
DOWNING John to Edey Nottingham 25 Jan 1791; Wm Bain sec; Mary Robins as to Edey's age; Guhu Johnson & Wm Jacob wits; m (1791) by E Baker.
DOWNING William to Martha Jacob 14 Jan 1772; d/o Philip Jacob dec'd; John Wise sec.
DOWTY See also DOUGHTY.
DOWTY Addison to Tabitha Milby 15 Jul 1778; Hezekiah Dowty sec.
DOWTY Addison to Seymour Heath 10 Jul 1779; d/o Wm Heath; Abel Abdeel sec.
DOWTY Archibald to Nancy Edmunds 24 Sep 1788; d/o David Edmunds dec'd; Peter Dowty sec; m (1788) by E Baker.
DOWTY Babel to Betsey Hickman 6 Jul 1798; Joseph Hanby sec; m (1798) by I Bratten.
DOWTY Eli to Nancy Floyd 9 Jan 1815; Arthur Cobb sec & as to Nancy's age; m bet 1 Jan - 13 Feb (1815) by I Bratten.
DOWTY Elisha to Elishe Jacob 21 Oct 1772; d/o Thomas Jacob con; Hezekiah Dowty sec.
DOWTY James to Susanna James 6 Dec 1821; d/o Andrew James sec; m 8 Dec 1821 by C Bonewell.
DOWTY James to Mary Rogers 9 Jan 1850; s/o Major Dowty dec'd; d/o John Rogers dec'd; Edward P Waddey sec & as to ages; m 9 Jan 1850 by P Warren.
DOWTY James P to Miss Sarah A Dunton 1 Mar 1847; s/o James Dowty sec & as to Sarah's age; d/o Benjamin F Dunton dec'd; Hamilton Neale wit; m 3 Mar 1847 by M Oldham.
DOWTY John to Sally Carpenter 24* Oct 1821; Shepherd Floyd sec; m 18* Oct 1821 by C Bonewell.
*discrepancy
DOWTY John A to Emily Godwin 27 Aug 1851; s/o James Dowty Sr; wid/o Griffin Godwin; m 28 Aug 1851 by P Williams.
DOWTY John W to Miss Susan Smith 22 Dec 1845; d/o Thomas Smith dec'd; Southey Rew sec & as to ages; m 24 Dec 1845 by P Warren Jr.
DOWTY Littleton to Susanna Smith 12 Mar 1821; George E Christian sec; m 14 Mar 1821 by C Bonewell.
DOWTY Major to Adah Andrews 30 Jun 1822; wid/o Southy Andrews; George Hickman sec & as to Major's age; m 1 Jul 1822 by C Bonewell.
DOWTY Major to Miss Elizabeth Mears 30 Jan 1841; d/o John Mears; Jacob Spady sec & as to Elizabeth's age; Geo F Wilkins wit; m 1 Feb 1841 by G C Wescoat.
DOWTY Martin to Miss Sally Dunton 21 Jul 1845; d/o Rickards Dunton Jr sec; James S Carpenter as to Martin's age; Wm S Christian wit; m 22 Jul 1845 by P Warren Jr.
DOWTY Michael to Peggy Jones 21 Dec 1790; Zorobabel Jones sec; m 21 Dec 1790 by C Simkins.
DOWTY Michael to Ann Dixon 9 Mar 1824; Ann wrd/o Jno W Dixon; T W Dixon & George F Wilkins secs; m Mar 1824 by L Dix.
DOWTY Michael to Ann Nelson 30 Sep 1830; d/o John Nelson Jr; Geo T Yerby sec; Angelo A Townsend as to Ann's age.
DOWTY Peter to Sinah Edmunds 8 Mar 1787; Elisha Dowty sec; m (1787) by E Baker.
DOWTY Peter to ____ 1 Dec 1807; John Hamby sec.
DOWTY Rowland to Mary Bratten 8 Dec 1817; d/o Isaac Bratten; James Dowty sec; m (1817) by I Bratten.
DOWTY Thomas to Sarah Belote 7 Jun 1791; wid/o Wm Belote; Wm Satchell Jr sec; Sarah Satchell wit; m 9 Jun 1791 by C Simkins.
DOWTY Thomas to Susanna Turner

2 Aug 1797; Geo Turner sec.
DOWTY Thomas to Susan Ogg 27 Dec 1813; Zachariah Wise sec; m (1813) by I Bratten.
DOWTY William to Elizabeth Edmonds 15 Dec 1823; d/o Thomas Edmonds con; Arthur & Teackle Roberts secs.
DRIGHOUSE George to Peggy Lang 2 Mar 1798; Abraham Lang sec (FN).
DRIGHOUSE Nathan Jr to Elizabeth Bingham 23 Jan 1794; wid; Reubin Read sec (FN); m 23 Jan 1794 by C Simkins.
DRIGHOUSE Nathan to Polly Jeffry 24 Jul 1810; Abraham Lang sec FN; m (1810) by J Elliott.
DRIGHOUSE William to Ann Bingham 25 Sep 1802; Samuel Beavans sec (FN).
DRISKILL Moses to Margaret Joynes 4 Nov 1795; John Dolby sec; m 1795 by J Elliot.
DRUMMOND Jas to Emily Bevans 9 Feb 1852; d/o Tom Bevans FN; m 14 Feb 1852 by Warren.
DRUMMOND William to Nanny Dunton 7 Jul 1759; d/o Elias Dunton Sr; John Waterfield Jr sec; Rob't Drummond wit.
DRUMMOND William S to Molly Savage 7 Jun 1809; Wm Savage sec.
DRYSDALE Thomas to Mary Anne Smith 22 Nov 1796; d/o Isaac Smith con; Wm Eyre sec.
DUN William to Mary Godferry 1 Oct 1709; Rob't Howson sec.
DUNCAN Thomas to Ann Susan Wheelor 27 Jun 1826; d/o Thomas Wheelor sec; m 30 Jun 1826 by P Williams Jr.
DUNSTAN Edward to Eliz Lingoe 12 May 1661. BK IX:114.
DUNTON Benjamin to Anne Jacob 15 Sep 1778; d/o Hancock Jacob Sr; Wm Waterfield sec.
DUNTON Benjamin to Sarah Garrison 3 Jun 1797; Dickie Dunton sec; m (1797) by I Bratten.
DUNTON Benj to Ann S Topping 22 Nov 1820; David Topping sec; m 30 Nov 1820 by L Dix.
DUNTON Benjamin to Mary T S Tankard 25 Mar 1828; d/o Dr John Tankard con (Mary's age 19y); George L E Tankard sec; m 27 Mar 1828 by G Wescoat.
DUNTON Benjamin F to Sally Churn 27 Mar 1816; Thomas S Brickhouse sec; m 3 Apr 1816 by C Bonewell.
DUNTON Carvey to Margaret Robins 20 Nov 1792; Carvey of Acc Co; Arthur Robins sec.
DUNTON Custis M to Elizabeth Custis Willis 9 Nov 1852; d/o Littleton & Mary A Willis of Acc Co. see BRec V2:125,128.
DUNTON Custis Mercer to Miss Caroline E Harmanson 14 Apr 1845; s/o Wm & Mary Dunton; Wm P Nottingham sec; m 15 Apr 1845 by J Ufford. see BRec V2:128.
DUNTON David A to Miss Bell Sarah Nottingham 19 May 1845; David wrd/o Thomas B Williams sec; d/o Jacob Nottingham dec'd; Wm P Nottingham as to Bell's age; Edw'd P Roberts sec; Geo W Brittingham wit; m 21 May 1845 by G G Exall.
DUNTON Edward M to Miss Ann S Stewart 13 Sep 1842; d/o James Stewart; Joshua G Stewart sec & as to Ann's age; Joshua Wescoat wit; m 15 Sep 1842 by G C Wescoat.
DUNTON Elias to Esther Waterfield 6 Oct 1750; wid/o (John Waterfield); Southy Satchell sec.
DUNTON Elias to Fanney Nottingham 25 Nov 1811; Thomas Nottingham sec; Hancock Jacob as to ages; m (1811) by J Elliott.
DUNTON George to Margaret Richardson 11 Jul 1814; John B Thomas sec; m (1814) by I Bratten.
DUNTON George W to Sally Benston 25 Oct 1808; Wm Andrews sec; m (1808) by I Bratten.

DUNTON George W to Arinthia B Downing 19 Dec 1831; d/o Dr Edm'd W P Downing sec; Jno C Jacob sec & as to Geo W's age; m 19 Dec 1831 by G Wescoat.

DUNTON Hancock to Sally Godwin 16 Feb 1802; Charles S Satchell sec; m (1802) by I Bratten.

DUNTON Isaac to Eliz Toleman 4 Apr 1785; Obed Cary sec.

DUNTON Isaac to Hannah White 19 Dec 1807; Wm White sec.

DUNTON Jacob to Betty Satchell 24 May 1763; Jacob orp; d/o Southey Satchell dec'd; Wm Satchell sec; Wm Drummond con for Jacob; Jno Waterfield & ____ McMullen wits.

DUNTON James M to Miss Susan Fitchett 2 May 1842; d/o Wm Fitchett dec'd; John Y Johnson sec & as to Susan's age; m 4 May 1842 by G C Wescoat.

DUNTON James S to Miss Mary B Church 24 Oct 1853; James P Douty as to Mary's age; m 26 Oct 1853 by M Oldham.

DUNTON John to Sukey Mills 22 Dec 1800; Wm Graves sec; m 1800 by J Elliott.

DUNTON John to Nancy Roberts 27 Aug 1816; Teackle Roberts sec.

DUNTON John R to Emeline Dunton 12 Sep 1831; Emeline wrd/o Alexander W Ward sec; Wm Dunton also sec; m Sep 1831 by L Dix. BRec V2:29 states Jno Rickets Dunton s/o Wm & Mary m 13 Sep 1831; Emeline R Dunton d/o Geo & Marg't Dunton.

DUNTON Mathew H to Polly N Brickhouse 14 Apr 1807; Thos Jacob Jr sec; Geo Brickhouse con for Polly N; m (1807) by J Elliott.

DUNTON Michael to Rosey Mathews 26 May 1779; d/o John Custis Mathews dec'd & his wife Martha con; Wm Waltham sec; Wm Jacob wit.

DUNTON Michael to Anne Nottingham 22 Jan 1780; wid; John Stratton Jr sec.

DUNTON Michael to Peggy Griffin 13 Dec 1791; Kendal Belote sec.

DUNTON Michael Sr to Sarah Bell 3 Jul 1792; wid/o Thomas Bell dec'd (1791); Nath'l Holland sec; m Jul 1792 by C Simkins.

DUNTON Richard T to Miss Vianna Wescoat 2 Jan 1849; d/o Edmund Wescoat; John E Winder sec; Wm Hamby as to Vianna's age; m 3 Jan 1849 by P Warren; see Brec V 12: 121

DUNTON Ricketts to Ann Jacob 18 Aug 1722; wid; Jacob Stringer & Edw'd Carter secs.

DUNTON Rickards Jr to Sophia Harmanson 7 Sep 1774; d/o Capt Matthew Harmanson; Wm Waltham sec; Abel Upshur wit; (m 8 Sep 1774. see BRec V2:128; V8:112).

DUNTON Rickards Jr to Rosanna Clegg 13 Aug 1796; John Macgawan sec; m 13 Aug 1796 by C Simkins.

DUNTON Rickards Jr to Sinah Benthall 20 Oct 1803; George Bell sec.

DUNTON Rickards Jr to Lucy Carpenter 5 May 1807; Littleton Kendall sec.

DUNTON Rickards to Charlotte Harrison 26 Apr 1808; d/o Robert H Harrison con; Caleb Core sec; m (1808) by I Bratten.

DUNTON Rickards Jr to Susan Simkins 24 Dec 1817; Henry B Kendall sec; m 27 Dec 1817 by C Bonwell.

DUNTON Rickards to Harriet Hall 20 Dec 1827; d/o Thomas Hall; Henry B Kendall sec & as to Harriet's age; Smith Nottingham & Jno S Dix wits; m Dec 1827 by L Dix.

DUNTON Samuel Washington to Margaret G Badger 5 Jul 1841; s/o Wm & Mary Dunton; d/o Thomas W Badger con; George & & Joseph E Bell wits; George Bell sec; m 7 Jul 1841 by P Warren Jr. see BRec V8:113.

DUNTON Selby to Elizabeth Kellam 16 Apr 1808; Laban Hickman sec; m (1808) by J Elliott.
DUNTON Severn to Agness Grice 25 Jun 1785; Wm Ward sec.
DUNTON Severn to Mary Bryan 10 Apr 1792; wid/o Levin Bryan; Wm Stith sec; m (1791) by E Baker.
DUNTON Severn to Sally Dunton 13 Oct 1821; wid/o George Dunton; Wm Richardson sec; m 20 Oct 1821 by L Dix.
DUNTON Smith L to Ann A Ward 3 Mar 1834; d/o Littleton Ward dec'd; George D White sec; m 7 Mar 1834 by G Wescoat.
DUNTON Southy to Peggy Dalby 20 Dec 1790; d/o John Dalby con; Thos Underhill sec.
DUNTON Thomas to Sukey Bell 16 Jul 1794; John Goffigon sec; m (1794) by E Baker.
DUNTON Thomas to Polly Hanby 26 Mar 1800; Thomas Dalby sec; m 1800 by I Bratten.
DUNTON Thomas Jr to Sarah Joynes 19 Feb 1808; John R Waddey sec; m (1808) by J Elliott.
DUNTON Thomas K to Emiline Fitchett 10 Oct 1832; d/o Joshua & Martha Fitchett. see BRec V2:23,128.
DUNTON Waterfield to Susanna Waterfield 17 May 1756; d/o Jacob Waterfield con; Isaac Dunton sec; Henry Bryant & Rich'd Smith wits.
DUNTON William to Nancy Bryan 10 Dec 1827; wid/o Henry Bryan; James Dunton sec; John S Heath as to Wm's age; Ves Ellis & Thos Young wits; m 1827 by G C Wescoat.
DUNTON William M to Rosa Fitchett 13 Feb 1832; Rosa wrd/o James Dowty sec; m 13 Feb 1832 by L Dix.
DUNTON William M to Harriet S Andrews 13 Feb 1837; d/o Isaac Andrews sec; m 14 Feb 1837 by J Cunningham.

DUPARK Thomas to Elizabeth Powell 13 Nov 1661. Bk IX:114.
DYE Daniel to Nora Irevane 4 Aug 1661. BK IX:114.

E

EAST Southy W to Elizabeth Yetman 26* Mar 1824; wid/o John Yetman; Edm'd W P Downing sec; m 24* Mar 1824 by C Bonewell. *discrepancy
EDMONDS, EDMUNDS.
EDMONDS John to Ann Benston 21 Aug 1826; Shepherd Andrews sec.
EDMONDS John to Rosy Dennis 29 Dec 1830; d/o Michael Dennis dec'd & wrd/o John Adams sec; Archibald Dennis as to John's age; m 29 Dec 1830 by G Wescoat.
EDMONDS Thomas to Peggy Hanby 3 Feb 1798; Joseph Hanby sec; m (1798) by J Elliot.
EDMUNDS Thomas to Rosey Dennis 22 Oct 1800; Joseph Hanby sec; m 1800 by I Bratten.
EDMUNDS William Jr to Susan Scarborough 4 Dec 1815; Edmund Scarborough sec; m 6 Dec 1815 by Joshua Burton.
ELLEGOOD, ELLIGOOD.
ELLIGOOD John to Elinor Jacob 21 Apr 1727; Wm Brooke & Jos Sheppard secs; lic 21 Apr 1727 CT ret Oct 1727.
ELLEGOOD John to Susanna Wilkins 12 May 1748; wid/o (Jonathan Wilkins); Benja Scott sec; Catherine Blaikley wit.
ELLEGOOD John to Esther Wilkins 19 Mar 1752; spinster; Alex Kemp sec; Salathiel Harrison wit; John Wilkins con.
ELLEGOOD John to Nanny Powell 15 Mar 1764; John of Worcester Co, MD; d/o Abel Powell dec'd; Adderson Nottingham sec.
ELLIGOOD Jonathan to Esther Floyd 28 Jan 1788; wid/o Wm Floyd; Nath'l Wilkins Jr sec.
ELLEGOOD Peter Norly to Margaret Forse 25 Nov 1735; wid; (no sec

given); Jno Dillion wit; lic 25 Nov 1735 CT ret Oct 1736.

ELLIGOOD William to Sarah Powell 14 Sep 1768; William of Worcester Co, MD; d/o Abel Powell dec'd; Adderson Nottingham sec; Joachim Michael wit.

ELLIOTT, ELLIOT, ELLET.

ELLIOT John to Mary Abdeel 30 Aug 1792; wid; Henry Smaw sec; m (1792) by E Baker.

ELLIOTT John to Polly Nolen 18 Dec 1801; Levin Scott sec; m 1801 by I Bratten.

ELLIOTT John J to Miss Caroline Wingate 5 May 1845; d/o Hickson Wingate; Littleton Townsend as to ages; Wm S Wilkins sec; m 7 May 1845 by P Williams.

ELLIOTT John T to Mary B Snead 16 Jan 1808; d/o Adah Snead con; L Upshur Sr con for John T who is a minor; Maj Pettit sec.

ELLIOTT John T to Juliet Upshur 22 Feb 1814; Caleb B Upshur sec; m 22 Feb 1814 by Thos Davis.

ELLIOTT John T to Miss Margaret E Downes 13 Jan 1834; John wrd/o Wm S Smith sec; Margaret wrd/o John E Nottingham sec; m 16 Jan 1834 by L Dix.

ELLIOTT John W to Louisa Travis 1 Dec 1834; d/o Dennard Travis con; Nathaniel Hickman sec & as to John's age; Daniel Fitchett & John Costin wits; m 3 Dec 1834 by P Williams.

ELLIOTT Thomas to Keziah Turner 10 Aug 1784; Robert Oag sec.

ELLET Thomas to Sally Widgeon 1 Aug 1801; Daniel Fitchett gdn/o Thomas con; Wm Carpenter sec; m 1801 by I Bratten.

ELLIOTT Thomas W to Susan Evans 12 Aug 1834; d/o John Evans dec'd & wrd/o Nathaniel Hickman sec & as to Thomas' age; John Belote wit; m 14 Aug 1834 by P Williams.

ELLIOTT Thomas W to Miss Susan Ann Speakman 9 Nov 1840; d/o Shepherd Speakman; John McCown sec & as to Susan's age; m 11 Nov 1840 by P Williams.

ELLIOTT Thomas W to Miss Nancy Smith 12 Sep 1845; Nancy orp/o Hannah Smith dec'd; Daniel Fitchett gdn/o Nancy con; Wm T Fitchett sec; Wm J Bowdoin wit; m 17 Sep 1845 by P Williams.

ELLIOTT William to Rose Johnson 16 Jul 1774; d/o John Johnson dec'd; John Johnson sec.

ELLIOTT William to Peggy Costin 25 Mar 1833; wid/o Henry Costin; Nathaniel Hickman sec & as to William's age; m 28 Mar 1833 by P Williams.

ELLIOTT William C to Rachel Hill 11 Aug 1823; Daniel (George?) Eshon sec & as to Rachel's age; m 11 Aug 1823 by S Wilmer.

ELLIOTT William W to Miss Harriet A Rolly 9 Oct 1848; d/o William Rolly; John T Hallett sec & as to Harriet's age; Wm T Nottingham wit. see BRec V2:150.

ERVIN, IRVIN See KERVIN.

ESDEL See ISDEL.

ESHON Daniel to Elizabeth Wheelor 23 Nov 1808; Charles Dillon sec.

ESHON George to Mary Wise 27 Dec 1820; Charles Bonwell sec.

ESHON Thomas to Miss Caty Roberts 20 May 1845; d/o William Roberts dec'd; Charles Kelly sec & as to Caty's age; m 20 May 1845 by G C Wescoat.

EVANS Arthur to Adah Kemp 12 Sep 1777; wid/o (John Kemp); Rob't Bell sec.

EVANS Arthur to Nelly Dixon 21 Jun 1796; (wid/o John Dixon); Nathan Griffeth sec; m (1796) by E Baker.

EVANS Edward to Louisa Bowdoin 4 Jun 1805; d/o Peter Bowdoin con; John K Evans sec; m (1805) by J Elliott.

EVANS Isaac to Lucinda Evans 11 Aug 1817; Hancock Jacob sec; m 13 Aug 1817 by C Bonewell.

EVANS John to Joan Munes 13 May 1660. BK IX:92.

EVANS John to Peggy Simkins 17 Feb 1774; d/o Wm Simkins con; Thos Underhill sec.

EVANS John to Santekey Moore 17 Nov 1800; Isaac Nottingham sec; m 1800 by J Elliott.

EVANS John to Ann Toleman 2 Jun 1802; Thos Dunton sec; m (1802) by J Elliott.

EVANS John to Susan Mills 3 Jul 1816; Abram Costin gdn/o Susan sec & con; Agnes Mills con for Susan also; Wm L & Ann Evans wits; m 4 Jul 1816 by C Bonewell.

EVANS John to Catherine Dowty 24 Dec 1817; Thomas Dowty sec; m 30 Dec 1817 by C Bonewell.

EVANS John to Betsy Spady 13 Apr 1840; wid/o Thomas Spady; Wm W Elliott sec & as to John's age; Daniel Fitchett wit; m 23 Apr 1840 by P Williams.

EVANS John K to Margaret Jacob 7 Apr 1807; Robert Jacob sec; (m 8 Apr 1807. see BRec V1:49).

EVANS Levin to Anne Mary Pitts 17 May 1755; spinster; Littleton Wilkins & John Frazer secs.

EVANS Richard to Eliz Goffigon 31 Dec 1782; d/o & wrd/o Tabitha Biggs con; Alexander Boyd sec.

EVANS Thomas to Mary Milbourne 29 May 1827; d/o Thomas Milbourne con; Angelo A Townsend sec; Catherine Evans wit; m May 1827 by L Dix.

EVANS Thomas to Sally Milbourn 2 Nov 1830; d/o Thomas Milbourn sec.

EVANS Thomas to Laura E Custis 19 Jun 1841; Laura wrd/o Sylvester M Kelly sec; Jno W Nicholson as to Thomas' age; Elisha D Cottingham wit; m 20 Jun 1841 by P Warren Jr.

EVANS Thomas E to Miss Juliet S Upshur 28 Jan 1839; Juliet wrd/o Abel P Upshur Esq con; Smith S Nottingham sec; John R Bowdoin wit; (m 30 Jan 1839. HunParReg:35).

EVANS Thomas S to Mary Ann P Ridley 11 May 1832; d/o Wm W Ridley sec; m 6 Jun 1832 by P Williams.

EVANS Wm to Adah Widgeon 26 Aug 1765; d/o Jonah Widgeon dec'd; Thos Bullick sec.

EVANS William to Rebecka Wood 21 May 1790; wid/o Wm Wood; Thos Suttie sec; m 24 May 1790 by C Simkins.

EVANS William to Miss Sally Costin 8 Sep 1824; s/o William S Evans; Joseph Warren as to Sally's age wit/by Wm S Evans & Sally Evans; William Dixon sec; m Sep 1824 by L Dix.

EVANS William S to Sophia Moore 2 Mar 1805; John Evans sec; m (1805) by J Elliott.

EVANS William S to Nancy Fitchett 8 Feb 1809; d/o Joshua Fitchett Sr & his wife con; James Travis sec; m (1809) by J Elliott.

EWELL John to Esther A Belote 26 Jan 1830; d/o Laban Belote con; Thos Smith Jr sec; Smith Belote wit.

EWING David to Ann Hopkins 1 Aug 1821; wid/o Wm W Hopkins; Wm P Copes sec; m 11 Aug 1821 by C Bonewell.

EWING Gustavus to Elizabeth James 7 Jun 1760; wid/o (Rob't James); John Harmanson sec.

EWING John to Jane Holbrooke 28 Nov 1785; Maddox Andrews sec; (L?) Fulwell con as to John.

EWING John to Polly McDaniel 29 Feb 1812; Nath'l Freshwater sec; m (1812) by I Bratten.

EWING John to Margaret A Matthews 14 Jul 1826; William Matthews sec; m 14 Jul 1826 by S S Gunter.

EWING Victor to Margaret Matthews 27 Jan 1817; Preson Savage sec; m 29 Jan 1817 by C Bonewell.

EYRE See also AYRES.

EYRE Ellegood to Esther Saunders 17 Mar 1777; d/o James Saunders; Benja Wilkins sec.

EYRE John to Ann Upshur 24 Feb 1800; Littleton Upshur sec; (m 26

EYRE Littleton to Bridget Harmanson 15 Jan 1734; (d/o Col Geo Harmanson*); Wm Tazewell sec; Gertrude Harmanson con for gr/son Littleton; Neech Eyre & Henry Harmanson wits. *North WB 18:123.

EYRE Neech to Anne Mifflin 12 Mar 1732; Peter Bowdoin sec.

EYRE Neech to Isabell Harmanson 21 Mar 1734; John Stratton sec; John Frazer wit.

EYRE Severn to Margaret L Taylor 28 Jan 1760; s/o Littleton Eyre. see BRec V5:165.

EYRE Thomas to Mary Ann Dunton 8 Jan 1838; d/o Matthew H Dunton sec; Obed Twiford wit; Edward Bool as to Thomas' age; m 9 Jan 1838 by G Wescoat.

EYRE William to Grace Dumcombe Taylor 26 Sep 1796; s/o Severn & Margaret Eyre. see BRec V5:153,162.

EYRE William L to Mary Burton Savage 10 Mar 1828; John Eyre sec; (m 12 Mar 1828. see BRec V5:162).

F

FATHERY, FATHERLY.

FATHERY Ebinezer to Amy Barret 8 Feb 1784; Southey Goffigon sec.

FATHERLY Jacob to Esther Bell 20 Sep 1787; Rob't Brickhouse sec.

FATHERLY Jacob to Miss Elizabeth Halcy 13 Jan 1840; Elizabeth wrd/o Azariah Williams sec; Walter W Widgeon as to Jacob's age; Edwin Goffigon wit; m 15 Jan 1840 by W A Dix.

FATHERLY Jacob to Elizabeth Gilden 1 Jun 1846; wid/o Wm Gilden; Wm T Goody sec & as to Jacob's age; m 1 Jun 1846 by G C Wescoat.

FATHERLY John to Sally Bearcraft 9 Apr 1816; Wm Frost sec; m 15 Apr 1816 by C Bonewell.

FARTHERY Matthew to Weltha Woodward 30 Jan 1799; Jacob Mills sec; m 31 Jan 1799 by A Foster.

FATHERY Mathew to Rachel Frost 26 Dec 1809; Wm Frost sec; m (1809) by J Elliott.

FATHERLY Matthew to Nancy Wilson 14 Nov 1814; John Nelson Jr sec; m (1814) by J Elliott.

FATHERLY William to Susan Matthews 11 Nov 1834; d/o Wm Matthews; Thomas Young sec; Hez P James as to Susan's age; P P Mayo wit; m 12 Nov 1834 by G Wescoat.

FENN Andrew to Jane Major 8 Dec 1661. BK IX:114.

FINNEY Edward O to Margaret S Thomas 9 Jun 1828; d/o John B Thomas sec.

FINNEY William to Joanna Stott 24 Dec 1746; William of Acc Co; wid/o (Johathan Stott); Peter Hog sec; Benoni Clay & David Jones wits.

FINNEY William R to Rosey Johnson 10 Dec 1810; Arthur R Savage sec; m 19 Dec 1810 by Thos A Elliott.

FIRKETTLE, See THURGETTLE.

FIRKETTLE Hamon to Frances Cowdry 13 May 1709; Hillary Stringer & Josias Cowdry secs; Sarah Palmer wit.

FISHER Caleb to Elizabeth Downing 6 Sep 177_ (paper torn; read by S Nottingham in 1929 as 1774); d/o Zerobable Downing; Wm Downing sec.

FISHER Caleb to Elizabeth West 2 Oct 1793; Elijah Baker sec; m (1793) by E Baker.

FISHER Edwin J to Anna M Cutler 12 Dec 1844; wid/o William W Cutler; Miers W Fisher sec; m 12 Dec 1844 by J Ufford.

FISHER Esme to Margaret Roberts 16 Apr 1765; wid/o (Francis Roberts); Thos Fisher Jr sec.

FISHER George to Susanna Joynes 13 Oct 1789; Wm Fisher sec.

FISHER James to Mary White 13 Dec 1791; d/o Wm White dec'd; Geo Melhollomes sec.

FISHER James to Sally Frost 18 Jan 1804; Robinson Custis sec; m (1804) by J Elliott.

FISHER John R to Melinda D Heath 8 Feb 1819; Wm R Fisher sec; m 10 Feb 1819 by C Bonewell.

FISHER John R to Edney (Edna) Henderson 4 Jan 1840; Miers W Fisher sec; m 6 Jan 1840 by G C Wescoat.

FISHER Miers W to Juliet B Harmanson 6 Oct 1829; (wid/o Jno H Harmanson); John Ker sec; m 8 Oct 1829 by S S Gunter. see BRec V4:107.

FISHER Reuben to Mary M Ross 18 Feb 1835; d/o John Ross dec'd; George T Belote sec & as to ages; m 18 Feb 1835 by G Wescoat.

FISHER Samuel P to Susan Pettit 13 Jun 1825; Wm M Pettit sec & gdn/o Susan; m 14 Jun 1825 by S S Gunter.

FISHER Thomas to Sarah Turner 1 Aug 1754; con/o Thos & Susanna Knightfor her son Thos; wid/o (George Turner)*; Wm Major Jr sec; Littleton Savage & Thos Dunn & Peggy Major wits. *North Co OB 24:356.

FISHER Thomas Jr to Margaret Christian 15 May 1770; d/o Michael Christian con; Joachim Michael sec. see BRec V7:151.

FISHER Thomas B to Sallie Addison 1830; s/o Wm & Mary Fisher. see BRec V1:2.

FISHER Wm to Rose Christian 25 Sep 1776; d/o William Christian dec'd; Thos Fisher Sr sec; Jno Michael con gdn/o Rose; Hez Pitts & Wm Jefres wits.

FISHER William to Sally Johnson 12 Feb 1789; d/o Powell Johnson dec'd; Wm Wilkins Sr sec; (m 18 Feb 1789. see BRec V1:2.)

FISHER William R to Edith Esther Williams 11 Mar 1822; con Margaret Williams gdn/o Edith orp/o Samuel P Fisher sec; m 27 Mar 1822 by L Dix. see BRec V1:2.

FITCHETT Charles to Peggy Powell 22 Nov 1797; d/o George Powell Sr con; Joshua Fitchett sec; m (1797) by E Baker.

FITCHETT Christopher to Leah Costin 8 Sep 1823; d/o William sec; m Sep 1823 by L Dix.

FITCHETT Daniel to Ann Widgen 24 Dec 1821; d/o Nancy Widgen con; Southey Spady sec; Jacob Nottingham wit.

FITCHETT Edward C to Miss Mary W Dunton 24 Jan 1853; d/o Thooms K Dunton con; Legustus Roberts as to Edward's age; Azariah Williams & Geo J Thomas wits; m 26 Jan 1853 by P Warren.

FITCHETT Edward G to Miss Elizabeth Kelly 23 Jul 1850; d/o Obed Kelly; Denward Fitchett as to Edward's age; Wm J Nottingham wit; m 24 Jul 1850 by P Warren.

FITCHETT George P to Mary S Williams 30 Aug 1830; d/o & wrd/o Margaret Williams; Sam'l L Floyd sec; Thomas Powell as to Geo P's age; Thomas D Fitchett wit; m 1 Sep 1830 by P Williams.

FITCHETT Henry to Anne Heritage 21 Dec 1789; Wm Clay sec; m (1789) by E Baker.

FITCHETT Jacob to Mary Bull 29 Dec 1830; wid/o Richard Bull; John Ewell sec.

FITCHETT James to Miss Elizabeth Jane Bell 13 Dec 1852; d/o Jesse Bell dec'd; Littleton Mears as to Elizabeth's age; m 13 Dec 1852 by P Warren.

FITCHETT James M to Susanna Rogers 13 Feb 1809; Geo Bell sec; Jas M Fitchett app't gdn/o Susanna orp/o John Rogers; m (1809) by J Elliott.

FITCHETT John R to Miss Fannie O Simkins 30 Jun 1851; d/o Dr Jesse J Simkins con; John A Simkins & Andrew J Nottingham wits; m 3 Jul 1851 by J Rawson. Hun Par Reg:35.

FITCHETT Jonathan to Elizabeth Nottingham 15 Jan 1783; John

Nottingham sec.
FITCHET Jonathan to Nancy Tyson 30 Nov 1787; d/o Nath'l Tyson sec.
FITCHETT Joshua to Sukey Dixon 12 Nov 1782; Ralph Dixon sec.
FITCHETT Joshua Jr to Polly Dixon 25 Jul 1801; Severn Savage sec; m Jul 1801 by C Simkins.
FITCHETT Nathaniel P to Sally H Jacob 15 Dec 1834; s/o Thomas Fitchett con; Sally wrd/o John Addison con; Rickard P Read sec; Geo W Brittingham & Victor A Nottingham wits; (m 18 Dec 1834. see BRec V6:21).
FITCHETT Ralph D to Mary E Fitchett 23 Oct 1828; d/o Thomas Fitchett Sr sec; m 30 Oct 1828 by P Williams. (BRec V6:21 states Mary Elizabeth).
FITCHETT Nehemiah to Rachel Stringer 22 Apr 1762; wid/o (John Stringer); John Smaw sec; m 25 Jul 1762; North Co Pk 60 Aug CT "Downs vs Fitchett".
FITCHETT Nehemiah to Elizabeth Flood 15 Jul 1752; spinster; John Flood sec.
FITCHETT Patrick H to Susan Williams 1 Jan 1830; d/o Samuel Williams dec'd; John Spady Jr sec; Benja Williams as to ages; m 6 Jan 1830 by P Williams.
FITCHETT Robert to Sally Warren 25 Nov 1782; Henry Smaw sec.
FITCHETT Robert to Frances Wilkins Widgeon 27 Dec 1790; Joshua Fitchett sec; Wm Willis gdn/o Frances con; m (1790) by E Baker.
FITCHETT Robert to Fanny Giddens 19 Jul 1806; Isaac Nottingham sec; m (1806) by J Elliott.
FITCHETT Robert to Patsey O'dear 11 Dec 1809; Wm S Evans sec; m (1809) by J Elliott.
FITCHETT Robert to Elizabeth Clay 8 Nov 1824; wid/o James Clay; Thomas Moore sec.
FITCHETT Robert to Elizabeth Griffith 22 Dec 1840; wid/o Wm Griffith; George O'Dear sec & as to Robert's age; m 29 Dec 1840 by P Williams.
FITCHETT Robert W to Miss Elizabeth A Griffith 11 Feb 1850; John H Griffith gdn/o Elizabeth sec; m 12 Feb 1850 by P Williams.
FITCHETT Thomas to Hannah Powell 14 Sep 1805; Joshua D Fitchett sec; m (1805) by J Elliott.
FITCHETT Thomas Jr to Elizabeth Fitchett 1 Jan 1836; wid/o Robert Fitchett; Thomas R Jarvis sec; m 5 Jan 1836 by P Williams.
FITCHETT Thomas D to Miss Lucy Ann Nottingham 8 Dec 1834; d/o Jacob Nottingham dec'd; George P Fitchett sec; m 11 Dec 1834 by L Dix.
FITCHETT Thomas J to Miss Elcana B Parsons 21 Dec 1848; d/o Mrs Sally Parsons; Samuel H Parson sec & as to ages.
FITCHETT William to Sally Hunt 27 Jun 1815; Arthur Simkins sec; m (1815) by J Elliott.
FITCHETT William to Elizabeth Elligood 15 Jun 1818; John Adams sec; m 17 Jun 1818 by C Bonewell.
FITCHETT William J to Mary W Ward 31 Dec 1836; d/o Jane W Harrison con & orp/o Tully S Ward; Wm H Bell sec & as to Wm's age; m 31 Dec 1836 by G Wescoat.
FITCHETT William P to Elizabeth Ann Williams 27 Oct 1838; s/o Martha Fitchett con; d/o Ann J Williams con; James D & Benja S Williams wits; Thomas K Dunton sec; m 31 Oct 1838 by L Dix. see BRec V1:37.
FITCHETT William Thomas to Maria Susan Nottingham 1 Dec 1852; d/o Wm J & Susan B Nottingham; m by Rev Mr Cummings (poss in Suffolk).
FITCHEW Henry to Betsey Wilson 23 Oct 1797; Matthew Floyd sec; m (1797) by J Elliott.
FITCHEW Henry to Cassey

Nottingham 17 Dec 1800; Custis Kendall sec; m 1800 by J Elliott.

FITCHEW John to Molly Luke 25 Aug 1795; John Dolby sec; m 1795 by I Bratten.

FITZHUGH Dr Philip Aylett to Miss Georgianna Tankard 16 Apr 1849; George P Scarburgh sec; m 16 Apr 1849 by J Ufford.

FLETCHER Charles to Esther Harrison 1 Aug 1822; Major Dowty sec & as to ages; m 1 Aug 1822 by C Bonewell.

FLETCHER Charles W to Margaret Scott 17 Sep 1838; d/o John Scott; James S Carpenter sec & as to Margaret's age; m 18 Sep 1838 by G C Wescoat.

FLETCHER James to Nancy Churn 13 Jan 1796; Wm Fletcher sec.

FLETCHER Jesse to Betsey Barecraft 18 Dec 1806; John Scott sec.

FLETCHER John T to Miss Rachel P Horton 10 Jun 1850; Rachel wrd/o John T. Fletcher; Nathan F Cobb sec; m 10 Jun 1850 by P Williams.

FLETCHER Nathan R to Miss Margaret E S Johnson 9 Oct 1840; d/o Jeptha Johnson sec; Jacob R Ashby as to Nathan's age; m 15 Oct 1840 by S T Ames.

FLETCHER Richard T to Miss Sally Webb 7 May 1845; d/o James S Webb sec & as to Richard's age; Wm P Nottingham wit; m 8 May 1845 by P Warren Jr.

FLETCHER Saml to Mary Parkerson 2 Jul 1834; wid/o Geo Parkerson; John Robins sec; m 6 Jul 1834 by G Wescoat.

FLETCHER Stephen to Susanna Churn 12 Mar 1790; Archibald Dowty sec; m 15 Mar 1790 by C Simkins.

FLETCHER William to Sarah Churn 13 Jan 1796; James Fletcher sec.

FLETCHER William to Mary Stakes 6 Sep 1799; Wm Hanby sec; m (1799) by I Bratten.

FLETCHER William H to Esther Mears 16 May* 1835; wid/o James Mears; Samuel C Fletcher sec & as to Wm's age given on 16 Jun* 1835; m 18 Jun 1835 by G Wescoat. *discrepancy

FLOOD John to Frances Warren 11 Jul 1752; wid/o (Mathew Warren); Nehemiah Fitchett sec.

FLOOD Samuel to Sarah Chance 20 Apr 1787; Eyrs Stokley sec.

FLOYD Berry to Lavinia Nottingham 23 Dec 1829; d/o Levin Nottingham dec'd & wrd/o Benja N Scott; Severn Nottingham sec & as to Berry's age; Jno Goffigon Jr & James Saunders wits; m 24 Dec 1829 by P Williams.

FLOYD Charles to Sarah Williams 8 Dec 1762; d/o Jacob Williams dec'd; Thos Wilson sec.

FLOYD Charles to Elizabeth Tankard 3 Mar 1778; d/o John Tankard sec.

FLOYD Frederick to Comfort Downing 30 Aug 1800; Johannes Johnson sec; m 1800 by J Elliott.

FLOYD Ishaman (Ishmail) to Sally Liverpool 8 Jul 1820; Josiah Liverpool sec (FN); m 8 Jul 1820 by C Bonewell.

FLOYD John to Mary Floyd 14 Feb 1765; d/o Matthew Floyd Jr dec'd; Jno Harmanson sec.

FLOYD John Jr to Mary Brickhouse 21 Aug 1773; d/o John Brickhouse Sr sec.

FLOYD John to Molly B Savage 12 Jan 1818; Michael Savage Sr sec; m 14 Jan 1818 by C Bonewell.

FLOYD John K to Ann Stoackley Teackle 26 Jul 1802; d/o Thomas Teackle of Acc Co con; Thos Lyt Savage sec; m (1802) by J Elliott; (m 28 Jul 1802. see BRec V8:139).

FLOYD Major to Nancy Willis 11 Oct 1800; Matthew Floyd sec; m 1800 by J Elliott.

FLOYD Major to Sally Moore 16 Dec 1817; Wm E Nottingham sec; m 20 Dec 1817 by C Bonewell.

FLOYD Matthew to Sarah Robins 22 Dec 1790; wid; Coventon Simpkins sec; m 25 Dec 1790 by

C Simkins.

FLOYD Matthew to Nancy Wilson 31 Jul 1794; Wm Roberts sec; m (1794) by E Baker.

FLOYD Matthew to Elizabeth H Kendall 15 Feb 1797; d/o Thomas Kendall con; Thos Wilkins sec; m Feb 1797 by C Simkins.

FLOYD Matthew to Peggy Roberts 29 Dec 1802; Wm Rooks sec.

FLOYD Matthew to Nancy Clay 19 Nov 1816; Thomas Powell sec; m 21 Nov 1816 by Rob't Windsor. (MinRet states "Sally" Clay).

FLOYD Matthew to Elizabeth Wilkins 9 Dec 1816; Edward Joynes sec; m 9 Dec 1816 by C Bonewell.

FLOYD Mathew to Nancy Williams 17 Jul 1821. Peter Williams Jr gdn/o Nancy con; Azariah Williams sec; Abner Thurtin wit; m 19 Jul 1821 by L Dix.

FLOYD Samuel L to Mary R Wise 16 Oct 1829; d/o Dr Tully R Wise dec'd; Nathl Winder sec.

FLOYD Shepherd B to Susan Freshwater 5 Sep 1813; Susan wrd/o Wm Stokely con sec; Thos L Nolen wit; m (1813) by J Elliott.

FLOYD William to Esther Kendall 14 Apr 1772; d/o John Kendall dec'd; Samuel Williams sec.

FLOYD William to Sukey Kendall 23 Dec 1801; Reuben Frost sec; m (1801) by J Elliott.

FLOYD William to Frances Hallet 7 May 1805; John Hallet sec; m (1805) by J Elliott.

FLOYD William to Mary Custis 28 Dec 1813; Major Floyd sec; m (1813) by J Elliott.

FLOYD William of Major to Margaret Joynes 10 Dec 1827; Margaret wrd/o Daniel Fitchett sec; Matthew Floyd as to Wm's age; Wm Dunton wit; m 24 Dec 1827 by P Williams.

FLOYD William H to Sarah Ann Stockley 23 Sep 1839; d/o Charles B Stockley sec; Geo F Wilkins as to William's age; m 26 Sep 1839 by S T Ames.

FLOYD William Satchell to Miss Ann T Smith 13 Jan 1834; s/o Jno K & Ann Floyd; d/o Isaac Smith sec; (m 15 Jan 1834. see BRec V8:139,142).

FOOKES (FOWKES) Thomas to Ann Waddelow 30 Sep 1660. BK IX:92.

FORMICOLA Serafino to Matilda Newman 12 Jul 1774; Serafino of York Co; wid; Teackle Robins sec.

FOSCOAT Simon to Ann Cook 30 Jan 1660/1661. BK IX:92.

FOSSETT John to Rhoda Lambertson 21 May 1661. BK IX:114.

FOUSHEE William to Isabella Harmanson 6 Mar 1775; William of Bor of Norfolk; John Staughton Harmanson sec.

FOWKES See FOOKES.

FOX John to Priscilla Widgeon 22 May 1824; wid/o John Widgeon; Littleton Upshur sec; m 22 May 1824 by S Wilmer.

FOX William to Adah Andrews 13 Feb 1804; Jacob Roberts sec; m (1804) by I Bratten.

FOX William to Anne W Travis 3 Sep 1834; wid/o Elliott Travis; Thomas Powell sec; Zorobabel Gibb as to Wm's age; m 5 Sep 1834 by P Williams.

FOX William G to Miss Esther Ann Fox 21 Feb 1846; d/o John D Fox sec; John H Duncan as to Wm G's age; m 25 Feb 1846 by P Warren.

FOXCRAFT Lyt Isaac to Bridget Charleton 23 Apr 1661. BK IX:114.

FRANCIS John to Ibby (Elizabeth) Shephard 28 Dec 1792; wid; Abraham Lang sec (FN; m Dec 1792 by C Simkins.

FRANCIS Thos to Tabby Press 26 Dec 1796; Edmund Press sec (FN); m (1796) by C Simkins.

FRANCIS Thomas to Chrysanna Collins 11 Aug 1825; Wm Francis sec (FN).

FRANCIS William to Polly Jacob 30

Dec 1791; Abraham Lang sec (FN); m 30 Dec 1791 by C Simkins.

FRANCIS William Jr to Margaret Bingham FN 26 Dec 1829; Severn Wickes sec; m 31 Dec 1829 by P Williams.

FRASER Collin to Ellenor Waterfield 11 Jan 1769; Jno Waterfield Jr sec; Wm Harmanson wit.

FREEMAN Absolem to Polly West 17 Apr 1805; Samuel Stevens sec.

FRESHWATER Edward to Susan Harrison 27 Dec 1831; d/o Newton Harrison sec; Geo F Wilkins as to Edward's age.

FRESHWATER Edward to Miss Fanny Richardson 30 May 1843; d/o ___ Richardson dec'd; James Williams sec & as to Fanny's age; James Dunton wit; m 30 May 1843 by P Williams.

FRESHWATER Jacob to Mary Nelson 24 Mar 1763; d/o John Nelson dec'd; Jno Wilkins blacksmith sec.

FRESHWATER Nathaniel to Elizabeth Clegg 14 Apr 1802; Jas Powell con for Elizabeth; John Simkins sec; m (1802) by I Bratten.

FRESHWATER William Jr to Nancy Mills 11 Dec 1786; Nancy wrd/o Southy Spady con & sec.

FRESHWATER William to Betsey Wilkins 11 Nov 1800; Wm Scott sec; m Nov 1800 by C Simkins.

FROST Francis to Miss Emma S Dunton 29 Jun 1852; d/o Rickets Dunton con; John H Powell & C Brickhouse wits; m 30 Jun 1852 by P Warren.

FROST John to Betsey Knight 1 Mar 1791; Severn Nottingham sec; m (1791) by E Baker.

FROST John to Tabby Dowty 12 Aug 1799; Thos Jacob sec; m (1799) by J Elliot.

FROST John Jr to Frances Wise 31 Dec 1817; Stephen Wilkinson sec; m 31 Dec 1817 by C Bonewell.

FROST John to Smarta Wilson 9 Jul 1818; Thomas Peed sec; m 15 Jul 1818 by C Bonewell.

FROST Joseph to Elenor Walker 27 Nov 1782; d/o John Walker con & states "she is at age"; Stuart Saunders sec.

FROST Josephus S to Miss Elizabeth Susan Scott 22 May 1846; d/o John Scott dec'd; Obediah Scott sec & as to ages; Geo P Upshur wit; m 26 May 1846 by P Williams.

FROST Nathaniel to Peggy Williams 18 Dec 1798; Wm Scott sec; m Dec 1798 by C Simkins.

FROST Reubin to Emily Wingate 27 Dec 1842; d/o Daniel Wingate sec; Victor A Nottingham as to Reubin's age; m 29 Dec 1842 by G Bradford.

FROST Robert to Esther Rippin 4 Jul 1836; d/o William Rippin dec'd; Severn Wilkins sec & as to ages.

FROST Robert to Sarah Ann Wingate 5 Aug 1839; d/o Daniel Wingate sec & as to Robert's age; Griffith Morgan wit; m 11 Aug 1839 by W A Dix.

FROST Capt William to Sally Russell 1 Jun 1808; d/o Robert Greenway & wife (m/o Sally) con; John Boggs sec; m (1808) by J Elliott.

FULWELL John Lewis to Margaret Costin 24 Jun 1761; d/o Jacob Costin dec'd; Nath'l Savage sec.

FULWELL Dr Victor Augustus to Elizabeth Simkins 12 Sep 1795; Coventon Simkins gdn/o Elizabeth con; Wm Simkins sec; m Sep 1795 by C Simkins.

G

GALE, See also GAYLE.

GALE Christopher to Margaret Abbot 3 Dec 1808; Joshua Garrison sec.

GARDINER Walter C to Elizabeth Fulwell 2 May 1804; Arthur Simkins sec; m (1804) by J Elliot.

GARDNER William to Tinsey

Bingham (FN) 25 Nov 1797; Isaac Stephens sec; m (1797) by I Bratten.
GARRELL Thomas to Marg Knight 29 May 1661. BK IX:114.
GARRETT Charles to Miss Leana Bool 10 Jan 1853; d/o George Bool dec'd; Jno T Charnick as to Leana's age; Edwin Goffigon wit.
GARRET George to Susan Bird 24 Dec 1825; Wm Carmine sec & as to ages; m 1825 by G C Wescoat.
GARRETT Richard to Polly Robins 9 Sep 1816; Major F Richardson sec; m 9 Sep 1816 by C Bonewell.
GARRETT Robert M to Miss Susan C Winder 2 Jun 1835; d/o John H Winder; Levin Y Winder sec.
GARRIS Isaiah to Lavinia Terrier 13 Jun 1842; James M Wilson gdn/o Lavinia sec; m 13 Jun 1842 by P Warren.
GARRIS William to Elizabeth Gooldsburry 24 Sep 1796; Coventon Stott sec; m (1796) by I Bratten.
GARRISON Abel to Margaret Floyd 8 Aug 1775; d/o John Floyd dec'd; John Widgen Jr sec.
GARRISON Bagwell to Catharine Mathews 21 Mar 1809; John Ames sec.
GARRISON George to Sarah Dunton 13 Dec 1785; Dicke Dunton sec.
GARRISON James to Sally Jacob 7 Aug 1797; Richd Jacob sec; (m 12 Aug 1797. see BRec V1:29).
GARRISON James R to Susan P Tankard 14 Dec 1833; James of Acc Co; Susan 18y & d/o John Tankard con; Elijah Floyd sec & as to James' age; John W Tankard wit; m 18 (Dec) 1833 by W B Snead. see BRec V2:18.
GARRISON William B to Susan S Mears 14 Feb 1833; d/o Richard Mears dec'd; Thomas Young sec & as to ages; m 21 Feb 1833 by W B Snead.
GARRISON William B to Margaret S Johnson 14 Mar 1836; d/o Richard Johnson dec'd; George S Garrison sec & as to ages; Thos A Coleburn wit; m 15 Mar 1836 by G Wescoat.
GASCOIGNE, GASCOYNE.
GASCOYNE Henry to Sarah Upshur 14 Apr 1752; wid/o (Thos Upshur); Esau Jacob sec.
GASCOYNE Henry to Sarah Stott 13 Jul 1773; d/o Laban Stott con; Joachim Michael sec.
GASCOYN Thomas to Sarah Andrews 8 Jan 1722; Thos Johnson & Jno White secs; lic 8 Jan 1722. CT ret Oct 1723.
GASCOYNE William to Anne Harmanson 17 Jan 1769; d/o Matthew Harmanson Gent dec'd; Dickie Galt sec.
GALT Dickie to Leah Benthall 13 Jan 1761; d/o Azel Benthall sec.
GAYLE, See also GALE.
GAYLE Christopher to Mary Ann Steaphens 20 Dec 1798; David Topping sec; Rachel Cowles con for Mary Ann; m (1798) by J Elliot.
GAYLE Christopher to Ann Stevens 22 May 1802; John R Waddy sec; m (1802) by J Elliott.
GAYLE Joseph to Margaret Cook 22 May 1794; David Topping sec; m May 1794 by C Simkins.
GAYLE Joseph to Peggy Jacob 14 Apr 1801; Richards Dunton Jr sec; m 1801 by I Bratten.
GELDING See GILDING.
GEORGE Willis to Miss Catharine Smith 29 Dec 1800; Major Pettit gdn/o Catharine con; Thomas James sec.
GIBB Flavious J to Emmy J Hoshier 17 Aug 1843; d/o Mahala Hosier con; John T Johnson sec & as to Flavious' age; Edw'd P Roberts & Thos N B Roberts wits; m 19 Aug 1843 by G C Wescoat.
GIBB Zorobabel to Ann Evans 16 Mar 1827; d/o John Evans con; Henry B Kendall sec; Thos Milbourn wit; m Mar 1827 by L Dix.
GIBBONS Jonathan to Frances (Fanny) Gault 8 Feb 1792; Jonathan of Delaware; d/o Sarah

Jacob con; John Carpenter sec; m (1792) by E Baker.

GIDDENS, GIDDINGS.

GIDDENS Benjamin to Betsy West FN 16 Feb 1826; Samuel Scisco sec & as to ages; m 18 Feb 1826 by S S Gunter.

GIDDENS Daniel to Sally Custis 29 Dec 1824; d/o Abram Custis FN & age 23y acc'd to mother; Benjamin Giddens sec & as to Daniel's age.

GIDDENS Henry to Milly Moor 16 Feb 1786; Jacob Fathery sec; Thos Nottingham Jr con as to Milly.

GIDDENS Henry to (Betsey Evans) 24 Aug 1795; Arthur Evans sec; John Evans con; m Aug 1785 by C Simkins. (bride's name shows on MinRet).

GIDDENS Henry to Betsey Jones 24 Feb 1823; George Eshon gdn/o Henry con; Thomas Eshon sec; m 26 Feb 1823 by C Bonewell.

GIDDENS Henry to Elizabeth Matthews 25 Jul 1826; wid/o Teackle Matthews; James Young sec; m 25 Jul 1826 by S S Gunter.

GIDDENS Henry to Sally Williams 14 Sep 1829; widower; d/o James Williams sec.

GIDDENS Thomas to Betsey Harrison 18 Jul 1801; Johannes Johnson sec; m (1801) by J Elliott.

GILDEN, GILDING, GILDON.

GILDING Charles to Mary Dixon 8 Jun 1771; d/o John Dixon dec'd; Richard Smith sec.

GILDING Charles to Peggy Turner 22 Dec 1798; Christopher Gayle sec; m 1798 by J Elliot.

GILDING Charles to Sally Jacob 5 Nov 1803; Teackle Roberts sec; m (1803) by I Bratten.

GILDING John to Nancy Core 4 Aug 1803; Severn Nottingham sec; Robins Mapp gdn/o John con; m (1803) by I Bratten.

GILDON John to Rosey Clark 12 Nov 1827; Wm W Ridley sec & as to Rosey's age; Nath'l Ames & Major Wescoat wits; m 1827 by G C Wescoat.

GILDON William C to Elizabeth Clarke 14 Oct 1828; s/o John Gildon sec; Elizabeth wrd/o Littleton K Godwin sec; m 15 Oct 1828 by G Wescoat.

GILLEY Thomas to Mary Manlow 23 Nov 1661. BK IX:114.

GILMER William to Mary Ann Drysdale 15 Apr 1799; Isaac Smith Sr sec.

GILSON George to Miss Kesiah Abdell 11 Jun 1838; d/o Abel Abdell dec'd; Samuel Bunting sec & as to ages.

GLADSON, GLADSTONE.

GLADSTONE William to Ann Teackle 27 Nov 1832. see BRec V2:93.

GLADSON Capt William to Sarah Metcalf (bet 1846 - 1851). Homes Presb Ch Rec:12.

GLANVILLE Edmund to Anna Katharina Thurmur 30 Oct 1758; Edmund of York Co; wid; John Dolby Jr sec.

GLANVILLE Edmund to Margaret Scott 24 Dec 1778; d/o Zerobabel Scott; Walter Hyslop sec.

GLEASON, GLEESON, GLESON.

GLEESON James to Adah Bell 8 Oct 1793; d/o Joab Bell; Geo Bell sec; m Oct 1793 by C Simkins.

GLESON John to Elizabeth Dodd 10 Jan 1770; Rob't Polk sec.

GLEASON John to Eliz Bullock 10 May 1785; Wm Jefferys sec.

GLEESON John Sr to Rachel Fitzgerald 24 May 1798; John Carpenter Sr sec; m (1798) by I Bratten.

GLEASON Peter to Sally Francis 5 Feb 1825; s/o Sarah Gleason as to Peter's age; d/o John Francis sec.

GLEESON Thomas to Polly Caple 24 Oct 1794; James Gleeson sec.

GLEESON William C to Polly Bell 13 Dec 1823; d/o George Bell sec; m Dec 1823 by L Dix.

GODDAY See GOODDAY.

GODWIN Archibald to Vianna Gray Jacob 9 Jul 1776; wid/o (Esau Jacob); Wm Wood sec.

GODWIN Charles to Elizabeth Wilson 1 Jan 1836; wid/o Thomas Wilson; John Tyson sec & as to Charles' age; Jno Casey wit; m 7 Jan 1836 by W B Snead.

øGODWIN Daniell to Elishaba Benthall 12 Jan 1724; George Lucar & wife con for Elishaba; Devorax Godwin & Geo Lucar secs.

øGODWIN Daniel to Susanna Preeson 5 May 1724; Thos Savage Jr & Godfrey Pole secs; lic 5 May 1724 CT ret Oct 1724.

GODWIN Daniel to Sarah Cowdry 30 Sep 1779; wid/o Thos Cowdry; Archibald Godwin sec.

GODWIN Devorax to Esther Bailey 27 Aug 1763; d/o Isaac Bailey dec'd; Daniel Eshon sec.

GODWIN Devorax to Sally Floyd 3 Mar 1807; Ezekiel Badger sec; m (1807) by J Elliott.

GODWIN Devorax to Margaret Jacob 16 Jun 1838; d/o Teackle Jacob sec; Edmund S Godwin as to Devorax's age; m 18 Jun 1838 by G C Wescoat.

GODWIN Devorax to Maria Underhill 6 Jan 1846; wid/o Michael Underhill; Southey S Wilkins sec; m 7 Jan 1846 by P Warren.

GODWIN Edmund to Nancy Grey Godwin 23 Oct 1797; Archibald Godwin sec; m Oct 1797 by C Simkins.

GODWIN Edmund S to Susan T Melhollomes 14 Apr 1834; d/o Thomas Melhollomes sec & as to Edmund's age; Obedience R Johnson wit; m 17 Apr 1834 by W B Snead.

GODWIN Edmund S to Rosy P Mears 9 Jan 1837; d/o Jamima Mears; John G Turner sec & as to ages; m 9 Jan 1837 by G Wescoat.

GODWIN Edwin to Mary B Nottingham 3 Jul 1821; Thomas N Williams sec; m 4 Jul 1821 by L Dix.

GODWIN Griffin F to Miss Emily Wilkins 31 Oct 1846; d/o Hetty Wilkins con; James H Stewart sec; Wm J Wilkins wit; m 4 Nov 1846 by P Warren. see BRec V4:45.

GODWIN John to Polly Haggoman 19 Aug 1823; John b 16 Dec 1800; s/o Laban Godwin; d/o Robert Haggoman sec; m 20 Aug 1823 by C Bonwell.

GODWIN Joseph P to Miss Arinthia Roberts 1 Jan 1848; d/o Sally Roberts con; Thomas Smith Jr sec; Michael Dowty & Wm Christian wits; m 3 Jan 1848 by P Warren.

GODWIN Laban to Letty Floyd 18 Feb 1800; d/o John Floyd con; George Holt sec; Margaret Holt wit; m Feb 1800 by C Simkins.

GODWIN Laban to Ann A Ward 22 Feb 1828; George T Yerby sec; Elizabeth Bool as to Ann's age.

GODWIN Littleton to Ann Dalby 9 Nov 1801; John Dalby sec; m (1801) by J Elliott.

GODWIN Littleton to Sukey (Susan) Johnson 18 Oct 1813; John Warren sec; m (1813) by J Elliott.

GODWIN Smith P to Ann Powell 18 May 1833; Ann wrd/o Joseph W Thomas sec.

GOFFIGON Edwin to Louisa C Spady 1 Jan 1839; Jacob E Nottingham sec & as to ages; m 8 Jan 1839 by P Williams.

GOFFIGON Frederick J to Miss Mary E Nottingham 15 Oct 1851; d/o James Nottingham con; W J Goffigon & N G Burris wits; m 23 Oct 1851 by P Williams. see BRec V10:53.

GOFFIGON James to Mary Floyd 27 Sep 1755; spinster; Anne Holt wid sec.

GOFFIGON James to Polly Goffigon 21 Dec 1802; d/o Nathl Goffigon con; Obediah Hunt sec; m (1802) by J Elliott.

GOFFIGON John to Nancy Bell 19

May 1792; d/o Robert Bell dec'd & con/o her gdn Thos Jarvis; Wm Jarvis sec; m May 1792 by C Simkins; (m 26 May 1792. see BRec V1:107).

GOFFIGON John to Sally Goffigon 18 Apr 1796; John Nelson sec; (m 19 Apr 1796. see BRec V1:107).

GOFFIGON John Jr to Diana D Segar 15 Nov 1831; Diana wrd/o John Segar sec; m Nov 1831 by L Dix.

GOFFIGON John Sr to Miss Susan Goffigon 9 Jan 1832; Nath'l S Goffigon sec; m 10 Jan 1832 by P Williams.

GOFFIGON Nathaniel to Frances Dunton 19 Dec 1772; d/o Levin Dunton Sr con; Sam'l Aitchison sec; (m 20 Dec 1772. see BRec V1:107; V10:53).

GOFFIGON Nathaniel S to Miss Emily Goffigon 27 Nov 1837; d/o James Goffigon; m 30 Nov 1837 by P Williams.

GOFFIGON Obed to Mary Trower 14 Sep 1829; d/o John Trower sec; Wm Dixon as to Obed's age; m 16 Sep 1829 by P Williams.

GOFFIGON Capt Peter to Sally Costin 6 Apr 1781; d/o Abraham Costin con; Walter Hyslop sec.

GOFFIGON Southy to Margaret Evans 18 Nov 1769; James Drummond sec.

GOFFIGON Southey to Esther Goffigon 23 Nov 1805; d/o Nathaniel Goffigon con; Samuel Williams sec; m (1805) by J Elliott.

GOFFIGON Thomas to Bridget Elliott 10 Mar 1781; wid/o Wm Elliott; Wm Rascoe sec.

GOFFIGON Thomas to Peggy Wilson 23 Jul 1785; Daniel Benthall sec.

GOFFIGON William to Polly Dixon 14 Apr 1806; Custis Hyslop sec; m (1806) by J Elliott.

GOFFIGON William J to Miss Arinthia S G Burris 11 Sep 1837; Arinthia wrd/o John Goffigon Sr sec & wit; as to William J's age; N L Goffigon wit; m 14 Sep 1837 by L Dix.

GOLDSMITH John to Mary Longo 13 Dec 1660. BK IX:92.

GOODAKER Thomas to Elizabeth Pott 18 May 1661. BK IX:114.

GOODDAY Reuben to Betsey Kendall 20 Jan 1808; Henry Smaw sec; m (1808) by I Bratten.

GOODDAY Reubin to Hetty Harman 2 Apr 1816; Reavil Watson sec; m 4 Apr 1816 by C Bonewell.

GORTHAN John to Bridget Darcy 28 Apr 1661. BK IX:114.

GRAVES See also GROVES.

GRAVES John Jr to Molly Pratt 28 Jan 1799; Wm Wilson sec; m (1799) by I Bratten.

GRAVES William to Mary Murry 7 Feb 1778; John Scott sec.

GRAVES William to Peggy Warren 23 Dec 1800; John Dunton sec; m 1800 by J Elliott.

GRAVES William to Sukey Warren 3 Aug 1808; Marriot Parsons sec; m (1808) by J Elliott.

GRAY, See also GREY.

GRAY John to Jane Benian 7 Feb 1661/1662. BK IX:114.

GRAY John to Delitha Heath 31 Oct 1816; d/o Patience Heath con as gdn; Robert A Joynes sec; m 7 Nov 1816 by C Bonewell.

GREEN George to Ann Benson 19 Dec 1798; George of Acc Co; George Kellam of Acc Co sec; m 1798 by J Elliott.

GREEN Hillary to Tamar Pitts 12 Apr 1757; wid; Holloway Bunting sec.

GREENAWAY Robert to Leah Scott 28 Jun 1788; Nath'l Goffigon sec; m (1788) by E Baker.

GREENWAY Robert to Susanna Rippen 9 Apr 1798; James Dolby sec; m (1798) by I Bratten.

GREENWAY Robert to Elizabeth Bearcraft 15 Feb 1817; Thos G Scott sec.

GREY, See also GRAY.

GREY George to Mahalah Byrd 27 Jun 1825; d/o Peggy Byrd con; Wm Byrd wit; Thos Byrd sec; m

1825 by G C Wescoat.
GRIFFETH, See GRIFFITH.
GRIFFIN Moses Jr to Nancy Costin 13 Jan 1800; Nathan Griffin sec; m Jan 1800 by C Simkins.
GRIFFITH, GRIFFETH
GRIFFITH Benjamin to Lilly Miller 9 Dec 1783; John Harwood sec.
GRIFFITH Benjamin to Rachell Havard 11 Jan 1808; John Winder sec; m (1808) by J Elliott.
GRIFFITH Benjamin to Sally Travis 11 Oct 1832; d/o Elliott Travis dec'd & wrd/o Dennard Travis con; Thomas Powell sec & as to Benja's age (Dennard Travis appt'd gdn 13 Feb 1826); m 13 Oct 1832 by P Williams.
GRIFFITH Charles to Sally More 28 Apr 1817; d/o Mathew More & Ann (prob his wife) con; John More sec; Robert Greenway wit.
GRIFFITH Jeremiah to Elizabeth Dixon 1 Sep 1832; s/o Moses Griffith con; d/o Wm Dixon con; Christopher D Fitchett sec; Jno Spady wit; m 13 Sep 1832 by P Williams.
GRIFFITH John to Nancy Costin 4 Jun 1791; wid/o Wm Costin; John Pratt sec; m 11 Jun 1791 by C Simkins.
GRIFFITH John to Nancy Willams 13 May 1809; Wm Stokely sec; m (1809) by J Elliott.
GRIFFITH John Jr to Mary Frost 26 Dec 1815; William Frost sec & as to Mary's age; m (1815) by J Elliott.
GRIFFITH John Jr to Ann Griffith 8 Sep 1828; d/o John Griffith Sr sec; Thos Hallett as to John Jr's age; J R Potter & John S Dix wits.
GRIFFITH John H to Elizabeth Ridley 9 Apr 1838; d/o Wm W Ridley sec; Thomas S Evans as to John's age; m 17 May 1838 by P Williams.
GRIFFITH Littleton to Peggy Wilson 13 Dec 1813; Josiah Willis sec; m (1813) by J Elliott.
GRIFFITH Littleton to Polly Collins 9 Jun 1817; John Collins sec; m 12 Jun 1817 by C Bonewell.
GRIFFETH Moses to Elenor Ellegood 13 May 1752; spinster; John Ellegood sec.
GRIFFITH Nathan to Sally Costin 27 May 1797; Moses Griffith Jr sec; m (1797) by E Baker.
GRIFFITH Nathan to Fanny Griffith 8 Feb 1838; d/o Moses Griffith con; Thomas S Evans sec; Rob't F Williams wit; m 21 Feb 1838 by P Williams.
GRIFFITH Thomas to Miss Mary Ann Kelly 13 Feb 1836; d/o Ann Kelly con; James B Nottingham sec; Severn E Nottingham wit; m 16 Feb 1836 by P Williams.
GRIFFITH Thomas to Mary Jacob 15 Sep 1841; d/o John Jacob Sr dec'd; Joshua Nottingham sec & as to ages; m 16 Sep 1841 by P Warren Jr.
GRIFFITH Thomas L to Elizabeth Parkerson 23 Dec 1837; Wm W Wilson sec & as to Thomas' age; Joshua Nottingham as to Elizabeth's age; m 27 Dec 1837 by G Wilshire.
GRIFFITH Thomas L to Mary Ann Saunders 4 May 1844; d/o John Saunders dec'd; David B Ball sec & as to Mary Ann's age; m 28 May 1844 by J D Curtis.
GRIFFITH William to Sally Snail 22 Jun 1791; Jno Graves Jr sec; m (1791) by E Baker.
GRIFFITH William to Sally Williams 24 May 1799; Azariah Williams sec; m 30 May 1799 by C Simkins.
GRIFFITH William to Elizabeth Griffith 20 Sep 1828; d/o Moses Griffith con; George O'Dear sec; Benja Griffith as to William's age; Obed Goffigon wit; m 25 Sep 1828 by P Williams.
GROTEN Kendall to Leah Spady 15 Aug 1815; Joshua Garrison sec.
GROTEN Kendall to Betsey Wilson 26 Mar 1818; Silas Jefferson sec; m 26 Mar 1818 by C Bonewell.
GROTEN Thomas to Elizabeth

Custis 12 Dec 1796; Geo Scott sec; m Dec 1796 by C Simkins.

GROVES, See also GRAVES.

GROVES John to Anne Wilson 26 Nov 1785; s/o Peter Groves con; Wm Stoyte sec; Naney Wilson as to Anne's age.

GUNTER Benjamin T to Miss Frances Ellen Fisher 22 Jan 1853; d/o John R Fisher; Geo G Savage as to ages; Jas G Floyd wit; m 23 Jan 1853 by Wm Laws.

GUNTER Stephen S to Tamar Pearson 7 Jan 1814; d/o Thos Pearson dec'd & his wife Adah (now w/o Jonathan Stott) con; Issachar Lewis sec; Tamer is 18y; John Tankard wit; m bet 1 Jan - 14 Feb (1814) by I Bratten.

GUNTER John W F to Sarah A Johnson 12 Dec 1836; s/o Stephen S Gunter dec'd & Tamer Gunter con; d/o Wm P Johnson dec'd & Margaret R Johnson con; Smith Belote sec; Obed R Johnson & Edw'd M Dunton wits; m 21 Dec 1836 by W B Snead.

GUNTER Joseph S M to Louisa B Johnson 30 Dec 1837; d/o Wm P Johnson dec'd; Thomas Pearson sec & as to ages; Joshua P Wescoat wit; m 1 Jan 1838 by G Wilshire.

GUNTER Joseph S M to Esther A Ewell 2 Aug 1845; wid/o John Ewell; H Neale wit; John Sterling sec; m 10 Aug 1845 by P Warren Jr.

GUNTER Stephen C to Miss Tabitha S Belote 12 Feb 1849; Laban Belote gdn/o Tabitha sec; Rhuben Gooday as to Laban's age; Jos P Godwin wit; m 14 Feb 1849 by P Warren.

GUSTIN Isaac to Jenney Bingham (FN) 13 Nov 1804; Jacob Floyd sec; m (1804) by I Bratten.

GUSTIN Jacob to Sarah Morris (FN) 28 Jul 1820; John Simkins sec; m 29 Jul 1820 by C Bonewell.

GUSTUS Abel to Abigail Stephens 6 Sep 1806; York Stepney sec (FN); m (1806) by I Bratten.

GUTRIE Esau to Absel Pool 23 Dec 1803; Esau of Acc Co; Moses Bucner sec; m (1803) by J Elliott.

GUY Harmanson to Adah Harmanson 6 Jan 1778; (d/o Patrick Harmanson dec'd) & her gdn John Harmanson con; John Burton sec.

GUY Henry to Adah Harmanson 18 Oct 1755; d/o Matthew Harmanson Gent dec'd; John Harmanson sec.

GUY John to Susanna Burton 27 Sep 1760; d/o John Burton Gent dec'd; Griffin Stith sec; John Kendall con to John Guy to marry "my kinswoman Susanah"; Adderson Nottingham & Howson Mapp wits.

GUY John to Elizabeth James 14 Feb 1791; d/o Thos James; Coventon Simkins sec; m 15 Feb 1791 by C Simkins.

GUY Matthew to Margaret Harmanson 25 Dec 1787; d/o John Harmanson Esq dec'd; John Kendall Jr sec.

H

HACK Peter to Sally Upshur 23 Oct 1786; Peter of Acc Co; d/o Thos Upshur con; John Upshur Jr sec.

HAGGOMAN John Jr to Betty Jacob 11 Mar 1755; d/o Hancock Jacob con; Henry Tomlinson sec; Jas Parker & Eyre Jacob & Elias Dunton wits.

HAGGOMAN Robert to Catharine Snead 10 Mar 1786; Maddox Andrews sec.

HAGGOMAN Robert to Mary MacDaniel 7 May 1799; Rickards Dunton Jr sec; m (1799) by J Elliot.

HAGGOMAN William to Margaret Michael 13 Jan 1755; wid/o (Joachim Michael); John Haggoman Jr sec; Esau Jacob wit.

HALE, See also HALL.

HALE (HALL?) James to Esther Scott 9 Sep 1791; John Dennis sec; m (1791) by E Baker.

HALEY Benjamin to Peggy Dawson 17 Nov 1803; Isaac Nottingham sec; m (1803) by J Elliott.
HALEY Benjamin to Miss Patsy Collins 18 Nov 1845; d/o Nathaniel Collins dec'd; Walter W Widgeon sec & as to Patsy's age; Wm A Smith as to Benja's age; Wm (J?) Bowdoin wit.
HALEY Robert to Peggy Costin 30 Jul 1807; Zorobabel Roberts sec; m (1807) by J Elliott.
HALEY Robert to Miss Nancy Mills 2 Sep 1824; James Costin sec & as to Nancy's age; m Sep 1824 by L Dix.
HALEY William to Miss Margaret Ann Costin 9 Oct 1848; William wrd/o John W Elliott sec; d/o Coventon R Costin con; John T Hallett sec; Thos F Spady & Wm H Mason wits; m 11 Oct 1848 by P Williams.
HALL, See also HALE.
HALL Daniel Roles to Susanna Guy 5 Feb 1772; wid/o John Guy; Samuel Aitchison sec.
HALL Daniel Roles to Susanna Wilkins 22 Nov 1780; d/o Jno Wilkins; John Stratton Jr sec.
HALL John R to Lucretia Bell 3 Jun 1816; Wm Dunton sec; Geo Brickhouse as to Lucretia's age being over 22y; m 6 Jun 1816 by C Bonewell.
HALL Robert to Esther Evans 10 Jul 1793; Jno Elliot gdn/o Esther con; she 17y old & orp/o Thos Evans; Wm Roberts sec; m (1793) by E Baker.
HALL Thomas to Esther Dunton 8 Oct 1793; Edward Bishop sec; m Oct 1793 by C Simkins.
HALL Thomas E to Lisha Jones 29 Dec 1825; John McCowan sec & as to ages; m Dec 1825 by L Dix.
HALL William to Lucretia Jones 29 Dec 1823; James H Jones br/o Lucretia as to her age; James Saunders sec; m Dec 1823 by L Dix.
HALLETT Edward M to Miss Lucy Ann Dixon 14 Nov 1853; d/o W Dixon con; Wm J Scott wit; Edw'd C Fitchett as to Edward M's age.
HALLETT Michael to Eliza Jacob 11 Oct 1824; Eliza wrd/o John Simkins sec; m Oct 1824 by L Dix.
HALLETT Thomas to Sally Trower 14 Aug 1815; John Trower sec.
HALLETT Thomas D to Sally Trower 12 Nov 1817; George Powell sec; m 13 Nov 1817 by C Bonewell.
HALLETT Thomas to Tamer Trower 13 May 1822; Nelley Trower states Tamer is 22y on 12 Mar; Micheal Hallet sec; Daniel Fitchett & Micheal Hallett wit; m 15 May 1822 by L Dix.
HALLETT William to Clear Dixon 4 Aug 1775; d/o John Dixon con; Jno Biggs sec.
HAMILTON, See also HAMPLETON.
HAMILTON Andrew to Ann Preeson 6 Mar 1706; wid; Wm Waters & John Luke secs; Rob't Denham & Henry Custis wits.
HAMILTON Andrew to Peggy Wheelor 25 Dec 1806; Nathaniel Jones sec; m (1806) by J Elliott.
HAMILTON Andrew to Mary G Williams 2 Dec 1823; John Moore sec & as to Mary's age; John Stockly wit.
HAMILTON Bowdoin to Susey Robins 26 Dec 1797; Wm Robins sec; m (1797) by I Bratten.
HAMMON Phillip to Mary Collever 13 Jan 1708/1709; Sam'l Palmer sec; James Watt wit.
HAMPLETON Bowdoin to Betsey Hosier 16 May 1821; Major Abdeel sec & as to Betsey's age; m 17 May 1821 by C Bonewell.
HAMPLETON James to Susan Bell 16 Dec 1839; d/o Thomas Bell dec'd; Elias Roberts sec & as to ages; m 18 Dec 1839 by P Williams.
HAMPLETON James to Miss Betsy Thurston 11 Sep 1843; Thomas K Dunton sec & gdn/o Betsy; m 11 Sep 1843 by P Williams.
HAMPLETON John to Mary Bell 3

Mar 1838; d/o Thomas Bell dec'd; Thomas S Brickhouse sec & as to ages; m 7 Mar 1838 by P Williams.

HAMPLETON William to Miss Molly Rippin 13 Dec 1824; Molly wrd/o John Wilkins sec; Teackle Roberts as to Wm's age.

HAMPLETON William to Margaret Williams 15 Dec 1832; d/o John Williams dec'd; Legustus Roberts sec & as to ages; m 20 Dec 1832 by P Williams.

HAMPLETON William to Miss Keziah Bell 8 Jan 1850; d/o John Bell dec'd; Edward T Robins sec & as to ages; Eldred R Holt wit; m 16 Jan 1850 by P Williams.

HANBY John to Leah Taylor 13 Mar 1809; Edmund Bell sec.

HANBY John to Sukey Taylor 12 Apr 1830; wid/o George Taylor; John M Wilkins sec; m 15 Apr 1830 P Williams.

HANBY John J to Rosina J Dalby 11 Jan 1841; d/o James Dalby; Southy Rew as to ages; Devorax Warren sec; m 11 Jun 1841 by J T Hazzard.

HANBY Joseph to Bridget Dalby 19 Jan 1791; Isaac Bull sec; m (1791) by E Baker.

HANBY Thomas to Sukey O'dear 13 May 1815; Peter Williams sec & as to Sukey's age.

HANBY William to Adelia Moore 19 May 1788; wid; Walter Hyslop sec.

HANBY William to Elizabeth James 15 Dec 1792; Wm Toleman sec; m Dec 1792 by C Simkins (MinRet states "Bridget" James).

HANBY William Jr to Polly James 21 Oct 1797; Thos Addison sec; m (1797) by J Elliot.

HANBY William to Rosey Scott 22 Aug 1798; Jno Speakman sec.

HANBY William to Joanna Williams 20 Apr 1802; Azariah Williams sec; m (1802) by J Elliott.

HANBY William to Mary Anne Wescoat 10 Dec 1833; d/o Edmund Wescoat con; Smith Bell sec; Thos W Rayfield wit; m Dec 1833 by L Dix.

HANBY William to Elizabeth Wescoat 24 Oct 1842; d/o Edmund Wescoat; Thomas Smith Jr sec & as to Elizabeth's age; m 26 Oct 1842 by P Warren.

HANDY William W to Miss Sally T B Upshur 7 Oct 1834; d/o John Upshur Sr; Wm S Savage sec & as to Sally's age.

HARLOW David to Molly Cary 3 Oct 1808; Wm Rippin sec; m (1808) by J Elliott.

HARMAN Emanuel to Lishe Webb; m May 1791 by C Simkins.

HARMON George to Anne Elliot 15 Feb 1775; d/o James Elliot sec.

HARMAN George to Peggy Smith 9 Mar 1797; Thos Dixon Jr sec; m (1797) by J Elliot.

HARMAN Keley to Leah Savage 13 Jun 1821; Leah wrd/o Calvin H Read sec; m 14 Jun 1821 by C Bonewell.

HARMAN Thomas to Bridget Bell 23 Nov 1811; Anthony Bell sec; m (1811) by J Elliott.

HARMANSON Henry to Rose Harmanson 7 May 1736; Wm Tazewell sec; Geo Douglas wit; m 7 May 1736; CT Ret 1736.

HARMANSON Henry to Lucretia Respess 14 Feb 1764; d/o John Respess con; John Harmanson sec; Devorax Godwin wit.

HARMANSON Henry to Elizabeth Robins 27 May 1789; Rob't Nottingham sec.

HARMANSON Henry Jr to Sarah Robins 19 Apr 1794; Henry Harmanson Sr sec; m Apr 1794 by C Simkins.

HARMANSON John to Isabell Harmanson 8 Oct 1723; spinster; Thos Harmanson sec; Jno Robins wit; lic 8 Oct 1723; CTret Oct 1724.

HARMANSON John to Margaret Wilkins 13 Oct 1823; Johannis Johnson sec & as to Margaret's age; m 14 Oct 1823 by C Bonewell.

HARMANSON John H to Catharine Coleburn 27 Feb 1806; Catharine wrd/o Geo Coleburn of Acc Co con; John Simkins sec; Jno S Wilkins & Jas Poulson wits; m (1806) by I Bratten.

HARMANSON John H to Juliet B Holland 1 Nov 1823; Nathaniel Holland sec; m 5 Nov 1823 by S S Gunter. see BRec V5:180.

HARMANSON Mathew to Rachel Roberts 9 Apr 1740; spinster; Thos Cable & Wm Taxewell & Geo Holden & Thos Preeson secs; Marg't Cable & Esther Preeson wits; m 9 Apr 1740; CT ret 1740.

HARMANSON Matthew to Catherine Robins 3 Jan 1791; d/o Henry Harmanson & gdn con; Matthew Guy sec.

HARMANSON Mathew to Elizabeth B Kendall 13 Dec 1798; d/o Lucretia Kendall con; Henry Harmanson sec; Margt Kendall wit; m 13 Dec 1798 by A Foster.

HARMANSON Patrick to Elishe Kendall 14 Mar 1758; wid/o (Geo Kendall)*; John Harmanson sec; Thos Respess wit. *North Co XIX:399.

HARMANSON William to Margaret Mapp 13 Sep 1774; John Staughton Harmanson sec.

HARMANSON William to Joanna Satchell 31 Dec 1777; Jno Savage Jr sec.

HARMANSON William to Margaret C Mapp 19 Dec 1825; d/o Margaret Mapp con & who states dau's age is 21y; Victor Mapp wit; George F Wilkins sec; m 23 Dec 1825 by S S Gunter.

HARMANSON Wm P to Sally Wilson Smith 26 Nov 1803; Wm Fisher sec; m (1803) by Bratten.

HARRISON Abel to Mary Carpenter 20 Dec 1797; John Carpenter sec; m (1797) by I Bratten.

HARRISON Abel to Polly Miles 10 Oct 1808; Southey Webb sec; m (1808) by I Bratten.

HARRISON Abel to Nancy Chance 20 Mar 1812; Wm G Harrison sec.

HARRISON Arthur to Kitty Lewis 10 Aug 1813; Arthur Cobb sec con & as to Kitty's age; m (1813) by I Bratten.

HARRISON Carvey to Caroline Joynes 28 Oct 1842; d/o Thomas Joynes dec'd & wife Leah Joynes con; Victor A Nottingham sec & as to Carvey's age; R J Poulson & N B Townsend wits; m 2 Nov 1842 by P Williams.

HARRISON Carvey to Miss Nancy Nottingham 10 Nov 1848; d/o Harrison Nottingham; Leonard B Nottingham sec; Mrs Betsy Belote as to Nancy's age; m 11 Nov 1848 by H Dalby.

HARRISON Isma to Anne Dillion 19 Nov 1832; d/o Charles Dillion sec & as to ages.

HARRISON James to Susan Chance 19 Dec 1816; Wm Smith sec; m (1816) by R Windsor.

HARRISON Jesse to Jane Ward 24 Apr 1832; wid/o Tully S Ward; Edward R Turner sec; m 24 Apr 1832 by G Wescoat.

HARRISON Joseph to Anne Flybrass 24 Jan 1661/1662. BK IX:114.

HARRISON Keley to Caty Ashby 9 Mar 1818; Reavil Watson sec.

HARRISON Newton to Tamar Edmunds 26 Dec 1805; Sarah Edmunds con for Tamar dated 9 Jan 1806; Thos Edmunds sec; m (1806) by I Bratten.

HARRISON Newton to Nancy Bradford 24 Apr 1837; wid/o Abel Bradford; Nathaniel J Winder sec; m 27 Apr 1837 by P Williams.

HARRISON Robert A to Elizabeth Belote 30 Sep 1791; d/o Levin Belote dec'd; Laban Stott sec; m (1791) by E Baker.

HARRISON Robert H to Polly Ewing 5 Sep 1816; Charles West sec.

HARRISON Robert Hutchison to Sally Dowty 24 Nov 1788; Seth Powell sec.

HARRISON Seth to Molly Anderson 29 Mar 1810; Thos S Brickhouse

sec; m (1810) by J Elliott.
HARRISON Wm to Anne Green 1 Jul 1776; Wm Nottingham sec.
HARRISON William G to Susanna Dowty 7 Feb 1810; Peter M Clegg sec.
HART Stephen to Susanna Nottingham 6 Oct 1777; d/o Rich'd Nottingham con; Jno Hamilton sec; Chas Satchell wit.
HASLOP, see also HYSLOP.
HASLOP Custis to Susanna Holland 12 Jun 1787; Benja Griffith sec; (m 17 Jun 1787. see BRec V5:180).
HATTON William P to Miss Ann Eliza James 4 Jun 1853; Francis B Mapp as to ages; Eldred R Holt wit; m 5 Jun 1853 by M Oldham.
HAVARD William to Rachel Dennis 28 Mar 1786; Whittenton Stripe sec; Joseph Dennis con.
HAYES Robert to Ann Draiton 20 Nov 1660. BK IX:92.
HAYES Robert to Jane Erristall 17 Jul 1661. BK IX:114.
HAYS John to Nancy Christian 6 Sep 1777; John of Rockbridge Co, VA; d/o Michael Christian con; Wm Steele sec. see BRec V7:151.
HAZARD Thomas to Mary Bowdoin 15 Nov 1746; Thomas of Road Island; spinster d/o Peter Bowdoin Gent dec'd; P Norly Ellegood & John Kendall secs; Jno Savage wit & as to Thomas' age.
HEATH Augustus C E to Edith E Fisher 17 Jul 1830; wid/o Wm R Fisher; Isaac Andrews sec; m 18 Jul 1830 by G Wescoat.
HEATH Carey to Sally Pratt 4 Mar 1822; wid; John Bull sec; m 4 Mar 1822 by S Wilmer.
HEATH George to Peggy Savage 4 Aug 1800; James Heath sec; m 1800 by J Elliott.
HEATH James to Mary Guy 17 Mar 1778; wid; Major Wilkins sec.
HEATH James to Patience Tankard 14 Nov 1780; Jacob Abdeel sec.
HEATH James to Sally Turner 18 Feb 1794; d/o John Turner dec'd; Wm Roberts Jr sec.
HEATH John S to Mary Anno 30 Apr 1811; Thomas Nottingham sec; m (1811) by J Elliott.
HEATH Josiah to Mary Floyd 17 Dec 1778; wid/o John Floyd; Henry Bryan sec.
HEATH Luke to Bridget Dunton 28 Sep 1763; d/o Elias Dunton dec'd; Wm Christian sec.
HEATH Rufus to Susan T W Brickhouse 21 Sep 1835; d/o John N Brickhouse con; Isaac Andrews sec & as to Rufus' age; Eadieth S Brickhouse wit; m 24 Sep 1835 by P Williams.
HEATH Seth to Grace Elliott 26 Nov 1798; d/o John Elliott con; Zorobabel Jones sec; m Nov 1798 by C Simkins.
HEATH William Sr to Mary Carpenter 1 Jul 1769; wid/o (John Carpenter)*; Thomas Dalby sec. *North Co WB 23:374.
HEATH William to Henrietta Joyne 21 Sep 1770; d/o Edmund Joyne; Edmund Glanville sec.
HEATH William to Polly Dennis 27 Dec 1826; Wm Martin sec & as to ages; m 28 Dec 1826 by S S Gunter.
HEATH William to Miss Patsy Dennis 8 Dec 1845; d/o Reubin Dennis; Wm Dennis sec; m 10 Dec 1845 by P Warren Jr.
HENDERSON, See also HINDERSON.
HENDERSON John to Maria Sturgis 23 Dec 1816; Thos E Addison sec; m 26 Dec 1816 by C Bonewell.
HENDERSON John M to Miss Louisa W Addison 11 Sep 1837; d/o John Addison dec'd; Teackle W Jacob sec & as to ages; m 12 Sep 1837 by G Wescoat.
HENDERSON John T to (Miss) Rachel Scott 24 Aug 1829; Thos C Hunt sec & as to Rachel's age; m 26 Aug 1829 by G Wescoat.
HENDERSON John T to Sally Ross 11 Feb 1840; wid/o John Ross;

James Sturges of John sec.
HENDERSON Robert to Nancy Jacob 2 Jun 1795; John Gleeson sec; m 1795 by I Bratten.
HENDERSON Thos to Rosey Fisher 12 Feb 1798; Geo Melholloms sec; m 1798 by J Elliot.
HENDERSON Thomas to Rosey Parramore 29 Dec 1812; Thomas W Badger sec; m (1812) by I Bratten.
HENDERSON William to Susanna Stott 20 Dec 1821; Wm C Watson sec; m 20 Dec 1821 by C Bonewell.
HENDERSON Zorobabel to Edna Ward 13 Dec 1811; d/o Golding Ward con; Joshua Garrison sec; Alex W Ward & Tully S Ward wits.
HENRY James to Susanna Harmanson 25 Dec 1786; d/o John Harmanson Esq dec'd; Nath'l Darby sec.
HERITAGE Freshwater to Anne Eshon 11 Apr 1783; Obed Cary sec.
HETH See HEATH.
HICKISON Robert to Elizabeth Crew 5 May 1661. BK IX:114.
HICKMAN Ed to Elishe Thompson 21 Jul 1814; Wm Clarke sec; m (1814) by I Bratten.
HICKMAN Nathaniel to Louisa Dawson 22 Jun 1818; Wm E Nottingham sec; m 28 Jun 1818 by W Costin.
HICKMAN Nathaniel to Rachel Griffith 11 Mar 1823; wid; John S Spady sec.
HICKMAN Nathaniel to Sally Elliott 2 Sep 1826; wid/o Thomas Elliott; John N Stratton sec; m 7 Sep 1826 by P Williams Jr.
HILL Rev Charles to Miss Susan S Wescoat 11 Mar 1850; d/o Hezekiah P Wescoat Sr sec; John B Maddux sec; L Harmanson wit; H P Wescoat as to Charles' age; m 14 Mar 1850 by J B Maddux.
HILL Joseph to Margaret Nottingham 30 Oct 1820; John Adams sec; m 30 Oct 1820 by C Bonewell.
HINDERSON Gilbert to Mary Major 25 Mar 1660. BK IX:92.
HITCHENS, HITCHINGS.
HITCHENS David to Rosey Kellam 1 Jan 1847; s/o Frances Hitchens con; d/o Margaret Costin con; John G Parsons & Luther W Roberts secs; Sam'l Parsons & Chas A Richardson wits; m 1 Jan 1847 by P Williams.
HITCHENS David R to Margaret Dixon 11 Jun 1821; Wm S Evans app't gdn/o David 11 Jun 1821 con; Margaret wrd/o Wm Goffigon con; Wm Dunton & Wm Downes & W E Jacob & W M Pettit & Jno Carpenter wits; m 14 Jun 1821 by L Dix.
HITCHINGS George to Frances Widgeon 24 Jan 1807; John Williams sec; m (1807) by J Elliott.
HODGE John to Nancy Smith 28 Mar 1794; d/o James Smith; Wm Bain sec; m Mar 1794 by C Simkins.
HOLBROOK Samuel to Peggy Stott 16 Jul 1763; d/o Laban Stott con; Walter Hyslop sec; Archibald Roberts & Abel (Holt?) wits.
HOLLAND Edward to Clara J West 15 Sep 1840. see BRec V3:148.
HOLLAND John to Margaret Wilkins 22 Mar 1775; d/o John Wilkins blacksmith sec.
HOLLAND Nathaniel to Susanna Bryan 20 Dec 1788; d/o Henry Bryan late of North Co dec'd; Walter Hyslop sec; (m 20 Dec 1788. see BRec V3:148,180).
HOLMES Edward to Elizabeth Parsons 25 Jul 1772; d/o Wm Parsons; Wm Floyd sec.
HOLT Albert G to Miss Emory S Roberts 3 Oct 1853; m 5 Oct 1853 by J Rawson.
HOLT George to Anne Custis 31 Dec 1757; d/o Edmund Custis dec'd; Adderson Nottingham sec.
HOLT George to Elizabeth Ann Savage 2 Sep 1824; Wm Nottingham gdn/o Elizabeth con

& sec; m 2 Sep 1824 by L Dix.
HOLT Martin to Adah Mapp 18 Feb 1769; d/o Howson Mapp dec'd; Howson Mapp sec.
HOLT Martin M M to Esther W Dixon 9 Dec 1820; Abram Costin gdn (of whom?) & sec; Laban Godwin sec; m 21 Dec 1820 by C Bonewell.
HOLT Stuart to Anne Johnson 11 Jan 1772; d/o Benjamin Johnson con; Stephen Sampson sec.
HOLT Stuart to Elizabeth Nelson 7 Feb 1783; wid/o Southy Nelson; Jno Lewis Fulwell sec.
HOLT Capt Stuart to Susannah Moore 28 Apr 1784; d/o Arcadia Moore con; John Savage sec.
HOOKS Samuel to (Nancy Justice) 11 Feb 1795; Michael Mathews sec; m Feb 1795 by C Simkins (bride's name shows on MinRet).
HOPKINS Maximilian to Elizabeth Armistead 9 Jul 1799; Nath'l Darby sec.
HOPKINS William W to Ann W Fisher 28 Apr 1810; Geo Fisher sec.
HORNER Benjamin to Margaret Hitchens 19 Jun 1821; Thomas Williams Jr sec & as to ages; Wm G Smith wit.
HORNSBY William to Susanna Carpenter 28 Apr 1787; wid/o Charles Carpenter; Kendall Addison sec.
HOSIER, HOZIER.
HOZIER Emanuel to Betsey Collins 9 Nov 1797; Preeson Abdil sec; m (1798) by I Bratten.
HOSIER John to Nancy Kellum 8 Jun 1819; Wm Mathews sec.
HOSIER John to Mahala Waterfield 22 Dec 1824; d/o Meshack Waterfield con; John Bool wit; Major Bool sec; m bet 15 Jun - 22 Dec 1824 by G C Wescoat.
HOZIER Thomas to Adah Dunton 26 Dec 1804; Stephen Waistcoate sec.
HOUSE William to Susanna Press 27 Aug 1788; d/o Edmund Press sec (FN).
HOWELL Custis to Rachel Beavans 2 Oct 1837; d/o Molly Beavans sec FN; Dilly Howell (alias Dilly Simkins) as to Custis' age; Montcalm Oldham sec; Jno S Wilkins wit; m 6 Oct 1837 by W B Snead.
HOWELL Jesse to Margaret Maley 9 Dec 1780; Henry Guy sec.
HOWELL John to Margaret Pitts 10 Sep 1771; d/o Jacob Pitts dec'd; Jackson Rodgers sec.
HOWELL John to Patsey Kelly 16 Sep 1806; John Waterfield sec; m (1806) by I Bratten (MinRet shows "Betsey" Kelly).
HOWELL William to Elizabeth White 16 Nov 1797; Hezekiah Pitts sec; m (1797) by J Elliot.
HUBBERD Edmund to Anne Scott 3 Oct 1785; Abel Garrison sec.
HUDSON, see also HUTSON.
HUDSON Nicholas to Elizabeth Freeman 16 Feb 1661/1662. BK IX:114.
HUGHS John to Mary Stockley 16 Oct 1779; Thos Bullock sec.
HUGHS John Sr to Mary McDonald 6 Jan 1781; wid/o Hugh McDonald; Nath'l Stevenson sec.
HUNT Azariah to Frances Benthall 31 Jan 1759; d/o Azel Benthall sec; Nath'l Stratton wit.
HUNT Azariah to Sarah Bishop 3 Aug 1771; wid; Douglas Willett sec; Joachim Michael wit.
HUNT Hillery to Delitha Lucre 28 Jan 1796; Obediah Hunt sec.
HUNT John G to Mary E Nottingham 21 May 1827; Mary wrd/o Leonard B Nottingham sec; m May 1827 by L Dix.
HUNT Obediah to Nancy Goffigon 29 Nov 1796; Nath'l Goffigon gdn/o Nancy con; Benja Griffith sec; m 30 Dec 1796 by C Simkins.
HUNT Obediah to Nancy Mathews 7 Oct 1803; d/o Mary Mathews con; Michael Dunton sec; Wm Goffigon wit; m (1803) by J Elliott.
HUNT Obediah to Margaret M

Nottingham 18 Dec 1819; Southey Goffigon sec; m 23 Dec 1819 by C Bonewell.
HUNT Thomas to Frances Goffigon 18 May 1791; d/o Nathaniel Goffigon con; Walter Hyslop sec.
HUNT Thomas O to Margaret B Nelson 26 Nov 1832; d/o Southy Nelson dec'd; Smith Nottingham sec; Dr Jesse Simkins as to Margaret's age; m Nov 1832 by L Dix.
HURTT William M to Miss Peggy T Savage 10 Apr 1848; Walter Raleigh gdn/o William sec; m 19 Apr 1848 by P Warren.
HURTT William Morgan to Elizabeth Ward 11 Jul 1846; William b 4 Apr 1823 s/o Elizabeth C Hurtt, he of Kent Co, MD, now living near Eastville VA; d/o Stephen Ward dec'd; Joshua P Wescoat sec; Unital (sp?) Gannett (Garrett?) wit.
HUTSON Jesse to Margaret Holbrook 23 Oct 1767; wid/o Samuel Holbrook; Jno Mapp sec.
HYSLOP, See also HASLOP.
HYSLOP Harvey to Miss Nancy Pratt 12 Sep 1842; d/o Sarah Pratt con; Thos K Dunton sec; Azariah Thurston wit.
HYSLOP John A to Nancy Parsons 13 May 1811; Custis Hyslop sec; m (1811) by J Elliott.
HYSLOP John C to Nancy Whitehead 22 Dec 1814; d/o John Whitehead con; Thos Graves sec.
HYSLOP John C to Anne Hayley 30 Jul 1823; d/o Robert Hayley sec.
HYSLOP Littleton to Mary Travis 11 Jul 1825; Mary wrd/o said Litleton, who was adjudged by clerk to be 21y; Thos L Evans sec.
HYSLOP Walter to Anne Bryan 3 Oct 1782; wid/o Henry Bryan; Wm Stith sec.

I

INQUEST Frederick to Lavenia Ann Speakman 2 Dec 1845; d/o Wm S Speakman sec; m 25 Dec 1845 by P Williams.
IRVIN See KERVIN
ISDEL, ISDELL, ISDALE, ESDEL, ISDOL.
ESDEL Edward to Elizabeth Floyd (undated - in 1786-1787 bundle); wid/o Charles Floyd; Wm Roberts sec.
ISDOL Gorge to Ether Green 23 Jun 1715; d/o George Green; Wm Nottingham sec.
ISDEL James to Lovey Mears 9 Aug 1824; Lovey wrd/o said James; Wm Roberts sec; m 9 Aug 1824 by C Bonewell.
ISDALE John to Mary Bunting 22 Aug 1821; wid; James Dennis sec; m 23 Aug 1821 by C Bonewell.
ISDALE Mathew to Leah Jeffries 3 Dec 1807; Isaac Nottingham gdn/o Leah con; John Jacob sec.
ISDALE Nathaniel to Betsey Luke 10 Jan 1799; Levin Belote sec; m (1799) by I Bratten.
ISDALE William to Nancy Dunton 10 Jun 1822; wid/o John; Wm Roberts sec; m 13 Jun 1822 by C Bonewell.
ISDELL William to Miss Sally Savage 27 Jan 1852; d/o Mrs Rosey M Savage wid gdn con; James Dennis wit.
ISHON Daniel to Margaret Howell 29 Jul 1660. BK IX:92.
ISHON Daniel to Susanna Thomas 9 Feb 1661/1662. BK IX:114.

J

JACKSON Geo W to Louisa Evans 13 Jul 1816; George (batch); Louisa (wid); Edw'd H C Wilson sec; m 13 Jul 1816 by R Symes.
JACKSON James to Sabra Kellum 1 Jun 1793; d/o Stephen Kellum dec'd; Michael Mathews sec; m Jun 1793 by C Simkins.
JACKSON James to Rose Kellum 26 Dec 1794; d/o Stephen Kellum dec'd; George Willis sec; m 1795 by I Bratten.
JACOB Arthur to Sally Thomas 13

Feb 1822; John K Floyd sec & as to Sally's age; m 14 Feb 1822 by C Bonewell.

JACOB Edward to Susan Jacob 9 Nov 1840; d/o William Jacob; George N Bool as to Susan's age; Littleton Wilson sec & as to Edward's age; Geo S Savage wit; m 11 Nov 1840 by W A Dix.

JACOB Esau to Betty Haggoman 4 Jun 1741; d/o John Haggoman con; Thomas Gibbons & Jonathan Porter secs (con slip is dated 31 May 1742).

JACOB Esau to Vianer Gray Pitts 12 Nov 1762; d/o Major Pitts dec'd; Walter Hyslop sec.

JACOB Esau to Margaret Joyne 21 Oct 1789; Jacob Abdeel sec.

JACOB George T to Miss Elizabeth S Dunton 16 Sep 1846; George orp/o Teackle Jacob dec'd & wrd/o Devorax Godwin sec; d/o Matthew Dunton dec'd; James Fitchett sec & as to Elizabeth's age; Wm P Nottingham wit; m 16 Sep 1846 by P Warren.

JACOB Hancock Jr to Sarah Harmanson 21 Dec 1773; Wm Harmanson sec; Jno Michael wit.

JACOB Hancock to Ann James 20 Jun 1803; Hancock Dunton sec; m (1803) by I Bratten.

JACOB Isaac to Anne Savage 31 Mar 1750; wid/o (John Savage); Nehemiah Fitchett sec; Thos Stratton wit.

JACOB James to Patience Only 23 Dec 1809; Cudjo Stephens sec (FN); m (1809) by J Elliott.

JACOB James to Emeline Johnson 19 Dec 1838; d/o James Johnson sec FN; Peggy Jacob as to James' age; Smith Nottingham sec; m 20 Dec 1838 by G C Wescoat.

JACOB John to Peggy Turner 29 Apr 1767; John of Acc Co; d/o George Turner dec'd; Wm Major sec.

JACOB John to Nancy Abdell 15 Mar 1804; Killiam Lankford sec; m (1804) by J Elliott.

JACOB John to Polly Wilson 19 Apr 1830; d/o Moses Wilson sec & as to Polly's age; m 21 Apr 1830 by P Williams.

JACOB John to Catharine Barcroft 21 Jun 1841; widr; spinster; Joshua Nottingham as to Catharine's age; Smith S Nottingham sec; m 23 Jun 1841 by P Williams.

JACOB John C to Emily Nottingham 4 Nov 1828; s/o Thos Jacob; Emily orp/o Wm Nottingham & wrd/o Rob't B Nottingham sec; Geo P Jacob as to John's age.

JACOB John C to Miss Tabitha R Cutler 8 Dec 1852; Litt W Young gdn/o Tabitha con; m 9 Dec 1852 by J Rawson.

JACOB Richard to Adriana Mapp 17 Jan 1749; wid/o (Samuel Mapp); John Flood sec.

JACOB Richard to Harriot Rooks 11 Sep 1837; wid/o John Rooks; Thos Smith Jr sec; Littleton Wilson as to Richd's age; m 14 Sep 1837 by W B Snead.

JACOB Robert to Anne Jacob 9 Jun 1764; wid/o (Isaac Jacob); John Stratton sec.

JACOB Robert to Elizabeth Hack 2 Jan 1789; (in Acc Co?). see BRec V1:49.

JACOB Robert C to Margaret S Wilkins 16 Dec 1833; Margaret wrd/o George F Wilkins sec; John Kendall as to Rob't's age; m 19 Dec 1833 by W B Snead.

JACOB Teackle to Peggy Widgeon 14 Apr 1818; James Travis sec; m 15 Apr 1818 by C Bonewell.

JACOB Teagle to Margaret Addison 27 Mar 1783; wid; Elisha Dowty sec.

JACOB Thomas to Nancy Abdeel 20 Aug 1788; wid; Teagle Jacob sec; m (1788) by E Baker.

JACOB Thomas to Mary Gilden 23 Apr 1790; wid/o Charles Gilden; Teackle Jacob sec; m (1790) by E Baker.

JACOB Thomas to Sally Savage 24 Jul 1795; Robins Mapp sec; m

1795 by J Elliot.

JACOB Thomas Jr to Henrietta Parramore 14 Dec 1801; Thos Parramore Sr sec; m 1801 by I Bratten.

JACOB Thomas to Sally White 23 Apr 1805; s/o Teackle Jacob; Thomas Jacob Jr sec; m (1805) by I Bratten.

JACOB Thomas to Elizabeth White 28 Jul 1821; Calvin H Read sec; m 28 Jul 1821 by L Dix.

JACOB Thomas L to Elizabeth Ann Wilkins 25 Sep 1838; Thomas wrd/o Edward W Nottingham sec; d/o Wm E Wilkins con; Edward R Waddey sec; Rosey L Costin wit; m 27 Sep 1838 by L Dix.

JACOB William to Mary Jacob 17 Dec 1766; d/o Hancock Jacob; Edmund Glanville sec.

JACOB William to Mary Bell 10 Jan 1775; (d/o Thos & Mary Bell); Wm Waltham sec.

JACOB William to Leah Gault 27 Aug 1784; Rickards Dunton Jr sec.

JACOB William to Peggy Henderson 4 Jul 1795; Kendall Belote sec; m 1795 by J Elliot.

JACOB William to Elizabeth Andrews 22 Aug 1816; Wm White sec; m 24 Aug 1816 by C Bonewell.

JACOB William W to Miss Sally Ann Godwin 18 Nov 1844; d/o Edwin Godwin; Edw'd R Waddy as to ages; Elijah Brittingham Jr wit; Wm T Nottingham sec; m 20 Nov 1844 by G G Exall.

JAMES Abel to Margaret Abdel 5 Jun 1790; Abel of Isle of Wight Co; wid; Thomas James Jr sec; m (1790) by E Baker.

JAMES Abel to Ann Craik 13 Dec 1824; wid/o Wm Craik; Thos E Addison sec & as to Ann's age; m 23 Dec 1824 by S S Gunter.

JAMES Andrew to Sally James 23 Jan 1800; John Ross sec; m (1800) by J Elliott.

JAMES Edmund P to Sally Bird (Byrd) 7 Jun 1827; d/o John Bird dec'd; Wm Byrd sec & as to Sally's age; S E Parker & John Ker wits; m 1827 by G C Wescoat.

JAMES Hezekiah P to Margaret Trower 11 Jun 1838; d/o John Trower Sr sec; John S James as to Hezekiah's age; m 13 Jun 1838 by P Williams.

JAMES John to Esther Dolby 20 Oct 1796; Henry Smaw sec; m 20 Oct 1796 by C Simkins.

JAMES John to Nancy Bell 15 Mar 1824; Edward Kellam sec & as to Nancy's age; John James made his oath as of age; m 16 Mar 1824 by C Bonewell.

JAMES John to Miss Nervilla Belote 21 Jan 1853; d/o Kendall Belote con; Wm James as to John's age; Edw'd V Addison & John R Nottingham & Emery L Roberts wits; m 22 Jan 1853 by P Warren.

JAMES John S to Margaret C James 9 Oct 1827; Margaret wrd/o Margaret Savage con; Arthur R Savage sec & as to John's age; Jeptha Johnson & Hez P James wits; m 1827 by G C Wescoat.

JAMES Levin T to Miss Lavenia C Floyd 14 Aug 1848; Wm J James sec & as to Lavenia's age; m 23 Aug 1848 by M Oldham.

JAMES Robert to Sarah Tilney 5 Jun 1751; wid; Jacob Marshall sec; Mathew Moor wit.

JAMES Robert to Elizabeth Christian 15 Dec 1753; spinster; Esau Jacob sec; Isaac Dunton wit.

JAMES Robert to Rosey Dowty 18 Dec 1820; Andrew James sec; m 21 Dec 1820 by C Bonewell.

JAMES Thomas to Rebecca Maddux 17 Nov 1714; wid/o (Thos Maddux)*; Francis Wainhouse Jr sec; John Custis Mathews wit.
*North Co XIX:317.

JAMES Thomas to Kessey Jacob 6 Feb 1764; d/o Hancock Jacob con; Isaac Clegg sec.

JAMES Thomas Sr to Mary Heath 7 Jul 1764; wid/ Luke Heath sec.

JAMES Thomas to Elizabeth Dunton 13 Dec 1774; d/o & orp/o Wm Dunton; Wm Jacob sec; Rickards Dunton Jr wit.

JAMES Thomas to Nancy Taylor 13 Jul 1807; Robert Walker sec; m (1807) by I Bratten.

JAMES William to Sukey Smith 25 Sep 1798; Thomas James sec; m 1798 by J Elliot.

JAMES William to Margaret Major 2 Jun 1806; s/o Thomas James Jr con; Thomas James Jr gdn/o Margaret con; John Simkins sec; m (1806) by I Bratten.

JAMES William to Susan Ann Wilson 25 Nov 1828; d/o Arthur A Wilson con; Luther Ball sec; Benja Dalby as to William's age; m 26 Nov 1828 by P Williams.

JAMES William to Fanny Tyson 22 Apr 1844; wid/o Samuel Tyson; Joshua P Wescoat sec; m 24 Apr 1844 by J Ufford.

JAMES William J to Elizabeth A Johnson 12 Mar 1834; d/o Jeptha Johnson con; Hez P James sec; Margaret Savage wit; m 16 Mar 1834 by G Wescoat.

JAMISON John to Adah Clegg 13 Aug 1751; Isaac Clegg br/o & gdn/o Adah spinster con; Henry Tomlinson sec.

JARVIS George T to Miss Sally F Goffigon 8 Mar 1847; d/o Southy Goffigon dec'd; Nathaniel S Goffigon sec.

JARVIS Jesse Nelson to Virginia Adams Dalby 9 Apr 1849; s/o Wm & Elizabeth Jarvis; d/o Benj J (con & sec) & Mary Ann Dalby; Wm T Fitchett as to Jesse's age; T F Spady wit; (m 11 Apr 1849. see BRec V1:101, V9:81).

JARVIS William to Anne Sinior Bell 26 May 1789; d/o Thomas Bell dec'd; Wm Jarvis sec; m (1789) by E Baker; (m 28 Sep 1789. see BRec V2:81).

JARVIS William to Sarah Hunt 26 Dec 1780; (wid/o Azariah Hunt);

Wm Rasco sec.

JARVIS William to Fanny Hunt (Goffigon*) 14 Dec 1795; Hillary Hunt sec; m Dec 1795 by C Simkins. *Both Wm Jarvis & Jno Goffigon Bible rec state Wm Jarvis m 15 Dec 1795 Frances Goffigon. Both bond & MinRet states Fanny Hunt. see BRec V1:107, V9:80.

JARVIS William Jr to Nancy Wilkins 25 Aug 1798; Wm Wilkins sec; Elizabeth Wilkins con for Nancy; (m 30 Aug 1798. see BRec V9:80).

JARVIS William to Elizabeth U Robins 14 May 1808; d/o John Robins con; Arthur Simkins sec; m (1808) by J Elliott; (m 19 May 1808. see BRec V9:80).

JARVIS William Jr to Margaret Williams 14 Sep 1812; d/o Margaret Williams con; Jno Nelson Sr sec; Ann Bayton & James Williams wits; m (1812) by J Elliott; (m 24 Sep 1812. see BRec V2:81, 144).

JARVIS William W to Leah Turpin 13 Oct 1823; s/o William Jarvis Sr; wid/o Thomas H Turpin; Smith Nottingham & Wm Jarvis Sr secs; m 23 Oct 1823 by S S Gunter.

JEFFERSON Peter to Polly Freshwater 18 Oct 1813; Thomas ___ sec; m (1813) by J Elliott.

JEFFERSON Silas to Polly Costin 15 Mar 1814; d/o Wm Costin Sr con; Lawrance Enholm sec; m (1814) by J Elliott.

JEFFRY Littleton to Nancy Collins 18 Sep 1810; Jas Jacob sec FN.

JEFFERY Littleton to Lurany Collins 13 Jun 1827; d/o Peggy Collins; Nathan Drighouse & Mack Collins secs (FN); m 13 Jun 1827 by P Williams.

JEFFERY Solomon to Tinsey Jacob 16 Jan 1788; Wm Satchell Jr sec (FN).

JEFFERY Solomon to Nancy Collins (FN) 3 Dec 1816*; Mack Collins sec; m 4 Dec 1817* by C

Bonewell. *discrepancy

JEFFERYS William to Sarah Bullock 18 Sep 1781; d/o Thos Bullock; Wm Wood sec.

JEFFRIES William to Polly Bingham 26 Jan 1803; Samuel Beavans sec (FN); m (1803) by J Elliott.

JENKINS George to Miss Charlotte Terrier 27 Apr 1838; Wm S Floyd gdn/o Charlotte sec; m 30 Apr 1838 by W G Jackson.

JENNE William to Margaret Fisher 12 Feb 1782; wid/o Thos Fisher; Jno Darby sec.

JENNE William to Betsy Ewing 20 Jul 1787; David Jones sec.

JOHNSON Abel B to Susan Dalby 13 Feb 1822; d/o Branson Dalby dec'd; Charles B Stockly sec & as to Susan's age; m 13 Feb 1822 by C Bonewell.

JOHNSON Benjamin to Rose Hunt 30 Jul 1773; wid/o (Obediah Hunt)*; John Smith sec; CR PK 81 Mar 1774 "Johnson et al vs Hunt."

JOHNSON Christopher to Susanna Stith 10 May 1780; Christopher of MD; d/o Griffin Stith Sr; Thorowgood Smith of Acc Co sec.

JOHNSON Edmund Jr to Polly Dowty 22 Jun 1781; d/o Hezekiah Dowty; Addison Dowty sec.

JOHNSON Edmund to Anna Smaw 5 Nov 1807; Henry Smaw sec; m (1807) by J Elliott.

JOHNSON Edmund to Mary Savage 27 Oct 1818; Preson Savage sec; m 29 Oct 1818 by C Bonewell.

JOHNSON Edmund S to Jane Dunton 25 Apr 1774; d/o Wm Dunton dec'd; John Blair sec.

JOHNSON Edward to Sally Bull 2 Nov 1840; Michael Bull as to Sally's age; Jacob Spady sec & as to Ed's age; John Simkins wit; m 4 Nov 1840 by W A Dix.

JOHNSON Edward N to Mrs Mahala Waterfield 12 Mar 1827; Jno W Leatherbury as to Edw'd's age; Harrison T Rayfield sec; P Mayo & Ves Ellis wits; m 1827 by G C Wescoat.

JOHNSON George R to Elizabeth S Johnson 23 Mar 1842; d/o John Johnson dec'd; John C Mapp Jr as to ages; Nathan R Fletcher sec.

JOHNSON Isaac to Matilder Stuard 9 Jan 1812; Elibet W Stuard (Stuart?) gdn/o Matilder con; James Johnson sec; Devorax Godwin wit; m (1812) by J Elliott.

JOHNSON Ismay to Rachel Darby 1 Aug 1761; wid/o (Benjamin Darby); James Peterkin sec.

JOHNSON James to Betsey Stott 2 Oct 1794; George Lewis sec.

JOHNSON James to Elizabeth Giddens 22 Jul 1806; Wm R Finney sec.

JOHNSON James to Mary Barlow 16 Jan 1809; Edward Ironmonger sec; m (1809) by J Elliott.

JOHNSON James of Isaac to Ann Godwin 8 May 1810; Henry Scarborough sec.

JOHNSON James Sr to Susanna Elligood 25 May 1813; Thos S Satchell sec.

JOHNSON Jehu to Rose Shores 13 Mar 1797; Geo Melholloms sec; m (1797) by J Elliot (MinRet states "John" Johnson).

JOHNSON Jeptha to Rosanna James 18 Aug 1807; Revil Watson sec; m (1807) by I Bratten.

JOHNSON Jeptha to Mrs Polly Bishop 7 Nov 1851; m 9 Nov 1851 by M Oldham.

JOHNSON Johannes to Ansly Savage 12 Jul 1785; Hezekiah Pitts sec.

JOHNSON Johannes to Elizabeth Stripe 13 Aug 1821; Charles West sec; m 15 Aug 1821 by C Bonewell.

JOHNSON John to Margaret Jacob 11 Oct 1774; wid/o (John Jacob); Alexander McLaughlin sec.

JOHNSON John to Eliza Downes 21 Feb 1827; Eliza wrd/o Nathaniel Dalby sec; m 21 Feb 1827 by S S Gunter.

JOHNSON John to Miss Elizabeth Belote 17 Apr 1843; d/o Susan Belote; Wm Dennis sec & as to Elizabeth's age; m 18 Apr 1843 by P Warren Jr.

JOHNSON John P m Keziah Watson 17 Apr 1794 by C Simkins.

JOHNSON John P to Catherine Ames 11 Jan 1798; John Milby sec; m (1798) by J Elliot.

JOHNSON John T to Susan Fitchett 29 May 1842; d/o William Fitchett Sr dec'd; Alexander W F Mears sec & as to John T's age; Joshua P Wescoat wit.

JOHNSON John Y to Louisiana W Trower 24 Dec 1833; Louisiana wrd/o William Costin sec; Obedience R Johnson as to John's age; m 26 Dec 1833 by P Williams.

JOHNSON Joshua to Esther Savage 12 Aug 1788; John Robins sec; m (1788) by E Baker.

JOHNSON Laban to Anne Gascoigne 14 Feb 1775; wid/o (Wm Gascoigne); Wm Harmanson sec.

JOHNSON Laban S to Elizabeth Waples 18 Feb 1820; Thomas West sec.

JOHNSON Laban S to Miss Elizabeth W Stott 11 Feb 1839; John W Leatherbury sec & as to Elizabeth's age.

JOHNSON Moses to Sarah Nottingham 12 Nov 1767; d/o Isaac Nottingham; Wm Major sec; Rob't Pitts wit.

JOHNSON Moses to Sarah Powell 24 Jul 1770; d/o George Powell dec'd; Jonathan Johnson sec.

JOHNSON Obadiah to Leah Abdell 30 Nov 1824*; Leah wrd/o Wm P Johnson sec; m bet 13 Jan - 30 Dec 1825* (?). *discrepancy

JOHNSON Obedience to Elishe Godwin 8 Feb 1772; d/o Devorax Godwin con; Rob't Polk sec.

JOHNSON Obedience R to Mary A T Young 18 Dec 1836; wid/o James Young; Robert B Savage sec; m 22 Dec 1836 by W B Snead.

JOHNSON Powell to Elizabeth Goffigon 22 Dec 1768; d/o James Goffigon dec'd & wrd/o Southy Goffigon con; Thos Underhill sec.

JOHNSON Richard to Polly B Bloxom 29 Aug 1812; Thomas Johnson bro/o & gdn/o Polly con; Nath'l West sec; m (1812) by I Bratten.

JOHNSON Robinson to Mary Johnson 3 Aug 1786; wid/o Edmund Johnson; Wm Jenne sec.

JOHNSON Samuel to Agatha Gildon 12 Sep 1723; sis/o Charles Gildon; Mathew Harmanson Gent & Jno Waterson secs; Thos Lucor wit; lic 12 Sep 1723. CT Ret Oct 1723.

JOHNSON Solomon to Adah Johnson 4 Jun 1770; d/o Obedience Johnson dec'd; Moses Johnson sec.

JOHNSON Thomas to Sally Fitchew 31 Aug 1795; Joseph Hanby sec; m 1795 by I Bratten.

JOHNSON Thomas to Peggy Wheeler 24 Mar 1796; Wm Hanby sec; m 1796 by E Baker.

JOHNSON Thomas to Sarah Nelson 29 Nov 1802; spinster; Jno Goffigon sec; Isaac Smith wit; m (1802) by J Elliott.

JOHNSON Thomas to Feriba Dalby 13 Jun 1807; David Harlow sec; m (1807) by J Elliott.

JOHNSON Thomas Jr to Frances Wescoat 7 Mar 1814; d/o Wm Wescoat con sec; Thos U Teackle wit; m (1814) by I Bratten.

JOHNSON Thomas E to Mary A Knight 10 Aug 1840; Thomas wrd/o John Simkins sec; d/o Wm Knight dec'd; Smith Nottingham sec; m 11 Aug 1840 by S T Ames.

JOHNSON William to Elishe Haggoman 15 Mar 1757; d/o Silvanus Haggoman; Esau Jacob sec.

JOHNSON William to Hannah Andrews 16 Sep 1775; Nath'l Powell sec.

JOYNES John Littleton to Miss Catharine S Floyd 30 Dec 1851; Cath wrd/o Mrs Lavinia Floyd; Wm T Campbell as to John's age; Wm J Nottingham wit; m 30 Dec 1851 by P Warren.

JOHNSON William to Hannah Carter 26 Apr 1794; George Savage sec; m Apr 1794 by C Simkins.

JOHNSON William R to Miss Margt D Brickhouse 17 Dec 1842; d/o Thomas S Brickhouse; Smith L Brickhouse sec & as to ages; m 20 Dec 1842 by P Williams.

JOLLIFF Richard m Eskey Ames Sep 1800 by C Simkins.

JONES Cave to Mary Upshur 14 Jan 1794; Cave of Acc Co; John Upshur Jr sec.

JONES David to Sarah Allegood 24 Aug 1759; d/o John Allegood dec'd; James Peterkin sec; Joachim Michael & Jno Stith wits; Sarah states that she is of age.

JONES David to Esther Mapp 2 Dec 1788; wid/o Wm Mapp; John Dennis sec; m (1788) by E Baker.

JONES Isaac to Smart Waterfield 25 Jun 1790; Peter Warren sec; Smart states that she is 21y, has no parents nor gdn; John Caple wit; m 26 Jun 1790 by C Simkins.

JONES James to Lucy Dowty 13 Feb 1815; d/o Archabald Dowty con; Shepherd Floyd sec; m (1815) by J Elliott.

JONES John to Nancy Stripe 28 Aug 1801; John Scott sec; m 1801 by I Bratten.

JONES John to Letitia M Godwin 26 Jul 1837; d/o Littleton Godwin dec'd; Thomas Smith Jr sec & as to ages; m 27 Jul 1837 by W B Snead.

JONES John W to Catherine S Floyd 25 Jun 1823; d/o John K Floyd sec; m 25 Jun 1823 by S Wilmer. see BRec V8:139.

JONES Littleton to Margaret Groves 30 Apr 1791; d/o Peter Groves who states that she is of age; Moses Wilson sec; m (1791) by E Baker.

JONES Major to Esther Waterfield 10 Jul 1787; Thos Jones sec; m (1787) by E Baker.

JONES Nathaniel to Sally Griffith 5 Jun 1797; d/o S(ary?) Griffith con; Littleton Jones sec; m (1797) by E Baker.

JONES Obediah to Elizabeth Caple 12 Jul 1798; d/o Catharine Caple con; Mathias Jones sec.

JONES Richard to Margaret Clegg 6 Mar 1812; Stuart Sanders sec; m (1812) by J Elliott.

JONES Richard to Sally Whitehead 11 Dec 1815; John Warrington sec; m (1815) by J Elliott.

JONES Thomas to Sarah Parkerson 10 Jun 1878; Major Jones sec; m (1787) by E Baker.

JONES Thomas to Sally Caple 3 Jun 1793; Littleton Jones sec; Mager Caple con; m (1793) by E Baker.

JONES Thomas to Elisa Simkins 13 Jan 1823; John Simkins sec; m 16 Jan 1823 by C Bonewell.

JONES William to Elishe Joyne 11 Dec 1779; Jacob Moor sec.

JONES William to Anne Groves 24 Dec 1791; wid; Thos Jones sec; Wm Jones states that his father gives con; m (1791) by E Baker.

JONES William to Nancy McCrady 5 Mar 1803; James Fisher sec; m bet 1 Jan - 9 May (1803) by J Elliott.

JONES Zorobabel to Susanna Mapp 16 Jun 1790; David Jones sec; Wm Simkins gdn/o Susanna con; m (1790) by E Baker.

JONES Zorobabel to Adah Heath 28 Sep 1798; d/o Bridget Heath gdn con; David Topping sec; m 1798 by J Elliot.

JOURDEN George to Susanna Caul 10 Apr 1765; d/o Daniel Caul; Henry Jourden sec.

JOURDEN Thos to Eliz Warren 18 Jun 1765; wid; John Luker sec.

JOYNE, JOYNES.

JOYNE Edmund to Esland Rogers

28 Nov 1752; Edmund mariner; spinster; Edward Holbrooks sec; Willcock Macky wit.

JOYNES Edmund to Mary Scott 22 Dec 1787; Hancock Jacob sec; m (1787) by E Baker.

JOYNES Edmund to Peggy Michael 28 Dec 1792; d/o John Michael Jr; Arthur Rodgers sec; m Dec 1792 by C Simkins.

JOYNES Edward to Nancy Kendall 31 Oct 1809; Seth Warren sec; m (1809) by J Elliott.

JOYNES Edward J to Sally Wescoat 12 Dec 1831; s/o Rob't A Joynes sec; Sally wrd/o Rob't A Joynes; m Dec 1831 by L Dix.

JOYNES George to Betsey Purnal Major 19 Dec 1799; Arthur Roberts Jr sec; m (1799) by J Elliot.

JOYNE Harmanson to Sarah Carpenter 2 Jan 1756; d/o Stephen Carpenter dec'd; Patrick Harmanson sec; Jno Harmanson wit.

JOYNE John to Rachel Andrews 14 Dec 1756; (s/o Edward Joyne); spinster; Littleton Andrews sec; John Goffigon wit.

JOYNES John Jr to Luranar (Lauranna) Kellum 29 Sep 1778; (s/o John & Rachel Joynes); Smith Kellum sec.

JOYNES John Jr to Peggy Floyd 29 Dec 1796; (s/o John & Rachel Joynes); Wm Joynes sec; m [(1796) by J Elliott].

JOYNES John Jr to Elishe Willis 28 Aug 1820; Marrot Willis con; Danil Smaw sec; m 30 Aug 1820 by C Bonewell.

JOYNES Kendall to Sally Milby 6 Mar 1797; John Milby sec; m (1797) by J Elliot.

JOYNES Levin S to Maria S Baptist 29 Jan 1824; Edward R Boisnard sec; m 29 Jan 1824 by S Wilmer.

JOYNES Nathaniel m Sally Griffith (1798) by E Baker.

JOYNES Robert A to Elizabeth (Bell) Widgeon 1 Nov 1821; wid/o Thomas Widgeon; Thomas Mehollomes sec; m 3 Nov 1821 by L Dix.

JOYNES Robert A to Margaret Ann (Godwin) Matthews 9 Sep 1835; wid/o Levin Matthews & 3rd wife of Robert A; John Lecato sec; m 9 Sep 1835 by G Wescoat. see BRec V11:8.

JOYNES Shepherd Abel to Peggy Smith Cooper Walter 8 Aug 1825; (s/o John Jr & Peggy Joynes); d/o Solomon Walter sec (& Sally Bunker Walter, his wife); Thos Meholloms as to Shepherd's age; m 12 Aug 1825 by S S Gunter.

JOYNES Thomas M to Leah Wise 9 Nov 1818; Stephen S Gunter sec; m 15 Nov 1818 by C Bonewell.

JOYNES Tully W A T to Sabra P Fitchett 24 Jun 1844; James H Stewart sec; Gracy Fitchett as to Sabra's age; m 25 Jun 1844 by G G Exall.

JOYNE Watkins to Rachel Brickhouse 17 Dec 1764; d/o Major Brickhouse dec'd; Charles Floyd sec.

JOYNE William to Mary Parsons 31 Dec 1779; d/o John Parsons; Walter Hyslop sec.

JOYNE Wm to Margaret Tankard 3 Jun 1789; d/o ___ Tankard dec'd; John Tankard gdn/o Margt con; Jacob Roberts sec.

JOYNES William to Sukey Floyd 1 Jan 1827; Nathaniel B Hickman sec & as to ages; m 4 Jan 1827 by P Williams.

JUDAH Mark to Adah Pool 14 Jul 1823; Adah wrd/o said Mark; George Pool & Isaac Thompson secs; m 14 Jul 1823 (Blacks) by S Wilmer.

JUSTICE Ralph to Sarah Marshall 13 Mar 1738; d/o Thomas Marshall con; John & Thomas Marshall secs; Geo Kendall wit.

K

KELLAM, KELLUM.

KELLUM Augustus J F to Mary E Goffigon 12 Nov 1838; Mary

wrd/o Wm Goffigon con; Thos H Sr & Severn F & Michael P Kellam wits; Major D Colonna sec & as to Augustus' age; m 14 Nov 1838 by P Williams.

KELLUM Charles to Sally Howell 11 Apr 1796; Wm Howell sec; m (1796) by I Bratten.

KELLUM Custis to Margaret Dunton 9 Sep 1817; Levin Lewis sec; m 11 Sep 1817 by C Bonewell.

KELLUM Edmund to Mary Pearson 13 Apr 1825; George T Outten sec & as to ages.

KELLUM Edward to Sally Nottingham 5 Dec 1814; d/o Wm Nottingham con; Thos Jacob sec; Joshua Fitchett wit; m (1814) by J Elliott.

KELLAM Edward to Sarah Wilkins 4 Apr 1838; wid/o John Wilkins of John; Edmund R Custis sec; m 4 Apr 1838 by P Williams.

KELLAM Edward to Vianna Underhill 5 Sep 1842; d/o William Underhill dec'd; Calvin H Savage sec & as to ages; m 7 Sep 1842 by G C Wescoat.

KELLUM Evans to Elizabeth Costin 13 Jul 1820; Thomas Peed sec.

KELLUM James to Peggy Dorman 10 Oct 1801; John Dunton sec; m 1801 by I Bratten.

KELLAM James to Rose Costin 3 Feb 1819; d/o Wm Costin con; Silas Jefferson sec; James Costin wit.

KELLAM James L to Susan Ann Goffigon 28 Feb 1837; Thomas A Coleburn sec; Obadiah Goffigon as to Susan's age; m 28 Feb 1837 by P Williams.

KELLAM Jesse to Mary J Mears 16 Jan 1830; d/o Richard Mears of Wm con; Egbert G Bayly sec & as to Jesse's age; Elizabeth M Burton wit; m 20 Jan 1830 by E Stevenson.

KELLAM John H to Miss Mary A Evans 20 Jan 1852; s/o Wm H Kellam con; Mary wrd/o Alfred Parker; Jos S Widgeon & Wm T Kellam wits; m 27 Jan 1852 by P Warren.

KELLAM John to Eliza Harrison 10 Dec 1832; illegitimate d/o Peggy Clegg sec; m 15 Dec 1832 by G C Wescoat.

KELLUM Lewis to Nancy Nortrip 30 Aug 1830; wid/o Daniel Nortrip; John Robins sec & as to ages; E C Wilkinson & Nath'l Holland wits; m 30 Aug 1830 by G Wescoat.

KELLUM Lewis to Lovey Collins 13 May 1850; d/o Maria Collins sec FN; John W Leatherbury sec; m 18 May 1850 by Warren.

KELLUM Nathl to Rosey Addison 11 Jan 1786; Abel Kellum sec.

KELLAM Robert to Sally Stott 22 Sep 1798; Wm Stratton sec; m (Apr?) by C Simkins.

KELLAM Samuel to Elizabeth Downing 4 Mar 1816; Edmund Downing gdn/o Elizabeth con; Thos Scarbrough sec; m 6 Mar 1816 by Joshua Burton.

KELLAM Samuel E D to Miss Louisa Kendall 11 Sep 1848; d/o Mrs Catharine H G Kendall con; Alex w F Mears sec; John Lecato as to Samuel's age; Fred B Fisher wit; m 13 Sep 1848 by M Oldham.

KELLAM Severn F to Martha Goffigon 22 May 1838; Martha wrd/o Severn E Nottingham sec; Levin Ames as to Severn's age; m 22 May 1838 by P Williams.

KELLUM Shadrack to Leah Mapp 12 Oct 1779; d/o Howson Mapp dec'd; Howson Mapp sec.

KELLAM Shepherd to Polly Ashby 25 Mar 1819; Robert Ashby sec.

KELLUM Stephen to Eliz Belote 10 May 1845; wid/o Benjamin Belote; Edward Rayfield sec; m 10 May 1845 by G C Wescoat.

KELLUM Teackle to Betsey Floyd Smith 22 Apr 1801; Zerobabel Jones sec; m Apr 1801 by C Simkins.

KELLAM Thomas to Mary L Tyler 22 Jan 1850; d/o Benjamin Tyler sec & as to Thomas' age; Jno Nicholson wit; m 23 Jan 1850 by

P Warren.

KELLAM Thomas H to Elizabeth B Dorsey 22 Jan 1819; Peter Bowdoin sec; m 23 Jan 1819 by C Bonewell. see BRec V1:49.

KELLAM Thomas H to Mrs Harriet B D Parramore 24 Feb 1837; Wm H Parker sec; m 28 Feb 1837 by W B Snead.

KELLUM Walter to Sarah Turpin 27 Jan 1801; (wid/o John Turpin); Ismay Johnson sec.

KELLAM William H to Catherine West 28 Dec 1825; Catherine wrd/o Abel Bradford sec.

KELLUM Wm H to Mahala F Mears 8 Nov 1830; d/o Richard Mears sec; (Nehimiah?) Elliott wit.

KELLAM William T to Emily S Willis 26 Apr 1853; Custis Willis gdn/o Emily con; Jno H Kellam as to Wm's age; m 27 May 1853 by P Williams.

KELLY, KELLEY.

KELLY Abel to Rosey Savage 27 Aug 1850; d/o Caleb Savage dec'd; Wm Lewis as to Abel's age; m 28 Aug 1850 by M Oldham.

KELLEY Alexander to Henrietta Stott 25 Oct 1780; Wm Waterfield sec.

KELLY Charles to Elizabeth Roberts 8 Jun 1826; d/o Nancy Isdell con; Wm Isdell sec & as to ages of both being upwards of 20y; Nathin H Dunton wit.

KELLY Charles to Eliza Ann Brown 11 Jul 1836; d/o Allen Brown; Charles Dillion sec & as to Charles' age; m 27 Jul 1836 by W B Snead.

KELLY James to Peggy Joynes 20 Dec 1808; Wm Savage sec.

KELLY Jas to Miss Mary Taylor 18 Dec 1849; d/o John Taylor sec; Obed Kelly as to James' age; m 19 Dec 1849 by P Warren.

KELLY John to Sally Churn 29 Dec 1840; d/o John Churn lately dec'd; Wm M Savage sec & as to ages; m 30 Dec 1840 by G C Wescoat.

KELLY Laban to Ann Goffigon 28 Nov 1814; Abram Costin sec & as to Ann's age; m (1814) by J Elliott.

KELLY Sylvester M to Elizabeth B Fitchett 30 Dec 1846; wid/o Thomas Fitchett Jr; John S Turpin sec; m 31 Dec 1846 by P Williams.

KELLY Timothy to Elizabeth Bradford 14 Mar 1825; Wm Mear of Thos sec & as to ages; m 1825 by G C Wescoat.

KELLY Timothy to Elizabeth Taylor 7 May 1842; d/o George Taylor dec'd; Thomas Kelly sec; m 8 May 1842 by G C Wescoat.

KELLY Thomas to Margaret J Kelly 28 Mar 1842; s/o Jesse Kelly dec'd; d/o Stephen Kelly dec'd; Arthur E Roberts sec & as to ages; m 29 Mar 1842 by G C Wescoat.

KELLY Thomas to Miss Margaret Ann Savage 24 Mar 1845; d/o Mrs Mary Savage con; Alex W F Mears sec; m 24 Mar 1845 by G C Wescoat.

KELLY Thomas B to Sophia Savage 26 Sep 1836; wid/o John Savage; Samuel G Carpenter sec & as to Thomas' age; m 28 Sep 1836 by G Wescoat.

KELLY William T to Miss Kiturah Churn 19 Dec 1848; d/o William Churn; Thomas N B Roberts sec & as to Wm's age; m 20 Dec 1848 by P Warren.

KEMP John to Adah Dunton 11 Mar 1769; d/o Stephen Dunton sec.

KENDALL Custis to Elizabeth Bowdoin; spinster; 11 Apr 1746 d/o Peter Bowdoin); Isaac Nottingham sec. CR PK 33 Sep 1747 "Bowdoin Adm vs C Kendall."

KENDALL Custis to Elizabeth W Jarvis 20 Feb 1816; Wm Jarvis Sr sec.

KENDALL George Mason to Elishe Harmanson 17 Mar 1740; d/o Elizabeth Harmanson con; John Marshall sec; P Norly Ellegood & Thos Cable wits; m 17 Mar 1740.

CT ret 1740.

KENDALL Henry B to Catherine Dalby 4 Oct 1814; Custis Kendall sec; m (1814) by J Elliott.

KENDALL John to Elizabeth Harmanson 15 Sep 1741; d/o Elizabeth Harmanson con; Littleton Eyre & Geo Kendall secs; Eleshe Stringer wit.

KENDALL John to Sarah Satchell 22 Jan 1768; d/o Southy Satchell dec'd; Wm Satchell sec.

KENDALL John Jr to Lucretia Guy 3 Nov 1779; d/o Henry Guy dec'd & bro/o Henry Guy gdn con; Edmund Glanville sec.

KENDALL John to Miss Sally Simkins 3 Jul 1802; s/o Lucretia Kendall con; John Simkins sec; Mathew Harmanson Sr wit; m Jul 1802 by C Simkins.

KENDALL John C to Juliet J Andrews 24 Sep 1845; wid/o Isaac Andrews; Alex W F Mears sec; m 24 Sep 1845 by P Warren Jr. see BRec V2:41-2.

KENDALL John W to Susanna Harmanson 5 Feb 1802; d/o Henry Harmanson con; John R Waddey sec; m (1802) by I Bratten.

KENDALL Lemuel to Susanna Robins 10 May 1738; Lemuel of Acc Co; Thos Cable sec; Thos Preeson & Jas Gibson wits.

KENDALL Littleton to Mary Holt 1 Dec 1755; d/o Geo Holt dec'd; John Harmanson sec.

KENDALL Littleton to Sally Dixon 21 Jul 1807; Thos V Custis sec; m (1807) by J Elliott.

KENDALL Littleton Jr to Maria Robins 28 Feb 1809; d/o John Robins con; Geo T Kendall sec; m (1809) by J Elliott.

KENDALL Thomas to Anne Wilkins 27 Nov 1776; d/o Jno Wilkins OP Gent; Jno Respess sec.

KENDALL Thomas to Elizabeth Matthews 11 Sep 1793; wid/o John Matthews; Geo Savage sec; m Sep 1793 by C Simkins.

KENDALL Thomas L to Susan W Heath 2 Apr 1849; wid/o Rufus Heath; William J Bowdoin sec; m 2 Apr 1849 by J Ufford.

KENDALL William to Jane Parks 16 Oct 1706; s/o Col William Kendall dec'd; (d/o Chas Parks*); Sam'l Palmer sec; Elizabeth Nighell wit. *North Co XIX:143.

KENDALL William to Nancy Parsons 17 Oct 1771; Henry Bryan sec.

KENDALL William Jr to Mary Waggoman (Haggoman?) 13 Apr 1774; Obedience Johnson sec.

KENDALL William to Susan Dalby 21 Jan 1818; Edward Kellum sec; m 22 Jan 1818 by C Bonewell.

KENNARD William to Anne W Stratton 5 Mar 1827; Henry Tazewell sec; m 8 Mar 1827 by S S Gunter.

KENNARD William B to Miss Margaret Nottingham 29 Oct 1844; d/o Thomas Nottingham dec'd; Tully A T Joynes sec; Devorax Warren as to Margaret's age.

KER Edward to Miss Caroline T Rutter 16 Oct 1850; (s/o John Ker Sr); Peter B Smith as to Caroline's age; m 17 Oct 1850 by A Weed.

KER George to Sarah Parker 6 Jan 1796; (m poss Acc Co). see BRec V7:172.

KER George to Miss Sarah C Winder 2 Oct 1849; (s/o John Ker Sr); d/o Nath'l J & Sarah U Winder sec con; (m 3 Oct 1849. see BRec V7:174.

KER Hugh to Annie E Yerby 3 Sep 1852; m MD 200 yards from VA line by Rev Waters. see BRec V1:65, V7:174.

KER Dr John Sr to Mary (Jacob) Waddey 15 May 1822; Mary wrd/o John E Nottingham sec; m 15 May 1822 by S Wilmer. see BRec V9:14.

KER John Jr to Cecelia Willig 21 Apr 1847; m in Baltimore, MD. see BRec V1:65, V7:174.

KERBY Robert to Elizabeth

Marshall; spinster; d/o John & Mary; s/o Thomas; 18 Jun 1744; John Custis sec.

KERVIN, KERWIN (ERVIN?).

KIRVEN Andrew to Anne Luke 4 Aug 1783; Charles Satchell Jr sec.

KERVIN* Andrew to Susannah Grise 2 Dec 1783; d/o ___ (unsigned) con; John Dalby sec. *This could be read as Ervin.

KILLMAN Charles to Rosy Ann Wingate 5 Jan 1836; d/o James Wingate sec & as to Charles' age; m 7 Jan 1836 by P Williams.

KING John to Jane Bishop 8 Oct 1660. BK IX:92.

KIMMEY Benson to Elizabeth C Bedell 15 Mar 1838; wid/o James Bedell; Christofer D Fitchett sec & as to Benson's age; m 7 Apr 1838 by P Williams.

KIMMEY Benson to Eliza Elliott 28 Mar 1844; wid/o James Elliott; Samuel W Williams sec; m 28 Mar 1844 by P Williams.

KINCAID John to Margaret Preeson 1 May 1730; (wid/o Zerubable Preeson); Thomas Cable sec; Wm Kendall wit.

KNIGHT Henry to Hamutal Knight 22 Oct 1756; wid/o (Dixon Knight)*; John Moor sec; *North Co OB 14:384.

KNIGHT John to Mary Benthall 28 May 1777; d/o Wm Benthall dec'd; Wm Jarvis sec.

KNIGHT John to Molly Floyd 24 Feb 1790; d/o Charles Floyd sec.

KNIGHT John to Betsey Wheelor 2 Feb 1808; Michael Dunton sec; m (1808) by J Elliott.

KNIGHT Kendall to Leah Nelson 10 Nov 1834; d/o John Nelson Sr; Thomas J Nottingham sec & as to ages; Thomas Young wit; m 13 Nov 1834 by L Dix.

KNIGHT Thomas to Susanna Fisher 19 Aug 1751; wid; Tilney Michael sec.

KNIGHT Thomas to Margaret Belote Dec 1794; by C Simkins.

KNIGHT Thomas to Eliza Trower 1 Jan 1828; d/o John Trower sec; m Jan 1828 by L Dix.

KNIGHT William to Sally Kendall 28 Dec 1808; Nath'l Widgeon sec; m (1808) by J Elliott.

KNOWER John to Anne Fitchew 23 Feb 1835; John wrd/o Thomas Nottingham sec; d/o Vussy Fitchew con; Joseph Godwin sec; Nath'l B Townsend wit; m 5 Mar 1835 by L Dix.

KUNNELOE Hugh to Mariam Haey 14 Oct 1660. BK IX:92.

L

LANE Ezekiel to Hannah Harmanson 12 Nov 1763; Ezekiel of Worcester Co, MD; wid; Mich'l Christian sec.

LANE William to Margaret Fulwell 7 Oct 1789; William of Gloster; d/o John Lewis Fulwell sec.

LANKFORD Killiam to Eleanor Cable 2 Dec 1803; John Jacob sec; m (1803) by I Bratten.

LAURENCE Levin to Susanna Eshon 18 Feb 1780; wid; James Williams sec.

LEATHERBURY James M to Elizabeth Powell 13 Aug 1838; wid/o Thomas Powell; Thomas K Dunton sec; m 16 Aug 1838 by L Dix.

LEATHERBURY John W to Sally C West 30 Nov 1818; d/o Charles West con; Jacob Nottingham Jr sec; Thos S Satchell wit. (m 2 Dec 1818 BRec V 12: 108.

LEATHERBURY Perry to Agnes Roberts 9 Jan 1770; wid; Edmund Leatherbury sec.

LEATHERBURY William J to Miss Virginia S Harmanson 13 Jul 1846; s/o John W Leatherbury sec; d/o Wm Harmanson sec; m 15 Jul 1846 by M Oldham.

LECATO John to Sally Dennis 27 Nov 1833; Sally wrd/o John W Leatherbury sec; Abel James as to John's age; m 2 Dec 1833 by G Wescoat.

LECATO John to Elizabeth S Wyatt 8 Feb 1848; d/o John Wyatt dec'd; Wm K Matthews sec & as

to Elizabeth's age; Lewis N Matthew sec.
LEMOUNT Hardes to Elizabeth Pigot 6 Dec 1758; wid; Southey Goffigon sec.
LEWIS George to Margaret Nottingham 10 Nov 1789; Thos Nottingham sec; m (1789) by E Baker.
LEWIS Issachar to Hannah Tankard 17 Apr 1811; John Tankard sec.
LEWIS Thomas to Sarah Williams 25 Jan 1800; John Frost sec; m (1800) by I Bratten.
LILLISTON Edmund to Sukey Costin 2 Feb 1811; d/o Samuel Costin dec'd; Arthur Simkins sec; James Travis & John Simkins as to Sukey's age; m bet 1 Jan - 8 Apr (1811) by J Elliott.
LILLISTON Jacob D to Elizabeth Turpin 15 Apr 1837; d/o Elizabeth Turpin sec; Henry P Lilliston sec; m 19 Apr 1837 by W B Snead.
LILLISTON Robert C to Nancy Cox (Cocks) 19 Nov 1806; Geo Beloate gdn/o Nancy con; Wm P Harmanson sec.
LITTLETON Edward to Mrs Frances Robins 7 Mar 1660/1661. BK IX:92.
LIVERPOOL Daniel to Elishe Drighouse 25 Jun 1799; Josias Liverpool sec (FN); m Jun 1799 by C Simkins.
LIVERPOOL Henry to Kesiah Becket 17 Mar 1789; Solomon Liverpool sec (FN); m (1789) by E Baker.
LIVERPOOL Josiah to Betsey Moses (FN) (1798) by J Elliott.
LOCKWOOD Amos to Joice Twiford 8 Jul 1794; Isaac Rose sec.
LUKE Daniel to Mary Walter 25 Jun 1772; d/o John Walter con; John Dalby sec.
LUKE Daniel to Molly McCrady 25 May 1796; Esau Jacob sec.
LUKE Daniel to Sally Bell 17 Apr 1799; Littleton Dennis sec; m (1799) by J Elliot.
LUKE George W to Catherine Lingo 14 Mar 1811; d/o Margaret Lingo gdn/o Catherine con; John Rafield sec; m bet 1 Jan - 8 Apr (1811) by J Elliott.
LUKE Isaac to Elizabeth Wilson 5 Jan 1780; Wm Cable sec.
LUKER, LUCRE.
LUKER John to Elizabeth Mapp 31 Dec 1763; d/o Howsen Mapp dec'd; John Dolby sec.
LUKER John to Patience Lawrence Jun 1793; by C Simkins.
LUKER John W to Miss Elizabeth N Scott 18 Nov 1826; Levin Nottingham sec; m Nov 1826 by L Dix.
LUKER Walter to Sukey Hunt 24 Dec 1791; Nath'l Goffigon gdn/o Sukey orp con; Jno Goffigon sec; Edmund Hubberd wit; m (1791) by E Baker.
LUKER Walter to Sally Dunton 18 Aug 1812; Edmund Joynes sec; m (1812) by J Elliott.
LUKER Walter H to Margaret S Moore 24 Dec 1838; d/o Matthew D Moore sec; m 27 Dec 1838 by P Williams.
LUNN John to Sally Roberts 11 May 1807; Levi Richardson sec; m (1807) by I Bratten.
LYON George A to Anna Glowina Savage 12 Jun 1815; Severn E Parker sec; (m 14 Jun 1815. see BRec V5:155, V9:12).
LYON James to Sarah Eyre 16 Jul 1799; John Eyre sec.

M

MCCOWAN See MCKOWN.
MCCREADY Ezekiel to Mary Gladston 13 May 1786; d/o Wm Gladston dec'd; Dan'l Benthall sec; John Evens as to Mary's age.
MCCROSKEY Samuel Smith to Elizabeth Bowdoin 24 Nov 1780; Griffin Stith Jr sec.
MCDANIEL Charles to Molly Hickman 3 Apr 1802; Robert Haggoman sec; m (1802) by I Bratten.
MCDONALD William Gibb to Sarah Michael 21 Sep 1771; d/o Tilney Michael dec'd; Wm Kendall Jr

MCDONALD William Gibb to Hannah Bell 1 Jul 1773; d/o George Bell dec'd; Samuel Atchison sec.

MCGREGOR James to Sally Jacob 23 Jun 1795; Abel Savage sec; m 1795 by I Bratten.

MCKOWN, MCCOWAN, MECOWN.

MCKOWN Edward to Sarah Ann Heath 18 Nov 1837; d/o John S Heath dec'd; Wm W Scott sec & as to ages; m 21 Nov 1837 by L Dix.

MCKOWN Edward to Susan Ann Biggs 4 Apr 1843; d/o John W Biggs dec'd; Severn Wilkins sec & as to Susan's age; m 5 Apr 1843 by P Warren.

MCCOWN John to Esther Downs 28 Sep 1791; Wm Smith sec; m (1791) by E Baker.

MECOWN (MCCOWN) John to Grace Jones 22 Jun 1818; Thos Speakman sec; m 25 Jun 1818 by W Costin.

MCCOWN John M to Nancy Griffeth 21 Dec 1802; Peter Wilkins sec; m (1802) by J Elliott.

MCKOWN John Thomas to Sally S Joynes 16 Jan 1843; d/o Mrs Elisha Joynes con; Severn Wilkins sec & as to John Thomas' age; Luther Nottingham wit; m 18 Jan 1843 by P Williams.

MCCOWAN William to Elizabeth Ann Costin 9 Aug 1828; wid/o Patrick F Costin; James Sanford sec; m Aug 1828 by L Dix; (m 14 Aug 1828. see BRec V4:75).

MCKOWN William C to Miss Margaret Ann Wilkins 11 Jan 1847; Margaret wrd/o said William C; John W Williams sec; John McKown as to Wm C's age; m 12 Jan 1847 by P Warren Jr.

MACKY Willcock to Desdemona Jackson 19 Sep 1752; William Sargant Kitteridge sec.

MAHIER Richard to Mary Savage 20 Apr 1719; James Forse & Thomas Savage Jr secs; Thos Waters wit.

MAIL George to Miss Betsy Lewis 21 Mar 1848; Robert Bell sec & as to ages; Wm T Fitchett wit; m 22 Mar 1848 by M Oldham.

MAJOR John to Anne Johnson 11 Oct 1791; d/o Obedience Johnson dec'd; Caleb Savage sec; m Oct 1791 by C Simkins.

MAJOR Littleton to Sarah Dunton 5 Sep 1790; d/o Jacob Dunton dec'd; Wm Dixon sec.

MAJOR Littleton to Louisa Morris FN 10 Jun 1829; d/o Levin Morris sec; Geo Bool as to Littleton's age; m 12 Jun 1829 by G Wescoat.

MAJOR Smith to Betsey Crippen 14 Mar 1796; John Turner sec; m (1796) by J Elliot.

MAJOR William to Rachel Underhill 25 Jun 1798; Arthur Roberts sec.

MAJOR William L to Elizabeth Costin 9 Feb 1829; William orp/o William & wrd/o* James Kellam of A (Acc Co); d/o Wm Costin Sr sec; m 11 Feb 1829 by P Williams. * gdn choice made Acc Co 27 Aug 1827.

MANN William to Margt Kellum 23 Apr 1790; John T Turner sec; m 12 Jun 1790 by C Simkins.

MANN William to Eulalie Donjeux 13 Nov 1800; John Brickhouse Jr sec.

MAPP Alfred N H to Miss Laura S Savage 3 Sep 1851; Laura wrd/o John C Mapp Jr con & as to Alfred's age; m 4 Sep 1851 by P Warren.

MAPP Howson to Bridget Westerhouse 25 Sep 1759; d/o Wm Westerhouse; Thos Luker sec.

MAPP John to Betty Haggoman 16 Feb 1765; wid; Thos Burk sec.

MAPP John C to Cassandra James 21 Dec 1813; Leavin J Thomas sec; m (1813) by I Bratten.

MAPP John C to Polly Jefferson 11 Oct 1838; wid/o Silas Jefferson; Thomas Nottingham sec; m 11 Oct 1838 by P Williams.

MAPP John C Jr to Malana Savage 6

Jun 1849; wid/o Severn Savage; Alfred N H Mapp sec; m 7 Jun 1849 by M Oldham.

MAPP Laban to Elizabeth J Kellam 13 Jul 1835; Laban wrd/o John R Fisher sec; George T Belote sec & as to Elizabeth's age.

MAPP Laban to Phebe Robertson 10 Dec 1838; Phebe wrd/o Joseph E Bell sec.

MAPP Robins to Jane Holbrooke 12 Nov 1755; d/o Rev'd John Holbrooke dec'd; John Harmanson sec.

MAPP Robins to Margaret Mathews 14 Jan 1789; Edward Robins sec; Benjamin Dunton con (for Marg't?).

MAPP Robins to Margaret C Leatherbury 21 May 1838; Col John W Leatherbury br/o Margaret sec & as to her age; m 24 May 1838 by W G Jackson.

MAPP Robins W W to Miss Harriet Fitchett 28 Dec 1852; d/o Mrs Leah Thurston con; Wm K Knight & Azariah Thurston wits; Wm T Sturgis as to Robin's age.

MAPP Samuel to Jane Baker 1 Jul 1776; wid; Rich'd Nottingham sec.

MAPP Samuel to Susanna Godwin 26 Jan 1786; Seth Powell sec.

MAPP Victor A to Miss Hannah E Scott 20 Dec 1830; Hannah wrd/o George F Wilkins sec.

MAPP Victor A to Eliza Ann Scott 3 Jul 1832; Eliza wrd/o Geo F Wilkins sec; m 4 Jul 1832 by P Williams.

MAPP William to Esther Moor 28 Sep 1770; wid/o Mathew Moor; Howson Mapp sec.

MAPP William to Nancy Hall 5 Aug 1852; d/o John Hall dec'd; Sam'l James Turner as to Nancy's age; m 25 Aug 1852 by P Warren.

MAPP William M to Elizabeth D Hallett 30 Nov 1821; Isaac W Avery sec; Michael Hallett states Elizabeth's age as 21y on 16 Oct 1821; John Bowle & Robert (Halet?) wits; m 1 Dec 1821 by L Dix.

MAPP William W to Miss Margaret A Hallett 21 Jan 1843; d/o John Hallett sec; Rich'd H Read swears to Wm W's age; m 24 Jan 1843 by P Williams.

MARSHALL Jacob to Margaret Roberts 29 Dec 1749; Jacob of Worcester Co, MD; wid; John Marshall sec.

MARSHALL Thomas John to Sarah Darby 12 Feb 175_; spinster; Henry Barlow sec; Peter Warren wit.

MARSHALL William to Mary Parker 12 May 1660. BK IX:92.

MARTIN James to Sukey (Susanna) Richardson 31 Dec 1822; Sukey wrd/o Severn Martin con; Luke Martin sec; m 31 Dec 1822 by C Bonewell.

MARTIN John to Parmer Satchell 7 Sep 1785; Peter Bowdoin sec.

MARTIN John S to Miss Susan Dunton 1 Sep 1851; d/o Wm M Dunton; Jas Fitchett as to Susan's age; m 2 Sep 1851 by P Warren.

MARTIN Louis to Polly Harrison 17 Sep 1778; d/o Salathiel Harrison dec'd; Stephen Ward sec.

MARTIN Luke to Elishe Freshwater 8 Jun 1786; d/o Mary Greenaway con (also signed by Rob't Greenaway); Thos Wilson sec.

MARTIN Luke to Molly Barret 6 Jan 1789; d/o David Barret; Jas Wood & Wm Phabin secs; m (1789) by E Baker.

MARTIN Luke to Mary Dalby 12 Jun 1792; Nath'l Powell sec; m 14 Jun 1792 by C Simkins.

MARTIN Severn to Mary Dunton 12 Aug 1822; Mary wrd/o Seldon S Ridley con; Johannis Johnson sec; Chas Bennett wit; m 22 Aug 1822 by C Bonewell.

MARTIN Smith K to Mary Ann Badger; d/o Nath'l & Mary Badger; m 2 Dec 1840. BRec V6:114.

MARTIN Thomas to Sally Craick 20

Jul 1821; Thomas of Onancock; David Ross sec & as to Sally's age; m 26 Jul 1821 by C Bonewell.

MARTIN William to Rosey Clegg 22 Dec 1827; d/o Major Clegg dec'd; Hezekiah Dalby sec & as to Rosey's age; m 24 Dec 1827 by S S Gunter.

MARTIN William B to Betsy Bloodsworth 1 Feb 1837; Pitt Price Bloodsworth sec & as to Betsy's age.

MASLIN, MASLING, MAZLIN.

MASLING Thomas to Elizabeth Pigot 10 Jul 1773; wid/o (John Pigot); Jno Lewis Fulwell sec; Abel Upshur wit.

MASLIN Thomas to Susanna Scott 27 Apr 1787; (wid/o John Scott); Smith Griffeth sec.

MASLIN Thomas to Betty Wheeler 19 Jul 1792; Jas Weir sec; m Jul 1792 by C Simkins (MinRet states "Betsy" Wheeler).

MASLIN Thomas to Mary Bell 20 Dec 1817; James Dalby sec; m 21 Dec 1817 by S W Woolford.

MAZLIN William to Nancy Pearson 24 Dec 1827; wid/o Thomas Pearson; William James sec; m 1827 by G C Wescoat.

MAZLIN William to Elizabeth B Young 23 Sep 1834; d/o Richard Young; Benja J Dalby sec & as to Elizabeth's age.

MASON George to Susanna Wilkins 17 Aug 1805; Johannes Wise sec; m (1805) by J Elliott.

MASON John to Susan Mathews 15 Jul 1813; d/o Sally Mathews con; Charles H Mason & Sam'l H Mathews secs; m (1813) by I Bratten.

MASON William H to Miss Elizabeth Ann Moore 12 Dec 1848; d/o Matthew D Moore sec; m 13 Dec 1848 by P Warren.

MASON Zorobabel A to Ann E S Addison 19 Dec 1837; d/o Wm Addison con; Edward C Thomas sec; Michael R Matthews sec & as to Zorobabel's age; Susan Bailey wit; m 20 Dec 1837 by G Wescoat.

MATHEWS, MATTHEWS.

MATHEWS Custis to Sarah Dixon 8 Dec 1772; d/o John Dixon dec'd; Charles Gilding sec.

MATHEWS Custis to Sarah Andrews 11 Jun 1777; wid; Rich'd Smith sec.

MATTHEWS Isaiah to Juliet Becket FN 24 Dec 1838; Rolla Thompson as to ages; George F Wilkins sec; m 24 Dec 1838 by S T Ames.

MATTHEWS Jacob to Susan Upshur FN 13 Jan 1840; George Stevens as to Susan's age; Hez P Wescoat as to Jacob's age; Wm J Fitchett sec; m 15 Jan 1840 by G C Wescoat.

MATHEWS John Custis to Elizabeth Barlow 5 Nov 1789; Michael Mathews sec; m (1789) by E Baker.

MATHEWS Jonathan to Margaret Johnson 1 Aug 1775; (wid/o John Johnson); Obed Cary sec.

MATHEWS Jonathan to Sarah Turner 13 Apr 1790; wid/o Samuel Turner; Obed Cary sec; m 3 May 1790 by C Simkins.

MATTHEWS Levin to Mary Nottingham 11 Jan 1779; d/o Addison Nottingham dec'd; Wm Waterfield sec.

MATTHEWS Levin to Margaret Ann Godwin 20 Dec 1825; Robert A Joynes gdn/o Margaret sec; m Dec 1825 by L Dix; (m 26 Dec 1825. see BRec V11:8).

MATTHEWS Lewis R to Adah Dunton 1 Mar 1820; John Whitehead sec.

MATTHEWS Lewis R to Harriet P Hadlock 5 Apr 1830; d/o Robert Hadlock con; John T Wilson sec; John W Leatherbury wit; m 6 Apr 1830 by G Wescoat.

MATHEWS Michael to Sally Barlow 13 Jul 1790; Littleton Upshur gdn/o Sally con; Teackle Turner sec.

MATTHEWS Michael to Lovy Roberts 29 Jul 1833; wid/o Arthur

Roberts; Wm H Bell sec; m 2 Aug 1833 by G Wescoat.

MATTHEWS Michael R to Elizabeth Mister 26 Apr 1847; d/o Wm Mister dec'd; Wm M Dunton as to Elizabeth's age; Thomas Smith sec; m 26 Apr 1847 by G C Wescoat.

MATTHEWS Samuel to Penda Read 16 Oct 1819; Isaac Read sec; m 21 Oct 1819 by C Bonewell.

MATHEWS Samuel H to Vienna Westcot 27 Nov 1816; Geo C Wescoat sec; m 28 Nov 1816 by C Bonewell.

MATHEWS Samuel (H?) to Henrietta Coleburn 6 May 1818; Richard Coleburn sec; John A Coleburn wit; m 7 May 1818 by C Bonewell.

MATHEWS Samuel H to Margaret Jackson 1 Jan 1819; Sam'l Dennis sec.

MATHEWS Teackle to Betsey Wheelor 17 Dec 1811; James Dalby sec & with Henry Fitzhugh as to Betsey's age; m (1811) by J Elliott.

MATTHEWS Teackle to Betsy Johnson 28 Jun 1824; John Johnson br/o Betsy states she is considerably older than 21y - older than he sec.

MATHEWS Wm to Violetta Booll 25 Apr 1798; Meshack Waterfield sec; m 1798 by J Elliot.

MATHEWS William to Sally Wright 8 Aug 1803; Major Andrews sec; m (1803) by C Fisher.

MATTHEWS William K to Eliz Ann Savage 23 Sep 1845; d/o Major Savage con; Lewis N Matthews sec & as to Wm's age; John T Elliott wit; m 24 Sep 1845 by G C Wescoat. see BRec V9:164.

MAYO Peter P to Leah C Upshur 7 Jul 1824; A P Upshur sec; m 9 Jul 1824 by M B Chase.

MAYO Peter P to Anne E Upshur 27 Mar 1841; d/o Col Littleton Upshur dec'd; John L Upshur sec; (m 28 Mar 1841. HunParReg:35).

MAZLIN See MASLING.

MEARS Alexr W F to Miss Susan F Hopkins 17 Nov 1840; James L Kellam sec & as to Susan's age; m 18 Nov 1840 by S T Ames.

MEARS Elisha W to Ann N Powell 25 Jan 1833; d/o George Powell dec'd; Joshua B Turner sec & as to ages.

MEARS George M to Miss Elizabeth Ann Savage 10 Dec 1849; George wrd/o Nathan F Cobb; d/o John M Savage sec & as to Elizabeth's age; m 20 Dec 1849 by P Warren.

MEARS George M to Miss Ellen A Dowty 7 Nov 1853; Rich'd T Dunton as to ages; C F Anderson wit.

MEARS George T to Pamela Richardson 10 Dec 1840; d/o Wm Richardson dec'd; James Dalby as to grd's age; Wm Mears as to George's age; Wm Mears sec.

MEARS George W to Adah Andrews 24 May 1841; d/o Shepherd Andrews con; Arthur T Roberts sec & as to George's age; Elijah Brittingham & Wm J Fitchett wits; m 25 May 1841 by G C Wescoat.

MEARS James to Anne Floyd 2 Jun 1834; d/o Shepherd B Floyd dec'd & wrd/o Wm L Eyre sec; Thos Smith Jr as to Anne's age.

MEARS James G to Esther Carpenter 17 Jun 1829; d/o John Carpenter (Hog Island) con; Ely Dowty sec; Jas Barcroft & Jno Robins as to James G's age; m 19 Jun 1829 by G Wescoat.

MEARS James W to Miss Caroline Bishop 6 Dec 1848; d/o Wm Bishop dec'd; John Mears sec & as to ages; m 7 Dec 1848 by P Warren.

MEARS John to Emeline Johnson alias Emeline Bingham 15 Jan 1838; d/o Lucretia Bingham FN; Joshua K Roberts sec.

MEARS John to Miss Rosey Abdell 13 Dec 1841; d/o Peggy Abdell; Major Dowty sec & as to ages;

Jno W H Parker wit; m 17 Dec 1841 by P Warren Jr.

MEARS Littleton to Mary Edna Garrett 10 Oct 1853; Mary wrd/o said Littleton; m 12 Oct 1853 by H Dalby. see BRec V1:103.

MEARS Reubin to Sophia Scott 21 Feb 1825; Levin Beach sec & as to ages; m 3 Mar 1825 by S S Gunter.

MEARS Robert to Adah Stott 25 Dec 1829; wid/o Jonathon Stott; Wm Wyatt Jr sec; m 25 Dec 1829 by G Wescoat.

MEARS Shadrack to Sally Fletcher 26 Sep 1807; Charles Floyd sec.

MEARS Shadrack to Jemima Wescoat 9 Oct 1811; George Wescoat sec; m 10 Oct 1811 by Thos A Elliott.

MEARS Thomas C to Frances L Johnson 3 Apr 1837; wid/o Thomas Johnson Jr; Smith S Nottingham sec; m 4 Apr 1837 by W B Snead.

MEARS William to Betsey Watson 20 Apr 1816; Isachar Lewes sec; m 28 Apr 1816 by C Bonewell.

MEARS William to Rosey Nottingham 17 Apr 1837; wid/o Severn Nottingham; Benjamin J Dalby sec; m 19 Apr 1837 by W B Snead.

MECKAEL See also MICHAEL.

MECKAELL (MICHAEL) John to Hellen Cornagh 24 Mar 1660/1661. BK IX:92.

MELBOURN See MILBOURN.

MELHOLLOMS, MEHOLLOMS, MAHOLMS.

MELHOLLOMS George to Esther Core 26 Oct 1791; Jacob Roberts sec.

MELHOLLOMS George to Nancy Hampleton 28 Mar 1807; Arthur Cobb sec; Jeheu Johnson as to age of Nancy who "is living at my house."

MEHOLLOMS Stringer to Bridget Edmunds 9 May 1781; d/o David Edmunds con; John Mehollams sec; Thos Upshur con as to Stringer.

MELHOLLOMS Thomas to Nancy Joynes 19 Aug 1801; John Bird sec; m (1801) by J Elliott.

MEHOLLOMES William W to Margaret Stockley 28 May 1840; d/o Charles B Stockley; John Stockley sec & as to Margaret's age; L B Nottingham wit.

MELSON Caleb to Catherine B Vaughn 13 Dec 1824; Wm S Smith sec & as to Catherine's age; m Dec 1824 by L Dix.

MELSON James T to Miss Susan E Maslin 7 Mar 1853; S S Brickhouse as to ages; m 7 Mar 1853 by J Rawson.

MELSON Smith to Esther Bell 4 Feb 1804; Smith of Acc Co; John Stratton sec.

MELSON Thomas J to Miss Mary J Mazeline 26 Feb 1852; R W Powell as to Thomas' age; m 26 Feb 1852 by P Warren.

MELVIL Hezakieh to Bridget Morris (FN) 2 Jan 1786; Reuben Reid sec.

MELVIN George to Agnes Clegg (FN) 24 Dec 1794; James Dolby sec; m Dec 1794 by C Simkins.

MICHAEL See also MECKAEL.

MICHAEL Joachim to Mary Blaikley Stith 12 Apr 1770; d/o Griffin Stith; Rob't Polk sec.

MICHAEL John to Margaret Christian 16 Feb 1767; John (b 3 Feb 1745/1746 test by Azel Benthall clerk to vestry Hungers Parish) s/o Joachim & Peggy Michael; d/o Wm Christian con; Jno Blair sec.

MICHAEL John Jr to Rose Wainhouse 23 Jan 1771; John Michael Sr sec.

MICHAEL Thos to Comfort Waterson 30 Dec 1747; (d/o John & Eliz*) spinster; Levi Moor sec; Azel Benthall wit. *Whl:153.

MICHAEL Tilney to Mary Rascoe 28 May 1760; wid; James Peterkin sec; Jno Buckner Stith wit.

MICHAEL William Wainhouse to Margaret Downing 11 Feb 1772; d/o Zerobabel Downing con;

Teackle Robins sec.

MILBOURN John C to Mary Williams 12 May 1823; Peter Williams as to Mary's age; Ezekiel Delastatious sec & as to John Milbourn's age; m May 1823 by L Dix.

MILBY Adiel to Elizabeth Christian 8 Jan 1770; d/o Wm Christian; John Michael sec.

MILBY John to Sarah Turner 13 Aug 1754; wid/o Edw'd Turner; Gilbert Milby sec; Littleton Andrews wit.

MILBY John to Leah Coward 18 Sep 1756; wid/o (Samuel Coward)*; John Stratton sec. *North Co OB24:385.

MILBY John to Nancy Aimes 27 Aug 1793; Wm Christian gdn/o John orp con; Coventon Simkins sec; m Aug 1793 by C Simkins.

MILES Richard to Eliza Richardson 3 Jul 1838; d/o Elizabeth Richardson con; John W Leatherbury sec; m 5 Jul 1838 by G C Wescoat.

MILES William to Mrs Sally Read 28 Jan 1834; wid; Wm Joynes sec; John C Terrier wit; m 30 Jan 1834 by P Williams.

MILES William to Nancy Haley 3 Dec 1835; wid/o Rob't Haley; Jeremiah Griffeth sec.

MILLENER Smith to Jenney Dunton 8 Jun 1808; James Travis sec; m (1808) by J Elliott.

MILLER Dr Mathias H to Miss Catharine F Jones 6 Nov 1848; d/o Catharine S Weisiger (formerly Catharine S Jones) con; Mrs Thos B Rowe sec & as to Mathais' age; m 6 Nov 1848 by J Ufford.

MILLS Edmund to Susanna Fitchett 23 Feb 1761; d/o Nehemiah Fitchett; Savage Cowdrey sec.

MILLS Jacob to Comfort Willis 18 Dec 1789; d/o Josias Willis; George Willis sec; m (1789) by E Baker.

MILLS Jacob to Agnes Graves 17 Sep 1795; John Graves Sr sec; m (1795) by E Baker.

MILMAN Ephraim to Rachel Dowty 17 Sep 1791; Ephraim of Acc Co; Wm Bloxom sec; m (1791) by E Baker.

MINGO Ewell to Sukey Church 11 Jan 1828; d/o Isaac Church FN; William Stephens (Church Neck) sec; Sukey 22y; John B Ross & Abel Church wits.

MINGO John to Adah Collins 14 Dec 1816; Isaac Stephens sec (FN).

MINSON John G to Emilene Sanford 14 May 1838; d/o Robert Sanford con; Teackle W Jacob sec; Jos E Bell & James H Sanford wits; m 16 May 1838 by G C Wescoat.

MINSON John G to Margaret S Brickhouse 29 Jul 1846; wid/o Albert Brickhouse; Wm P Nottingham sec; m 29 Jul 1846 by G C Wescoat.

MINTER John P to Miss Harriet Wilkins 24 Jun 1847; d/o John Wilkins Sr; Wm W Elliott as to John P's age; Wm H Kendall sec & as to Harriet's age.

MINTER William B to Polly Elliott 18 Jun 1838; Nathaniel Hickman gdn/o Polly sec & as to William's age; m 21 Jun 1838 by P Williams.

MISTER John to Miss Nancy Horner 5 Oct 1853; d/o Susan Horner con; Gilbert Mister wit; Wm J Haley as to John's age; m 5 Oct 1853 by P Williams.

MITCHELL Wm D to Eliz Fitzhugh 26 Nov 1823; d/o of Henry sec; m Nov 1823 by L Dix.

MOOR, MOORE.

MOORE Abraham to Betsey Hanby 8 Feb 1800; Thomas Lewis sec; m Feb 1800 by C Simkins.

MOORE Abraham to Betsy Taylor 24 Jul 1812; Thomas Lewis sec.

MOORE Abram to Lavinia Isdell 18 Sep 1828; Lavinia wrd/o William Welsh sec; m 20 Sep 1828 by G Wescoat.

MOORE Abram to Elisha Williams 1 Jan 1842; d/o Peter Williams dec'd; Benjamin Nottingham sec

& as to Elisha's age; George Bool as to Abram's age; Obed Twiford wit; m 2 Jan 1842 by P Williams.

MOORE Edward to Elizabeth Turner 2 Jun 1661. BK IX:114.

MOORE George W to Emily S Rooks 22 Dec 1842; s/o Matthew D Moore sec; d/o John Rooks dec'd; Richard Jacob as to Emily's age; m 22 Dec 1842 by P Warren.

MOORE Jacob to Agnes O'dear 17 Jan 1780; wid/o Joseph O'dear; Ralph Dixon sec.

MOOR Jacob to Elizabeth Wilkins 7 Feb 1789; wid/o Joachim Michael Wilkins; Nath'l Powell sec; m (1789) by E Baker.

MOOR Jacob to Peggy Robins 2 Nov 1792; wid/o Mack (Mark?) Robins; Henry Smaw sec; m (1792) by E Baker.

MOORE John to Elizabeth Twiford 8 Feb 1780; John of James City Co; Golding Ward sec.

MOORE John to Susey Pratt 11 Nov 1800; Wm Wilson sec; m Nov 1800 by C Simkins.

MOORE John to Peggy Roberts 16 Mar 1802; Samuel Costin gdn/o Peggy con; William Havard sec; m (1802) by J Elliott.

MOORE John to Nancy Collins 4 Jan 1825; wid/o John Collins; James Willis sec; m Jan 1825 by L Dix.

MOORE John to Miss Eliza Willis 18 Dec 1850; d/o Wm Willis dec'd; Wm C Nottingham as to Eliza's age; m 18 Dec 1850 by P Williams.

MOORE John C to Angeline Griffith 12 Jan 1841; d/o Mrs Mary Pettitt con; Elias Roberts sec & as to John's age; m 12 Jan 1841 by P Williams.

MOORE John D to Miss Fanny Copes 15 Jan 1844; d/o Levin Copes dec'd; Wm Downes as to Fanny's age; Matt D Moore sec; m 17 Jan 1844 by G G Exall.

MOOR Levi to Sarah Waterson 25 Sep 1744; George Kendall sec.

MOORE Lewis to Ellen Dalby 19 Aug 1848; wid/o Nathaniel Dalby; Lloyd Q Moore sec; John Willis as to Lewis' age; Thos H Nottingham wit; m 19 Aug 1848 by S C Boston.

MOORE Lloyd to Miss Emory Casey 13 Nov 1848; s/o Matthew D Moore sec; Emory wrd/o Wm G Costin sec; m 15 (Oct?) 1848 by C Hill.

MOORE Mack to Sally Dalby 30 Dec 1836; d/o Mrs Peggy Dalby; Wm Welch sec & as to ages; Wm S Floyd wit; m 31 Dec 1836 by W B Snead.

MOOR Matthew Jr to Peggy Wilkins 14 Apr 1752; spinster; John Stratton sec.

MOOR Mathew to Esther Joyne 20 Jan 1764; d/o Edmund Joyne dec'd; Edw'd Homes sec; Douglas Willett con for Esther.

MOORE Mathew to Nancy Freshwater 13 Jan 1798; Jacob Moore sec; m (1798) by E Baker.

MOORE Mathew to Betsey Downs 22 Nov 1809; d/o Nancy Downs con; Robert Fitchett sec; m (1809) by J Elliott.

MOORE Peter to Mary Ann Bonwell 13 Jul 1824; s/o Mathey Moore as to Peter's age; Charles Bonwell gdn/o Mary Ann sec; Thomas Evans & Benja Kellum wits; m Jul 1824 by L Dix.

MOORE Richard to Polly Cullin 27 Feb 1796; Wm Hanby sec; m (1796) by E Baker.

MOORE Richard to Miss Lavenia Spady 8 Dec 1847; d/o Westerhouse Spady sec; m 8 Dec 1847 by H Dalby.

MOORE Socrates to Arinthia C Melborne 13 Feb 1849; d/o John Melborne dec'd; Samuel Savage sec & as to ages; Ellison S Nottingham wit; m 15 Feb 1849 by H Dalby.

MOORE Thomas to Sally Stripe 6 Jan 1802; Charles Dillon sec; m bet 1 Jan - 8 Mar (1802) by J Elliott.

MOORE Thomas to Elishe Scott 6

Apr 1812; Nath'l Bishop sec; m (1812) by J Elliott.

MOORE Thomas to Catharine Spady 27 Jun 1827; Thos Kellum sec & as to Catharine's age; m 6 Jul 1827 by P Williams.

MOORE Thomas of John to Miss Sarah Ann Bool 14 Sep 1846; d/o Spencer Bool; Wm Kennard sec & as to Sarah's age; Lewis Moore as to Thomas' age; m 16 Sep 1846 by H Dalby.

MOORE Thomas to Miss Rosey E Spady 29 Dec 1852; d/o Westerhouse Spady con; Zerababel Gibb as to Thomas' age; Wm H Cottingham & Jno R Trower wits; m 30 Dec 1852 by H Dolby.

MOORE Thomas D to Drusilla Groten 6 Jan 1841; d/o Thomas Groten; James G Groten as to Drusilla's age; Thomas E Evans sec; Richard Mapp wit; m 6 Jan 1841 by J T Hazzard.

MOORE William to Peggy Dixon 6 Mar 1780; Nath'l Wilkins Jr sec.

MOOR William to Margaret Wood 5 Jan 1782; d/o Wm Wood con; Stuart Holt sec.

MOOR William to Santica Dixon 29 Aug 1783; Christopher Dixon sec.

MOORE William D to Angeline B Brickhouse 7 Dec 1831; d/o Thomas S Brickhouse sec; m 7 Dec 1831 by P Williams.

MORRIS George to Mary Stevens (FN) 19 Oct 1785; David Jones sec.

MORRIS Henry to Adah Pool FN 24 Dec 1851; Horace Stephens as to ages; m 25 Dec 1851 by P Warren.

MORRIS Isaac to Juno Read 24 Oct 1823; Juno wrd/o said Isaac; Wm Stephens sec FN; m 25 Oct 1823 by S S Gunter.

MORRIS Jacob to Phillis Only 23 Aug 1802; York Stepney sec (FN); m (1802) by C Fisher.

MORRIS Revel to Dilly Drighouse (FN) 7 Sep 1801; James Smith sec; m 1801 by I Bratten.

MORRIS Stockley to Chilamethia Read FN 21 May 1831; Jacob Thompson sec; m 25 May 1831 by P Williams.

MOSES Daniel to Rachel Teague 25 Sep 1802; Levin Morris sec.

MOSES Ezekiel to Diana Becket 22 Aug 1791; wid/o Mark Becket (FN); Wm Stith sec.

MOSES George to Sarah Pool 13 Mar 1848; s/o Jenny Moses sec; Sarah wrd/o Peggy Ames sec FN; Wm T Leatherbury sec; m 16 Mar 1848 by P Warren.

MOSES Mark to Mary Becket 13 Dec 1785; Isaac Becket sec (FN).

MOULTON E L to Miss Mary J Gadd 5 Feb 1852; m 5 Feb 1852 by H Dalby.

MURRAY James to Hannah Savage 16 May 1764; James of Dorchester Co, MD; d/o Thomas Savage Gent dec'd; Edward Noel of Dorchester Co, MD, sec.

N

NEALE Presley to Susanna Satchell 12 Sep 1780; d/o Charles Satchell; Rob't Brickhouse sec.

NEDAB Abraham to Lurey Bingham 29 Dec 1813; d/o Tinsey Weeks con (FN); Stephen Nedab sec; Jno S Heath wit; m (1813) by I Bratten.

NELSON Charles to Sally Fisher 14 Mar 1821; W R Fisher gdn/o Sally con; John Nelson Jr sec; Samuel P Fisher wit; m 17 Mar 1821 by L Dix.

NELSON James to Mary Hamilton 11 Jul 1780; d/o Andrew Hamilton; Wm Abdeel sec.

NELSON James F to Miss Sallie E Wilson 22 Dec 1851; d/o James B Wilson con; Wm H Trower as to James' age; Frances D Brickhouse wit; m 23 Dec 1851 by H Dalby.

NELSON John to Sarah Goffigon 17 Oct 1772; d/o James Goffigon dec'd; Southy Goffigon sec.

NELSON John to Adah Carpenter 6

Jul 1790; Wm Carpenter sec; m (1790) by E Baker.

NELSON John to Lear Wilkins 20 Jun 1800; James Goffigon sec; m Jun 1800 by C Simkins.

NELSON John Jr to Jenney Wilkins 12 Jan 1805; John R Waddey sec; m (1805) by J Elliott.

NELSON John Sr to Rosy Goffigon 8 Dec 1813; Abram Costin sec; m (1813) by J Elliott.

NELSON John Jr to Catherine S Teackle 18 Jun 1827; Wm S Floyd sec & as to Catherine's age; m 18 Jun 1827 by S S Gunter.

NELSON John Sr to Miss Elizabeth Biggs 9 Dec 1833; John W Biggs sec & as to Eliz's age; m 19 Dec 1833 by P Williams.

NELSON Southey to Eliz Willett 5 May 1770; d/o Thomas Willett dec'd; Samuel Williams sec.

NELSON Southey to Sally Joynes Brickhouse 17 Nov 1803; (d/o Geo & Mary); Geo Brickhouse sec; m (1803) by J Elliott. BRec 11: 43.

NICHOLSON James Macon to Arinthia Darby Parker 21 Jun 1838; John Eyre sec; m 21 Jun 1838 by W G Jackson. see BRec V7:151.

NICHOLSON John W to Miss Elizabeth Stewart 11 Oct 1841; d/o James Stewart sec.

NICHOLSON William J to Elizabeth A Martin 27 Nov 1849; wid/o Peter Martin; Caleb R Savage sec; Wm (W?) Thomas wit; m 29 Nov 1849 by M Oldham.

NIVISON John to Sarah Stratton 6 Dec 1781; John of Greensville Co; d/o John Stratton Sr Esq; Wm Stith sec.

NOLEN Lewis to Molly Warren 8 Dec 1789; Dan'l Benthall sec; m (1789) by E Baker.

NOTTINGHAM Adderson to Barbary Powell 15 Jul 1763; wid; Walter Hyslop sec.

NOTTINGHAM Addison to Peggy White 25 Apr 1826; Peggy b 7 Dec 1804, d/o Susannah White con; Elias Dunton sec; m Apr 1826 by L Dix.

NOTTINGHAM Benjamin to Frances Williams 26 May 1828; s/o Elisha Nottingham con; d/o Peter Williams Sr sec; John Spady Sr & Richard Bell & Jno S Dix & Luther H Read wits; m 26 May 1828 by P Williams.

NOTTINGHAM Cornelius to Miss Mary Rooks 8 Dec 1845; Mary wrd/o Wm J Fatherly sec & as to Cornelius' age; Wm P Nottingham wit; m 8 Dec 1845 by P Warren Jr.

NOTTINGHAM Edward T to Maria Goffigon 2 Apr 1839; d/o Wm Goffigon dec'd & sis/o Obadiah Goffigon sec & as to Maria's age; Victor A Nottingham as to Edward's age; m 3 Apr 1839 by P Williams.

NOTTINGHAM Edward W to Henrietta P Jacob 9 Nov 1830; d/o Thomas Jacob con; Richard Cutler sec; Jno C Jacob & Rob't B Nottingham wits.

NOTTINGHAM Edward W to Miss Harriet Spady 18 Sep 1844; Piner W Clark sec; m 18 Sep 1844 by P Williams.

NOTTINGHAM Ellison S to Miss Margaret S Brickhouse 10 Dec 1849; Ellison wrd/o Jacob Nottingham sec; d/o Elam L Brickhouse sec; m 12 Dec 1849 by M Oldham. see BRec V7:145.

NOTTINGHAM George L - name changed to George L UPSHUR.

NOTTINGHAM Harrison to Elizabeth Andrews 8 Sep 1817; Thomas Smith sec; m 10 Sep 1817 by C Bonewell.

NOTTINGHAM Harrison to Patsey Hickman 9 Sep 1822; John Warren sec & as to ages; gives Patsey's age as about 26y; m 21 Sep 1822 by L Dix.

NOTTINGHAM Isaac to Sarah Freshwater 31 Aug 1748; d/o Mark Freshwater con; Jas Westwood of Eliz City sec; Mary Waterson & Thos Bullock wits.

NOTTINGHAM Isaac to Mary Kendall 23 Nov 1763; wid/o (Littleton Kendall*); John Glisan sec. *North Co MBk 27:265.

NOTTINGHAM Isaac to Sophia Dixon 12 Sep 1792; Wm Hallet sec; m (1792) by E Baker.

NOTTINGHAM Jacob to Sarah Jarvis Bell 14 Jul 1804; (d/o Rob't & Mary (Jarvis) Bell); Wm Nottingham Sr sec; m (1804) by J Elliott.

NOTTINGHAM Jacob Jr to Rosey G Wescoat 14 Jun 1824; Rosey wrd/o Geo C Wescoat sec; m bet 15 Jun - 22 Dec 1824 by G C Wescoat.

NOTTINGHAM Jacob E to Ann Spady 21 Jan 1828; d/o Southy Spady con; Thomas Powell sec; Jno G Smaw & Wm Kennard wits; (m 23 Jan 1828. see BRec V1:15).

NOTTINGHAM James to Ann Costin 18 Sep 1827; Ann wrd/o Thomas Downes sec; Smith Nottingham as to James' age; m Sep 1827 by L Dix.

NOTTINGHAM John to Peggy Nottingham 27 Dec 1788; d/o Severn Nottingham con; Isaac Bratten sec; m (1788) by E Baker.

NOTTINGHAM John to Betsy Taylor 8 Dec 1789; d/o Thos Teackle Taylor & wife con; James Dolby sec.

NOTTINGHAM John to Nancy James 28 Dec 1802; Major Taylor sec.

NOTTINGHAM John E to Elizabeth P Upshur 30 Dec 1820; Littleton Upshur sec; m 30 Dec 1820 by S Wilmer.

NOTTINGHAM John E to Caroline S F Luker 4 Jun 1831; s/o Severn E; d/o Walter Luker dec'd; Thomas Young gdn/o Caroline con; James Saunders sec; Jno T & Ezekiel Young wits.

NOTTINGHAM John E to Mrs Mary Ann Burris 26 Oct 1839; John D Williams sec; m 30 Oct 1839 by W A Dix.

NOTTINGHAM John E Jr to Miss Sally S Kennard 20 Oct 1851; Wm Alex Thom wit; (m 22 Oct 1851 by J Rawson. HunParReg:35).

NOTTINGHAM John R to Susan Ann Cutler 3 Dec 1849; s/o Jacob Nottingham sec & as to age; d/o William W Cutler dec'd; late wrd/o Edwin J Fisher; Wm Hanby as to Susan's age; m 6 Dec 1849 by M Oldham.

NOTTINGHAM Joseph to Amelia Roberts 14 May 1793; wid/o Moses Roberts; Severn Widgeon sec; m (1793) by E Baker.

NOTTINGHAM Joseph to Polly Dixon 12 May 1828; Joshua Nottingham sec; John Bishop as to Polly's age; m 12 May 1828 by P Williams.

NOTTINGHAM Joseph D to Polly Widgeon 17 Jan 1823; s/o Joseph; Polly orp/o Severn Widgeon & wrd/o Nathaniel Widgeon sec; Susan Savage & Thos L Savage wits.

NOTTINGHAM Joseph (W?) to Anne Jacob 1 Jan 1794; Geo Lewis sec; m Jan 1794 by C Simkins.

NOTTINGHAM Joseph W to Sarah Ann Griffith 25 Nov 1845; d/o Wm Griffith & wrd/o Thomas Griffith con; Thos K Dunton sec; Charles A Richardson wit; m 27 Nov 1845 by P Williams.

NOTTINGHAM Joseph W to Miss Frances Griffeth 14 May 1849; Frances wrd/o Thos Griffeth con; Thomas M Wilkins sec.

NOTTINGHAM Joshua to Mary Bearcraft 16 Jan 1817; Joseph Nottingham sec.

NOTTINGHAM Joshua to Margaret Parkerson 28 Feb 1829; d/o George Parkerson sec; Thos Brickhouse sec; m 4 Mar 1829 by P Williams.

NOTTINGHAM Leonard B to Emeline Waddey 20 Nov 1827; Emeline wrd/o John Ker sec; m 20 Nov 1827 by S S Gunter. see BRec V9:14.

NOTTINGHAM Leonard J to Miss Ellen S Floyd 1 Mar 1853; John S Parker gdn/o Ellen con; (m 2 Mar 1853 by J Rawson. HunParReg:35).

NOTTINGHAM Levin to Sally Hubbard 11 Mar 1811; Peter Wilkins sec; m (1811) by I Bratten.

NOTTINGHAM Luther to Miss Emiline Nottingham 25 Dec 1837; Jesse J Simkins gdn/o Luther con; George P Fitchett gdn/o Emiline con; Severn E Bowdoin sec; m 26 Dec 1837 by P Williams. see BRec V9:102.

NOTTINGHAM Lloyd C to Miss Virginia S W Roberts 3 Oct 1863; d/o Mrs Sally A Roberts con; John R Nottingham as to Lloyd's age; Virginia L Leatherbury & Albert G Holt wits; m 5 Oct 1853 by J Rawson.

NOTTINGHAM Luther to Miss Catherine E Dalby 1 Oct 1849; widower; d/o Hezekiah Dalby; Wm L Dalby sec & as to Catherine's age; m 2 Oct 1849 by J B Maddux.

NOTTINGHAM Nathaniel to Mary Jacob 17 Aug 1799; Jos W Nottingham wrd/o Mary con; Nath'l Bryon sec; m (1799) by J Elliot.

NOTTINGHAM Richard to Elizabeth Wilkins 10 Jul 1764; d/o Watkins Wilkins dec'd; John Wilkins blacksmith sec; Mathew Moor con.

NOTTINGHAM Richard to Mary Evans 18 Dec 1776; d/o Arthur Evans dec'd; Edmund Glanville sec.

NOTTINGHAM Richard to Anne Harrison 18 Jan 1785; d/o Salathiel Harrison dec'd; Branson Dalby sec. see BRec V1:78.

NOTTINGHAM Richard to Nancy Bullock 28 Dec 1805; Joseph Nottingham sec; m (1805) by J Elliott.

NOTTINGHAM Richard to Susanna Cox 30 Aug 1806; Wm Harrison sec; m (1806) by I Bratten.

NOTTINGHAM Richard to Mary B Fisher 28 Jul 1811; d/o Sally Y Fisher; Thomas Johnson Jr sec; John Andress wit; m (1811) by J Elliott.

NOTTINGHAM Richard to Mary Stead Pinckney Gardiner 19 Jul 1814; d/o Wm C Gardiner con; Nath'l Widgeon sec; John Whitehead wit; m (1814) by J Elliott.

NOTTINGHAM Capt Robert to Elishe Stringer 16 Nov 1741; wid/o (Jacob Stringer); George Mason Kendall sec.

NOTTINGHAM Robert to Anne Johnson 12 Apr 1785; Hezekiah James sec.

NOTTINGHAM Robert B to Mary Jacob 1 Oct 1828; d/o Thomas Jacob con; Robins Mapp sec; Sam'l S Stott wit.

NOTTINGHAM Samuel Y to Leah F Carpenter 5 Jun 1826; sis/o Samuel G Carpenter con; John Gayle & J W Wilkins wits; Wm Nottingham sec; m 5 Jun 1826 by S S Gunter.

NOTTINGHAM Severn to Elizabeth Evans 10 Feb 1769; d/o Arthur Evans dec'd; Jacob Nottingham sec.

NOTTINGHAM Severn to Nancy Waterfield 5 Oct 1790; John Williams Jr sec.

NOTTINGHAM Severn to Betsey Bell 6 Dec 1802; John Nottingham sec; m (1802) by J Elliott.

NOTTINGHAM Severn to Rosy Smith 6 May 1828; d/o Thomas Smith Sr; John Ker sec; John Jacob as to Rosy's age.

NOTTINGHAM Severn E to Bridget Goffigon 20 Mar 1830; d/o Wm Goffigon dec'd & wrd/o John Goffigon con; James Saunders sec; Smith Nottingham as to Severn E's age; m 25 Mar 1830 by P Williams.

NOTTINGHAM Smith to Sally Williams 3 Mar 1810; Wm Williams sec; m (1810) by J

NOTTINGHAM Smith to Esther S B Nottingham 23 Jun 1830; d/o Wm Nottingham; Leon B Nottingham sec; Jno W Leatherbury as to Esther's age; (m 24 Jun 1830. see BRec V10:104).
NOTTINGHAM Smith B to Polly Elliott 4 Apr 1826; Polly wrd/o Daniel G Smaw sec; m Apr 1826 by L Dix.
NOTTINGHAM Thomas Jr to Peggy Johnson 8 Nov 1776; d/o Wm Johnson dec'd & wrd/o M Christian con; Rich'd Nottingham sec.
NOTTINGHAM Thomas to Patsey Costin 18 Apr 1801; d/o Francis Costin con for "Patey"; Westerhouse Widgeon sec; m 1801 by I Bratten.
NOTTINGHAM Thomas to Nancy Floyd 8 May 1809; Jas Floyd sec; m (1809) by I Bratten.
NOTTINGHAM Thomas to Peggy Turner 13 Oct 1812, Littleton Kendall Sr sec.
NOTTINGHAM Thomas to Susan Biggs 21 Dec 1815; d/o Nancy Biggs con for "Sukey"; Jacob Watson sec; John Biggs wit; m (1815) by J Elliott.
NOTTINGHAM Thomas to Peggy Frost 23 Jul 1822; Peggy wrd/o Obed Hunt sec; m 25 Jul 1822 by L Dix.
NOTTINGHAM Thomas to Harriet Addison 23 Feb 1828; d/o William Addison con; Thos B Fisher sec; Geo W Dunton wit; m 1828 by G C Wescoat.
NOTTINGHAM Thomas H to Miss Jenny Nottingham 11 Dec 1849; d/o Nathaniel Nottingham dec'd; Joseph E Bell sec; m 12 Dec 1849 by P Williams.
NOTTINGHAM Thos J to Catherine E Nottingham 24 Dec 1828; Catherine wrd/o John W Biggs sec & as to Thomas J's age.
NOTTINGHAM Thomas J L L to Tabitha S West 28 Nov 1831; d/o Charles West; Smith Nottingham sec; Thos Nottingham & Robins Mapp wits; Chas West as to Tabitha's age; (m 30 Nov 1831. see BRec V1:19; V5:1).
øNOTTINGHAM Thomas W to Elizabeth Snead 20 Dec 1836; wid; Wm Spady sec.
NOTTINGHAM Victor A to Miss Edith S Nottingham 23 May 1842; Leonard B Nottingham sec; m 23 May 1842 by P Warren.
NOTTINGHAM William to Leah Walter 16 Nov 1768; d/o John Walter; Edmund Glanville sec.
NOTTINGHAM William to Peggy Fitchet 6 Jul 1795; Wm Eyre sec; m (1795) by E Baker.
NOTTINGHAM Wm to Elishe Parks Wingate 21 Apr 1797; Wm Wingate sec; m (1797) by E Baker.
NOTTINGHAM William to Molly Bell 6 Feb 1798; Thomas Jarvis sec.
NOTTINGHAM William Jr to Margaret Turner 27 Aug 1802; Nathaniel Bryan sec; m (1802) by I Bratten.
NOTTINGHAM William of Robert to Susan Hyslop 5 Jul 1817; d/o Susanna Hyslop her curator; James Travis sec & as to Susan's age; Abram Costin wit; m 10 Jul 1817 by C Bonewell.
NOTTINGHAM William to Sally Jones 8 Nov 1823; Thos W Nottingham br/o William as to his age; Teackle Jones bro/o Sally as to her age; Thos W Nottingham & Teackle Jones secs.
NOTTINGHAM William to Elizabeth Snead 10 Sep 1838; Thomas J Nottingham gdn/o Elizabeth sec; m 11 Sep 1838 by L Dix.
NOTTINGHAM William C to Miss Elizabeth S Wilkins 4 Dec 1848; s/o Benja J Nottingham sec; Elizabeth wrd/o Thos M Wilkins sec; John Willis wit.
NOTTINGHAM William E to Margaret S Wilson 6 May 1814; d/o Anne Wilson con; Wm

Savage Jr sec; John L Wilson & Wm Hitchen wits; m (1814) by J Elliott; (m 11 May 1814. see BRec V9:102).

NOTTINGHAM William J to Susan Bishop Woodhouse 8 Mar 1829; (m poss in Norfolk). see BRec V7:63.

NOTTINGHAM Wm J to Margaret M Upshur 19 Dec 1837; d/o Wiliam M Upshur dec'd; Edwin J Fisher sec & as to ages; m 20 Dec 1837 by G Wescoat.

NOTTINGHAM William P to Miss Charlotte L Winder 28 Nov 1837; d/o John H Winder; Leonard B Nottingham sec; m 30 Nov 1837 by L Dix.

NOTTINGHAM William T to Miss Margaret S Williams 19 Nov 1844; d/o Ann J Williams con; Robert J Nottingham sec; David A Dunton & Jas B Dalby wits; m 20 Nov 1844 by P Williams. see BRec V1:3.

NOTTINGHAM William T to Lucy Ann Carpenter 31 Aug 1852; d/o Sam'l G Carpenter dec'd; James M Brickhouse as to Lucy's age; m 1 Sep 1852 by P Warren.

NUTALL Chas to Ansley Mathews 18 Sep 1804; Major Pettit sec.

NUTHALL John to Jane Johnson 12 Sep 1660. BK IX:92.

NUTTS Edmund to Mary Bibbins 18 Jun 1800; Nanny Bibbins con; Southy Collins sec; m 1800 by J Elliott.

O

OAGE Robert to Esther Turner 28 Nov 1788; d/o John Furbush Turner; John Tompkins sec.

OAST William to Margaret Campbell 13 Apr 1829; Margaret wrd/o William J Campbell sec; m 14 Apr 1829 by G Wescoat.

O'DEAR, ODEAR.

ODEAR George to Miss Elizabeth Smith 8 Sep 1834; d/o George Smith dec'd; Thomas Griffith sec & as to Elizabeth's age; m 16 Sep 1834 by P Williams.

O'DEAR George to Lilly Griffith 1 Sep 1838; d/o Moses Griffith con; Robert F Williams sec; Nathan Griffith & Victor A Nottingham wits; m 6 Sep 1838 by P Williams.

ODEAR John to Esther Phaben 2 Jul 1788; Wm Phaben sec; m (1788) by E Baker.

O'DEAR John to Patsey Whaley 1 Jan 1810; Robert Fitchett sec; m (1810) by J Elliott.

O'DEAR Joseph to Molly Nagle 24 Dec 1799; John K Floyd sec; m (1799) by I Bratten.

ODEAR Stephen to Susan Parsons 9 Apr 1832; Susan wrd/o Wm Whitehead sec; Matthew D Moor as to Stephen's age; m 9 Apr 1832 by P Williams.

O'DEAR William to Susey Williams 9 Jan 1804; Nathaniel Benthall sec; m bet 1 Jan - 13 Feb 1804 by J Elliott.

OLDHAM Leroy to Jenney Wheelor 1 Oct 1806; Wm Andrews sec; m (1806) by J Elliott. see BRec V6:82.

OLDHAM Montcalm to Maria A Harmanson 3 Dec 1835; Montcalm wrd/o John Ker sec; Maria wrd/o Wm W West sec; m 9 Dec 1835 by J Lewis.

OLIVER Joseph to Elizabeth Watson 23 Aug 1806; Branson C Dalby sec.

ONLY John Wesley to Ailsey Guy 10 Nov 1851; d/o Mary Guy con FN; E J Fisher & W M Dunton wits; m 13 Nov 1851 by M Oldham.

ONLY William to Catharine Benson 1 Dec 1803; Wm Parramore sec; m (1803) by I Bratten.

OSBURN Nehemiah to Polly Willis 6 Apr 1821; George Hitchens sec; m 24 May 1821 by L Dix.

OUTTEN, OUTEN.

OUTTEN George F to Ann S Williams 27 Mar 1827; Leon'd B Nottingham sec; m 27 Mar 1827 by L Dix.

OUTTEN Isaac to Sally Wingate 1 Jan 1844; s/o Jacob Outten sec;

d/o Wm Wingate dec'd; Abram Moore as to Sally's age; Benja Nottingham sec; m 3 Jan 1844 by P Williams.

OUTEN Jacob to Susan Saunders 14 Jul 1817; Michael Savage sec; m 14 Jul 1817 by C Bonewell.

OUTTEN James to Mary L Outten 22 Mar 1831; s/o John & Sallie Outten; d/o Abraham & Sophia Outten. see BRec V9:93.

OUTTEN John to Susan Mears 30 Dec 1833; d/o Susan Mears con; Thomas Smith Jr sec; John Roberts wit & as to John's age.

OUTTEN Timothy to Betsey Moore 13 Feb 1796; Joseph O'dear sec.

OUTTEN Timothy to Kesiah Mathews 23 Jun 1810; James Williams sec; m (1810) by J Elliott.

OWEN Thomas to Elishe Wilson 21 Jul 1744; Thomas of Somerset Co, MD; wid; Rich'd Nottingham sec.

P

PAINE Daniel to Peggy Pool 13 Feb 1815; Charles Pool sec; m (1815) by J Elliott.

PARKER Clement to Elizabeth Core 25 Oct 1798; Rich'd Nottingham sec; m 1798 by J Elliot.

PARKER George to Amie Major 18 Dec 1721; Wm Major sec; Isaac Dix wit.

PARKER George to Adah Bagwell 8 Mar 1756; s/o George & Sarah Parker; d/o Thos & Elizabeth Bagwell. see BRec V5:168.

PARKER George to Margaret Eyre 12 Oct 1786; George of Acc Co; d/o Severn Eyre Esq dec'd & wrd/o Littleton Eyre con; Thos Lytt Savage sec. see BRec V5:167.

PARKER George m (2) Elizabeth Stith 25 May 1802; wid/o Griffin Stith & d/o Isaac & Elizabeth Smith; Thos Lyt Savage sec. see BRec V5:167.

PARKER George to Susan Savage 19 May 1813; wid/o Wm B Savage & d/o Isaac & Elizabeth Smith. see BRec V5:167.

PARKER Jacob G to Ann Gertrude Stratton 29 Jan 1811; d/o John Stratton; John B Taylor sec; m 5 Feb 1811 by Thos Davis. see BRec V10:81.

PARKER James to Nancy Vermillon 29 Nov 1806; Laban Godwin sec; m (1806) by J Elliott.

PARKER John Andrews to Harriet B Darby 29 May 1802; John of Acc Co; d/o Col John & Esther (Christian) Darby; Nathaniel Darby sec; (m 2 Jun 1802. see BRec V9:151).

PARKER John Stratton to Ann Elizabeth Floyd 16 Dec 1839; (s/o Dr Jacob G & Anne (Stratton) Parker); d/o Mrs Anne S Floyd sec; m 18 Dec 1839. HunParReg:35. see BRec V8:139.

PARKER Severn E to Maria Teackle Savage 13 Jul 1811; George Parker sec; m 17 Jul 1811 by Rev Thos Davis. see BRec V5:155; V9:12.

PARKER Thomas J m Anne M Gault 23 Dec 1817 by R Symes; batch & spinster.

PARKER Tully W to Miss Peggy T Evans 22 Jan 1840; James B Poulson & Edward R Waddey sec & as to ages; Thos E Evans wit; m 28 Jan 1840. HunParReg:35.

PARKER William A to Margaret A Parramore 2 Dec 1811; Abel P Upshur sec; (m 4 Dec 1811. see BRec V2:41).

PARKER William A to Juliet J Scarborough 23 Jul 1833. see BRec V2:41.

PARKERSON, see also PARKINSON.

PARKERSON George to Mary Tylor 4 Oct 1820; Samuel H Mathews sec; m 5 Oct 1820 by C Bonewell.

PARKERSON George to Mary Harrison 18 Jan 1825; Samuel H Matthews sec & as to Mary's age; m 18 Jan 1825 by S S Gunter.

PARKERSON George to Miss Margaret Spady 3 Feb 1852; d/o Margaret Spady con; Jno L Dalby wit; Jno Moore as to George's age; m 5 Feb 1852 by H Dalby.

PARKERSON James to Elizabeth Holland 1 Aug 1787; wid/o John Holland; James Hawkins sec.

PARKERSON Joseph to Lydia Smith 13 Dec 1754; wid; Thos Dolby sec; Isaac Dolby wit.

PARKERSON Levin to Hannah Brown 26 Dec 1834; d/o Nathaniel Brown dec'd; George Charnock sec & as to Levin's age; Elijah Brittingham as to Hannah's age; Smith L Nottingham wit; m 28 Dec 1834 by G Wescoat.

PARKERSON William to Peggy Fletcher 21 May 1804; Robert Peak sec.

PARKHURST William C to Mary E Jarvis 4 Jan 1834; d/o William B Jarvis dec'd & Margaret his wife con; John Kendall sec; Thos F Spady wit; m 16 Jan 1834 by P Williams.

PARKINSON George to Mary Jacob 19 Aug 1806; John Wescoat Jr sec.

PARKINSON Jas to Nancy Johnson 5 Feb 1815; Levin Beach sec; m (1815) by C Bonewell.

PARKINSON Wm to Peggy Dowty 13 Dec 1813; Thos Henderson sec; m (1813) by J Elliott.

PARKINSON William to Betsey Stott 23 May 1817; Arthur Cobb sec; m 24 May 1817 by C Bonewell.

PARRAMORE Thomas to Esther Burton 22 Dec 1787; d/o John Burton dec'd; John Guy sec.

PARRAMORE Thomas Jr to Mary Darby 22 Apr 1797; Nath'l Darby sec; m Apr 1797 by C Simkins.

PARRAMORE William to Sarah Seymour 22 Oct 1763; William of Acc Co & s/o Thomas Parramore Gent also of Acc Co; d/o Digby Seymour Gent dec'd; Michael Christian sec.

PARROTT George to Adah Lewis 3 Apr 1804; Michael Dunton sec; m (1804) by J Elliott.

PARSONS Archibald to Margaret Floyd 24 Jul 1838; wid/o Wm Floyd of Major; Wm Miles sec; m 26 Jul 1838 by P Williams.

PARSONS Carvey to Rosey Collins 23 Dec 1824; s/o John Parsons who states Carvey b 27 Jun 1804; Jno Spady Jr wit; Wm Parsons sec & as to Rosey's age.

PARSONS Capt Francis W to Rosy Ann Elliott 17 Oct 1843; d/o Mrs Rachel Elliott con; Elias Roberts sec & as to Francis' age; m 17 Oct 1843 by P Williams.

PARSONS John to Susanna Costin 27 Sep 1803; John of Acc Co; Francis Costin sec; m (1803) by J Elliott.

PARSONS John to Sally Warren 7 Nov 1836; d/o Joseph Warren sec; George Somers as to John's age; John Simkins wit; m 1 Dec 1836 by P Williams.

PARSONS Marrot to Elizabeth Homes 4 Oct 1803; Wm Parsons gdn/o Elizabeth con; Geo Smith sec; m (1803) by J Elliott.

PARSONS Thomas to Anne Wise 26 May 1772; s/o Sarah Parsons con; d/o Col John Wise dec'd & Isaac Avery gdn/o Anne con; Wm Kendall sec.

PARSONS Thomas to Nancy Hyslop 11 May 1805; Custis Hyslop sec; m (1805) by J Elliott.

PARSONS William Jr to Sarah Cable 13 Feb 1749; William of Eliz City Co; d/o Margaret Cable con; Thos Preeson sec; Jno Tompkins & Jane Holbrook & Geo Holden wits.

PARSONS William to Mary Costin 11 Mar 1783; d/o Francis Costin con; Laban O'dear sec.

PARSONS William to Susan Elliott 8 Nov 1830; d/o Jeremiah Elliott sec; Thos Roberts Jr as to Wm's age; m 10 Nov 1830 by P Williams.

PAULIN (PAULING) Joseph W to Elizabeth Rush 30 Oct 1851; wid/o Thomas Rush; (m 30 Oct 1851 by J Rawson. HunParReg:35).

PEAK Robert to Elishe Smith 8 Mar

1800; David Harlow sec.

PEAK Robert to Seymour Dowty 18 Nov 1800; Thomas Dunton sec; m Nov 1800 by C Simkins.

PEAK Robert to Molly Campbell 10 Dec 1805; David Harlow sec; m (1805) by J Elliott.

PEAK Robert to Sukey Jarvis Flood 25 Jul 1807; Rich'd Young sec; m (1807) by J Elliott (MinRet shows Sukey Jarvis "Floyd").

PEAK Thomas to Sally McCrady 10 Mar 1797; Rich'd Nottingham sec; m (1797) by E Baker.

PEARSON, See also PIERSON.

PEARSON Joseph J to Letitia M Jones 1 Jan 1850; wid/o John Jones; Joseph B Brittingham sec; Wm T Pearson as to Joseph J's age; m 2 Jan 1850 by P Warren.

PEARSON Patrick to Polly A Craik 11 Jun 1821; Thomas E Addison gdn/o Polly sec & con; Chas Satchell & Wm Savage & Wm Watson wits; m 12 Jun 1821 by C Bonewell.

PEARSON Patrick to Elizabeth Dennis 9 Aug 1824; Thomas E Addison gdn/o Elizabeth sec; m 9 Aug 1824 by C Bonewell.

PEARSON Thomas to Nancy Megriger (McGregor) 18 Jan 1814; d/o Sally Megriger con; Major Pettit sec.

PEARSON Thomas to Sally Belote 27 Dec 1838; d/o Kendall Belote dec'd; Wm H Floyd sec & as to ages; Joseph Widgen wit; (m 28 Dec 1838. HunParReg:35).

PEARSON Thomas J to Miss Emeline Pearson 18 Jan 1848; d/o Patrick Pearson dec'd & Eliz his wife con; John Belote sec & as to Thomas' age; J P Wescoat & Nath'l J Bradford wits; m 18 Jan 1848 by P Warren.

PECK Noble to Nancy Warren 24 Jun 1852; wid/o John P Warren.

PEED Thomas to Susan Trower 28 Jun 1821; wid/o (Wm Trower); Silas Jefferson sec; m 28 Jun 1821 by L Dix.

PEED William J F to Miss Virginia T Costin 21 Dec 1841; Wm Costin gdn/o Wm J F con; Virginia wrd/o James H Costin sec; John H Spady sec; Robert Trower wit; m 23 Dec 1841 by G C Wescoat.

PETERKIN James to Anne Holt 20 Jan 1758; wid; John Harmanson sec.

PETTIT, PETTITT.

PETTIT Bartholomew to Leah Pitts wid/o John; d/o Leah Milby; 4 Feb 1765; Bartholomew of Norfolk Co; Wm Pettit sec. CR PK 67 Sep 1768 "J Pitts vs B Pitts;" see also xxxiii-R: 499.

PETTIT Jacob to Nancy Pettit 15 Dec 1810; Abel Harrison sec; m (1810) by C Bonnewell.

PETTITT John Jr to Adah Pettitt 11 Jan 1780; d/o John Pettitt Sr; Levin Mathews sec.

PETTIT Laban to Joanna Wilkins 29 Jul 1768; Walter Hyslop sec.

øPETTIT Major to Susanna Bradford 17 Sep 1795; Esau Smith sec; m Sep 1795 by C Simkins.

PETTITT Stewart B to Mary Griffith 19 Aug 1829; Wm Martin sec & as to Mary's age.

PETTIT Stuart to Peggy Dustin 9 Oct 1787; Isaac Bell sec.

PETTIT Thomas to Ann Custis 24 Sep 1767; d/o Robinson Custis dec'd; Henry Bryan sec.

PETTIT Thomas to Polly Stakes 23 Oct 1797; Solomon Richardson sec; m Oct 1797 by C Simkins.

PETTIT William Jr to Mary Custis 17 Jun 1754; wid/o (Robinson Custis*); Wm Westerhouse sec; Littleton Savage wit. *North Co OB24:130, 201, 360.

PETTITT William Major to Sarah Frances Cooper Tankard 15* Nov 1823; d/o John, Sarah b 1 May 1806; Wm P Johnson sec & as to Wm's age; George L E Tankard & Susan C Pettitt wit; m 10* Nov 1823 by S S Gunter. *discrepancy

PHABON Paul to Mary Wilson 31 May 1779; wid; Littleton Wilson sec.

PHILIPS Zorobabel to Miss Margaret Nottingham 26 Dec 1848; d/o Benja Nottingham con sec; Geo W Brittingham as to Zorobabel's age; L H Read wit.

PIERSON, See also PEARSON.

PIERSON George to Sally Dolby 6 Apr 1797; John James sec; m (1797) by I Bratten.

PIGOT John to Peggy Nottingham 7 Sep 1787; Abel Nottingham sec.

PIGOT Capt Ralph to Mary Bullock 21 Oct 1724; Ralph of Portsmouth Co; spinster; Godfrey Pole & Abraham Bowker both of Portsmouth Co secs.

PITTS George to Elizabeth Dewey 14 Jul 1783; d/o Nancy Dewey who states Elizabeth's age as 22y; Maddox Fisher sec.

PITTS Jacob to Rachel Kelly 27 Dec 1742; Rob't Kerby sec; Esther Preeson & Elisabeth Cable wits.

PITTS John to Nancy Major 10 Dec 1798; (wid/o John Major); Maxamilian Hopkins sec; m 1798 by J Elliot.

PITTS John to Peggy Stevens FN 11 Jan 1838; Geo Simkins as to ages; Smith S Nottingham sec; m 12 Jan 1838 by G Wescoat.

PITTS Purnal to Elizabeth Gilden 13 Sep 1791; d/o Charles Gilden dec'd; Wm Stith sec; m Sep 1791 by C Simkins.

POOL Anderson to Catharine Drighouse 23 Jun 1800; Jacob Holland sec (FN); m Jun 1800 by C Simkins.

POOL Charles Leven to Anne Driggus 1 Jan 1820; Cudjo Stephens sec (FN); m 4 Jan 1820 by C Bonewell.

POOL George to Comfort Weeks 10 May 1793; Abraham Lang sec (FN); m (1793) by E Baker.

POOL George to Patience Stephens 27 Sep 1819; Daniel Pool sec; m 29 Sep 1819 by C Bonewell.

POOL Isaac to Sophia Morris 17 Dec 1811; John Upshur sec.

POOL Littleton to Sinah Clayton 27 Apr 1818; Abel Stokeley sec; m 30 Apr 1818 by C Bonewell.

POOL Marshall to Margaret Weeks 27 Dec 1817; d/o James Weeks con; John Weeks sec; Rich'd Young wit; m 27 Dec 1817 by C Bonewell.

POOL Seth m Nancy Cutlar Jan 1794 by C Simkins.

POOL Solomon to Nancy Anthony 10 Dec 1827; s/o George Pool sec (FN); d/o Abel Anthony sec (FN); m 1827 by G C Wescoat.

POOL William to Rosey Baker 24 Jul 1827; s/o Charles Pool sec; d/o Thomas Baker sec.

POTTER Edmund to Mary Floyd 30 May 1752; Edmund of Acc Co; spinster; John Floyd sec; Watkins Joyne wit.

POULSON George to Rachel Church FN 17 Jan 1853; Joseph Pool as to ages; m 19 Jan 1853 by M Oldham.

POULSON James to Elizabeth Guy 8 Mar 1798; Robert James sec; m (1798) by C Simkins.

POULSON James B to Elizabeth P Williams 20 May 1829; d/o Margaret Williams sec; m 28 May 1829 by P Williams.

POULSON John to Elizabeth Cutler 20 Nov 1810; John of Acc Co & br/o Erastus Poulson his choice as gdn on 29 Sep 1807 con; Jno Young gdn/o Elizabeth by choice on 29 Jan 1810 con; John & Elizabeth gdn papers in Acc Co; Henry Scarborough sec.

POULSON Samuel to Jenny Bradford 23 Oct 1814; John T Elliott sec; m (1814) by I Bratten.

POWELL Abel to Margaret Savage 2 Nov 1812; Littleton Savage sec.

POWELL George to Molly Nottingham 22 Jun 1776; d/o Jacob Nottingham; Rich'd Nottingham sec.

POWELL George to Mary P Nottingham 29 Dec 1818; Abram Costin sec; m 6 Jan 1819 by W Costin.

POWELL James to Sukey Fitchett 24 Feb 1800; Robert Rogers sec;

m 1800 by J Elliott.
POWELL James to Sukey Trower 9 Sep 1805; James Johnson sec; m (1805) by J Elliott.
POWEL Nathaniel to Susanna Milby 11 Aug 1772; Susanna orp/o John Milby; Wm Taylor sec.
POWELL Nathaniel to Rose Dunton 7 Oct 1784; Joseph Milhas sec.
POWELL Lyt Nichicolas to Agnes Stratton 6 Jun 1661. BK IX:114.
POWELL Robert to Betsey Collins 24 Jan 1820; James Jacob sec; m 26 Jan 1820 by C Bonewell.
POWELL Seth to Elizabeth Dowty 18 Mar 1791; John Kendall Jr sec; m 18 Mar 1791 by C Simkins.
POWELL Seth to Elizabeth Powell 15 Oct 1810; Geo Powell sec; m (1810) by J Elliott.
POWELL Thomas to Elizabeth Costin 18 Feb 1832; d/o Abram Costin dec'd & wrd/o Jesse J Simkins sec; m 22 Feb 1832 by P Williams.
POYNTER Thomas to Frances Innis 9 Apr 1661. BK IX:114.
PRATT James to Margaret Bull 13 Feb 1826; Margaret wrd/o Joshua K Roberts sec; Wm Pratt as to James' age; Thos R Joynes wit; m 13 Feb 1826 by L Dix.
PRATT John to Nancy Williams 7 May 1796; Moses Griffith sec; m (1796) by E Baker.
PRATT John to Miss Sarah Hanaford 14 Sep 1824; niece/o Patsey Fitchett as to age; Joshua Fitchett wit; Christopher Fitchett sec; m Sep 1824 by L Dix.
PRATT Scarborough to Sally Johnson 25 Mar 1799; Wm Rippen sec; m Mar 1799 by C Simkins.
PRATT William to Anne Rippin 9 Mar 1779; d/o Wm Rippin sec.
PRATT Zorobabel to Elishe Widgeon 6 Jan 1814; Nath'l Widgeon sec; m bet 1 Jan - 14 Feb (1814) by J Elliott.
PREESON Thomas to Esther Cable 12 Mar 1738; (s/o Zerubabel*); d/o Thomas Cable con; Geo Kendall sec. *North Co Land Causes:49.
PRENTIS Joseph to Margaretta Bowdoin 11 Dec 1778; d/o John Bowdoin dec'd & wife Grace con; Sam'l Smith McCroskey sec.
PRESS Edmund to Nancy Collins 14 Feb 1832; d/o Peggy Collins of Old Town FN; Sam'l Bevans Sr gdn/o Edmund sec; Wm Francis sec; Levin Winder as to Nancy's age.
PRESS George to Mary Baker 15 Nov 1831; wid/o Thomas Baker; John Bevans sec & as to George's age (FN).
PRESS Littleton to Molly Fisherman 14* Dec 1790; Reubin Reed sec (FN); m 11* Dec 1790 by C Simkins. *discrepancy
PRICE Alfred G to Miss Esther M Kellam 25 Dec 1850; d/o Edmund Kellam dec'd; m 25 Dec 1850 by H Dalby.
PRITCHARD John H & Caroline James 3 Sep 1832; d/o Thomas James; James Charnock sec & as to ages.
PUGH Francis to Farabee Savage 8 Sep 1722; spinster; James Forse & Thos Savage Gent secs.
PUGH Theophilus to Esther Robins 9 Feb 1738; Theophilus of Nansemond Co; d/o Col Jno Robins con; Edward Robins sec; Thos Preeson & Wm Burton wits.

R

RABYSHAW William to Grace Harmanson 19 Mar 1709/1710; wid; John Mapp sec; Jos Tollman wit.
RAFIELD, RAIFIELD, RAYFIELD, REAFIELD.
RAFIELD Charles to Susanna Jones 5 Aug 1791; d/o Issac Jones; Edmund Aimes sec; m (1791) by E Baker.
RAYFIELD Dennard to Mary S Brickhouse 4 Sep 1832; d/o Thomas S Brickhouse; Thomas Smith Jr sec & as to ages; m 8 Sep 1832 by P Williams.

RAYFIELD Harrison T to Janette H Stott 28 Apr 1820; Laban Stott sec; m 4 May 1820 by C Bonewell. see BRec V1:22.

RAYFIELD Harrison T to Margaret Ann Johnson 28 Feb 1825; Margaret wrd/o said Harrison; Spencer Bool sec; m 1825 by G C Wescoat.

RAIFIELD John to Peggy Luke 28 Sep 1801; d/o Daniel Luke; L Upshur gdn/o Peggy con; Thomas Dixon sec; m (1801) by J Elliott. See also WB 32: 180.

RAYFIELD John H to Eliza Fitchett 30 Dec 1837; d/o Susan Fitchett con; Wm J Fitchett sec & as to John's age; James Fitchett wit; m 30 Dec 1837 by G Wescoat.

RAYFIELD John H to Mary S Rayfield 17 Feb 1847; wid/o Dennard Rayfield; James Fitchet sec; m 17 Feb 1847 by P Warren Jr.

REAFILD Thos to Nancy Thomas 6 Apr 1798; Wm Thomas sec; m (1798) by I Bratten.

RAYFIELD Thomas W to Margaret Waterfield 22 Aug 1839; d/o Thomas Waterfield; Wm Savage sec & as to Margaret's age.

RAYFIELD Wesley to Miss Letta Lewis 1 Aug 1849; d/o William Lewis con; John H Rayfield sec & as to Wesley's age; Rich'd T Dunton & Wm Beach & Wm W Jacob wits; m 1 Aug 1849 by M Oldham.

RASCO, RASCOE.

RASCOE James to Joanna Stott 12 Jun 1770; d/o Jonathan Stott dec'd; Leaven Widgen sec.

RASCO William to Anne Hunt 5 Nov 1779; d/o Thomas Hunt dec'd; Samuel Johnson sec.

RASCO William to Sally Dunton 19 Nov 1799; Dickie Dunton sec; m (1799) by I Bratten.

RASIN Thomas Savage to Susanna Reynolds 16 Apr 1770; Thomas of Kent Co, MD; Nath'l Lytt Savage sec.

READ, REED, REID.

READ Calvin H to Margaret L Powell 20 Jan 1817; (wid/o Abell); Thomas Jacob sec.

READ Edmund to Nancy B Ward 9 Feb 1818; Wm M Scarborough sec; m 11 Feb 1818 by J Burton.

REED Isaac to Betty Stevens 2 Jul 1793; Ralph Collins sec (FN); m Jun 1793 by C Simkins.

READ John to Sally Parsons 25 Sep 1810; Wm Parsons sec; m (1810) by J Elliott.

READ John W to Adah S Mears 7 Jan 1845; wid/o George Mears; Walter Raleigh sec & as to John's age.

READ Littleton S to Mary W Fisher 10 Jan 1844; s/o Margaret L Read con; d/o Wm R Fisher dec'd & wrd/o Thomas B Fisher con; Leonard B Nottingham & Alex W F Miers secs; Peter B Savage & C F Anderson wits; m 10 Jan 1844 by P Warren Jr.

READ Luther H to Mary Simkins 14 Nov 1808; John Simkins sec; m 16 Nov 1808 by Rev Dr Walter Gardiner. see BRec V1:99.

READ Richard H to Miss Margaret D Jacob 10 Feb 1835; d/o Hancock Jacob dec'd; George W Brittingham sec & as to Margaret's age; Nath'l P Fitchett wit; (m 11 Feb 1835. see BRec V1:30; V2:4).

READ Richard H to Margaret S Read 12 Feb 1844; d/o Calvin H Read dec'd; Peter B Savage sec & as to Margaret's age; Jos W Widgeon wit; m 14 Feb 1844 by P Warren Jr.

READ Richard P to Sally C Henderson 29 Apr 1839; wid/o Wm Henderson; Wm Goffigon sec; (m 14 May 1839. HunParReg:35).

READ Spencer (alias Wickes) to Priscillia Custis (alias Becket) 17 Dec 1832; d/o Sarah Becket sec FN; Jas Carter as to Spencer's age; m 19 Dec 1832 by W B Snead.

READ Thomas to Mary Satchell FN

19 Apr 1851; Betty Read as to Thomas' age; m 20 Apr 1851 by P Warren.
REID Victor F to Ann Walter Smith 20 Nov 1852; d/o Cap't George Smith dec'd; Wm S Parsons as to Ann's age; m 27 Nov 1852 by P Williams.
RESPESS John to Elizabeth Kendall 30 Apr 1766; wid; John Guy sec.
RESPASS John to Susanna Luker 9 Jul 1791; Elijah Baker sec; m (1791) by E Baker.
RESPASS Mathew to Sophia Harmanson 23 Jul 1790; d/o Henry Harmanson; Nath'l Goffigon sec; m (1790) by E Baker.
RESPASS Thomas to Esther Burton d/o Eliza Harmanson 16 Dec 1746; wid; Wm Scott sec; Peter Hog wit.
REVEL John B to Rosey D Seymour 16 Sep 1816; Wm A Christian sec.
REVELL John B to Ann W Hopkins 9 Dec 1820; Wm A Christian sec.
REW Southy to Elizabeth G Smaw 24 Dec 1828; wid/o John Smaw; Luther Ball sec; m 25 Dec 1828 by P Williams.
RICHARDSON Albert G to Rebecca Bell 11 Dec 1843; Rebecca wrd/o Jacob Nottingham sec & as to Albert's age; m 13 Dec 1843 by P Warren Jr.
RICHARDSON Charles A to Nancy Costin 13 May 1844; wid/o Wm Costin; James M Savage sec & as to Charles' age; Wm J Fitchett wit; m 15 May 1844 by P Williams.
RICHARDSON Edward J to Miss Margaret Evans 11 Nov 1837; Margaret wrd/o Edmund S Godwin sec; John Roberts as to Edward's age; m 13 Nov 1837 by W B Snead.
RICHARDSON Eli to Polly Currie 23 Mar 1799; Sol Richardson sec; m (1799) by I Bratten.
RICHARDSON George to Eliza J Bell 22 Jan 1828; d/o Anthony Bell sec & as to George's age.
RICHARDSON John to Kesiah Dalby 19 Feb 1802; Severn Dalby sec; m (1802) by I Bratten.
RICHARDSON John to Rosey Pratt 13 Dec 1831; d/o & wrd/o Elishe Pratt con; John Tyson sec; John Widgeon wit; Wm Richardson as to John's age.
RICHARDSON John to Sarah Ann Evans 14 Aug 1843; Sarah orp/o Wm Evans dec'd; John W Elliott sec & as to Sarah's age; m 31 Aug 1843 by P Williams.
RICHARDSON Jonathan to Fanny Johnson 5 Jan 1818; John Sturgis sec; m 8 Jan 1818 by J Burton.
RICHARDSON Levi to Susey Russel 9 Aug 1805; Moses Roberts sec; m (1805) by I Bratten.
RICHARDSON Levi to Rachel Ward 11 Jul 1814; Wm Roberts sec; m (1814) by I Bratten.
RICHARDSON Major to Sally Haggoman 9 Jan 1827; Henry B Kendall sec; John D Turpin as to ages; Henry B Kendall wit; m 9 Jan 1827 by S S Gunter.
RICHARDSON Smith B to Ann Ames 23 Jul 1835; d/o James Ames dec'd; Nath'l Ames sec & as to ages; m 23 Jul 1835 by L Dix.
RICHARDSON Solomon to Esther Roberts 2 Nov 1797; Moses Roberts sec; m (1797) by I Bratten.
RICHARDSON Thomas to Miss Sally Wyatt 25 Dec 1837; d/o Mrs. Susan Wyatt; Wm Beach sec & as to ages; m 25 Dec 1837 by G Wescoat.
RICHARDSON Wm to Peggy Dolby 24 Dec 1812; James Dolby sec.
RICHARDSON William to Elizabeth Dunton 7 Aug 1815; Allen Brown sec.
RIDING Thomas to Rose Yardly 4 Jan 1661/ 1662. BK IX:114.
RIDLEY Seldon S to Ann Rodgers 1 Feb 1819; John Widgeon sec; m 11 Mar 1819 by C Bonewell.
RIDLEY Seldon S to Susanna Belote

21 Nov 1821; d/o Laban Belote con & gives her age as 21y past Oct; Benjamin Dunton sec; Henry Gidings wit; m 22 Nov 1821 by C Bonewell.
RIDLEY William P to Esther Belote 14 Oct 1844; Esther wrd/o said William P; Thomas Smith Jr sec; Teackle J Turner as to Wm P's age; m 16 Oct 1844 by P Warren Jr.
RIDLEY William W to Sally Powell 10 Dec 1811; George Powell sec.
RIDLEY William W to Elizabeth Savage 27 Jan 1817; Preson Savage Jr sec; m 29 Jan 1817 by C Bonewell.
RILEY George to Miss Catherine Horner 24 Aug 1853; (George of Acc Co); Wm Smith as to ages; Jos W Paulin wit; m 25 Aug 1853 by P Williams.
RILEY William G to Miss Elizabeth J Leatherbury 10 Jun 1845; William of Acc Co; d/o John W Leatherbury sec; (m 11 Jun 1845 by J Ufford. HunParReg:35).
RINGGOLD Thomas L to Miss Susan P B Upshur 27 Jul 1846; d/o Judge A P Upshur dec'd; Lieut George P Upshur gdn/o Susan sec; (m 2 Aug 1846 by J Ufford. HunParReg:35).
RIPPEN, RIPPIN.
RIPPEN David to Adah Downs 13 Jun 1805; Littleton Jones sec; m (1805) by J Elliott.
RIPPEN James to Nancy Stoit 14 Dec 1829; d/o John Stoit; George N Bool sec & as to James' age; Benja Thomas as to Nancy's age; m 24 Dec 1829 by P Williams.
RIPPEN John to Betty Elliot 22 May 1756; d/o Thomas Elliot con; Robins Mapp sec.
RIPPEN Thomas to Anne Wilkins 13 Nov 1792; d/o Major Wilkins con; Wm Scott sec; m (1792) by E Baker.
RIPPEN Thomas to Susanna Willis 18 Aug 1807; Marrot Willis sec; m (1807) by J Elliott.
RIPPIN Thomas to Margaret Williams 31 Dec 1839; d/o Peter Williams Sr dec'd; John Spady Jr sec & as to ages; Thomas D Fitchett wit; m 1 Jan 1840 by W A Dix.
RIPPIN Thomas to Ursula B Brickhouse 26 Dec 1843; d/o Thomas S Brickhouse; Victor A Nottingham sec; Geo T Scott as to ages; m 26 Dec 1843 by P Williams.
RIPPON Thomas to Miss Sarah E Tyler 2 Jun 1846; d/o Benjamin Tyler sec & as to Thomas' age; Matthew D Moor wit; m 4 Jun 1846 by P Williams.
RIPPIN William to Susanna Russel 17 Mar 1790; Wm Bain sec; m (1790) by E Baker.
RIPPIN William m Peggy Wilkins 1796 by E Baker.
ROBERSON, See also ROBERTSON, ROBINSON.
ROBERSON John Lilly to Peggy Roberts 24 Aug 1802; niece/o Moses Roberts con; Thos Lewis sec; Geo Abdell wit.
ROBERTS Arthur to Margaret Bagwell 3 Nov 1724; Arthur of Acc Co; (d/o Alex) spinster; Abel Upshur of Acc Co sec.
ROBERTS Arthur to Elizabeth Major 2 Mar 1793; (wid/o John Major); John Major sec; m Mar 1793 by C Simkins.
ROBERTS Arthur to Betsey Underhill 11 May 1795; Thos Underhill Jr sec; m 1795 by J Elliot.
ROBERTS Art to Nancy Stott 16 Dec 1808*; d/o Coventon Stott con; bond dated 16 Dec 1809*; George Fisher sec. *discrepancy
ROBERTS Arthur to Lovey Clegg 8 Mar 1824; wid/o Peter Clegg; Thomas J Wescoat sec.
ROBERTS Arthur B to Miss Lavenia Andrews 5 Mar 1849; d/o Shephard Andrews con; Wm J Leatherbury sec; W W Jacob & Piner Clark & S E D Kellam wits; m 7 Mar 1849 by M Oldham.
ROBERTS Arthur E to Elizabeth S

Pearson 9 Jun 1834; Arthur wrd/o Joshua K Roberts sec; d/o Wm Pearson sec.

ROBERTS Arthur E to Miss Margaret A S Smith 18 Apr 1842; d/o John C Smith sec; m 20 Apr 1842 by P Warren.

ROBERTS Arthur T to Catherine Bell 23 Dec 1829; d/o Jesse Bell con; Thomas Smith Jr sec & as to Arthur's age.

øROBERTS Arthur T to Eliza Andrews 26 Mar 1839; Eliza wrd/o Major Dowty sec; m 29 Mar 1839 by G C Wescoat.

ROBERTS Edmund to Esther Scarborough 10 Jan 1811. see BRec V3:50.

ROBERTS Edward Powell to Elizabeth A Fitchett 1 Nov 1843; wid/o Wm P C Fitchett; John T Wilkins sec; m 1 Nov 1843 by P Williams. see BRec V1:37; V3:50.

ROBERTS Edmund to Sarah Mapp 20 Dec 1814; d/o Margaret Mapp con; Wm White Jr sec; (m 22 Dec 1814. see BRec V3:50).

ROBERTS Elias to Ann Collins 17 May 1836; d/o Mary Collins con who was wid/o Nathaniel Collins; James Hampleton sec; m 19 May 1836 by P Williams.

ROBERTS Emmanuel to Rachel Powell 12 Feb 1760; d/o Abel Powell dec'd; Laban Stott sec; Custis Kendall wit.

ROBERTS Humphrey to Anne Mifflin 3 Jan 1759; Humphrey merchant of Norfolk Co; wid; James Peterkin sec.

ROBERTS Jacob to Sarah Taylor 25 Apr 1793; Jno Nottingham sec; m (1793) by E Baker.

ROBERTS Jacob to Lucy Gale 6 Mar 1797; John Milby sec; m (1797) by I Bratten.

ROBERTS John to Rachel Harrison 24 Feb 1787; Wm Roberts sec.

ROBERTS Legustis to Eliza Collins 11 Feb 1833; d/o Mary Collins con; Douglass Trower sec & as to Legustis' age; Walter W Widgeon wit; m 20 Feb 1833 by P Williams.

ROBERTS John to Sarah A Smith 10 Nov 1823; d/o Thos Sr sec; George Brickhouse as to John's age; m Nov 1823 by L Dix.

ROBERTS Leonard W to Miss Laura M Savage 13 Jan 1851; d/o Mrs. Mahala Savage; m 16 Jan 1851 by M Oldham.

ROBERTS Luther W to Elizabeth Wilson 10 Jun 1845; d/o James B Wilson con; Jno A Simkins & Wm T Nottingham secs; Matthew D Moore as to Luther's age; Rob't Fitchett wit; m 18 Jun 1845 by P Williams.

ROBERTS Moses to Susanna Dowty 12 Oct 1784; Hezekiah Dowty sec.

ROBERTS Moses to Milly Dalby 22 Feb 1787; Major Brickhouse sec.

ROBERTS Moses to Olive Snails 12 Aug 1791; John Widgeon sec.

ROBERTS Moses to Nancy Richardson 21 Jul 1802; Levi Richardson sec.

ROBERTS Moses to Sarah Harrison 24 Nov 1825; d/o Robert H Harrison; Wm Roberts sec; James Williams wit; R H Harrison as to Sarah's age; m 1825 by G C Wescoat.

ROBERTS Obedience Jr to Peggy Dalby 30 Apr 1785; Benja Dolby sec.

ROBERTS Teackle to Frances Courser 19 Jun 1794; Major Pettit sec; m Jun 1794 by C Simkins.

ROBERTS Teackle to Peggy Hutson 7 Nov 1801; James Johnson sec; m 1801 by I Bratten.

ROBERTS Teackle to Sally Broughton 19 Nov 1825; Edw'd Joynes sec & as to Sally's age; m 20 Nov 1825 by S S Gunter.

ROBERTS Thomas to Elizabeth Willis 1 Jan 1787; Jacob Spady sec; m (1787) by E Baker.

ROBERTS Thomas to Mary Walker 29 Mar 1794; Edward Williams sec; m Mar 1794 by C Simkins.

ROBERTS Thomas to Sally Griffin

17 Aug 1807; James Travis sec; m (1807) by J Elliott.

ROBERTS Thomas Jr to Charlotte Bell 23 Mar 1833; d/o Tinney Bell; Thomas Roberts Sr sec & as to ages; P W Anderson wit; m 27 Mar 1833 by P Williams.

ROBERTS William to Elizabeth Houghton 15 Aug 1778; wid/o Jacob Houghton; Thomas Bullock sec.

ROBERTS William Jr to Abigal Carpenter 9 Jul 1795; Stewart Pettit sec; m 1795 by I Bratten.

ROBERTS William to Peggy Miller 18 Dec 1804; Johannes Wise sec; m (1804) by J Elliott.

ROBERTS William to Sukey Dunton 22 Dec 1810; James Travis sec.

ROBERTS Zorobabel to Peggy Trower 20 Dec 1806; John Trower Jr sec; m (1806) by J Elliott.

ROBERTSON, See also ROBERSON, ROBINSON.

ROBERTSON William to Mary Abdell 30 Jan 1838; Laban S Johnson sec & as to ages; m 30 Jan 1838 by G Wescoat.

ROBINS Abraham J to Sally B Mears 20 Apr 1849; d/o Thomas C Mears sec; m 22 Apr 1849 by M Oldham.

ROBINS Arthur to Zillah Braiser 6 Jan 1783; John Sturgis sec.

ROBINS Arthur to Beckah Abdell 16 Oct 1800; d/o Jacob Abdell dec'd & con Jehugh Johnson her gdn; David Topping sec; Rosey Johnson & Nancy Hamilton wits; m 1800 by J Elliott.

ROBINS Arthur to Julia Ashby 12 Jun 1820; Wm Mears of Wm sec. see BRec V9:2.

ROBINS Edward T to Anne S Jacob 2 Jun 1829; d/o Robert Jacob dec'd; Wm W Wilkins sec.

ROBINS George M to Margaret Jane Bell 12 Nov 1838; d/o Mrs Tabitha Bell con; Hugh G Smith sec & as to George's age; Wm H Bell & George W Robins wits.

ROBINS George W to Miss Mary Susan Bell 1 Aug 1838; d/o Mrs Tabitha Bell con; Samuel G Carpenter sec; Wm H Bell wit; m 4 Aug 1838 by G C Wescoat.

ROBINS Isaac Dunton to Elizabeth F Smith 29 Sep 1808; s/o Thos & Lettice Robins; d/o Jno & Mary Smith. see BRec V4:1.

ROBINS Isaac Dunton to Miss Eliza E Ward 29 Apr 1853; s/o Isaac D & Bettie; d/o Albert D & Letitia R; Jno E Robbins as to ages (Mrs?) E Widgeon wit; (m 1 May 1853 at an Episcopal church in Belle Haven, VA. see BRec V4:3).

ROBINS James T to Sarah M Ketcham 12 May 1842; d/o Oliver Ketcham con; Kendall Addison sec & as to James' age; m 13 May 1842 by G C Wescoat.

ROBINS John Jr to Sarah Harmanson 8 Oct 1729; d/o Susanna Harmanson con; John Harmanson sec; Susanna Godwin wit.

ROBINS John Jr to Susanna Godwin 17 Jun 1734; d/o Susanna Godwin Powel (wid/o Devorax Godwin & w/o Jno Powel) con; Thos Cable sec; Isabell Harmonson & Levin Robinson wits.

ROBINS John to Sarah Harmanson 13 Mar 1749; spinster; Edward Robins sec; Katharine Robins con as to John; Margaret Robins wit.

ROBINS John to Jane Core 10 Dec 1810; s/o Thos Robins con for underage John; John Core sec; m 20 Dec 1810 by Thos A Elliott.

ROBINS John to Margaret Tignor 24 Mar 1824; Edw'd W Addison as to Margaret's age; Isaac Andrews sec; m 24 Mar 1824 by S S Gunter.

ROBINS John to Betsy Teagner (Tigner) 11 Mar 1839; John Stockley sec & as to Betsy's age.

ROBINS John A to Sally Giddens 27 May 1841; wid/o Henry Giddens; Devorax Warren sec; Geo F Wilkins as to John's age; Smith Belote wit; m 28 May 1841 by G

C Wescoat.
ROBINS John Edward to Margaret Abdell 31 Dec 1835; Margaret wrd/o Edmund W P Downing con; John S Robins sec & as to John's age; Geo Bigelow & L S Johnson wits; m 31 Dec 1835 by G Wescoat.
ROBINS Joshua to Sarah Green 12 Jul 1768; d/o Wm Green sec.
ROBINS Louis S to Miss Sarah Ann Roberts 3 Oct 1849; d/o Frank Roberts; William Beach sec & as to ages; Louis C H Finney wit; m 3 Oct 1849 by P Warren.
ROBINS Teackle to Elizabeth Stott 29 Apr 1772; d/o Wm Stott dec'd; Francis Andrew con for his "dau-in-law"; Wm Wainhouse Michael sec; Wm Downing wit.
ROBINS Temple N to Maria Smith 10 May 1819; Isaac Smith sec; m 13 May 1819 by C Bonewell.
ROBINS Thomas to Rachel Graves 22 Aug 1805; Johannes Wise sec.
ROBINS William to Sally Burris 10 Oct 1814; Wm Dixon Jr & Thos S Brickhouse secs & as to Sally's age.
ROBINSON, See also ROBERSON.
ROBINSON George L W to Polly Bell 1 Apr 1839; d/o Edmund Bell; Smith Bell sec & as to ages; m 1 Apr 1839 by J Walker.
ROBINSON George L W to Miss Margaret Bell 10 Apr 1841; d/o Edmund Bell dec'd; John H Powell sec & as to Margaret's age; Joshua P Wescoat wit; m 12 Apr 1841 by G C Wescoat.
ROE William to Miss Rosey Tatem 30 Dec 1845; d/o James Tatem dec'd; William Dennis sec & as to ages; m 31 Dec 1845 by P Warren Jr.
RODGERS, ROGERS.
ROGERS James W to Miss Maria Scott 29 Jan 1845; d/o Hillery Scott dec'd; James Douty sec & as to ages; m 29 Jan 1845 by G C Wescoat.
ROGERS John to Mary Hewes 5 Jan 1661/ 1662. BK IX:114.

ROGERS John to Ann Bell 9 Mar 1807; Kendall Richardson sec; m (1807) by I Bratten.
RODGERS John W to Mary M Thomas 2 Feb 1820; Anthony Bell sec.
ROGERS Major to Margaret Roberts 8 May 1753; spinster; Watkins Joyne sec; Tilney Michael & Mathew Benthall wits; Arthur Roberts con for Marg't; Joseph Laurence & Rachel Watson wits.
ROGERS Michael E to Elizabeth Isabella Carpenter 15 Oct 1841; d/o John Carpenter Sr dec'd; Robert N Rogers sec & as to ages; m 16 Oct 1841 by G C Wescoat.
ROGERS Nathaniel to Mary Johnson 12 Aug 1755; d/o Moses Johnson sec; Amos Johnson wit.
ROGERS Nathaniel to Ann Ritter Savage 22 Oct 1807; Nathaniel Savage sec; m (1807) by I Bratten.
RODGERS Richard to Sarah Kendall 5 Jan 1808; Richard of Acc Co; John Brickhouse sec; John Boisnard con as to Richard; Michael Dixon wit.
ROGERS Richard to Esther Floyd 11 Oct 1813; Esther wrd/o John Joynes sec con; Thos N Wedgeon wit.
RODGERS Robert to Susanna Walter 1 Dec 1785; Walter Hyslop sec.
RODGERS Robert to Anne Ash 6 Jan 1786; Robert of Acc Co; Wm Waterfield sec.
RONALD William to Elizabeth Kendall 10 Oct 1769; d/o George Kendall dec'd & John Respess gdn con; John Kendall sec. (MB 27:317).
ROOKS, ROOKES.
ROOKS Arthur to Ann Williams 8 Jan 1827; Ann wrd/o said Arthur; John Rooks sec & as to Arthur's age; m 1827 by G C Wescoat.
ROOKES John to Harriot Bull (min rec states Harriet Davis) 14 Apr

1817; Samuel S West sec; m 16 Apr 1817 by C Bonewell.
ROOKS Oliver to Miss Elizabeth Ann Nottingham 28 Dec 1846; d/o Joseph D Nottingham sec; Joshua Nottingham as to Oliver's age; m 29 Dec 1846 by H Dalby.
ROOKS Patrick to Sally Wheeler 1 Jan 1820; John Warren sec; m 6 Jan 1820 by C Bonewell.
ROOKS William to Bridget Dolby 8 Jan 1788; John Dolby sec.
ROOKS William Sr to Sally Godwin 17 Nov 1823; wid/o Deveraux; Johannis Johnson sec; m Nov 1823 by L Dix.
ROOKS William D to Miss Mary A Welche 18 Oct 1847; d/o Wm Welche con; John W Leatherbury sec; Rickards Dunton wit; m 19 Oct 1847 by H Dolby.
ROSE Isaac to Rosey Rose 15 Apr 1793; wid; Wm Stith sec; m Apr 1793 by C Simkins.
ROSE Isaac to Polly Joynes 13 Jul 1795; Geo Fisher sec; m 1795 by J Elliot.
ROSE Jacob to Rosanna Addison 14 Feb 1792; wid/o Littleton Addison; Sam'l Cox sec.
ROSE John to Polly Turner 11 Dec 1787; wid/o Edward Turner; Isaac Smith sec.
ROSE Samuel to Adah Pettit 22 Jan 1795; Andrew Stewart sec; m Jan 1795 by C Simkins.
ROSS David to Susanna Andrews 2 Mar 1808; Jesse Ross sec.
ROSS David to Nancy White 10 Feb 1817; George D White sec; m 19 Feb 1817 by C Bonewell.
ROSS Jesse to Miss Betsey Henderson 30 Dec 1852; d/o John T Henderson con; G A Brickhouse as to Jesse's age; Jno R Dunton & Edw'd V Addison & J J Martyne wits; m 30 Dec 1852 by M Oldham.
ROSS John to Nancy Hutson 8 Feb 1802; George Turner sec.
ROSS John Jr to Sally Roberts 9 Feb 1824; s/o John Ross Sr sec; Alexander W Ward gdn/o Sally sec; m 10 Feb 1824 by S S Gunter.
RUE See REW.
RUSH Thomas J to Elizabeth W Kellam 1 Sep 1842; d/o Edmond Kellam sec; A Gray (?) wit; m 1 Sep 1842 by P Warren.
RUSSEL Ignatius to Joanna Roberts 4 Mar 1784; Wm Roberts sec.
RUSSEL Ignatius to Susanna Odear 19 Jun 1787; Edward Williams sec.
RUSSEL John to Mary Annis 1 Jul 1814; George Eshon sec; m 3 Jul 1814 by Thos Davis.
RUSSELL Thomas to Delia Ball 5 Nov 1832; Wm James sec & as to Delia's age; m 8 Nov 1832 by W B Snead.

S

SALTS John to Clara Knight 27 Dec 1797; John Knight sec; m (1797) by E Baker.
SALT William to Peggy Luke 3 Jun 1765; d/o Daniel Luke dec'd; Joseph Dalby sec.
SALUSBURY William to Elizabeth Costin 4 Feb 1796; Abraham Costin sec; m (1796) by E Baker.
SAMPLE Billy to Christiana Weeks 26 Nov 1817; Frank Sample sec (FN); m (1817) by I Bratten.
SAMPLE Edmund to Nancy Beavans (FN) 14 Jan 1812; Abraham Lang sec; m (1812) by J Elliott.
SAMPLE John to Kesiah Beavans 13 Feb 1810; Isaiah Carter sec (FN); m (1810) by J Elliott.
SAMPLE John to Sally Drighouse alias Morris (FN) 5 Mar 1822; d/o Dilly Drighouse as to her age; Harold L Wilson sec; m 6 Mar 1822 by C Bonewell.
SAMPLE Littleton to Sukey Drighouse 22 Jun 1824; d/o Dilly Drighouse who states that Sukey is 21y (FN); Arthur Evans sec.
SAMPSON John to Anne Holt 28 Oct 1758; wid; Savage Cowdree sec; Elizabeth Stith wit.
SAMPSON Stephen to Anne Holt 7

Mar 1761; d/o George Holt dec'd; John Sampson sec; Mary Stith wit.

SAMPSON Stephen to Anne Pettitt 9 Jun 1779; wid/o Thomas Pettitt; John Mapp sec.

SANDERS See SAUNDERS.

SANFORD James to Sarah Bell 27 Nov 1797; Teackle Turner sec; m (1797) by J Elliot.

SANFORD James H to Sally Dalby 13 Jan 1825; d/o Henry Dalby con & states Sally "is arrived at age 21"; Robert Sanford sec & as to James' age; John Sanford & George Christian wits; m 1825 by G C Wescoat.

SANFORD Robert to Rachel Dalby 22 Nov 1814; Wm White Jr sec & as to Rachel's age; m (1814) by I Bratten.

SATCHELL Charles to Margaret Green 4 Feb 1778; Wm Harrison sec.

SATCHELL John to Elizabeth Green 13 Jan 1787; Wm Harrison sec.

SATCHELL John to Sally Barrett 17 May 1821; wid/o Wm Barrett; Warren H Pool sec; m 17 May 1821 by C Bonewell.

SATCHELL Peter to Mary Jane Satchell FN 24 May 1852; May Satchell as to ages; m 27 May 1852 by H Dalby.

SATCHELL Thomas Stokeley to Mary Satchell 22 Dec 1813; John R Waddey sec; m 1813 by Thos Davis.

SATCHELL William to Elizabeth Stringer 30 May 1796; (d/o John Stringer Sr); John Macgawan sec.

SAUNDERS James to Maria Nottingham 24 Jul 1820; Thomas Downs gdn/o Maria con; Thomas S Satchell sec; Jno N Scott & Wm Nelson wits; (m 27 Jul 1820. see BRec V1:111).

SAUNDERS John to Elizabeth Campbell 9 Mar 1786; John Welch sec.

SAUNDERS John to Kesiah Abdeel 12 Jul 1788; wid; Wm Rooks sec; m (1788) by E Baker.

SAUNDERS John to Mary Scott 24 Dec 1793; Michael Dixon sec; m Dec 1793 by C Simkins.

SAUNDERS John to Grace Wilson 14 Jan 1822; John & Grace both wrds/o Thomas Milbourn sec; m 17 Jan 1822 by C Bonewell.

SAUNDERS Macneal m Esther O'dear bet late 1797 - 12 Feb 1798 by J Elliott.

SAUNDERS Robert to Sarah Bowdoin 11 Feb 1795; John Eyre sec.

SAUNDERS Samuel to Molly Hampleton 24 Dec 1833; wid/o William Hampleton; Severn Wilkins sec & as to Samuel's age; m 26 Dec 1833 by L Dix.

SAUNDERS Stuart to Sally Clegg 17 Jan 1792; Hillary Clegg sec; m (1792) by E Baker.

SAVAGE Abel to Elizabeth Dunton 27 Nov 1776; Jno Lewis Fulwell sec.

SAVAGE Abel to Susannah Clegg 8 Sep 1789; wid; Thomas Bell sec; m (1789) by E Baker.

SAVAGE Albert to Emiline Trower 8 Nov 1841; d/o John Trower dec'd & wife Delitha con; Robert & John Trower wits; Obadiah Goffigon sec; Wm G Jackson as to Albert's age; m 10 Nov 1841 by P Williams.

SAVAGE Arthur to Elizabeth Smith 18 Jun 1794; d/o Caleb Smith con; Major Pettit sec; m Jun 1794 by C Simkins.

SAVAGE Arthur to Ann Dunton 8 Jun 1800; Dickie Dunton sec; m 1800 by J Elliott.

SAVAGE Arthur R to Sarah Rasco 9 Jun 1806; Obed Cary sec; m (1806) by I Bratten.

SAVAGE Arthur R to Catharine George 1 Jul 1812; niece/o Major Pettit con; Obedience White sec; m (1812) by I Bratten.

SAVAGE Caleb to Elishe Johnson 10 Dec 1784; (wid/o Obed Johnson); John Major sec.

SAVAGE Caleb to Elizabeth Jenne 2 Dec 1794; Major Pettit sec.

SAVAGE Caleb to Sally Clegg 26 Nov 1816; Rich'd Johnson sec; m 27 Nov 1816 by C Bonewell.

SAVAGE Caleb to Rosy M Johnson 23 Feb 1828; d/o John Johnson; Robt B Savage sec & as to Rosy's age; Jno N Stratton wit; m 1828 by G C Wescoat.

SAVAGE Capt Calvin H to Miss Emily Read 14 Nov 1837; Emily (orp/o Edmund Read) gdn* Wm Wyatt con; Albert G Ashby sec & as to Calvin's age; Thos Robins wit. (* Emily Read made choice in Acc Court 27 Mar 1837 of Wm Wyatt to be her gdn.).

SAVAGE Edward C to Miss Ann P Wescoat 10 Dec 1851; d/o John Wescoat dec'd; m 10 Dec 1851 by M Oldham.

SAVAGE George to Elizabeth Harmanson 11 Jan 1774; Elizabeth orp/o Kendall Harmanson; John S Harmanson sec.

SAVAGE George to Sarah Stith 19 May 1795; John Stratton sec.

SAVAGE George Jr to Nancy Booll 24 Dec 1800; Thomas Jacob sec; m 1800 by C Simkins.

SAVAGE George J to Sally T Dowty 23 May 1814; Wm White Sr sec; m (1814) by J Elliott.

SAVAGE George L to Rosey Dowty 27 May 1839; Rosey wrd/o James Dowty sec; H P Wescoat as to George's age; Leroy Oldham wit; m 29 May 1839 by W A Dix.

SAVAGE James to Elizabeth Savage 17 Jan 1832; Elizabeth wrd/o Rob't B Savage sec; m 17 Jan 1832 by G Wescoat.

SAVAGE James M to Mary Ann Underhill 8 Nov 1830; d/o James Underhill dec'd; Thos B Fisher sec & as to ages; m 9 Nov 1830 by G Wescoat.

SAVAGE James M to Miss Mary W Upshur 12 Sep 1836; d/o Wm M Upshur dec'd; Wm H Core sec & as to Mary's age; m 14 Sep 1836 by G Wescoat.

SAVAGE John to Dorothy Jordan 18 Nov 1660. BK IX:92.

SAVAGE John to Mary Godwin 14 Apr 1735; spinster; Gawton Hunt sec.

SAVAGE John to Rachel Belote 31 Jan 1763; d/o John Belote; Josiah Dowty sec.

SAVAGE John to Tabitha Belote 11 May 1764; wid/o (John Belote); Edw'd Belote sec.

SAVAGE John to Susanna James 11 Jun 1776; d/o Robert James dec'd; Solomon Bunting sec.

SAVAGE John M to Ann Smith 21 Dec 1825; Ann wrd/o Benjamin Dunton sec; m Dec 1825 by L Dix.

SAVAGE John W to Susan Ann Bull 16 Jan 1850; d/o Nancy Bull; John W F Gunter sec & as to ages; m 17 Jan 1850 by M Oldham.

SAVAGE Kiah (alias Hezekiah) to Peggy Anthony FN 10 Jan 1853; d/o Mary Anthony con; Thos B Jarvis as to Kiah's age; Kealy W Benson wit; m 12 Jan 1853 by M Oldham.

SAVAGE Littleton to Margaret Burton 14 Jan 1768; d/o Wm Burton Gent; Wm Kendall sec.

SAVAGE Littleton to Elizabeth Jacob 11 Dec 1792; George Lewis sec.

SAVAGE Michael to Betsey Mapp 7 Oct 1794; Joseph Nottingham sec.

SAVAGE Michael L to Miss Mary M Mears 22 Dec 1853; s/o Wm L Savage con; Nath'l J Bradford & Jos Pearson wits; Francis A Bunting as to Mary's age.

SAVAGE Michael R to Margaret Johnson 10 Mar 1817; Jeptha Johnson sec; m 12 Mar 1817 by C Bonewell.

SAVAGE Nathaniel to Margaret James 19 Dec 1812; Wm D James sec; m (1812) by I Bratten.

SAVAGE Peter B to Elizabeth Jane Read 21 Feb 1835; d/o Margaret L Read con; John D Upshur sec; Leah U Nottingham wit; m 4 Mar 1835 by L Dix.

SAVAGE Preson to Esther Jenney 11 Jun 1810; Hancock Dunton sec; m (1810) by J Elliott.

SAVAGE Preson Jr to Mahala Warren 1 Feb 1819; d/o Adah Warren her gdn & con; Wm W Ridley sec; Jno T Johnson wit; m 3 Feb 1819 by C Bonewell.

SAVAGE Reavel to Nancy Turner 10 Jun 1794; d/o John Furbush Turner con; John Boggs sec; m Jun 1794 by C Simkins.

SAVAGE Robert B to Rosy W Addison 16 Feb 1827; wid/o Thos E Addison; Isaac Andrews sec; m 1827 by G C Wescoat.

SAVAGE Robert B to Margaret S Matthews 16 Aug 1848; d/o Margaret Ann Joynes con who was wid/o Robert A Joynes; Obedience R Johnson sec; m 16 Aug 1848 by M Oldham. see BRec V11:8.

SAVAGE Robins M to Miss Rosey Ann Fisher 30 Jul 1849; d/o James Fisher; Geo Waterfield sec & as to Rosey's age; A C Garrett wit; m 1 Aug 1849 by M Oldham.

SAVAGE Samuel G to Elizabeth J M Mears 9 Oct 1837; Eliz wrd/o Heley D Bagwell sec; Thos A Coleburn as to Samuel's age; m 11 Oct 1837 by S T Ames.

SAVAGE Severn to Betsey Trower 23 Sep 1800; Lewis Nolen sec; m Sep 1800 by C Simkins; (m 25 Sep 1800 BRec V 12: 46.)

øSAVAGE Severn to Malana James 12 Dec 1831; Malana wrd/o John Simkins sec; m 12 Dec 1831 by G Wescoat.

SAVAGE Southy Littleton to Harriot Reynolds 25 Apr 1805; niece/o Susanna Taylor gdn con; Edward Evans sec.

SAVAGE Thomas Jr to Esther Littleton 27 Nov 1722; spinster; James Forse & Edw'd Mifflin secs; John Robins wit; lic 27 Nov 1722. CTRet Oct 1723.

SAVAGE Thomas D to Polly Wescoat 24 Dec 1832; d/o Patty Wescoat; John Roberts sec & as to ages; m 28 Dec 1832 by G Wescoat.

SAVAGE Thomas L to Louisa M Mayo 28 Jun 1831; Geo T Yerly sec; (m 29 Jun 1831. see BRec V9:12).

SAVAGE Thomas Lyttleton to Mary Burton Savage 21 May 1789; d/o Littleton Savage Esq con; Walter Hyslop sec; m by Rev Sam'l T McCroskey. see BRec V9:11.

SAVAGE Thomas Lyttleton to Margaret Teackle 7 Jan 1796; sis/o John Teackle Jr of Craddock con; James Lyon sec; m by Rev S T McCroskey. see BRec V5:155; V9:12.

SAVAGE Thomas Lyttleton to Lauretta A Winder 2 Apr 1851; s/o Thos L & Margaret (Teackle) Savage; d/o Jno H & Comfort (Gore) Winder; m by Rev D Totton. see BRec V9:13.

SAVAGE William to Peggy Savage 29 Jun 1779; Wm Satchill sec.

SAVAGE Wm to Comfort Michael 7 Nov 1797; Edmond Joynes gdn/o Comfort con; John Milby sec; m (1797) by J Elliot.

SAVAGE William to Susey Joynes 23 Dec 1806; Wm Dixon sec; m (1806) by I Bratten.

SAVAGE William to Betsey Knight 22 Jun 1817; Benj Scott sec; m 25 Jun 1817 by C Bonewell.

SAVAGE Wm Jr to Margt Nottingham 16 Jun 1821; wid/o Wm E Nottingham; Peter Wilkins sec; m 20 Jun 1821 by L Dix.

SAVAGE William to Miss Ritta Bool 27 Sep 1824; Isaac Andrews sec & as to Ritta's age; m bet 15 Jun - 22 Dec 1824 by G C Wescoat.

SAVAGE William to Margaret Henderson 8 Dec 1841; d/o John T Henderson; Wm Ridley sec & as to ages; m 10 Dec 1841 by G C Wescoat.

SAVAGE William B to Susanna Smith 12 May 1795; Wm Eyre sec; Litt Savage con for "Billy" to get license.

SAVAGE William K to Mary Savage 14 Dec 1812; Reavil Savage sec;

m (1812) by I Bratten.
SAVAGE William L to Ann Bunting 2 Jul 1833; d/o Jonathan Bunting dec'd; John S Bunting sec & as to ages; Edw'd W Nottingham wit; m 6 Jul 1833 by G Wescoat.
SAVAGE William Lyttleton to Sarah Chauncey 11 Jun 1840; d/o Elihu & Henrietta T Chauncey of Philadelphia. see BRec V5:155; V9:12.
SAVAGE William M to Miss Nancy S Addison 10 Mar 1834; Nancy wrd/o Rob't B Savage sec; James Savage as to Wm's age; Levin Richardson sec; m 14 Mar 1834 by G Wescoat.
SAVAGE William T to Elizabeth P Young 16 May 1825; d/o Thomas Young con; Isaac Andrews sec & as to Wm's age; m 1825 by G C Wescoat.
SAVAGE William T to Mary J Lewis 9 Jul 1849; d/o Wm Lewis con; Lewis M Matthew gdn/o William & Teackle W Jacob secs; Wm G Johnson wit; m 11 Jul 1849 by P Warren.
SCARBURG, SCARBOROUGH, SCARBORO.
SCARBURGH Charles to Bridgit Robins 20 Aug 1794; Carvy Dunton sec.
SCARBOROUGH Edmond to Elizabeth Parker 2 Oct 1810; Wm Clark sec; note reads, "I consent to marry Edmond Scarburg ... grant him a license" signed Elizabeth Parker (her mark); Wm G Pitts wit; m (1810) by C Bonnewell.
SCARBOROUGH Francis M to Susan B Fisher 22 Jan 1852; wid/o Sam'l P Fisher; m 22 Jan 1852 by J A Weed.
SCARBURGH John to Ann Kendall 26 Jun 1759; John of Worcester Co, MD; d/o John Kendall Gent con; Wm Wood sec.
SCARBOROUGH Capt John to Mary (Polly) Jacob 14 Jun 1784; Mary wrd/o Hezekiah Pitts con; Maddox Andrew sec.

SCARBURGH Samuel to Peggy Kendall 10 Apr 1759; Samuel of Worcester Co, MD; d/o John Kendall sec.
SCARBURGH William to Margaret Jacob 23 Apr 1776; William of Acc Co; d/o Abraham Jacob dec'd & con Isaac Clegg for his "dau-in-law"; John Wilkins of Occohannock sec.
SCHERER Dr George Nicholas Hack to Henrietta Sarah Jarvis 22 Oct 1850; d/o Wm & Marg't Jarvis. see BRec V2:82; V7:188.
SCHROEDER Henry B to Miss Elizabeth W Wilkins 7 Aug 1846; d/o William Wilkins Sr dec'd; Wm Shea as to Henry's age; Thomas Tyson sec; L Harmanson wit.
SCISCO, see SISCO.
SCOTT Rev A Francis to Miss Margaret E Holt 31 May 1852; d/o George Holt dec'd; m 31 May 1852 by P Warren.
SCOTT Benjamin to Sally Nottingham 23 Sep 1796; John Nottingham sec; m (1796) by I Bratten.
SCOTT Benjamin Jr to Elizabeth Waterfield 13 Jan 1818; Rich'd Dunton Jr sec; m 14 Jan 1818 by C Bonewell.
SCOTT Benjamin N to Mary Ann Goffigon 19 Jun 1824; James Goffigon sec; m Jun 1824 by L Dix.
SCOTT Daniel to Esther Warren 13 Feb 1788; d/o Hillery Warren; Isaac Bell sec; m (1788) by E Baker.
SCOTT Daniel to Susan Warrington 14 Feb 1834; d/o George Warrington; Edw'd Kellam (MBay) sec & as to ages; m 25 Feb 1834 by L Dix.
SCOTT George to Sarah Kemp 22 Dec 1790; Sarah wrd/o Arthur Evans sec; m (1790) by E Baker.
SCOTT George to Nancy T Kellum 15 Jul 1826; Shepherd B Floyd sec; m Jul 1826 by L Dix.
SCOTT George Thomas to Miss Virginia S Tyson 26 Jun 1839;

George wrd/o Geo F Wilkins con; d/o Wm Tyson sec; Thos L Kendall sec; Stoakley W Wilson wit; m 27 Jun 1839 by W A Dix.

SCOTT Hillary to Susan Hamby 20 Jan 1817; Sam'l S Stott sec; m (Jan 1817) by R Windsor.

SCOTT Hillary to Maria James 1 Jun 1818; Andrew James sec.

SCOTT James to Nancy Groten 20 Dec 1821; d/o Thomas Groten sec & as to age; John Evans wit; m 20 Dec 1821 by C Bonewell.

SCOTT James B to Miss Emily S Williams 2 Mar 1847; Nathl L Goffigon gdn/o James sec; John W Williams gdn/o Emily sec; m 9 Mar 1847 by P Williams.

SCOTT John to Susanna Hart (undated - in 1780-1782 bundle; S Hart: inv 1779); wid/o Stephen Hart; Abel Nottingham sec.

SCOTT John to Betsey Churn 4 Feb 1797; Wm Barecraft Jr sec; m (1797) by I Bratten.

SCOTT John to Peggy Salts 18 Aug 1801; Henry Smaw sec; m 1801 by I Bratten.

SCOTT John to Sally Chance 17 Jun 1806; John Trower sec; m (1806) by J Elliott.

SCOTT John Sr to Jenney Rogers 1 May 1810; Wm Powell sec; m (1810) by C Bonewell (MinRet states "Jane" Rogers).

SCOTT John N to Sally Powell 24 Jun 1820; Isaiah W Baker sec.

SCOTT John T to Mary Ann Nottingham 13 Apr 1835; John wrd/o Thomas Smith Jr sec; d/o Thomas Nottingham sec; (m 22 Apr 1835. see BRec V4:62).

SCOTT John T to Elizabeth Sabra Harmanson 25 May 1840; Edward P Roberts sec; m 27 May 1840 by W A Dix. see BRec V4:61.

SCOTT John T P to Virginia A J Nottingham 11 Jul 1842; Joshua B Turner gdn/o John sec; d/o Jacob Nottingham sec; m 13 Jul 1842 by G C Wescoat.

SCOTT Levin to Nancy Peaton 26 Jan 1818; Thos G Scott sec; m 29 Jan 1818 by S W Woolford.

SCOTT Levin T to Miss Sarah Spady 26 Dec 1843; d/o Wm Spady sec & as to Levin's age; Edward Holland wit; m 27 Dec 1843 by G G Exall.

SCOTT Michael to Nancy Whitehead 25 Jun 1790; Wm B Wilson sec; m (1790) by C Simkins.

SCOTT Obadiah to Elizabeth Heath 10 Sep 1838; d/o John S Heath dec'd; Edward Kellam sec & as to ages; Edm'd Roberts wit; m 13 Sep 1838 by L Dix.

SCOTT Thomas to Sarah Johnson 9 May 1772; d/o Thomas Johnson dec'd; Amos Underhill sec.

SCOTT Thomas to Nancy Kendall 8 Apr 1805; Geo Scott sec; m (1805) by J Elliott.

SCOTT Thomas to Sukey Hunt 8 Apr 1816; Walter Luker & (W?) Williams sec; m 11 Apr 1816 by C Bonewell.

SCOTT Thomas to Ann Mary Scott 26 Jun 1830; d/o John W Scott dec'd; Wm Whitehead sec & as to ages; m 30 Jun 1830 by P Williams.

SCOTT Thomas to Miss Rebecca Knight 28 Dec 1852; Jesse N Jarvis gdn/o Rebecca con; Leonard B & Leonard J Nottingham wits; m 29 Dec 1852 by H Dalby.

SCOTT Thomas W to Sally Holmes 14 Feb 1818; Silas Jefferson sec; m 14 Feb 1818 by C Bonewell.

SCOTT William Sr to Ann Davis 2 Jul 1709; wid; Wm Scott Jr & Gawton Hunt secs; Wm Kendall Jr wit.

SCOTT William Jr to Betty White 4 Apr 1764; d/o Wm White dec'd; Thomas Pettit sec.

SCOTT Wm to Betsy Hunt 20 Dec 1783; Southey Goffigon sec.

SCOTT Dr. William J to Martha E Dixon 2 Nov 1852; d/o W W Dixon con; Lucie A Dixon wit; Wm L Burras wit & as to Dr Wm J's age; m 3 Nov 1852 by P

Warren.

SCOTT William W to Nancy Scott 1 Jul 1819; Sarah Scott sec; m 1 Jul 1819 by C Bonewell.

SCOTT William W to Henny Mason 8 Oct 1832; d/o Arroda Mason ? - bond shows Martin; Levin Beach sec; Thos G Stockly as to Henny's age; m Oct 1832 by L Dix.

SCOTT Zorobabel to Mary Bell 16 Nov 1781; wid/o Thos Bell; Edmund Glanville sec.

SEATON Thomas to _____ 31 May 1787; Wm Warren sec.

SEGAR John to Sarah Fitchett 21 Jul 1828; wid/o William Fitchett; Luther H Read sec & as to John's age; Jno W Leatherbury wit; m Jul 1828 by L Dix.

SEYMOUR Digby to Rose Christian 10 Feb 1736; Neech Eyre sec; Geo Kendall wit.

SEYMOUR William D to Miss Anne U Bayly 4 Oct 1826; Richard D Bayly sec; m 10 Oct 1826 by S S Gunter.

SHEA William to Miss Ann Burnham 13 Nov 1844; Nathan R Fletcher sec & as to Ann's age; Jno S Turpin as to Wm's age; Geo G Booth wit; m 13 Nov 1844 by G G Exall.

SHEPHERD Hezekiah to Ibby Baker (FN) 28 Nov 1787; John Moore sec.

SHOWERS Wm to Nancy Langdon 29 Jun 1835; d/o Michael Langdon; Zorobabel Showers sec & Jacob Lurton as to ages; m 29 Jun 1835 by G Wescoat.

SIDELINGER Jeremiah to Miss Margaret S Wilkins 13 Apr 1852; d/o James C Wilkins; Wm B Savage as to Margt's age; m 8 Jun 1852 by M Oldham.

SIMKINS Arthur to Peggy Dolby 19 Aug 1761; John Mathews sec.

SIMKINS Arthur to Sally Jarvis 22 Apr 1801; Wm Jarvis sec; m Apr 1801 by C Simkins.

SIMKINS Coventon to Bridget Westerhouse 30 May 1781; d/o Wm Westerhouse dec'd & Henry Harmanson her gdn con; James Taylor sec.

SIMKINS Coventon to Margaret Satchell 21 Feb 1788; wid/o Charles Satchell; Wm Simkins Jr sec; m (1788) by E Baker.

SIMKINS George to Leah Stephens 29 Dec 1832; d/o Amy Stephens FN; Edw'd W Nottingham sec; James Simkins (FN) as to ages; m 30 Dec 1832 by W B Snead.

SIMKINS George to Leah Becket 25 Aug 1837; d/o Joshua Becket dec'd FN & sis/o Maria Scisco as to her age; Montcalm Oldham sec; m 26 Aug 1837 by W B Snead.

SIMKINS Jesse J to Frances D Goffigon 13 Aug 1830; d/o James Goffigon sec.

SIMKINS Dr Jesse J to Esther W Goffigon 29 Oct 1832; d/o James Goffigon con; John Segar sec; m Oct 1832 by L Dix.

SIMKINS Jesse J to Miss Laura Jarvis 13 Feb 1838; d/o Wm Jarvis Sr dec'd; Thomas R Jarvis sec & as to Laura's age; m 20 Feb 1838 by L Dix.

SIMKINS John to Sally James 27 Feb 1786; d/o Hezekiah James; Wm Simkins sec.

SIMKINS John to Anne W Powell 22 Apr 1800; Maximilian Hopkins sec; m Apr 1800 by C Simkins.

SIMKINS John to Peggy Harmanson 22 Dec 1802; Wm Bain sec; m (1802) by J Elliott.

SIMKINS John to Sarah Satchell 20 Dec 1808; Jacob G Parker sec.

SIMKINS John A to Elizabeth S Spady 1 Jan 1839; d/o Southy Spady con; Edwin Goffigon sec; m 10 Jan 1839 by P Williams.

SIMKINS John A to Margaret S Fitchett 22 Jun 1846; d/o Thos Fitchett con; Jno R Fitchett wit; Robert B Nottingham sec; m Jun 1846 by P Williams; (m 24 Jun 1846. see BRec V6:21).

SIMKINS Thomas D to Susan Brickhouse 17 Nov 1810; John Brickhouse gdn/o Susan con;

John Whitehead sec; m (1810) by J Elliott.
SIMKINS William to Anne Dunton 24 May 1769; d/o William Dunton; Elias Dunton Sr sec.
SIMKINS William to Sally Dunton 22 Sep 1783; Christopher Dixon sec.
SIMKINS William Jr to Peggy Dunton 17 Apr 1793; d/o Betty Dunton con; John Simkins sec; m Apr 1793 by C Simkins.
SIMPSON John to Elizabeth Byrd 2 Feb 1823; Litt Upshur gives Elizabeth's age as over 22y; Curtis Trehearn sec; m 2 Feb 1823 by S Wilmer.
øSIMPSON John to Fanny Waterford 18 Jan 1830; Peter Williams sec; m 21 Jan 1830 by P Williams.
SISCO, SCISCO.
SISCOE Daniel to Betsey Weeks 9 Dec 1794 (FN); Wm Roberts Jr sec; m Dec 1794 by C Simkins.
SISCO Henry to Maria Becket FN 11 Jan 1837; s/o Betty Sisco; Sally Wickes as to Maria's age; Betty Sisco & John S Parker secs; m 12 Jan 1837 by W B Snead.
SCISCO Samuel to Adah Collins FN 3 Jan 1835; George Perkins sec FN.
SMAW Daniel to Ann W Elliott 22 Dec 1820; Thomas W Scott & John Adams secs; m 27 Dec 1820 by L Dix.
SMAW George to Peggy Evans 19 Jan 1785; d/o Wm Evans dec'd; John Nelson sec.
SMAW George to Nancy Smaw 22 Jun 1795; John Nelson sec; m (1795) by E Baker.
SMAW Henry to Elizabeth Holland 17 Oct 1783; John Nelson sec.
SMAW John to Mary Griffeth 15 Jul 1786; d/o Daniel Griffeth con; Eyrs Stokley sec; m 1786 by E Baker.
SMAW John to Elizabeth O'dier 10 Dec 1823; Elizabeth b Jan 1802, d/o Mary O'dier; Thomas Knight sec; George Holt Sr & Hezekiah Dalby wits; m Dec 1823 by L Dix.
SMAW John to Elizabeth Dalby 26 Dec 1825; d/o James Dalby sec; m 28 Dec 1825 by J Henry.
SMAW John G to Miss Elmira Simkins 7 Jan 1835; d/o Thomas Simkins dec'd; Thos J Nottingham sec & as to Elmira's age; m 10 Jan 1835 by L Dix.
SMITH Caleb to Sarah Johnson 8 Jun 1779; wid; Thomas James sec.
SMITH Charles to Catherine Teackle 21 Mar 1786; Griffin Stith sec; con Litt Savage as to "Catey".
SMITH Charles to Mrs Hannah Powell 6 Nov 1802; Charles of Acc Co, s/o Chas Smith Sr con; John Simkins con for Hannah; Chas S Satchell sec.
SMITH George to Ann Ware 23 Sep 1660. BK IX:92.
SMITH George to Rebecca Sickles 14 Dec 1778; Solomon Bunting sec.
SMITH George to Esther Parsons 26 Dec 1787; Wm Parsons sec.
øSMITH George to Nancy Parsons 1 Jun 1802; Wm Parsons sec; m (1802) by J Elliott.
SMITH George to Sukey Costin 14 Apr 1806; John Griffith sec; m (1806) by J Elliott.
SMITH George to Patsy S Widgeon 24 Nov 1828; d/o Westerhouse Widgeon dec'd & Nancy his wife con; L B Nottingham sec; Nath'l & Walter W Widgeon wits; m Nov 1828 by L Dix.
SMITH Henry to Mary Ann Williams 13 Jan 1840; d/o Peter Williams; Azariah Williams as to Mary Ann's age; Walter W Widgen as to Henry's age; Edwin Goffigon sec; m 14 Jan 1840 by S T Ames.
SMITH Isaac Jr to Eliz Goffigon 24 Apr 1790; Geo Scott sec; m 8 May 1790 by C Simkins.
SMITH Isaac to Ann Teackle 6 Apr 1814; s/o Isaac & Elizabeth Smith; d/o John & Ann Teackle of Acc Co; m by Thos Davis. see BRec V2:110; V8:120.
SMITH James to Anne Anderson 15 Aug 1789; d/o Matthew Anderson con; Wm Trower sec;

Wm Parsons wit; m (1789) by E Baker.
SMITH James to Nancy Melholloms 4 Jan 1799; Joseph Hanby sec; m (1799) by I Bratten.
SMITH John to Sarah Johnson 9 Jan 1765; d/o Benja Johnson con; Francis Darby of Acc Co sec.
SMITH John to Elizabeth Johnson 8 Dec 1789; d/o Isaac Johnson; Wm Smith Jr sec; m (1789) by E Baker.
SMITH John to Nancy Stott 5 Jun 1802; James Johnson of Isaac sec; m (1802) by I Bratten.
SMITH John to Drusilla Dowty 12 Jan 1824; Drusilla wrd/o said John Smith; Thos W Badger states that John's late master, Levin Beach says that John is well above age 21y; Arthur Roberts sec; m Jan 1824 by L Dix.
SMITH John to Mrs Ann S Briggs 23 Jul 1839; con Wm Smith of George gdn/o said John; Wm S Parsons & Leonard B Nottingham secs.
SMITH John B to Miss Sarah Ann Kellam 3 Dec 1838; George F Wilkins sec; (m 6 Dec 1838. HunParReg:35).
SMITH John C to Miss Elizabeth Mears 12 Dec 1845; d/o William Mears dec'd; Wm B Upshur sec & as to Elizabeth's age; Piner W Clark wit; m 17 Dec 1845 by P Warren Jr.
SMITH Jonathan to Anne Westerhouse 21 Dec 1772; wid; John Dalby (Church Neck) sec.
SMITH Jonathan to Nancy Joynes 26 Jan 1798; Thos Costin sec; m (1798) by J Elliot.
SMITH Jonathan to Esther Savage 29 Aug 1799; Michael Dixon sec; m (1799) by I Bratten.
SMITH Joshua J to Margaret Floyd 18 Apr 1825; John Hallett sec & gdn/o Margaret; m Apr 1825 by L Dix.
SMITH Joshua J to Nicey H Stott 25 Dec 1827; d/o Laban Stott con;
Spencer Bool sec; Daniel Luke wit; m bet Feb 1826 - Mar 1828 by G C Wescoat; (m 28 Dec 1827. see BRec V1:22).
SMITH Richard to Susanna Dixson 17 Jan 1761; Benja Dixson sec.
SMITH Richard to Peggy Dixon 4 Apr 1792; d/o Tilney Dixon dec'd; Thos Dixon sec; m (1792) by E Baker.
SMITH Richard to Juliet E Heath 28 Mar 1819; Isaac Andrews sec; Wm Satchell gdn/o Juliet sec con.
SMITH Thos to Elizabeth Reynolds 21 Apr 1661. BK IX:114.
SMITH Thomas to Susanna Jacob 11 Sep 1770; d/o Esau Jacob; Jno Floyd sec.
SMITH Thomas to Susanna Johnson 9 Feb 1778; d/o Obediah Johnson; Thos Freshwater sec.
SMITH Thomas to Anne Pitts 27 Jun 1778; d/o John Pitts dec'd; Archibald Godwin sec.
SMITH Thomas to Esther Andrews 24 Dec 1790; John Smith sec; unsigned con for "my dau-in-law" to be married; Stephen Ward wit; m (1790) by E Baker.
SMITH Thomas to Lucy Respass 14 Oct 1817; Sophia Respass sec; m 15 Oct 1817 by S W Woolford.
SMITH Thomas Sr to Peggy Sturgis 14 Jan 1828; wid/o Jacob Sturgis; Edward R Turner sec; m 16 Jan 1828 by G Wescoat.
SMITH Thorowgood to Mary Blaikley Michael 28 Jun 1775; Thorowgood of Acc Co; (wid/o Jno Michael); John Lewis Fulwell sec.
SMITH William to Peggy Addison 28 Dec 1784; Wm Abdeel sec.
SMITH William to Mary Scott 23 Apr 1791; d/o Thomas Scott dec'd; Isaac Johnson sec; m 23 Apr 1791 by C Simkins.
SMITH William to Fanny Parsons 6 Sep 1813; Wm Parsons con for Fanny & sec; John Dunton & Elijah Baker wits.

SMITH Wm to Fanny Haley 21 Dec 1825; d/o Benj Haley; con Benj & Wm Griffith secs & wits.
SMITH William G to Elizabeth U Bowdoin 19 Nov 1825; d/o Peter Bowdoin sec; m 22 Nov 1825 by S S Gunter.
SNEAD Col Edward to Rose Christian 25 Sep 1776; Col Edward of Acc Co; d/o Dr Mich'l & Rose Christian. see BRec V7:151.
SNEAD Smith to Rosetta Christian 12 Feb 1783; Thos Parker of Acc Co sec.
SNEAD Thomas to Nancy Waddy 26 Feb 1800; Michael Mathews sec; m 1800 by J Elliott; (m 27 Feb 1800. see BRec V7:179; V9:14).
SNEAD Thos to Sarah Melholloms 12 Jun 1804; John Core sec.
SNEAD Tully S to Miss Frances S Costin 3 Mar 1852; d/o Wm G Costin.
SNEAD William to Adah Satchell 16 Jan 1788; d/o Wm Satchell Sr; Wm Satchell Jr sec.
SNEAD William to Susan Parsons 21 Sep 1833; William (sailor); wid/o Wm Parsons Jr; Edm'd R Custis sec & as to William's age; m 23 Sep 1833 by P Williams.
SNEAD William B to Emma E Gardner 1 Oct 1823; Emma wrd/o John Simkins con; George F Wilkins sec; Thomas Jones & C Satchell wits.
SNEAD William H to Sally Smith 13 Jun 1831; Zorobabel Chandler sec & as to ages.
SOMERS George S to Mary H Milbourn 5 Jan 1833; wid/o John C Milbourn; Jeremiah Griffith sec & as to George's age.
SOPER Cap't William to Miss Nancy Carpenter 7 Jul 1851; Jno F Bell as to Nancy's age; E J Spady wit; m 7 Jul 1851 by P Warren.
SORSBY Samuel to Kessy Richardson 14 Oct 1824; Jesse Bell sec & as to Kessy's age; m Oct 1824 by L Dix.
SPADY Benjamin to Adah Spady 10 Mar 1798; James Spady sec.
SPADY Benjamin to Polly Hamby 6 Nov 1827; Thomas Hamby sec & as to Polly's age; John Spady as to Benja's age; Jno Addison & Jno S Dix & Wm Jackson wits; m 9 Nov 1827 by P Williams.
SPADY Benjamin to Ann Scott 26 Dec 1843; wid/o Thomas Scott; Joseph Warren sec; m 26 Dec 1843 by P Williams.
SPADY Jacob to Sarah Roberts 18 Dec 1788; Westerhouse Widgen sec; m (1788) by E Baker.
SPADY Jacob to Anne Barnes 21 Jul 1830; d/o Preeson Barnes dec'd; Wm Dennis Jr sec & as to ages.
SPADY Jacob to Miss Elizabeth Fox 25 Sep 1848; James S Webb sec; Custis Trehearne as to Elizabeth's age; m 25 Sep 1848 by S C Boston.
SPADY James to Catherine Dolby 28 Mar 1785; John Dolby sec.
SPADY James to Mary Hughes 3 Jun 1796; Wm Carpenter sec; m (1796) by E Baker.
SPADY James to Leah Evans 17 Apr 1802; Robinson Custis sec; m (1802) by J Elliott.
SPADY James to Amelia Goffigon 16 Aug 1803; John Spady sec; m (1803) by J Elliott.
SPADY James to Peggy Willis 13 Dec 1828; d/o Thomas Willis con; Jas Williams sec; Wm Harmanson & Thos Stockley wits; m 15 Dec 1828 by P Williams.
SPADY James to Rosy Ann Becket FN 4 May 1839; George Simkins (FN) as to ages; John W Leatherbury sec; m 18 May 1839 by S T Ames.
SPADY John Jr to Leah Williams 8 Jan 1827; s/o John Spady Sr sec; Jno B Wilkins as to Leah's age; L B Nottingham & Wm P Johnson wits; m 11 Jan 1827 by P Williams.
SPADY John H to Margaret A Jarvis 24 Sep 1832; s/o Thomas S Spady sec; d/o Margaret Jarvis con; m 27 Sep 1832 by P

Williams.
SPADY Samuel to Polly Moore 15 Jan 1834; d/o Abram Moore; James Spady (of John) sec & as to Samuel's age; Charles Dillion as to Polly's age.
SPADY Samuel to Miss Esther Welch 11 Aug 1845; d/o William Welch; Mack Moore as to ages; Benjamin Nottingham sec; m 19 Aug 1845 by P Warren Jr.
SPADY Southy to Susanna Mills 21 Jan 1783; Jacob Spady sec.
SPADY Southy to Mary Joynes 10 Jan 1786; Wm Nelson sec.
SPADY Southy to Nancy Trower 11 May 1790; Robert Trower sec; m 28 May 1790 C Simkins.
SPADY Southey Jr to Rosa (Rosanna) Trower 18 May 1822; Rosa wrd/o Wm E Wilkins perm; Christopher Fitchett sec; Daniel Fitchett wit; m 23 May 1822 by L Dix.
SPADY Thomas to Mary Wheeler 8 Mar 1780; John Wheeler Sr sec.
SPADY Thomas to Sarah Green Williams 5 Dec 1809; Wm Wilson sec; con Ann Williams as to Sarah; m (1809) by J Elliott.
SPADY Thomas to Sally Fitchett 23 Jun 1810; d/o Joshua Fitchett Sr con; Wm Wilson sec; m (1810) by J Elliott.
SPADY Thomas to Betsy McCowan 8 May 1821; Moses Griffeth sec; m 10 May 1821 by L Dix.
SPADY Dr Thomas Fitchett to Maria Ann Jarvis 27 Mar 1843; d/o Elizabeth U Jarvis con; Nathaniel S Goffigon sec; Edwin Goffigon wit; m 28 Mar 1843 by P Williams. see BRec V1:24.
SPADY Thomas S to Elizabeth Williams 22 Nov 1823; d/o Margaret Williams who was app't gdn Jul 1807; Thomas Knight sec; m Nov 1823 by L Dix.
SPADY Westerhouse to Elizabeth Nottingham 20 Sep 1829; d/o & wrd/o Elisha Nottingham con; Benja Nottingham sec & as to Westerhouse's age; m 1 Oct 1829 by P Williams.
SPADY William to Susanna Caple 9 Jun 1796; John R Floyd sec; m 1796 by E Baker.
SPADY William to Margaret Nottingham 14 Jul 1823; Margaret wrd/o Wm Floyd sec.
SPEAKMAN John to Elizabeth Wilkins 12 Sep 1796; d/o Elizabeth Wilkins con & Stephon Wilkinson her gdn con; Thos Tyler sec; m (1796) by E Baker.
SPEAKMAN Thomas to Betsey Tylor 13 Jun 1796; Stephon Wilkinson sec; m (1796) by E Baker.
SPEAKMAN William to Caty Griffeth 31 May 1803; Thos Speakman sec; m (1803) by J Elliott.
SPEAKMAN William to Charlotte Jones 21 Dec 1820; d/o Littleton Jones con; Severn Wingate sec; John N Scott & George Taylor wits; m 21 Dec 1820 by L Dix.
SPEAKMAN William to Mary Ann Brown 13 Nov 1826; d/o Allen Brown sec; Jno W Wilkins wit; m 30 Nov 1826 by P Williams Jr.
SPENCER Moses to Anne Arnold 31 May 1769; John Burton sec.
SPENCER William to Mrs Eliza Whittington 14 Jun 1660. BK IX:92.
STANDLY Christofer to Ann Turner 4 Sep 1660. BK IX:92.
STARLING Wm to Marg't Edwards 20 Sep 1660. BK IX:92.
STEPHENS, See also STEVENS.
STEPHENS Ephraim to Leah Read FN 11 Dec 1832; Peter S Bowdoin sec; m 16 Dec 1832 by G Wescoat.
STEPHENS George to Caty Stephens FN 16 Jan 1823; d/o Dilly Stephens who states Caty b 17 Oct 1802; Major Scisco sec; (date of Bond 1823 - date of Dilly's consent 1824 - ??).
STEPHENS George to Mary Francis 18 Oct 1828; Mary wrd/o Samuel Beavans sec FN; m Oct 1828 by L Dix.
STEPHENS George to Louisa Collins FN 24 Sep 1852; Severn

Stephens as to ages; Thos W Upshur wit; m 24 Sep 1852 by P Warren.

STEPHENS Isaac m Adah Thompson (Blacks) 3 Jan 1817 by C Bonewell.

STEPHENS Isaac to Eliza Johnson 31 Dec 1838; d/o James Johnson & sis/o Emeline Jacob (late Emiline Johnson) FN as to Eliza's age; Sabra Stephens sec.

STEPHENS William to Elizabeth Dixon 29 Oct 1773; William of Gloucester Co; d/o John Dixon sec.

STEPHENS William to Caroline Press 13 Jul 1829; s/o Jinney; Caroline wrd/o said William (FN); William Stephens of Abigail sec; Jinney Stephens as to her son's age; m 16 Jul 1829 by P Williams.

STEPHENS William to Sally Pool 28 Dec 1848; s/o George Stephens sec; d/o Hessey Pool con FN; John S Turpin sec; James Poulson FN & Chas Brickhouse wits; m 29 Dec 1848 by H Dalby.

STEPNEY York to Peggy Lewis 6 Jun 1807; Jacob Morris sec; m (1807) by I Bratten.

STERLING John to Miss Elizabeth Seaton 16 May 1846; d/o Mrs Jenny Seaton; James Buntin sec & as to Elizabeth's age; m 16 May 1846 by P Warren.

STERLING Levi to Mary Ann Gunter 3 Oct 1838; Smith Belote gdn/o Mary con; John G Minson sec; Jos S M Gunter & Edm'd Roberts wits; m 5 Oct 1838 by G C Wescoat.

STERLING Severn H to Miss Cinthia Ann Ward 11 Jul 1843; d/o Alex W Ward sec; Severn states that he was b 21 Oct 1817; Jno T Wilkins & Wm White wits.

STEVENS, See also STEPHENS.

STEVENS Cugjo to Betsey Pool 20 Dec 1806; Charles Pool sec (FN); m (1806) by I Bratten.

STEVENS George to Eliz Collins 11 May 1838; d/o Ritta Collins sec; Smith S Nottingham sec; Ritta Collins as to George's age.

STEVENS Isaac to Rachel Tomson (FN) 22 Jan 1791; Coventon Simkins sec; m 30 Jan 1791 by C Simkins.

STEVENS Isaac Jr to Sabra Nutts 16 Aug 1809; Isaac Stevens Sr sec (FN).

STEVENS John to Betsey Thompson 7 Aug 1798; Ben Lewis sec (FN); m (1798) by I Bratten.

STEVENS Samuel to Nancy Lang 16 Jul 1797; Abraham Lang sec (FN); m Jul 1797 by C Simkins.

STEVENS Toby to Bridget Nutts (FN) 7 Sep 1804; Ben Dunton sec.

STEWART Geo m Elizabeth Collins 13 May 1838 by G C Wescoat.

STEWART John to Scarbrough Burton 27 Apr 1780; Nath'l Tyson sec.

STEWART John L to Susan Bool 15 Mar 1841; d/o Ezekiel Book dec'd; Joshua K Roberts gdn/o Susan sec; James Stewart as to John L's age of 23y. see BRec V1:40.

STEWART Joshua G to Miss Margaret Savage 9 Nov 1847; d/o Preson Savage dec'd; John W Nicholson sec; Teackle J Turner as to Margaret's age.

STITH Griffin Jr to Anne Stratton 24 Jun 1778; d/o Jno; Edw'd Robins Jr sec.

STOAKLEY, See also STOCKLEY.

STOAKLEY Thomas S to Hannah Scott 31 Jul 1798; Wm Scott Sr sec.

STOAKLEY Thomas S to Sarah Ann Scott 24 Nov 1829; d/o Thomas G Scott & wrd/o George F Wilkins sec; m 26 Nov by P Williams. see BRec V7:43.

STOAKLEY William to Adah Stratton 21 Jan 1774; d/o Benja Stratton; John Wilkins blacksmith sec; Wm Scott con as to William.

STOCKLEY, STOCKLY, STOKELY.

STOCKLEY Abel to Kesiah Pool 27 Jan 1802; Wm Hanby sec; m Jul 1801 by C Simkins (several entries in this period - 1801 - are confused in the MinRets).

STOKLEY Charles B to Drusilla Andrews 1 Dec 1813; Leroy Oldham sec; m (1813) by J Elliott.

STOCKLEY Charles B to Sarah Tatim 23 Dec 1843; d/o Polly Tatim dec'd; Branson Dalby sec & as to Sarah's age; m 24 Dec 1843 by G C Wescoat.

STOCKLY John Sr to Isabell Moore 14 Feb 1708/9; Wm Willett sec; Ellen C Moore wit.

STOCKLY John to Peggy Scott 9 Dec 1816; Samuel Stott sec; m 11 Dec 1816 by C Bonewell.

STOCKELY John to Polly Joynes 30 Jul 1839; s/o Chas B Stockley sec; d/o Robt A Joynes sec; m 31 Jul 1839 by S T Ames.

STOCKLY John Sr to Rachel Dennis 22 Sep 1846; wid/o Archibald Dennis; Wm W Mehollomes sec; m 22 Sep 1846 by G C Wescoat.

STOCKLEY Thomas m Mrs Freshwater Jul 1800 by C Simkins (see Wm Stockley to Nancy Freshwater; are these entries the minister's error?).

STOCKLEY Thomas G to Sally Booth 14 Mar 1831; d/o John Booth dec'd & wrd/o John Smith sec; m 14 Mar 1831 by G Wescoat.

STOKELY William to Betsey Mills 1 Jul 1808; John Dunton sec.

STOCKLEY William to Elizabeth Jarvis 30 Aug 1775; d/o Wm Jarvis; Wm Scott sec.

STOCKLEY Wm m Nancy Freshwater Jul 1800 by C Simkins.

STOIT See STOYT.

STOTT Abel to Sarah Watson 10 Feb 1789; Jacob Rose sec.

STOTT Abel to Barbara White 8 May 1826; s/o Eliz Parkinson as to his age; Barbara wrd/o Harrison Rayfield sec; Geo L E Tankard & John Tankard Beloate & Richard Young wits; m 1826 by G C Wescoat.

STOTT Abel to Margaret Tyson 17 Jan 1831; d/o John Tyson dec'd & wrd/o Thomas Tyson sec; m 19 Jan 1831 by G Wescoat.

STOTT Abel to Miss Margt H Wise 19 Feb 1844; d/o Peter Wise dec'd; James Window sec & as to Margt's age; John Eyre wit; m 29 Feb 1844 by P Warren Jr.

STOTT Bennet to Eliza Godwin (13 Feb 1826); Eliza wrd/o William Rooks Sr sec; J W Wilkins as to Bennet's age; m 15 Feb 1826 by L Dix.

STOTT Charles to Jenny Collins FN 31 May 1852; Horace Stephens as to Jenny's age; m 31 May 1852 by P Warren.

STOTT Coventon to Kesiah Fisher 17 Dec 1788; d/o Daniel Fisher dec'd; Abel Savage sec.

STOTT David to Elishe Hanby 14 Feb 1775; wid; Custis Mathews sec.

STOTT Isaac to Betsey Hughes 28 Nov 1804; John Rafield sec.

STOTT John to Susanna Smith 17 Aug 1759; wid; Jno Bowdoin sec.

STOTT John to Mary Dewey 4 Jul 1759; wid (Thos Dewey*); Jas Peterkin sec. *North Co WB 22:396, 497.

STOTT John Sr to Anne James 2 Jul 1763; d/o Thomas James con; Hezekiah James sec.

STOTT John to Sarah Wise 16 Sep 1775; wid/o John Wise; Francis Andrew sec.

STOTT John to Polly Waterfield 27 Jul 1787; Geo Willis sec.

STOTT John to Molly Giddens 5 Jul 1788; d/o John Giddens con; Jacob Waterfield sec; m (1788) by E Baker.

STOTT John to Hannah Warren 18 Feb 1796; Thos Johnson sec; m (1796) by I Bratten.

STOTT Jonathan to Susanna Hays 12 May 1761; wid; John Harmanson sec.

STOTT Jonathan to Anne Walter 21 Feb 1772; d/o John Walter; Elias Waterfield sec.

STOTT Jonathon to Adah Pearson

101

24 Mar 1802; (wid/o Thos Pearson); Patrick Carpenter sec; m (1802) by I Bratten.
STOTT Keley to Susanna Willis 23 Jun 1823; Susanna b 3 Jun 1802 d/o Josiah Willis dec'd; Nath'l Benson sec; N Winder & W W Wilkims wits; m Jun 1823 by L Dix.
STOTT Laban to Sarah Roberts 27 Jul 1752; spinster; Henry Tomlinson sec.
STOTT Laban to Susanna Belote 17 May 1793; Isme Heath sec; m (1793) by E Baker. see BRec V1:22.
STOTT Laban to Betsey Heath 11 Jun 1795; Wm Dorman sec; m 1795 by I Bratten. see BRec V1:22.
STOTT Laban Sr to Peggy Waterfield 15 Nov 1808; Zorobabel Jones sec; m (1808) by I Bratten; (m 21 Nov 1808. see BRec V1:22).
STOTT Laban W to Susan Roberts 3 Jul 1819; Jacob Nottingham Jr sec.
STOTT Samuel to Miss Ann Griffith 30 Jun 1846; d/o Charles & Sally Griffith dec'd; Mrs Rosey Parsons as to Ann's age; John Kendall sec; m Jun 1846 by P Williams.
STOTT Timothy B to Mahala Sturgis 9 Feb 1824; Mahala wrd/o Patrick Pearson sec who states that Mahala is over 21y; m 9 Feb 1824 by S S Gunter.
STOYT, STOYTE, STOIT, STOITE.
STOYT Benjamin to Mary Speakman 27 Dec 1820; d/o Thomas Speakman con; Wm Thomas sec; John Floyd wit; m 28 Dec 1820 by C Bonewell.
STOYTE John to Nancy Rutherford 11 Sep 1812; Southy Wingate sec; m (1812) by J Elliott.
STOIT Luther to Sally Jacob 3 Apr 1843; d/o John Jacob dec'd; Benj Tyler sec & as to Luther's age; Wm Warren as to Sally's age; Wm T Nottingham wit; m 4 Apr 1843 by P Williams.

STOITE Walter to Miss Margaret E Spady 8 Dec 1851; d/o Wm Spady dec'd; Luther Stoite as to Walter's age; Westerhouse Spady as to Margaret's age; George P Fitchett wit; m 10 Dec 1851 by P Williams.
STRATTON Benjamin to Susanna Henry 1 Jan 1789; wid; Matthew Guy sec.
STRATTON Benjamin to Margaret Mapp Harmanson 5 Jun 1794; Wm Harmanson sec.
øSTRATTON Benjamin to Esther Parsons 4 Sep 1799; (d/o Thos & Ann Parsons); John Stratton sec.
STRATTON Edward to Mary Ann F Wilson 13 Oct 1819; Jacob G Parker sec; m 13 Oct 1819 by C Bonewell. see BRec V2:49.
STRATTON John to Gertrude Tazewell 19 Feb 1754; spinster; John Harmanson sec.
STRATTON John Jr to Peggy Wilkins 25 Jan 1780; d/o John Wilkins OP con; Dan'l Roles Hall sec.
STRATTON Nathaniel to Elishe Hunt 28 Sep 1757; d/o Azariah Hunt dec'd; Isaac Jacob sec.
STRATTON William to Esther Guy 28 Apr 1787; d/o John Guy dec'd; Thomas Kendall sec.
STRATTON William to Adah Snead 11 Dec 1809; (wid/o Wm); Littleton Kendall Sr sec.
STRINGER Hillary to Alicia Harmanson 23 Jan 1722; spinster (d/o Geo Harmanson*); Argall Harmanson & Godfrey Pole secs; Geo Harmanson & Mich'l Christian wits; lic 23 Jan 1722 - CT ret Oct 1723. *North Co WB 18:123.
STRINGER Hillary to Margaret Kendall 12 Oct 1799; John Bowdoin sec.
STRINGER Hilary B to Sally B Parker 14 Apr 1814; Peter Bowdoin sec; m 14 Apr 1814 by Thos Davis.
STRINGER John to Rachel Wilkins 7 Nov 1760; d/o Jonathan Wilkins dec'd; Savage Cowdrey sec; Nath'l

Savage wit.
STRINGER John to Eliz Buckner Stith 7 Feb 1767; d/o Griffin Stith; Walter Hyslop sec; bond written 3/4 past 11 o'clock.
STRINGER John to Susanna Dalby 12 Nov 1778; wid/o John Dalby; Edmund Glanville sec.
STRINGER John to Mary Godwin 23 Feb 1785; d/o Archibald Godwin sec.
STRINGER Thomas to Frances Willis 24 Nov 1827; d/o Marriot Willis dec'd; Jno K Floyd as to Thomas' age; Ezekiel Young sec & as to Frances' age; m 24 Nov 1827 by P Williams.
STRINGER Thomas to Mary S Nottingham 5 May 1838; Edmund R Custis sec & as to Mary's age; Westerhouse Widgeon wit; m 22 May 1838 by P Williams.
STRINGER Walter to Caty McCowan 28 Dec 1830; d/o John McCowan sec & as to ages; m 30 Dec 1830 by P Williams.
STRINGER William S to Nancy Wilkins 8 Apr 1811; Marrot Willis sec with Josias Willis Jr as to Nancy as more than 23y; m (1811) by J Elliott.
STRIPE Littleton to Betsey Outten 20 Feb 1796; Wm Hanby sec.
STRIPE Peter to Kessy Dunton 15 Feb 1820; Charles Dillion sec; m 15 Feb 1820 by C Bonewell.
STRIPE Whittington to Mary Cox 25 Feb 1790; Wm Bain sec; m (1790) by E Baker.
STURGIS Jacob to Sarah Scott 10 Aug 1779; d/o Barthemy Scott; John Dowty sec.
STURGIS Jacob to Margaret Nottingham 10 Feb 1816*; Thos Scarbrough sec; m 13 Feb 1817* by Joshua Burton. *discrepancy
STURGIS James to Vianna Wescoat 22 Nov 1831; d/o John Wescoat dec'd; Wm Wyatt Jr sec & as to ages; Rob't Dashiel wit; m 22 Nov 1831 by G Wescoat.
STURGIS John to Dorothy Savage 1 Sep 1661. BK IX:114.
STURGIS Richard to Margaret Dalby 21 Jan 1787; Edmund Joynes sec.
STURGIS Samuel G to Mary Ann Lawson 13 Jun 1836; George D White sec & as to Mary Ann's age; Benj Floyd as to Samuel's age; m 15 Jun 1836 by G Wescoat.
STURGIS Thomas to Esther W Holt 22 Jul 1830; wid/o Martin M M Holt; George Holt Sr sec.
STURGIS William to Peggy Gascoyne 18 Feb 1764; d/o Henry Gascoyne; Ezekiel Bell sec.
STURGIS William to Sally Andrews 12 Apr 1824; Levin J Thomas sec; m 12 Apr 1824 by C Bonewell.
SWILLIVAN Dorman to Anne Manarrell 20 Oct 1661. BK IX:114.

T

TABB Thomas to Elizabeth Teackle 27 Dec 1790; d/o Caleb Teackle dec'd & con/o John Winder her gdn; John Stratton Jr sec.
TANKARD Azariah to Rachel Pettitt 3 Feb 1764; d/o Wm Pettitt dec'd; Howson Mapp sec.
TANKARD George L E to Anne K J Dunton 10 Apr 1826; Smith Nottingham sec; m 20 Apr 1826 by S S Gunter.
TANKARD John to Sarah Andrews 12 Feb 1778; (wid/o Southey Andrews); John Thomas sec.
TANKARD John to Zillah Turner Downing 10 Jan 1791; wid/o Arthur S Downing Sr; John Eyre sec; (m 17 Jan 1791. see BRec V2:18).
TANKARD John W to Susan W Taylor 13 Jun 1839. see BRec V2:19.
TATUM, TATEM.
TATUM James to Polly Brickhouse 18 Sep 1805; Thomas Jacob sec.
TATEM William T to Alichia Biggs 12 Dec 1838; d/o Christopher Biggs dec'd; Daniel Scott sec & as to

ages; m 22 Dec 1838 by P Williams (ret shows "Elisha" Biggs).

TAYLOR Abraham to Debora Kechine 3 Nov 1661. BK IX:114.

TAYLOR Bartholomew to Polly Evans 9 Apr 1805; d/o Richard Evans dec'd; Wm Carpenter as to Polly's age; Joshua Garrison sec.

TAYLOR Bartholmew to Mrs Nancy Rooks 8 Apr 1839; Wm J Fitchet sec & as to Bartholmew's age; m 11 Apr 1839 by W A Dix.

TAYLOR David C to Margaret S Dalby 24 Jun 1824; s/o Crippen Taylor as to his age; Jno B Thomas gdn/o Marg't con; Jno N Stratton & James Young sec.

TAYLOR George to Elizabeth Garris 28 Jan 1791; George of Acc Co; d/o Thos Garris (Garrott) dec'd; Rob't Brickhouse con as to Elizabeth; Thos Jacob sec; John West & George Bell wits; m (1791) by C Simkins.

TAYLOR George to Sarah Dalby 20 Aug 1799; Wm Teackle Taylor sec; m Aug 1799 by C Simkins.

TAYLOR George to Elizabeth Evans 2 May 1812; Bartholomew Taylor sec; m (1812) by I Bratten.

TAYLOR George to Sukey Scott 30 Jul 1821; wid/o Thomas Scott; Thomas Peed sec; m 1 Aug 1821 by C Bonewell.

TAYLOR James to Susanna Rasin 16 Jan 1774; Wm Harmanson sec.

TAYLOR James to Nancy Jacob 28 Dec 1808; Edward Joynes sec; m (1808) by J Elliott.

TAYLOR James to Esther Bryan 13 Jan 1816; John Taylor sec; m (1816) by C Bonewell.

TAYLOR John to Nancy Addison 25 Feb 1800; Thomas Addison con for Nancy; Major Andrews sec.

TAYLOR John to Polly Davis 17 Aug 1802; John Dalby sec; m (1802) to I Bratten.

TAYLOR John to Caty Savage 10 Apr 1809; John Turner sec.

TAYLOR John to Elizabeth Dowty 9 Mar 1818; Thos Dowty sec; m 11 Mar 1818 by C Bonewell.

TAYLOR John to Peggy Spady 17 Dec 1818 by W Costin.

TAYLOR John to Nancy Harrison 14 Jun 1826; d/o Abel Harrison sec; John is "son-in-law" of William Churn; James Floyd wit.

TAYLOR John to Miss Lucy Mazlin 27 Mar 1844; Wm H Floyd as to Lucy's age; Wm T Nottingham sec; Jno G Parsons wit; m 28 Mar 1844 by P Warren Jr.

TAYLOR John E to Eliza J Matthews m 20 Jun 1843; d/o Levin Matthews dec'd & wife Margaret Matthews (Joynes) con; R A Joynes wit; John G Nelson sec; m 27 Jun 1843 by G C Wescoat (m 28 Jun 1843 BRec 11:14.)

TAYLOR Joshua to Martha Sturgis 11 May 1775; Joshua of Acc Co; Martha (d/o or wid/o ?) of Wm Sturgis dec'd; Thos Hurst sec.

TAYLOR Louis B to Elizabeth B Burron 7 Jan 1839; s/o Bagwell & Lucretia Taylor; d/o Jno B & Sarah B Burron; (poss m in Acc Co). see BRec V2:22.

TAYLOR Major to Sally Luke 2 Oct 1802; Jacob Roberts sec; m (1802) by I Bratten.

TAYLOR Robert to Sarah Barraud 26 Sep 1771; d/o Daniel Barraud. see BRec V5:158.

TAYLOR Robert Barraud to Nancy Kitson 28 Jul 1796; d/o Thos & Martha (Willoughby) Kitson. see BRec V5:158.

TAYLOR Shadrack to Polly Richardson 7 Jan 1823; s/o Shadrack Taylor con; Custis Kellam sec; John W Wilkins wit; m 9 Jan 1823 by C Bonewell.

TAYLOR Thorogood to Susanna Rogers 10 Jan 1816; James N Fitchet sec & as to Susan's age; m bet 1 Jan - 19 Feb (1816) by I Bratten.

TAYLOR William to Henrietta Dunton 11 Feb 1773; d/o Stephen Dunton dec'd; Wm White Jr sec.

TAYLOR William to Sarah Wheeler 2 Nov 1780; Levin Lawrence sec.

TAYLOR William E to Margaret A Lyon 21 Feb 1831; d/o Dr James Lyon dec'd; John Eyre sec; (m 22 Feb 1831. see BRec V5:158).

TAYLOR William J to Virginia A Hunt 1 May 1848; d/o Mrs Mary E Hunt con; Lucy Ann Fitchett wit; David A Dunton sec; m 1 May 1848 by S C Boston.

TAZEWELL William to Sophia Harmanson 10 Jun 1723; (d/o Gertrude Harmanson); Thos Cable & Edw'd Carter secs; Elicia Stringer wit; lic 10 Jun 1723 - CT ret Oct 1723.

TEACKLE Abel Upshur to Rachel Gascoyne 7 Jul 1790; Abel of Acc Co; Wm Harmanson gdn/o Rachel & con; John Guy sec; m 8 (June?) 1790 by C Simkins (both clerk & gdn dated papers for Jul; prob min error).

TEACKLE Caleb to Elizabeth Harmanson 17 Dec 1771; Caleb of Acc Co; d/o George Harmanson; Wm Floyd sec.

TEACKLE George to Fanny B Bowdoin 8 Aug 1801; Peter Bowdoin sec.

TEACKLE John Jr to Anne Upshur 17 Dec 1783; Griffin Stith sec; John Upshur con as to Anne.

TEACKLE Littleton D to Elizabeth Upshur 27 May 1800; John Stratton sec; L Upshur con for "his two relatives."

TEAGUE (TEAGUL?) Abram to Martha ____ Jul 1792 by C Simkins.

TEAGUE Thomas to Keziah Scott 21 Feb 1767; Thomas of Acc Co; d/o Henry Scott; Solomon Scott sec.

TERRIER John C to Elizabeth Dixon 24 Oct 1827; Elizabeth wrd/o Thos S Brickhouse con; Smith Nottingham sec; Wm P Custis wit; m 1827 by G C Wescoat.

TERRILL George to Emily Ann Eyre 15 Jun 1830; s/o Wm & Jane Terrill; d/o Wm & Grace Eyre. see BRec V5:153.

THOM Dr William Alexander to Anne Parker 11 Apr 1844; (Dr Wm of Culpeper Co VA); (d/o Dr Jacob G & Anne Stratton Parker); Miers W Fisher sec; (m 18 Apr 1844 by J Ufford. HunParReg:35).

THOMAS Benjamin to Elizabeth D Broughton 14 Dec 1829; d/o Isaac Broughton dec'd; Rowland Dowty sec & as to Elizabeth's age.

THOMAS Benjamin to Miss Elizabeth H Warren 1 Apr 1842; d/o John Warren Jr sec; m 6 Apr 1842 by P Warren.

THOMAS George L J to Miss Mary Ann Ward 17 Sep 1850; d/o Albert D Ward; Kendall F Addison as to Mary's age; m 18 Sep 1850 by M Oldham.

THOMAS Harrison to Elizabeth Downing 23 Mar 1793; Elijah Baker sec; m (1793) by E Baker.

THOMAS James to Elizabeth S Turner 24 Nov 1842; d/o Edward R Turner sec; m 24 Nov 1842 by P Warren.

THOMAS John B to Elizabeth Rogers 26 Mar 1807; s/o Harrison & Tabitha Thomas; d/o Levin & Rachel Rogers; (m in Acc Co. see BRec V4:41).

THOMAS John B to Ann C Dunton 19 Jun 1822; d/o William who certifies as to Ann's age; John Hanby sec; m 19 Jun 1822 by C Bonewell. see BRec V2:128; V8:113.

THOMAS John B to Miss Harriet G Holland 1 Mar 1826; Edw'd R Boisnard & Nath'l Holland secs; m 1 Mar 1826 by S S Gunter. see BRec V5:180.

THOMAS John B to Catherine Sabra Dunton 2 Jul 1829; d/o Wm & Mary Dunton. see BRec V2:128; V8:113.

THOMAS John W to Sophia E Dunton 19 Sep 1836; d/o Major William Dunton dec'd; Samuel W Dunton sec & as to Sophia's age; John W Thomas wit; m 21 Sep 1836 by W B Snead. see BRec

V2:128; V8:113.
THOMAS Joseph W to Ailsie T Floyd 7 Oct 1830; wid/o Shepherd B Floyd; Wm J Campbell sec; m 7 Oct 1830 by P Williams.
THOMAS Leavin J to Salley Core 21 Dec 1813; d/o John Core con; John C Mapp sec; m (22 Dec 1813. see BRec V6:85).
THOMAS Levin J to Harriet P Matthews 8 Aug 1836; wid/o Lewis R Matthews; John W Tankard sec; m 10 Aug 1836 by G Wescoat.
THOMAS William to Polly Smith 4 Apr 1795; John Dixson sec; m 1795 by I Bratten.
THOMAS William to Frances Nottingham 1 Jul 1822; Frances wrd/o Jacob Nottingham Sr sec.
THOMPSON, THOMSON, TOMPSON, See also TOMPKINS.
TOMPSON Abram to Peggy ____; m 3 Nov 1790 by C Simkins. CT Ret 1790.
THOMSON Isaac to Leah Stivens 22 Sep 1792; Jacob Frost sec (FN); m Sep 1792 by C Simkins.
THOMPSON Isaac to Margaret Carter 9 Aug 1824; d/o Ezekiel Carter sec.
THOMPSON Isaac Sr to Lilly Stephens FN 26 Dec 1839; Henry Morris FN sec; m 28 Dec 1839 by Stames.
THOMPSON Jacob to Sukey Morris (FN) 26 May 1795; Thomas Lewis sec; m May 1795 by C Simkins.
THOMPSON Jacob to Tamar Stevens 26 Sep 1800; Johannes Johnson sec; m 26 Sep 1800 by C Simkins (MinRet shows "Amey" Stevens).
THOMPSON Jacob Jr to Mary Baker 20 Dec 1827; s/o Jacob Thompson Sr; d/o Thomas Baker; Jacob Sr & Thomas sec.
THOMPSON Raleigh to Peggy Collins FN 2 May 1835; d/o Little Peggy Collins dec'd; John S Parker sec; George Pool FN as to Raleigh's age; John Kendall as to Peggy's age; m 14 May 1835 by P Williams.

THOMPSON Robert to Eliza Watson 25 Jan 1819; Elijah Floyd sec & as to Eliza's age; m 27 Jan 1819 by J Burton.
THURGETTLE (FIRKETTLE) John to Dorothy Wilkison 26 Aug 1660. BK IX:92.
THURMER Robert to Anna Catharine Westerhouse 12 Oct 1756; d/o Wm Westerhouse; Dickie Galt sec; Mark Freshwater wit.
THURSTAIN, THURSTON, THURTON.
THURSTAIN Abner to Eliz Williams 25 Jan 1782; d/o Peter Williams dec'd; John Tyler sec.
THURSTAN Abner to Betsy Williams 26 May 1812; d/o Peter Williams Jr sec & con; Peter Williams & Thomas Scott wits; m (1812) by J Elliott.
THURSTON Azariah to Mary Ann Williams 24* Jun 1826; d/o Samuel S Williams sec; m Jun 1826 by L Dix; (m 8* Jun 1826. see BRec V6:122). *discrepancy
THURSTON Azariah to Susan A Williams 27 Jun 1842; d/o Capt Saml S Williams; Leonard B Nottingham sec; Benja Tyler as to Susan's age; Richard H Read wit; m 2 Jul 1842 by P Williams. see BRec V6:122.
THURSTON Azariah to Mrs Leah Fitchett 30 Nov 1848; wid/o Christopher Fitchett; Thomas K Dunton sec.
THURSTON James Benjamin to Sarah A Owens 28 Jun 1849. see BRec V6:121.
TILNEY Jonathan to Sarah Marshall 22 Jun 1742; Thos Cable sec; Jno Jones & Fielding Lewis wits.
TIMMONS Michael to Mary Sabrah 18 May 1799; Wm Havard sec; m May 1799 by C Simkins.
TOLEMAN William to Polly Heath 9 Jun 1792; Chas Stevenson sec; m Jun 1792 by C Simkins.
TOMPKINS John to Ann Custis 19 Feb 1747; wid/o (John Custis V); George Kendall sec; Elisabeth &

Sarah Cable wits.
TOPPING David to Rosey Stott 11 Apr 1801; Wm Bain sec.
TOWNSEND Angelo A to Adah Parrott 18 Oct 1823; wid/o George Parrott; Gilbert Townsend sec; m 23 Oct 1823 by S S Gunter.
TOWNSEND Angelo A to Martha Ann Eliza Holcroft 13 Jul 1832; d/o Wm Holdcroft sec; m 14 Jul 1832 by W B Snead.
TOWNSEND John to Eliza Wheatly 20 May 1660. BK IX:92.
TOWNSEND John to Eliz Danford 9 Feb 1661/1662. BK IX:114.
TOWNSEND Nathaniel B to Rebecca M Joynes 27 Mar 1829; d/o Edmund Joynes dec'd; Henry B Kendall sec & as to Nathaniel's age; Elizabeth Bull as to Rebecca's age.
TRAVIS Dennard to Rebekah Costin 14 Sep 1808; d/o Matthew Costin con; Wm S Evans sec; Henry Costin wit; m (1808) by J Elliott.
TRAVIS Dennard to Susan Whitehead 26 Jun 1821; John Whitehead Sr sec; m 5 Jul 1821 by L Dix.
TRAVIS Elliott to Polly Herbert 16 Jul 1813; s/o Shadrack Travis; Thos Graves sec & speaking for Shadrack con for Elliott; B Griffith con for Polly who is not of age; m (1813) by J Elliott.
TRAVIS Eliott to Ann Elliott 13 Aug 1821; Wm Goffigon sec; m 15 Aug 1821 by L Dix.
TRAVIS Elliott to Miss Mary Warren 5 Jan 1846; d/o Joseph Warren con; Leonard Warren sec & as to Elliott's age; Dennard Travis & Wm Whitehead wits; m 5 Jan 1846 by P Williams.
TRAVIS James to Sally Dunton 10 Nov 1792; Henry Giddens sec; m Nov 1792 by C Simkins.
TRAVIS John to Charlotte Whitehead 9 Sep 1850; wid/o Stephen Whitehead; m 9 Sep 1850 by P Williams.

TRAVIS Meshack to Adah Wilkins 26 Dec 1825; d/o John Wilkins Sr sec; m Dec 1825 by L Dix.
TRAVIS Meshack to Elizabeth Wilkins 8 Dec 1828; d/o John Wilkins Sr; Thomas Hallett sec & as to Elizabeth's age; m Dec 1828 by L Dix.
TRAVIS Shadrack to Charlotte Hyslop 9 Jan 1821; d/o Susana Hyslop con; John Evans sec; m 17 Jan 1821 by L Dix.
TRAVIS Shadrack to Mrs Sukey Nottingham 13 Nov 1826; Bowdoin Costin sec; Ves Ellis wit; m Nov 1826 by L Dix.
TRAVIS Thomas to Sally W Brickhouse 12 Jun 1843; s/o Mrs Susan Travis con; d/o Thomas S Brickhouse con; Leonard B Nottingham & James B Wilson secs; m 14 Jun 1843 by P Williams.
TRAVIS William to Sally O'dear 13 Apr 1818; Abram Costin sec; m 16 Apr 1818 by W Costin.
TRAVIS William to Miss Elizabeth Costin 11 Nov 1850; Elizabeth wrd/o Thomas K Dunton; m 12 Nov 1850 by P Williams.
TRAVIS William S to Miss Frances D Brickhouse 19 Dec 1853; Thomas Travis as to ages; Wm G Smith wit.
TREHEARN Custis (Curtis?) to Harriot A Johnson 9 Dec 1833; d/o Polly Johnson con; Peter P Mayo sec; Edm'd Roberts & John T Johnson wits; m 14 Dec 1823 by G Wescoat.
TROWER Douglass to Elizabeth Fitchett 10 Sep 1821; Wm Dixon gdn/o Elizabeth con; Thomas Hallett sec; John S Spady wit; m 13 Sep 1821 by L Dix.
TROWER John to Sarah Smith 11 Jun 1791; d/o Richard Smith sec con; m 11 Jun 1791 by C Simkins.
TROWER John to Delitha Belote 19 Oct 1805; James Johnson sec; m (1805) by J Elliott.
TROWER John to Miss Elizabeth S

Fitchett 23 Dec 1846; d/o Mrs Leah Fitchett gdn & con; John T Hallett sec; Thomas Knight wit.
TROWER Luke to Bethany Jefferey 13 Nov 1826; Bethany wrd/o Nathan Drighouse sec (FN); m Nov 1826 by L Dix.
TROWER Luke to Ann Collins 18 Feb 1845; wid/o Victor Collins FN; Joshua P Wescoat sec; m 20 Feb 1845 by G G Exall.
TROWER Robert to Nelly Costin 31 Oct 1795; David Topping sec; m (1795) by E Baker.
TROWER Dr Robert S to Miss Sally A James 6 Jun 1838; Sally wrd/o John S James sec; m 8 Jun 1838 by G C Wescoat.
TROWER William to Sukey Williams 6 Sep 1815; John Spady sec; m (1815) by J Elliott.
TROWER William H to Susan Ann Tyson 15 Dec 1849; d/o Thomas Tyson sec; m 19 Dec 1849 by P Warren.
TRUITT Solomon to Frances Smith 4 Apr 1751; Solomon of Sussex Co, PA; wid; Matthew Warren sec; Hugh Baker wit.
TUNNIL John to Nancy Taylor 31 May 1803; James Travis sec; m (1803) by I Bratten.
TURNER Branson to Leah Savage 21 Oct 1803; Samuel Minson sec; m (1803) by C Fisher.
TURNER Custis to Sally Drighouse 15 Nov 1831; d/o Nathan Drighouse sec FN; Jno W Leatherbury as to Custis' age.
TURNER Edward to Mary Addison 26 Oct 1781; d/o Littleton Addison sec.
TURNER Edward R to Margaret Brickhouse 27 Dec 1820; d/o George Brickhouse con for "Pegey"; Laurance Enholm sec; H L Wilson wit; m 27 Dec 1820 by L Dix.
TURNER James to Patsey Wyatt 27 Apr 1818; Wm Mathews sec & as to Patsey's age; m 29 Apr 1818 by C Bonewell.
TURNER James to Nancy Haggaman 2 Sep 1829; Nancy wrd/o Benja Dunton sec con; Rich'd Cutler & Edw'd W Nottingham wits.
TURNER James E to Elizabeth S Knight 29 May 1838; d/o Wm Knight dec'd; Rubin Goody sec & as to ages; m 30 May 1838 by G C Wescoat.
TURNER James E to Matilda Ann Ames 25 Jan 1849; d/o Samuel Ames; Levin S Ames sec & as to Matilda's age; Thos M Savage wit; m 27 Jan 1849 by H Dalby.
TURNER John to Salley Pitts 22 Apr 1790; d/o Jno Pitts dec'd; Salley writes her own con; Jno T Turner sec; Major Pitts wit; Hezekiah Pitts former gdn/o Salley as to age; m 3 May 1790 by C Simkins.
TURNER John E G to Nancy Savage 19 Aug 1852; widower; wid/o Wm M Savage; m 19 Aug 1852 by M Oldham.
TURNER John G to Margaret Ann Joynes 26 Nov 1834; John wrd/o Joshua B Turner sec; d/o Edward Joynes sec; Jas Goffigon wit; m 28 Nov 1834 by G Wescoat.
øTURNER Joshua to Bridget Turner 18 Apr 1815; Joshua Garrison sec.
TURNER Joshua B to Sally S Scott 2 Feb 1829; wid/o John N Scott; Nathaniel West sec; m 4 Feb 1829 by P Williams.
TURNER Nathaniel to Anne Dunton 1 Oct 1805; Joshua Garrison sec; m (1805) by I Bratten.
TURNER Revel to Betsey Palker (Parker?) 26 Aug 1790; Teackle Turner sec; Thos Addison gdn/o Revel con to marry Betsey "Parlker"; Wm Walstone wit; m (1790) by E Baker.
TURNER Teackle to Nancy Sandford 13 Jul 1790; Michael Mathews sec.
TURNER Teackle to Peggy Mapp 5 Feb 1798; John K Floyd sec.
TURNER Teackle J to Ann P Wescoat 5 Dec 1826; s/o John & Peggy Turner; d/o John & Rosey

Wescoat; Jacob Nottingham Jr sec; m Dec 1826 by L Dix (m 25 Dec 1832 BRec V 10:118.)

TURNER Theophilus to Sophia Turner 22 Jan 1759; d/o Edw'd Turner dec'd; Hezekiah Dowty sec.

TURPIN John to Sally B Gascoyne 27 Oct 1789; John Upshur Jr sec; Thomas Upshur Sr con as to Sally.

TURPIN John to Nancy Willet 9 Oct 1809; Henry Walker sec.

TURPIN John D to Eliz Willett 15 Jan 1819; Thos H Turpin sec; m 21 Jan 1819 by C Bonewell.

TURPIN John S to Miss Mariah S Powell 10 Apr 1847; Mrs Margaret MacIntosh as to Mariah's age; Lafayette Harmanson sec; Hamilton Neale wit; m 11 Apr 1847 by H Dalby.

TURPIN Thomas to Lear Willet 1 Dec 1812; John D Turpin sec; m (1812) by A Milvin.

TYLER, TYLOR.

TYLER Benjamin to Polly Bell 9 Aug 1824; Polly wrd/o said Benjamin; Allen Brown & Richard Bell as to Benja's age; Rich'd Bell sec.

TYLER John to Catharine Moore 7 Jan 1778; Wm Wilson sec.

TYLOR John to Betsey Speakman bet 1 Jan - 8 Mar 1802 by J Elliott.

TYLER John to Peggy Spady 14 Dec 1818; Thos Vichus sec; m 17 Dec 1818 by W Costin.

TYLER Thomas to Ann Bishop 1 Jan 1800; Wm Wilson sec; m Jan 1800 by C Simkins.

TYSON John to Mary Widgeon 14 Dec 1787; d/o John & Ann Widgeon; Elijah Baker sec; m (1787) by E Baker. see BRec V9:90.

TYSON John to Sally Knight 21 Dec 1814; d/o John Knight con; Nath'l Widgeon sec; Severn Wigeon wit; m (1814) by J Elliott.

TYSON John to Susan Widgeon 2 Feb 1820; Nathaniel Widgeon sec.

TYSON Luther to Miss Rosena T Ridley 27 May 1851; d/o Wm W Ridley dec'd; Wm T Carmine as to Rosena's age; Wm T Duncan as to Luther's age; Wm T Fitchett wit; m 28 May 1851 by P Williams.

TYSON Nathaniel to Judith Wilkins 13 Jun 1761; d/o John Wilkins Sr; J L Fulwell sec.

TYSON Robert to Miss Elizabeth Stoit 23 Dec 1848; d/o Benjamin Stoit dec'd; Wm Warren as to Robert's age; Joshua Nottingham sec & as to Eliz's age; m 25 Dec 1848 by P Williams.

TYSON Samuel to Frances Godwin 19 Jul 1828; Frances wrd/o Shepherd B Floyd sec & as to Samuel's age.

TYSON Thomas to Nancy Widgeon 20 Mar 1823; d/o Nathaniel Widgeon sec; m Mar 1823 by L Dix. see BRec V9:90.

TYSON Thomas to Miss Sarah E Nelson 3 May 1842; d/o John Nelson Jr; James S Wilson sec & as to Sarah's age; m 4 May 1842 by P Warren. see BRec V9:90.

TYSON William to Anne Biggs 23 Dec 1817; d/o Nancy Biggs con; John Biggs sec; Elizabeth Brown wit; m 25 Dec 1817 by C Bonewell.

U

UNDERHILL Daniel to Mary Tompson 27 May 1761; wid/o (Rob't Tompson); Thos Underhill sec.

UNDERHILL Edmund E W to Polly S Nelson 12 Aug 1833; d/o Southy Nelson dec'd; James M Savage sec & as to Polly's age; John Floyd as to Edmund's age; Alex W Ward wit; m 17 Aug 1833 by G Wescoat.

UNDERHILL Michael P to Maria J Nelson 1 Dec 1834; d/o Southey Nelson dec'd; Thomas O Hunt sec & as to Maria's age; Smith Nottingham wit; m 3 Dec 1834 by G Wescoat. see BRec V4:5.

UNDERHILL Thomas to Susanna Evans 14 Nov 1767; d/o Arthur

Evans dec'd; Edmund Glanville sec.

UNDERHILL Thomas to Susanna Barlow 13 Aug 1793; Michael Mathews sec.

UNDERHILL William to Mary Westcoat 9 Jun 1807; Robert Sanford sec.

UPSHUR Abel to Elizabeth Gore 15 Nov 1779; Abel of Acc Co; d/o Daniel Gore dec'd & con/o Alexr Stockly her gdn; Edward Robins sec; Litt Savage wit.

UPSHUR Arthur B to Elizabeth G Carpenter 27 Apr 1811; Rickards Dunton gdn/o Elizabeth & con; Thos Nottingham sec; Keley Stott wit; m 28 Apr 1811 by Thos Davis.

UPSHUR George to Mary Pool 22 May 1852; s/o Susan Upshur; d/o Hessy Poulson FN; m 26 May 1852 by M Oldham.

UPSHUR Dr George Littleton * to Miss Sarah (Andrews) Parker 8 Feb 1844; (s/o John E & Elizabeth (Upshur) Nottingham) of Norfolk VA; (d/o Dr Jacob G & Anne (Stratton) Parker); Alfred Parker sec; m 8 Feb 1844 by J Ufford. see BRec V10:75. * Name changed from Geo Upshur Nottingham.

UPSHUR George P to Peggy E Parker 25 Jun 1836; George of US Navy; d/o Severn E Parker sec; m 28 Jun 1836 at "Kendall Grove" by Wm G Jackson. see BRec V5:155.

UPSHUR John to Ann Emmerson 4 Dec 1763. see BRec V8:174.

UPSHUR John to Margaret Michael 17 Mar 1781; wid/o Wm Michael; Jno Stratton Sr sec. see BRec V8:174.

UPSHUR John Sr to Rosey Robins 23 Jul 1794; Arthur Rogers sec.

UPSHUR John Jr to Elizabeth Brown Upshur 22 Oct 1798; Custis Kendall sec; T Tompkins states Elizabeth's age as upwards of 22y.

UPSHUR John Brown to Mary Elizabeth Stith 11 May 1802; John of Acc Co; d/o Wm Stith dec'd & Isaac Smith her gdn con; Wm B Savage sec.

UPSHUR Thomas to Anne Stockley 29 Jan 1761; Nath'l & Mary Beavans gdns/o Anne con; David Edmunds sec; Nath'l Bell wit.

UPSHUR Thomas T to Elizabeth T Smith 8 Apr 1842; d/o Isaac Smith sec; Thos L Kendall wit; m 12 Apr 1842. HunParReg:35. see BRec V8:166.

UPSHUR William B to Miss Catharine T Neale 3 Nov 1851; d/o Mrs Elizabeth T Neale; m 6 Nov 1851 by J Rawson. HunParReg:35.

UPSHUR William M to Elizabeth White 2 Sep 1805; John Addison sec.

UPSHUR William S to Miss Anne S Wilson 28 May 1827; Peter P Mayo sec; m 6 Jun 1827 by S S Gunter.

V

VAWTER William to Margaret Bonewell 12 Jul 1726; spinster; Luke Johnson Gent sec; Wm Stokes wit.

VERMILLION Guy to Sinah Jacob 15 May 1782; wid; Geo Parker Jr sec.

VICCOUS John to Esther Clegg 4 Oct 1792; d/o Clark Clegg late of Northampton Co & wife Sarah con; Stuart Saunders sec; m (1792) by E Baker.

VICHUS Thomas to Sally Freshwater 14 Dec 1818; John Spady sec; m 24 Dec 1818 by C Bonewell.

W

WADDEY, WADDY, WADY.

WADDY Edward R to Harriet Nottingham 19 Oct 1824; Harriet wrd/o Wm Nottingham Jr sec; m Oct 1824 by L Dix; (m 22 Oct 1824. see BRec V1:64; V9:14).

WADDEY John to Elizabeth Wise Rodgers 18 Jun 1768. see BRec V7:179; V9:14.

WADY John R to Hannah White 29

Jan 1801; Wm Gillet sec; (m 4 Feb 1801. see BRec V1:64; V9:14).

WADDEY Thos to Adah Carpenter 1 Nov 1788; Wm Hornsby sec.

WADDEY William E to Miss Mary E Griffith 12 Nov 1849; John H Griffith gdn/o Mary & sec; m 13 Nov 1849 by P Williams. see BRec V1:62.

WAGGAMAN Henrick to Winnifred Schyn 31 Aug 1660. BK IX:92.

WAKEFIELD Peter to Lusey Weeks 7 Sep 1794; Nath'l Holland sec.

WALCH William to Mary Moore 16 Dec 1819; Charles Dillion sec; m 16 Dec by C Bonewell.

WALTER John to Susanna Stott 8 Dec 1767; wid; Wm Dunton Sr sec.

WALTER Solomon to Sarah Read 18 Dec 1819; Arthur Roberts sec.

WALTER Solomon to Patty Wescoat 29 May 1835; wid/o John Wescoat; Miers W Fisher sec; m 20 Jun 1835 by G Wescoat.

WALTHAM John to Anne Michael 26 Dec 1759; John of Acc Co; wid; Jas Peterkin sec.

WALTHAM John to Susanna Johnson 10 Feb 1778; d/o Obediah Johnson dec'd; Jonathan Smith sec.

WALTHAM William to Sarah Johnson 24 Feb 1780; Sarah wrd/o said William by will; d/o Obediah Johnson dec'd & wife Priscilla Johnson con; Mich'l Dunton Jr sec; Wm White wit.

WAPLES Joshua to Betsey Costin 12 Dec 1803; Wm Costin sec; m (1803) by J Elliott.

WARD Albert D to Lettitia R Badger 27 Sep 1827; d/o Nath'l & Mary Badger. see BRec V6:114.

WARD Alexr W to Jennet S Turner 13 Dec 1813; Jas Sanford sec.

WARD Alexander W to Anne Bell 11 Apr 1831; d/o Anthony Bell con; Wm H Bell sec; Geo Richardson wit; m 11 Apr 1831 by G Wescoat.

WARD Golding to Peggy Savage 24 Aug 1786; d/o Delither Savage con; Seth Powell sec.

WARD James to Betsey Abdell 19 Mar 1806; Stephen Ward sec; m (1806) by I Bratten.

WARD James to Susan Smith 16 Nov 1819; Jacob Pettit sec & as to Sukey's age; A Costin & Wm Wilkins Sr wits.

WARD James to Margaret A C ___ 6 Sep 1826; s/o Golding & Nancy. see BRec V2:89.

WARD James G to Miss Margaret Ann Ross 20 Oct 1852; d/o Jno Ross dec'd; Wm J Nottingham as to ages; Edwd U Addison wit; m 21 Oct 1852 by P Warren.

WARD James H to Mary Robins 27 Dec 1841; d/o Arthur Robins; Wm B Upshur sec & as to ages; m 29 Dec 1841 by P Warren Jr. see BRec V7:51.

WARD James H to Tabitha (Bicey) Wyatt Joynes 21 Nov 1849; widower. S A Joynes Family:20 (clerk's office).

WARD John A to Tinney Trader 23 Dec 1803; James Benson sec.

WARD Joseph to Miss Sarah Isdell 12 Aug 1850; Sarah wrd/o said Joseph; m 14 Aug 1850 by P Warren.

WARD Littleton to Anne Bell 21 Dec 1787; Wm Belote sec.

WARD Michael to Ann (Anna) Johnson 16 Mar 1822; d/o John P Johnson who certifies as to Ann's age; Michael R Savage sec; m 19 Mar 1822 by C Bonewell.

WARD Michael to Miss Mary Turner 9 Sep 1839; Newton Harrison as to Michael's age; John Segar sec & as to Mary's age; Edm'd Roberts wit; m 12 Sep 1839 by G C Wescoat.

WARD Robert B to Peggy Heath 26 Mar 1804; James Heath con as to Peggy; Thomas Johnson Jr sec; m (1804) by J Elliott.

WARD Samuel to Malinda Mears 9 Mar 1836; d/o John Mears; James S Carpenter sec & as to ages; m 9 Mar 1836 by W B

Mears.
WARD Stephen to Elizabeth Harrison 2 Apr 1774; s/o Wm Ward Sr con; d/o Salathiel Harrison who certifies as to her age; Elijah McLanachan sec; Wm Ward Jr wit.
WARD Stephen to Nancy Cook 6 Jun 1791; Abner Thurston sec; m 9 Jun 1791 by C Simkins.
WARD Stephen to Adah Hickman 2 Mar 1797; John Abdil sec; m (1797) by I Bratten.
WARD Stephen to Betsey Edmunds 19 Mar 1806; James Ward sec; m (1806) by I Bratten.
WARD Tully S to Jane Brickhouse 10 Jul 1815; George Brickhouse Sr sec.
WARD William to Elizabeth Johnson 8 Aug 1786; Littleton Ward sec.
WARD William to Catharine McCready (no date, in 1786-1787 bundle); Robert Nottingham sec.
WARD William to Agnes Melvil 7 Jan 1797; Charles Carpenter Jr sec; m (1797) by I Bratten.
WARD William H to Miss Mary Isdell 11 Feb 1850; d/o James Isdell dec'd; James Dennis sec & as to ages; Michael N Higgins wit; m 13 Feb 1850 by P Warren.
WARE William to Barbara Batson 5 Feb 1722; (wid/o Jacob Batson); Abraham Bowker & Jno Ellegood secs; lic 5 Feb 1722 CT Ret Oct 1723.
WARREN Argill to Elizabeth Marriner 15 Feb 1709/1710; wid; Rob't Wiggon sec.
WARREN Calvin Laws* to Miss Mary E Roberts 30 Jun 1852; d/o Edmund Roberts dec'd; Edward P Roberts as to Mary's age; m 1 Jul 1852 by P Warren. * see BRec V3:50.
WARREN Devorax to Esther Abdil 12 Apr 1802; Wm Rooks sec; m Apr 1802 by C Simkins.
WARREN Devorax to Sabra M Dix 18 Jan 1836; d/o Levin Dix sec; Edward Holt as to Devorax's age.
WARREN Devorax to Elizabeth B Nicholson 4 May 1842; Levin H Nicholson as to Elizabeth's age; John Ker sec; E D Cottingham wit; m 4 May 1842 by P Warren.
WARREN Henry to Rose Mary Campbell 28 Jul 1772; d/o Nicholas Campbell, Rose 23y; John Gleeson sec; Wm Gibb McDonald & Sarah Gibb wits.
WARREN Hezekiah to Adah Kellam 4 Dec 1794; Wm Thomas sec; m Dec 1794 by C Simkins.
WARREN Hillery to Anne Mary Dixon 11 Jul 1764; wid/o (John Dixon); Rich'd Smith sec.
WARRAN Hilray to Hannah Rafield 11 Dec 1787; Isaac Bell sec; m (1787) by E Baker.
WARREN Hillary to Juda Wilkins 13 Oct 1806; Wm S Speakman sec; m (1806) by J Elliott.
WARREN Hillary to Esther Widgeon 14 Feb 1814; John Tyler sec.
WARREN James to Esther Parsons 8 Mar 1832; d/o Marriott Parsons dec'd; Stephen Wilkinson sec & as to ages.
WARREN James to Miss Sally Parkerson 28 Dec 1846; d/o George Parkerson dec'd; Joseph D Nottingham sec & as to ages; m 29 Dec 1846 by H Dalby.
WARREN John to Miss Polly Floyd 11 Jun 1838; d/o Mrs Sally Floyd con; John W Elliott sec & as to John's age; Thos Dawson & Edw'd W Nottingham wits; m Jun 1838 by P Williams.
WARREN John to Sally Wood 16 Oct 1813; Patrick Rooks & Jacob G Parker secs.
WARREN John to Miss Tabitha M Bell 1 Jan 1848; s/o Patrick Warren Sr sec; d/o Anthony Bell dec'd; m 3 Jan 1848 by P Warren.
WARREN John to Emily Mister 12 Feb 1849; d/o Gilbert Mister sec; John C Parsons as to John's age; m 15 Feb 1849 by P Williams.
WARREN John P to Catherine Kellam 18 Apr 1832; d/o Charles Kellam dec'd; Jacob Waterfield

sec & as to ages.

WARREN John P to Nancy Darby 22 Jan 1838; wid/o John Darby; John R Fisher sec; m 23 Jan 1838 by G Wescoat.

øWARREN Joseph to Martha Lune -- - 1707; John Savage & Joshua Cowdey secs. (Bond badly damaged)

WARREN Joseph to Peggy Evans 7 Jan 1812; Wm S Evans sec; m (1812) by J Elliott.

WARREN Joseph to Elizabeth Travis 11 Dec 1843; d/o Shadrack Travis sec; m 28 Dec 1843 by P Williams.

WARREN Patrick to Betsey Williams 12 Mar 1810; Wm Downs sec; m (1810) by J Elliott.

WARREN Patrick Jr to Elizabeth Ann Scott 16 Jul 1838; (d/o Thos & Sally H Scott) & wrd/o Wm S Floyd sec; Devorax Warren as to Patrick's age; m 18 Jul 1838 by L Dix.

WARREN Peter to Rose Johnson 13 Feb 1750; (d/o John & Elizabeth Johnson); John Flood sec.

WARREN Peter to Rose Johnson 3 Nov 1774; wid; Griffin Stith Jr sec.

WARREN Seth to Betsey Caple 31 Oct 1809; Edward Joynes sec.

WARREN Seth to Betsy Jones 21 Dec 1809; John Warren sec; m (1809) by J Elliott.

WARREN Thomas to Esther Viccus 2 Dec 1801; Stuart Saunders sec; m (1801) by J Elliott.

WARREN Thomas to Miss Ann Floyd 8 Jun 1840; Ann wrd/o Thomas Hellett sec & as to Thomas' age; W W Cutler wit; m 8 Jun 1840 by P Williams.

WARREN Thomas P to Eliza E Henderson 20 Oct 1842; d/o Wm Henderson dec'd; Wm G Robinson as to Eliza's age; Walter Belote sec; m 20 Oct 1842 by P Warren.

WARREN William to Anne Wheeler 26 Jul 1788; Wm Stith sec; m (1788) by E Baker.

WARREN William to Peggy Travis 12 Feb 1821; Peter Williams sec; m 15 Feb 1821 by L Dix.

WARREN William to Fanney Clegg 1 Jan 1811; Walter Luker sec; m bet 1 Jan - 8 Apr (1811) by J Elliott.

WARREN William Jr to Rosey Bradford 16 Jan 1830; Wm Speakman sec; Benja Tyler sec & as to ages; m 18 Jan 1830 by P Williams.

WARREN William of Hilary to Anne Dix 28 Dec 1835; wid/o Isaac Dix; James Warren sec & as to William's age; m 30 Dec 1835 by L Dix.

WARREN William H to Angeline Moore 16 Aug 1852; wid/o Wm D Moore; m 17 Aug 1852 by P Williams.

WARRINGTON George to Nancy Barrett 20 Dec 1808; Thos Widgeon sec; m (1808) by J Elliott.

WARRINGTON George to Sally Toleman 8 Jan 1816; Jeptha Johnson sec & as to Sally's age; m bet 1 Jan - 12 Feb (1816) by C Bonewell.

WARRINGTON John to Elizabeth Willis 18 Jun 1810; Jos Warren sec; m (1810) by J Elliott.

WATERFIELD George to Miss Margaret Fatherly 24 Dec 1849; d/o John Fatherly dec'd; Major Taylor sec & as to ages; Thos H Bagwell wit; m 3 Jan 1850 by M Oldham.

WATERFIELD Jacob to Susanna Harrison 11 Jun 1748; spinster; Geo Holt sec; Cath Blaikley wit.

WATERFIELD Jacob to Sarah Joyne 21 Feb 1791; Elijah Watson sec.

WATERFIELD Jacob to Zipporah Crocket 14 Aug 1843; d/o Thomas Crocket; Teackle J Turner sec & as to ages; John Ker wit.

WATERFIELD Jacob to Sally Turner 4 Sep 1843; d/o James Turner (Occ) sec; m 6 Sep 1843 by G C Wescoat.

WATERFIELD John Jr to Mary Dunton 12 Feb 1754; d/o Richard Dunton con; Isaac Dunton sec; Elias Dunton Jr wit.
WATERFIELD John to Elizabeth Brickhouse 14 Jun 1803; John Brickhouse Jr sec.
WATERFIELD Meshack to Jane Salts 14 Jun 1785; Wm Waterfield sec.
WATERFIELD Meshack to Rachel Benthall 15 Jan 1790; John Waterfield sec; m 18 Jan 1790 by C Simkins.
WATERFIELD Meshack to Priscilla Bool 31 Jan 1797; James Dalby sec; m (1797) by J Elliot.
WATERFIELD Meshack to Sally West 15 Feb 1812; d/o Tamer West as to Sally's age; David Topping sec; Thomas Ames wit.
WATERFIELD Richard to Peggy Hutcheson m Sep 1793 by C Simkins.
WATERFIELD Southy to Peggy Wilkins 28 Dec 1771; d/o Wm Wilkins dec'd; Wm Trower sec; Wm Harmanson & Joachim Michael wits.
WATERFIELD Thomas to Mahala Heath 12 Aug 1816; Kendall Addison sec; m 21 Aug 1816 by Joshua Burton.
WATERFIELD William to Nancy Hunt 8 Jun 1779; d/o Azariah Hunt dec'd; Michael Dunton sec.
WATERS Edward to Margaret Waters 18 Aug 1731; John Custis sec.
WATERS Thomas to Susanna Stringer 20 Apr 1799; Wm W Wilson sec.
WATERS William to Mary Bayaton 4 Oct 1707; Andrew Hamilton sec.
WATERS William Gent to Margaret Robins 20 Mar 1728; spinster; Jno Robins Jr Gent sec; Geo Pole wit.
WATERS William to Rose Harmanson 10 May 1739; Joseph Cottman & John Maddox of Somerset Co Md secs.
WATERS Wm to Ann Jacob 13 Jul 1790; d/o Robert Clark Jacob sec. (Bond badly damaged)
WATSON Besial to Pattsey Dennis 7 Aug 1805; Major Dennis sec; m (1805) by I Bratten.
WATSON Bezel to Nancy Dennis 25 Jan 1815; Archibald Dennis sec & as to Nancy's age; m (1815) by C Bonewell.
WATSON Besey (Bezel) to Jinny Dennis 14 Apr 1816*; Wm Satchell sec; m 15 Apr 1817* by C Bonewell. *discrepancy
WATSON Edmund to Rosanna Andrews 26 Dec 1786*; d/o Sarah Abdell con; Wm Harrison sec & wit (*date of con; bond nd).
WATSON Edmund to Peggy Thomas 3 Feb 1801; Wm Thomas sec; m (1801) by J Elliott.
WATSON Edmund to Peggy Westcot 2 Aug 1802; Thomas Dowty sec; m (1802) by J Elliott.
WATSON Moses to Director Twiford 1 Jan 1730; Arther Roberts & Geo Nicholas Turner secs; Ebenezer Tollman wit.
WATSON Revel to Nancy Tankard 15 Jul 1794; Geo Holt sec; m (1794) by E Baker.
WATSON Revil to Eckay Jofflif 8 Jul 1811; Kendall Addison sec.
WATSON Wm to Elenor Johnson 17 Jul 1800; Benjamin Johnson sec; m 1800 by J Elliott.
WATSON William to Nancy Major 4 Sep 1821; Wm Savage sec & as to ages; m 6 Sep 1821 by C Bonewell.
WATTS, WATT.
WATTS David to Margaret Simkins 5 Sep 1799; Coventon Simkins sec; m Sep 1799 by C Simkins.
WATT James to Mason Kendall 2 Mar 1708/1709; Wm Kendall Sr sec; Sam'l Palmer wit.
WATTS John W to Sarah Boyd 24 Nov 1794; Nath'l Wilkins Jr sec; m (1794) by E Baker.
WATTS John Wilkins to Rachel Fitchett 25 May 1765; wid/o (Nehemiah Fitchett); John Smaw sec.

WEBB Aaron to Catharine Drighouse (FN) 31 Dec 1811; James Carter sec; m (1811) by J Elliott.

WEBB Charles to Sinah Sample FN 7 Jun 1791; Wm Satchell Jr sec; Chas Satchel wit; m 11 Jun 1791 by C Simkins.

WEBB James to Margaret Isdale 8 Oct 1821; Margaret wrd/o said James; Matthew H Dunton sec; m 8 Oct 1821 by C Bonewell.

WEBB James to Louisa Bell 9 Oct 1843; d/o John Bell dec'd; James S Carpenter sec & as to ages; Jas M Nicholson wit; m 11 Oct 1843 by P Warren Jr.

WEBB Levin to Mary Matthews FN 31 Dec 1851; George Guy as to Mary's age; Jno R Birch wit; m 1 Jan 1851 by M Oldham.

WEBB Southy to Ann Miles 26 Oct 1795; John Carpenter (Hog Island) sec; m 1795 by I Bratten.

WEBB Southey to Hessey Virginia Hargiss 16 Aug 1852; James S Bunting as to ages; James M Brickhouse wit; m 19 Aug 1852 by M Oldham.

WEEKS, WEICKS, See also WICKES.

WEICKS Cornelius to Nancy Howell FN 2 Sep 1848; Geo B Dunton sec & as to Nancy's age; Sylvester M Kelly wit; m 2 Sep 1848 by S C Bolton.

WEEKS Daniel to Nanny Morris 6 Jul 1803; Abraham Lang sec (FN).

WEEKS Ely to Molly Collins 8 Aug 1817; John Sample sec (FN); m 9 Aug 1817 by C Bonewell.

WEEKS Jacob to Tinsey Gardiner 21 Sep 1813; James Weeks sec (FN); m (1813) by I Bratten.

WEEKS James to Peggy Stephens 8 May 1810 (FN); Rich'd Johnson sec; Lucy Stephens states Peggy is 21y.

WEEKS John to Mary Weeks 20 Aug 1817; Samuel Bevans sec (FN); m 21 Aug 1817 by C Bonewell.

WEICKS John to Jane Brickhouse FN 13 Apr 1846; Jane wrd/o said John; Charles J D West sec; m 13 Apr 1846 by T T Moorman.

WEEKS Levi to Peggy Stephens 6 Jan 1809; James Travis sec.

WEEKS Nathaniel to Abigail Thompson 23 Dec 1822; Severn Weeks sec; m 26 Dec 1822 by C Bonewell.

WEICKS William to Betsy Moses FN 12 Jun 1848; s/o Marea Weicks sec; d/o Jenny Moses sec; Thomas L Kendall sec; Wm J Fitchett wit; m 12 Jun 1848 by B H Johnson.

WEEKS Zorobabel to Nancy (Ann) Beavens 3 Jan 1793*; Reubin Reed sec; m Jan 1794* by C Simkins. *discrepancy

WEISIGER Joseph K to Mrs Cath S Jones 23 Dec 1846; John S Parker sec; m 24 Dec 1846 by J Ufford. HunParReg:35.

WESCOAT, WESTCOTE.

WESCOAT Edmund to Polly Dunton 19 May 1796; Michael Dunton sec.

WESCOAT Edmund to Adah Abdell 25 Sep 1805; George Mehulloms sec.

WESCOAT Edmund P to Elizabeth Bunting 26 Jul 1819; d/o Nancy Bunting con; Wm Bunting sec; Wm G Pitts wit.

WESCOAT Rev George C to Mary Ann Johnson 26 Dec 1828; d/o Thomas Johnson Jr dec'd; Harrison T Rayfield sec. see BRec V2:131.

WESCOAT George M to Rosey Savage 22 Jan 1850; wid/o George L Savage; Joshua P Wescoat sec & as to George M's age; m 30 Jan 1850 by P Warren.

WESCOAT Hezekiah P to Susan Savage 24 Dec 1816; Michael R Savage sec; m 26 Dec 1816 by C Bonewell.

WESCOAT Hezekiah P Jr to Rosey J Andrews 14 Dec 1847; d/o Shepherd Andrews con; Fred B Fisher sec; Joshua P Wescoat as to Hezekiah's age; m 15 Dec 1847 by M Oldham.

WESTCOTE John to Esther Floyd 6 Apr 1774; wid; Jno Upshur sec.

WESCOAT John to Rosey Wescoat 9 Feb 1801; Edmund Wescoat sec; m (1801) by J Elliott.

WESCOAT John Jr to Patsey Harden 8 Apr 1806; John Carpenter gdn/o (not given) con 20 Mar and 7 Apr stating that Mr Pitts no longer opposes the marriage; Esau Godwin sec.

WESCOAT Joshua to Mary Pitts 14 Sep 1771; d/o Major Pitts dec'd; Robert Polk sec.

WESCOAT Joshua P to Miss Eleanor Dowty 20 Dec 1848; Benjamin Thomas gdn/o Eleanor con; Lafayette Harmanson sec; m 20 Dec 1848 by P Warren.

WESCOTE Littleton to Mary Jacob 1 Sep 1766; d/o Philip Jacob dec'd; Zerobabel Downing sec; Jos West & Jno Buckner Stith wits.

WESTCOAT Major to Polly Dowty 11 Jul 1812; Thos W Badger sec; Rowland Dowty as to Polly's age; m (1812) by I Bratten.

WESCOAT Nathaniel S to Miss Margaret E A Scott 19 Sep 1853; James W Rogers as to ages; Joshua P Wescoat wit; m 21 Sep 1853 by J Allen.

WESCOAT William to Sally Bloxom 9 Dec 1789; John Bloxom sec.

WEST Abel to Bridget Hutson 27 Dec 1808; Teackle Roberts sec.

WEST Charles to Joanna Dunton 16 Feb 1798; (d/o Jacob Dunton); Littleton Major sec.

WEST Charles J D to Miss Elizabeth R Pitts 14 Mar 1836; d/o Major S Pitts dec'd; John G Turner sec; Robins Mapp as to Charles' age; Thomas Smith Jr as to Elizabeth's age; Jos E Bell wit; m 16 Mar 1836 by W B Snead.

WEST Edward to Martha Vandegrot 6 Mar 1726; Gawton Hunt sec; Wm Tye wit; lic 6 Mar 1726 - CT ret Oct 1727.

WEST John to Nancy Becket 21 Aug 1805; Wm Drighouse sec (FN).

WEST John C to Elizabeth Snead 6 Jan 1801; Wm Gillet sec.

WEST John T to Sally Smith 11 Dec 1837; Sally wrd/o Walter W Widgen sec; Edward C Savage as to John T's age; m 21 Dec 1837 by W B Snead.

WEST Joseph to Anne Johnson 1 Sep 1766; wid; Littleton Wescote sec; Zero Downing & Jno B Stith wits.

WEST Joseph to Catharine Snead 13 Mar 1781; wid/o Thomas Snead; Jno Furbush Turner sec.

WEST Joseph to Nelly Martin 5 Nov 1817; James Johnson sec; m 5 Nov 1817 by C Bonewell.

WEST Nathaniel to Mary Smith Dolby 20 Nov 1810; Arthur B Upshur sec.

WEST Nathaniel to Mary Turner 29 Aug 1812; d/o John Turner con; Richard Johnson sec; m 2 Sep 1812 by Thos Davis.

WEST Nathaniel S to Eliza Ann Harrison 18 Sep 1843; d/o James Harrison; Wm P Ridley sec & as to ages; m 20 Sep 1843 by G C Wescoat.

WEST Samuel to Margt Fitchett 12 Sep 1815; Johannes Johnson sec; m (1815) by C Bonewell.

WEST Thomas to Margaret Nottingham 7 Apr 1814; Samuel Coward sec; Wm E Nottingham & Thos Copes as to Margaret's age; m (1814) by J Elliott.

WEST Thorowgood to Susanna Eshon 14 Jan 1786; Nath'l Holland sec; Walter Hyslop con as to Susanna (dated 14 Jan 1785).

WEST Toby to Thamar Thompson 22 Dec 1820; Job Upshur sec.

WEST William to Mahala Collins 6 Feb 1828; d/o John Collins dec'd FN; Robert Powell sec & as to ages; m 6 Feb 1828 by P Williams.

WESTERHOUSE Abraham to Anne Andrews 15 Feb 1770; (wid/o Wm Andrews); John Thomas sec.

WESTERHOUSE Reubin to Sarah Scott 11 Nov 1766; d/o Wm Scott

dec'd; Jno Waterfield Jr sec.
WESTERHOUSE William to Margaret White 23 Jul 1745; wid; Isaac Nottingham sec.
WESTERHOUSE William to Leah Mapp 13 Mar 1759; wid/o (Howson Mapp); Thomas Watts sec; Joachim Michael wit.
WESTERHOUSE William to Anne Jacob 12 Dec 1764; d/o Abraham Jacob dec'd; Edmund Glanville sec.
WHALEY Joshua to Leah Wheeler 25 Nov 1778; Wm Graves sec.
WHEELER James to Elizabeth Rippin 8 Dec 1778; d/o John Rippin dec'd; Wm Rippin sec.
WHEELER Jas to Elizabeth Soals 3 Sep 1781; Isaac Moor Jr sec.
WHEELER James to Naomi D Brickhouse 14 Dec 1835; Naomi wrd/o Wm W Scott sec; Wm Rooks Sr as to James' age; Wm W West wit; m 16 Dec 1835 by L Dix.
WHEELER John to Edith Luke 14 Jul 1772; d/o Daniel Luke dec'd; Joseph Dalby sec.
WHEELER John to Anne Scott 13 Jun 1777; wid; John Harwood sec.
WHEELOR John to Margaret Garret 24 Nov 1778; d/o Amos Garret; Joshua Whaley sec.
WHEELER John to Keziah Snale 24 Apr 1782; Henry Smaw sec.
WHEELER John to Betsey O'dear 22 Jun 1805; Mariot Willis sec; m (1805) by J Elliott.
WHEELER John T to Eliza Ann Dowty 8 Oct 1838; Eliza wrd/o James Dowty sec; Thomas A Wheeler as to John T's age; Washpon Ashly wit; m 10 Oct 1838 by L Dix.
WHEELOR Thomas to Betsey Wilson 21 May 1803; Geo Scott sec; m (1803) by J Elliott.
WHEELOR Thomas to Peggy Seaton 11 Jun 1810; Henry Smaw sec; m (1810) by J Elliott.
WHEELOR Thomas to Agnes Wilkins 8 Jun 1811; d/o Susan Wilkins as to Agnes' age; Nath'l Wilkins sec; John Wilkins Jr wit; m (1811) by J Elliott.
WHITE Edward T to Mahala Ann Savage 4 Dec 1839; d/o Mahala Savage gdn & con; James H White sec & as to Edward's age; Obediah Johnson wit; m 6 Dec 1839 by G C Wescoat.
WHITE George D to Margaret Waterfield 18 Dec 1816; Thos Waterfield sec; Peggy (Waterfield) Stott con as gdn/o both Margaret & Mary Waterfield, app't in 1808 before her own marriage; she & Laban Stott Sr now give their con; m 24 Dec 1816 by C Bonewell.
WHITE James H to Ann Wilkins 30 Aug 1837; d/o John Wilkins Jr; Thos Smith Jr sec & as to ages; m 7 Sep 1837 by W B Snead.
WHITE John to Sarah Deale 29 Jan 1789; wid; Wm Hays sec.
WHITE John to Susey Cary 10 Nov 1806; Johannes Johnson sec; m (1806) by I Bratten.
WHITE Joseph to Peggy Jacob 10 Jan 1775; d/o Hancock Jacob; Severn Nottingham sec.
WHITE Obedience to Nancy Heath 29 Oct 1813; Robert A Joynes sec; m (1813) by I Bratten.
WHITE Teagle to Elizabeth Pitts 28 May 1789; wid/o George Pitts; James Sanford sec.
WHITE Teackle S to Margaret Ward 29 Nov 1815; Obedience White sec; m (1815) by J Elliott.
WHITE Teackle S to Susan Kellam 24 Apr 1827; d/o Charles Kellam dec'd; Teackle J Turner sec & as to Susan's age; m 1827 by G C Wescoat.
WHITE Teackle S to Margaret J Harmanson 20 May 1843; George T Belote sec & as to Margaret's age; Patrick Warren wit; m 21 May 1843 by G C Wescoat.
WHITE Thomas to Esther Cowdry 4 Nov 1745; wid; P Norly Ellegood & Wm Bishop secs.
WHITE Thomas to Polly Thompson

17 Aug 1812; William Mathews sec; m (1812) by I Bratten.
WHITE Thomas to Polly Robins 2 Nov 1818; John R Fisher sec.
WHITE Thomas to Esther Abdel 26 Aug 1823; Esther 28y; Abbot Belote sec; m 27 Aug 1823 by C Bonewell.
WHITE William to Mary Moore 9 Feb 1661/1662. BK IX:114.
WHITE William to Rachel Jacob 17 Oct 1771; Wm Jacob sec.
WHITE William to Sarah L Sanford 3 Dec 1811; d/o James Sanford con; John C West sec.
WHITE William Sr to Eliz H Dunton 23 May 1814; Geo J Savage sec; m (1814) by I Bratten.
WHITE William to Elizabeth Eshon 25 Jul 1818; John Bull sec; m 27 Jul 1818 by C Bonewell.
WHITE William to Emeline Savage 20 Jan 1840; s/o William White; d/o Wm K Savage con; John C Mapp sec & as to William's age; Hez P James & Wm T Nottingham wits; m 20 Jan 1840 by G C Wescoat.
WHITEHEAD John to Sucky Smith 11 May 1790; d/o James Smith sec; m 12 May 1790 by C Simkins.
WHITEHEAD John Jr to Sally Goffigon 5 Jan 1813; John Griffeth sec; Abram Costin as to Sally's age; B Griffith wit; m (1813) by J Elliott.
WHITEHEAD John to Elizabeth Bain 25 Nov 1816; (batch); (wid); C B Upshur sec; m 1 Dec 1816 by R Symes.
WHITEHEAD Stephen to Charlotte Downes 24 May 1831; wid/o Capt Daniel Downes; Wm Whitehead sec; m 25 May 1831 by P Williams.
WHITEHEAD Thomas to Ann Milbourn 11 May 1829; Wm Whitehead gdn/o Thos sec; d/o Thomas Milbourn sec; 20 May 1829 by P Williams.
WHITEHEAD Thomas to Emeline Jones 25 Nov 1836; d/o Richard Jones dec'd; Jesse J Simkins gdn/o Emiline con sec; Benjamin Griffith wit; m 3 Dec 1836 by P Williams.
WHITEHEAD William to Lucretia Spady 6 Aug 1789; Jacob Spady sec.
WHITEHEAD William to Margaret Warrington 3 Dec 1821; Wm Parsons sec gives Margaret's age as 28y or more; m 6 Dec 1821 by L Dix.
WHITEHEAD William S to Miss Sally P Evans 8 Dec 1851; d/o Thomas S Evans; John G Dennis as to William's age; m 16 Dec 1851 by P Williams. see BRec V4:60.
WICKES, WICKS, See also WEEKS.
WICKES Edmund to Lucy Brickhouse (FN*) 27 Jul 1839; Leonard B Nottingham sec; Gabe Wickes as to Lucy's age; m 3 Aug 1839 by S T Ames. * Ephram Stephens certifies that Edm'd Wickes FN wants to mate with Lucy Brickhouse a slave formerly belonging to him and purchased in 1822 by the said Edm'd who now has legal title to her increase. Stephens doubts that clerk would grant license without his certificate. (Note that Bond indicates Lucy as a free negro.)
WICKES Edward to Lavinia Howell FN 30 Mar 1840; s/o Maria Wickes sec; d/o Sukey Wickes formerly Sukey Howell con; George Holt sec; m 1 Apr 1840 by S T Ames.
WICKES Gilbert to Lucy Scisco 20 Nov 1834; s/o Maria Wickes sec; d/o Rachel Scisco dec'd FN; Edmund Wickes sec; Betty Scisco as to Lucy's age; m 22 Nov 1834 by L Dix.
WICKES Isaac to Lauretta Powell (mulattoes) 26 Nov 1839; Leonard B Nottingham sec; m 26 Nov 1839 by S T Ames.
WICKES Jacob to Sukey Simkins 16 Feb 1827; s/o Betsey Wickes; d/o Dilly Simkins (FN); Short John Collins sec; Betsey & Dilly

as to ages; Henry B Kendall & Wm R Brounley wit.

WICKES Spencer to Sally Becket FN 22 Dec 1836; Juliet & Maria Becket as to Sally's age; Luther Nottingham sec; m 24 Dec 1836 by W B Snead.

WICKES Thomas to Rachel Ann Scisco 12 Oct 1830; Rachel wrd/o Isaac Stephens sec; Jno Collins as to Thomas' age (FN); Josiah T Polk wit.

WICKS William to Comfort Wicks 5 Mar 1822; Samuel Beavans sec.

WICKES William to Betsey Wickes (FN) 10 Oct 1826; Wm Sample sec; Wm Francis Jr as to Betsey's age.

WIDGEON, WIDGEN.

WIDGEON George F to Elizabeth Spady 13 Jan 1834; d/o Thomas S Spady con; Walter W Widgeon as to George's age; Thos W B Jarvis & Piner W Clarke wits; m 14 Jan 1834 by P Williams.

WIDGEON John to Adah Westerhouse 18 May 1765; d/o Thos Westerhouse dec'd; Rickards Dunton sec.

WIDGEN John to Anne Floyd 24 Mar 1770; d/o Mathew Floyd dec'd; Thos Widgeon sec.

WIDGEN John to Esther Ellegood 22 Aug 1772; wid; Wm Johnson Sr sec.

WIDGEON John to Bridget Robins 19 Jan 1792; Kendall Belote sec.

WIDGEON John to Priscilla Heath 10 Mar 1817; (wid/o Josiah Heath); John Taylor sec; m 12 Mar 1817 by G Bonewell.

WIDGEON John to Maria B Nottingham 3 Mar 1818; (d/o Jos Walter & Ann (Jacob) Nottingham); Thos Jacob sec; m 5 Mar 1818 by S W Woolford.

WIDGEON John Jr to Susan Taylor 5 Dec 1831; d/o Betsy Moore (formerly Betsy Taylor) dec'd; Abram Moore sec & as to ages.

WIDGEON Capt John to Elizabeth Widgeon 30 Sep 1844; wid/o Severn Widgeon; Robert B Nottingham sec; m 1 Oct 1844 by P Williams.

WIDGEON John S to Sarah Ann Jacob 16 Oct 1834; d/o Hancock Jacob dec'd; Robert C Jacob sec & as to Sarah's age.

WIDGEON Joseph to Peggy Russel 11 Dec 1787; Richard Savage sec.

WIDGEON Joseph S to Miss Margaret E Mister 28 Dec 1852; d/o Wm Mister con; Jno H Kellam & Purnall B Carey wits; J H Kellam as to Joseph's age.

WIDGEN Leaven to Susanna Wilson 13 Nov 1777; d/o Wm Wilson dec'd; Southy Nelson sec.

WIDGEON Littleton to Lovey Timmons 9 Mar 1807; Moses Horner sec; m (1807) by J Elliott.

WIDGEON Littleton to Tinney Biggs 2 Feb 1839; wid/o Christopher Biggs; John T West sec; m 6 Feb 1839 by S T Ames.

WIDGEON Nathaniel to Susanna Knight 11 Dec 1802; Wm Wilkins sec; m (1802) by J Elliott.

WIDGEON Robert to Nancy Wingate 23 Dec 1828; d/o Southy Wingate dec'd; John Tyson sec & as to ages; m 24 Dec 1828 by P Williams.

WIDGEON Robert to Miss Susan Jones 21 May 1840; Douglas Trower sec & as to Susan's age; Thos C Mears wit; m 21 May 1840 by W A Dix.

WIDGEN Severn to Rachel Willis 25 Nov 1778; d/o Josiah Willis; John Scott sec.

WIDGEN Severn to Molly Knight 30 Apr 1791; John Knight Jr sec; m (1791) by E Baker.

WIDGEON Severn to Elizabeth Salts 1 Jan 1828; d/o John Salts dec'd; Thomas Tyson sec & as to ages; m 1 Jan 1828 by P Williams.

WIDGEON Southy to Miss Mary Susan Nottingham 18 Dec 1851; d/o Joseph D Nottingham.

WIDGEON Thomas to Anne Stockley 3 Mar 1759; (wid/o Wm

Stockley); Edward Widgeon sec.

WIDGEON Thomas to Esther Nottingham 19 Nov 1805; Jos Nottingham sec; m (1805) by J Elliott.

WIDGEON Thomas to Elizabeth Bell 11 Jan 1807; Thomas Dunton sec; m (1807) by J Elliott.

WIDGEON Walter W to Susan Smith 12 Nov 1832; d/o George Smith Sr dec'd; Thos Griffith sec & as to ages; m 21 Nov 1832 by P Williams.

WIDGEN Westerhouse to Nancey Fitchett 5 Aug 1789; John Dennis sec; Daniel Fitchett con as to Nancey; m (1789) by E Baker.

WIDGEN Westerhouse to Sally Widgeon 11 Jul 1796; Elijah Baker sec; m (1796) by E Baker.

WIDGEN Westerhouse to Nancy Costin 3 Mar 1798; Francis Costin sec.

WIDGEON Westerhouse to Elizabeth Dunton 11 Feb 1828; Elizabeth wrd/o Shepherd B Floyd sec; Teackle Jacob as to Westerhouse's age.

WIDGEN William to Rachel Pitts 18 Apr 1761; wid/o (Jacob Pitts); John Glisan sec.

WILKERSON See also WILKINSON.

WILKERSON Stephen to Sally Biggs 26 Feb 1827; d/o Christopher Biggs sec; m 26 Feb 1827 by S S Gunter.

WILKINS Benjamin to Elishey Willis 26 Jul 1775; d/o Josias Willis con; Jno Widgeon Sr sec.

WILKINS Eleazer to Rachel Griffith 17 Jun 1772; d/o Nathan Griffith dec'd; Hezekiah Griffith sec.

WILKINS George F to Anne Snead 27 Dec 1817; (batch); (spinster); Wm Satchell sec; m 31 Dec 1817 by R Symes.

WILKINS George F to Margaret B Williams 28 May 1825; Margaret wrd/o Margaret Williams sec; m May 1825 by L Dix.

WILKINS James to (Nelly Griffith) 22 Dec 1807; Nathaniel Jones sec; m (1807) by J Elliott (above name of bride from MinRet).

WILKINS James to Miss Hetty Harman 9 Dec 1822; Edwin Godwin con as to James; James Saunders sec; Jas Goffigon & Patrick F Costin wits; m Dec 1822 by L Dix; (m 25 Dec 1822. see BRec V4:45).

WILKINS Joakim to Delitha Hunt 14 Dec 1801; Wm Jones sec; m (1801) by J Elliott.

WILKINS Joakim to Margaret Hunt 9 Jul 1839; wid/o Obediah Hunt; John M Wilkins sec; m 10 Jul 1839 by W A Dix.

WILKINS John Jr to Cath Custis 7 Sep 1748; wid/o (Edmund Custis); Henry Smaw sec.

WILKINS John Jr to Susanna Stratton 18 May 1752; spinster d/o Susanna Stratton con; Thomas Stratton sec; Solomon Warren wit.

WILKINS John to Smart Stockley 10 Jan 1764; John blacksmith; d/o Woodman Stockley dec'd; John Wilkins Jr sec.

WILKINS John Jr to Mary Pettitt 13 Jun 1769; wid/o (Wm Pettitt); Jno Blair sec.

WILKINS John to Sarah Hunt 30 Dec 1769; d/o Thomas Hunt dec'd; Obadiah Hunt sec.

WILKINS John (OP?) to Susanna Carpenter 15 Nov 1786; Charles Carpenter sec.

WILKINS John to Elizabeth Elliet 31 Mar 1794; Wm Scott Jr sec; m Mar 1794 by C Simkins.

WILKINS John to Betsey Goffigon 9 Nov 1803; David Rippin sec; m (1803) by J Elliott.

WILKINS John Jr to Mary Spady 3 Jul 1810; d/o Southy Spady con; Levin Nottingham sec; m (1810) by J Elliott.

WILKINS John Jr to Catherine Evans 22 Dec 1832; wid/o John Evans; Samuel W Dunton sec; m 26 Dec 1832 by W B Snead.

WILKINS John B to Polly Williams 22 May 1824; Christopher

Williams as to Polly's age; James Wilkins sec.

WILKINS John M to Miss Margaret Susan Williams 13 Jan 1836; James Saunders sec & gdn/o Margt; m 20 Jan 1836 by L Dix.

WILKINS John S to Elizabeth Wilkins 10 Nov 1795; d/o Wm Wilkins con; Thos Wilkins sec; m Nov 1795 by C Simkins.

WILKINS Dr John T to Miss Elizabeth A Roberts 5 Nov 1844; s/o Wm E & Nancy; d/o Sally Roberts con; Alex W F Mears sec & as to John's age; Esther W Roberts wit; m 6 Nov 1844 by P Warren Jr.

WILKINS Leonard T to Miss Sallie E Downing 18 May 1852; Wm E Brickhouse as to Sallie's age; m 19 May 1852 by P Warren.

WILKINS Major to Adah Fathery 22 Jul 1769; Jno Evans sec.

WILKINS Major to Mary Guy --- 1778; wid; Geo Harmon sec.

WILKINS Nathaniel to Susanna Wilkins 21 Dec 1779; d/o Wm Wilkins Sr con; Wm Willis sec; Nan Joyne wit.

WILKINS Nathaniel to Nancy Joynes 24 Aug 1818; Abram Costin sec; m 26 Aug 1818 by C Bonewell.

WILKINS Peter to Elishe Collins 19 Sep 1795; Thos Webb sec; m (1795) by E Baker.

WILKINS Robert to Elizabeth Harmanson 4 Nov 1793; d/o Henry Harmanson; Nath'l Holland sec; m 4 Nov 1793 by C Simkins.

WILKINS Robert to Nelly Jones 26 Nov 1827; d/o Nathaniel Jones dec'd; James Wilkins of Benja sec & as to ages; Daniel Fitchett & L B Nottingham secs; m Dec 1827 by L Dix.

WILKINS Robert to Elizabeth Parsons 7 Dec 1841; d/o Marriott Parsons dec'd; George F Wilkins sec; James Warren as to Elizabeth's age; m 8 Dec 1841 by P Warren Jr.

WILKINS Robert E to Mary Ann Fitchett 11 Nov 1844; d/o Daniel Fitchett sec; m 13 Nov 1844 by P Warren Jr.

WILKINS Severn to Rosy W Elliott 3 Apr 1832; d/o John Elliott dec'd; James Saunders sec & as to ages; m 5 Apr 1832 by L Dix. see BRec V1:43.

WILKINS Southey S to Miss Kiturah G Dunton 27 Mar 1843; d/o Benjamin F Dunton dec'd; John S Wilson sec & as to ages; m 29 Mar 1843 by P Warren Jr.

WILKINS Thomas M to Sarah E Saunders 22 Dec 1840; d/o James Saunders con; Victor A Nottingham sec & as to Thomas' age; Edw'd Holland & W W Wilkins wits; m 23 Dec 1840 by P Williams. see BRec V1:100, 111.

WILKINS Walter L to Patsy F Nottingham 22 Dec 1832; Patsy wrd/o Thomas J Nottingham sec & as to Walter's age; m Dec 1832 by L Dix (m 25 Dec 1826 BRec V 14:88.)

WILKINS William Jr to Agnes Stratton 9 Nov 1758; d/o John Stratton Gent dec'd; Nath'l Stratton sec; John Stith wit. see BRec V10:49.

WILKINS William Jr to Elizabeth Johnson 11 Aug 1773; wid; Wm Scott sec; m 12 Aug 1773. see BRec V10:50.

WILKINS William Jr to Frances Benthall 29 Sep 1778; d/o Wm Benthall dec'd; John Knight sec.

WILKINS William Jr to Peggy Scott 11 Jan 1790; d/o Wm Scott sec.

WILKINS William (OP) to Margaret Speakman 5 Mar 1793; James Floyd sec; m (1793) by E Baker.

WILKINS William OP to Sarah Fitchett 25 Jan 1802; Wm Hanby sec; m bet 1 Jan - 8 Mar (1802) by J Elliott.

WILKINS William to Susanna Godwin 9 Dec 1802; Nath'l Widgeon sec; m (1802) by I Bratten.

WILKINS William Elliott to Nancy Trower 26 Sep 1815; s/o John &

Betsey Wilkins; d/o John & Sally Trower; Thomas Dixon sec & as to Nancy's age; m 28 Sep 1815 by J Elliott. see BRec V2:60.

WILKINS William S to Miss Emily S Spady 25 Jun 1844; s/o William E Wilkins sec; d/o Mrs Rosey S Costin sec; m 26 Jun 1844 by P Williams.

WILKINS William W to Elizabeth C Kendall 26 Jun 1843; d/o Elizabeth W Kendall con; Robert E Wilkins sec; Thos E Evans wit; m 28 Jun 1843 by P Williams.

WILKINSON See also WILKERSON.

WILKINSON Stephen to Anne Speakman 3 Feb 1790; wid; Robert Fitchett sec; m (1790) by E Baker.

WILKINSON Stephen to Betsey Warren 25 Dec 1811; Wm Warren sec; m (1811) by J Elliott.

WILKINSON William to Mary Baike 15 Dec 1661. BK IX:114.

WILLETT, WILLET.

WILLETT Douglas to Henrietta Johnson 21 Jun 1760; d/o John Johnson dec'd; Amos Johnson sec; Adderson Nottingham wit.

WILLET Douglas to Betsey Savage 13 Jan 1796; d/o Abel Savage con but states her age as over 21y; Thomas Dunton sec.

WILLETT James R to Edy Wheeler 21 Mar 1827; Arthur A Wilson sec & as to ages; Smith Nottingham & Ellison A Hopkins wits; m 21 Mar 1827 by P Williams.

WILLIAMS Archibald to Mrs Margaret B McIntosh 22 Jul 1847; Jackson B Powell sec; m 23 Jul 1847 by H Dalby.

WILLIAMS Azariah to Anne Costin 14 Aug 1787; Benja Griffith sec.

WILLIAMS Azariah to Susan C Clay 17 Jan 1821; Peter Williams gdn/o Susan con; Matthew Floyd sec; George Sumers wit.

WILLIAMS Benjamin to Margaret Barnes 26 Jan 1829; John Spady Jr sec & as to ages; m 29 Jan 1829 by P Williams.

WILLIAMS Benjamin to Sukey Clegg 1 Jan 1838; d/o Wm Clegg dec'd; John Spady Jr sec & as to ages; m 1 Jan 1838 by P Williams.

WILLIAMS Benjamin to Sally Ann Jacob 30 Aug 1843; d/o Wm Jacob dec'd; Thomas L Griffeth as to Sally's age; Joshua P Wescoat sec; m 31 Aug 1843 by G G Exall.

WILLIAMS Christopher to Nancy Moore 11 Sep 182(6); d/o John Moore sec; Peter Moore wit; m Sep 1826 by L Dix.

WILLIAMS Custis F to Frances McCowan 27 Apr 1835; d/o Nancy McCowan; Elijah Brittingham Jr sec; Littleton Townsend as to ages; m 30 Apr 1835 by P Williams.

WILLIAMS Custis F to Elizabeth Griffith 4 Jul 1839; d/o Sally Griffith con; Elias Roberts sec; Benjamine Griffith wit; m 4 Jul 1839 by P Williams.

WILLIAMS Edward to Sarah Sanders 7 Aug 1778; d/o Richard Sanders sec.

WILLIAMS Goodwn G to Mary R Hulings 15 Aug 1848; s/o Thos N & Anne S Williams; d/o David W & Maria H P Hulings; m in Lewistown, Pa. see BRec V2:98.

WILLIAMS James to Margaret Johnson (undated in 1787 bundle); Wm Stith sec.

WILLIAMS James to Susey Mathews 23 Dec 1801; Thos Lewis sec; m 1801 by I Bratten.

WILLIAMS James to Suky Costin 14 Sep 1812; Southey Goffigon gdn/o James con; d/o Wm Costin Sr con; Wm Jarvis sec; Jas Johnson & Wm Jarvis Jr & Ann Bayton wits; m (1812) by J Elliott.

WILLIAMS James to Nancy Harrison 4 Feb 1840; s/o John G & Nancy; d/o Newton Harrison sec; Geo Warren as to James' age; m 4 Feb 1840 by J T Hazzard.

WILLIAMS James D to Miss Lavinia A W Dunton 10 Dec 1838; John

E Nottingham sec & gdn/o Lavinia.
WILLIAMS John to Edith Nottingham 11 Aug 1775; d/o Thomas Nottingham Sr; Thos Nottingham Jr sec; Samuel Williams con & Thos Nottingham con.
WILLIAMS John to Margaret Glanville 17 Aug 1787; Severn Nottingham sec.
WILLIAMS John to Margaret Goffigon 12 Jun 1793; Nath'l Goffigon gdn/o Margaret con; Hillery Hunt sec; m Jun 1793 by C Simkins.
WILLIAMS John to Nancy Hughes 24 Dec 1800; Wm Stokely gdn/o Nancy con; Chas Fitchett sec; m 1800 by I Bratten.
WILLIAMS John Jr to Peggy Powell 25 Aug 1804; Thomas Dowty sec; m (1804) by J Elliott.
WILLIAMS John to Esther Roberts 28 Dec 1829; d/o Teackle Roberts dec'd; Benja Dunton sec; Arthur T Roberts as to ages; m 29 Dec 1829 by G Wescoat.
WILLIAMS John to Mary Dillion 29 May 1833; d/o Charles Dillion sec; Moses Turner as to John's age.
WILLIAMS John A to Miss Sally M Trower 18 Feb 1846; d/o Douglass Trower dec'd; Mrs Elizabeth Trower as to Sally's age; Wm T Fitchett sec; G W Brittingham wit.
WILLIAMS John Green to Nancy Hitchins 12 Jul 1805; James Travis sec; m (1805) by J Elliott. see BRec V2:64.
WILLIAMS John L to Elizabeth Powell 21 Nov 1812; Thos Dowty sec; m (1812) by J Elliott.
WILLIAMS Rev John W M to Corinthia V J Read 21 Dec 1846; d/o Margaret L Read con; Richard T Read & Calvin Read wits; John H Winder sec; m 22 Dec 1846 by P Warren.
WILLIAMS Lloyd W to Maria Patton Hulings 5 Sep 1844; Lloyd of Norfolk, Va & s/o Thos N & Anne S Williams; d/o David W & Maria H P Hulings; m in Lewistown, Pa. see BRec V2:98.
WILLIAMS Peter to Elishe Dixon 16 Jun 1791; Thomas Downs sec.
WILLIAMS Peter to Betsey Trower 14 Nov 1808; Joseph Warren sec; m (1808) by J Elliott.
WILLIAMS Peter to Polly Hickman 7 Apr 1811; d/o Eliz Hickman con; Geo Powell sec; Ann Williams as to Peter's age; Nath'l Hickman & Robert Fitchett wits; m (1811) by I Bratten.
WILLIAMS Peter to Nancy Clay 28 Feb 1816; Thomas Powell sec.
WILLIAMS Samuel to Sarah Haggoman 7 Nov 1753; spinster; Geo Harmanson sec.
WILLIAMS Samuel to Sarah Dunton 4 Dec 1764; d/o Levin Dunton sec.
WILLIAMS Samuel to Margaret Nottingham 12 Dec 1772; d/o Thomas Nottingham sec.
WILLIAMS Samuel to Sukey Dixon 14 Jun 1799; Peter Williams sec; m (1799) by I Bratten.
WILLIAMS Samuel to Peggy Burris 21 Jan 1806; Levin Nottingham sec; Wm Jarvis in support of Samuel's application; m (1806) by I Bratten.
WILLIAMS Samuel to Elizabeth Mills 22 Mar 1833; d/o Jacob Mills dec'd; Gilbert Mister sec & as to ages; E R Waddy wit; m 26 Mar 1833 by P Williams.
WILLIAMS Seth to Rosy Roberts 20 Dec 1831; d/o Teackle Roberts dec'd; Stephen Wilkinson & James Williams secs & as to ages.
WILLIAMS Thomas to Elizabeth Timmons 21 Jul 1800; Wm Salusbury sec.
WILLIAMS Thomas to Sally A Luker 6 May 1814; Walter Luker sec; m (1814) by J Elliott.
WILLIAMS Thomas to Rachel Willis 14 Jan 1822; d/o Josias Willis dec'd; Josiah Willis sec & as to

Thomas' age; John Upshur Sr wit.

WILLIAMS Thomas B to Sarah Ann P West 30 May 1836; d/o Nathaniel West; Smith S Nottingham sec; Patrick H Fitchett as to Thomas' age; John T West br/o Sarah as to her age; m 1 Jun 1836 by W B Snead.

WILLIAMS Capt Thomas N to Anne S Nottingham 12 Feb 1814; d/o Wm Nottingham Sr sec con; John L Williams & Thos Nottingham wits; (m 17 Feb 1814. see BRec V2:98).

WILLIAMS William to Mary Nottingham 29 Apr 1786; d/o Thos Nottingham Sr as to her age; Thos Wilson sec.

WILLIAMS William to Lear Goffigon 3 Aug 1795; John Goffigon sec.

øWILLIAMS William to Ann (Nancy) Jacob Dunton 16 Dec 1806; Hancock Dunton sec; m (1806) by J Elliott.

WILLIAMS William H to Adah Widgeon 26 Sep 1833; Adah wrd/o Walter W Widgeon sec; m 2 Oct 1833 by P Williams.

WILLIAMS William N to Miss Rosina B Dunton 1 Aug 1842; John E Nottingham gdn/o Rosina sec; m 3 Aug 1842 by P Williams.

WILLIAMS William N to Miss Virginia U Fitchett 8 Sep 1851; d/o Daniel Fitchett; m 9 Sep 1851 by P Williams.

WILLIS Custis to Polly Fitchett 26 Apr 1812; Peter Bowdoin sec; m (1812) by J Elliott.

WILLIS Custis to Miss Emily S Moore 23 Nov 1852; d/o Mrs Angeline B Warren con; Sheppard Roberts wit; Luther Nottingham as to Custis' age; m 24 Nov 1852 by H Dalby.

WILLIS George to Jenny Jackson 26 Dec 1791; d/o Jonas Jackson; Wm Smith sec; m (1791) by E Baker.

WILLIS George to Catherine Smith 29 Dec 1800; Catherine wrd/o Major Pettitt con; Thos James sec; m 1800 by I Bratten.

WILLIS James to Lucretia Moore 24 Dec 1821; d/o John Moore sec; (m 27 Dec 1821. see BRec V1:91; V3:134).

WILLIS John to Peggy Clegg 25 Jan 1800; John Frost sec; m (1800) by J Elliott.

WILLIS John to Miss Arinthia Travis 29 Oct 1850; Arinthia wrd/o Leonard B Nottingham; m 30 Oct 1850 by H Dalby.

WILLIS Josiah to Elizabeth White 18 Feb 1788; d/o Levin White dec'd; Severn Widgen sec.

WILLIS Josiah to Elizabeth Rippin 24 Dec 1823; d/o Thomas; Thos Rippin as to ages; Thos Smith Jr sec.

WILLIS Leonard J to Miss Mary S Cottingham 20 Dec 1852; d/o Henry Cottingham con; Custis Willis as to Leonard's age; Luther Nottingham wit; m 21 Dec 1852 by P Williams. see BRec V1:90.

WILLIS Marrot to Sally Freshwater 23 Apr 1790; Severn Widgeon sec; m 28 Apr 1790 by C Simkins.

WILLIS Parker to Sarah Goffigon 15 Dec 1795; Samuel Costin sec; m (1795) by E Baker.

WILLIS Parker to Elishe Costin 27 Jul 1797; Rich'd Nottingham sec; m Jul 1797 by C Simkins.

WILLIS Thomas to Anne Knight 1 Nov 1792; Westerhouse Wid-geon sec; m (1792) by E Baker.

WILLIS Thomas to Elishe Graves (Groves) 11 Feb 1794; d/o Peter Graves; Littleton Jones sec; m (1794) by E Baker.

WILLIS Thomas to Susan Jones 1 Jan 1836; d/o Nathaniel Jones dec'd; John Spady Jr sec & as to Susan's age; m 2 Jan 1836 by L Dix.

WILLIS William to Margaret Ellegood 1 Sep 1775; d/o ___ dec'd; Rich'd Nottingham sec.

WILLIS William to Smart Dunton 3 Jan 1788; d/o Elias Dunton dec'd; John Scott sec.

WILLIS William to Sally Burke 23 Dec 1824; Moses Turner sec states Sally's age as 26y acc'd to her mother.

WILLIS William to Kessy Stripe 29 Jun 1830; wid/o Peter Stripe; James Williams Sr sec; m 1 Jul 1830 by P Williams.

WILLIS William to Polly Nottingham 30 Nov 1836; wid/o Joseph Nottingham; Smith Nottingham sec; m 1 Dec 1836 by L Dix.

WILLY George to Elizabeth Jones 12 Dec 1835; d/o Richard Jones dec'd; N J Winder sec; Moses Turner as to ages; m 16 Dec 1835 by L Dix.

WILSON Arthur to Nancy Wheelor 20 Dec 1806; Leroy Oldham sec; m (1806) by J Elliott.

WILSON Edward B to Elizabeth S S Floyd 20 Dec 1843; d/o Shepherd B Floyd dec'd; Kendall Groten sec & as to ages; m 21 Dec 1843 by P Warren Jr.

WILSON Edward H C to Sally Stratton 5 May 1818; (d/o John Stratton); Jacob G Parker sec.

WILSON Harold Luther to Leah L Savage 6 Jan 1814; m 1814 by Thos Davis. see BRec V8:8; V9:12.

WILSON Henry P C to Susan E Savage 15 Jun 1824; Henry of Somerset Co, Md; d/o Thos L & Margaret (Teackle) Savage; Peter Bowdoin sec; m 16 Jun 1824 by M B Chase. see BRec V9:13.

WILSON James to Mary Tyson 18 Dec 1816; John Tyson sec; m 19 Dec 1816 by C Bonewell.

WILSON James to Sukey Spady 12 Sep 1821; Sukey wrd/o Henry B Kendall sec; m 12 Sep 1821 by C Bonewell.

WILSON James B to Anne H Brickhouse 25 Nov 1843; d/o Thomas S Brickhouse; Rob't J Nottingham sec & as to Anne's age; Thos H Nottingham wit; m 28 Nov 1843 by P Williams.

WILSON James S to Elizabeth A Dix 30 Aug 1842; wid/o Wm A Dix; John Bishop sec; m 31 Aug 1842 by P Williams.

WILSON John C Jr to Mary Ann Savage 9 May 1818; Caleb B Upshur sec.

WILSON John S to Nancy Tilghman 26 Jun 1821; Dennard Travis sec & with John Whitehead as to Nancy's age; m 28 Jun 1821 by L Dix.

WILSON John S to Keturah Churn 1 Jan 1833; George Holt Jr sec; John M Savage as to ages; m 2 Jan 1833 by W B Snead.

WILSON Littleton to Margaret Floyd 9 Oct 1815; Shepherd B Floyd sec; m (1815) by J Elliott.

WILSON Littleton to Polly Wilkins 8 May 1837; wid/o John Wilkins; George P Upshur sec; m 8 May 1837 by W B Snead.

WILSON Moses to Sally Wingate 8 Mar 1803; David Topping sec; m bet 1 Jan - 9 May 1803 by J Elliott.

WILSON Moses to Betsey Dunton 3 Feb 1813; Shepherd B Floyd sec; m (1813) by J Elliott.

WILSON Moses to Adah Knight 28 Dec 1830; d/o Wm Knight dec'd & wrd/o Thomas Tyson sec; m 29 Dec 1830 by P Williams.

WILSON Samuel to Peggy Custis 25 Mar 1760; d/o (John Custis dec'd) & Ann Custis Tompkins who states Peggy is of age; Levin Gale sec; Littleton Dennis & Wm Hayward & Levin Wilson wits.

WILSON Spencer to Frances Watts 22 Sep 1774; d/o Thomas Watts dec'd; Wm Waltham sec.

WILSON Spencer to Susanna Andrews 17 Sep 1778; d/o Wm Andrews dec'd & Ann Westerhouse as to Susanna's age of 21y; John Wheeler sec.

WILSON Spencer to Nancey Stott 17 May 1788; d/o Thos Stott dec'd & sis/o John Stott con who states her age as 21y on 15 Nov last (i.e. 1787); Wm Thomas & Jacob Roberts wit; Michael Dunton Sr sec; m (1788) by E

Baker (MinRet shows "Wm" Wilson).
WILSON Stockly to Sarah Wilson 21 Sep 1785; Henry Warren sec.
WILSON Stockley to Smart Wilkins 19 Apr 1787; Argyl Wilkins sec.
WILSON Stockley W to Mary W Rayfield 17 Jun 1822; d/o John Rayfield con sec; Dennard Rayfield & Wm Thomas & Joseph Jester secs; m 19 Jun 1822 by L Dix.
WILSON Thomas to Ann Scott 26 Dec 1787; d/o Zorobabel Scott dec'd; Rich'd Nottingham sec; m (1787) by E Baker.
WILSON Thomas to Elizabeth Cobb 8 Jun 1824; d/o Southey Cobb con; Wm Kellum sec; C B Stockley & LeRoi Oldham & Isaiah (Baker?) secs; m 8 Jun 1824 by C Bonewell.
WILSON William to Molly Spady 10 Feb 1795; d/o Abraham Spady con; Azariah Williams sec; m (1795) by E Baker.
WILSON William Jr to Adah Pratt 18 Nov 1797; Charles Dillon sec; m (1797) by I Bratten.
WILSON William to Polly Wilson 23 Dec 1814; Thos G Scott sec; m (1814) by J Elliott.
WILSON Wm (shipwright) to Margaret Kellam 26 Jan 1835; Matt D Moore sec & as to Margt's age; Montcalm Oldham sec.
WILSON William to Ann Harrison 14 Dec 1835; Ann wid/o Isma Harrison; Charles Dillion sec; m 16 Dec 1835 by P Williams.
WILSON William Bishop to Nancy Freshwater 17 May 1790; Marrot Willis sec.
WILSON William T to Miss Polly Frost 8 Oct 1839; Wm W Wilson sec & as to Wm T's age; John S Wilson as to Polly's age; m 10 Oct 1839 by P Williams.
WILSON William W to Peggy Custis Tompkins 14 Jan 1795; d/o T Tompkins con; Thos Parramore Sr sec.
WILSON William Washington m @1800 Nancy Dillon. see BRec V5:113.
WINDER John H to Sally C Snead 4 Nov 1816; C B Upshur sec; m 4 Nov 1816 by R Symes.
WINDER Nathaniel J to Margaret S Bowdoin 21 Nov 1821; Peter Bowdoin sec; m 21 Nov 1821 by C Bonewell.
WINDER Nathaniel James to Sarah Upshur Bayly 18 Oct 1826; s/o John & Susanna Winder; d/o Richard D & Sarah D Bayly. see BRec V7:158.
WINDER Richard H to Miss Elizabeth L Custis 2 Feb 1849; s/o Sarah U Winder sec; James J Ailworth gdn/o Elizabeth sec; m 13 Feb 1849 by J Ufford.
WINDOW Levin to Elizabeth Ann Andrews 28 May 1838; d/o Shepherd Andrews con; Edward J Joynes sec & as to Levin's age; John R Dunton wit; m 30 May 1838 by G C Wescoat.
WINGATE, WINGET.
WINGATE Daniel to Comfort Willis 27 Dec 1815; d/o Marrot Willis con; John Floyd sec; Wm Sav-age Jr wit; m (1815) by J Elliott.
WINGET George to Mary Miller 22 Jun 1786; James Wilson sec; m (1786) by E Baker.
WINGATE Jacob to Nice Wilson 11 Mar 1796; Matthew Floyd sec; m (1796) by I Bratten.
WINGATE James to Nancy Scott 13 Jan 1812; Benja Griffith sec; m (1812) by J Elliott.
WINGATE James to Mahala Clegg 1 Jan 1833; d/o Major Clegg dec'd; Thos Whitehead sec; Nath'l Dalby sec & as to Mahala's age; m 3 Jan 1833.
WINGET John to Sarah Wattson 27 Feb 1760; d/o Robert Wattson con; Azariah Hunt sec; James Cox & Wm Watson wits.
WINGATE Severn to Nancy Moore 1 Jan 1833; d/o Abram Moore; George Holt Jr sec; John Spady as to Nancy's age; m 1 Jan 1833 by L Dix.

WINGATE Southy to Peggy Costin 11 Jan 1808; John Spady sec; m (1808) by J Elliott.

WINGATE Thomas to Arady Deare 1 Aug 1789; d/o Wm Deare con; John Stoyte sec; m (1789) by E Baker.

WINGATE William to Amey Tylor 24 Dec 1807; John Spady sec; m (1807) by J Elliott.

WISE Johannes to Peggy Dunton 23 Jan 1799; James Travis sec; m Jan 1799 by C Simkins.

WISE John Jr to Sarah Batson wid/o Ralph; d/o Jno & Eliza Waterson; m 2 Jan 1765; John of Acc Co; Custis Matthew sec.

WISE Tully (R?) to Mary Bowdoin 11 Feb 1795; John Eyre sec.

WISE Tully R to Mary Fisher 7 Dec 1797; John Macgowan sec.

WISE Tully R to Anne K Evans 18 Nov 1834; d/o John K Evans dec'd; Wm Lytt Savage sec; Geo T Yerby as to Anne's age; (m 19 Nov 1834. see BRec V1:52).

øWISE Zackariah to Cassey Dalby 21 Jan 1801; Severn Nottingham sec; m Jul 1801 by C Simkins.

WISE Zachariah to Fanny Bishop 10 Jan 1814; Teackle Roberts sec.

WISELY Ronald to Ann Fitchett Dixon 8 Aug 1808; Jacob (Mills?) sec; m (1808) by J Elliott.

WOLFORD Roger to Mary Denwood 1 Mar 1660/ 1661. BK IX:92.

WOOD William to Bridget Batson 7 Jun 1760; Jno Harmanson sec.

WOOD William to Rebecca Scott 12 Jan 1786; Kendall Godwin sec.

WOODARD John to Rebecca Chandler 12 Jun 1708; Capt John Luke sec; Thos Church Sr wit.

WORSER Jacob to Esther Trower 1 Oct 1811; James Jacob sec; m (1811) by J Elliott.

WRIGHT John to Betsey Dunton 17 Feb 1802; John Simkins sec; m bet 1 Jan - 30 Mar (1802) by J Elliott.

WRIGHT Thomas to Margaret Belote 16 Dec 1793; d/o George Belote sec.

WYATT Arthur M to Miss Emory V Downing 6 Dec 1852; Arthur of Acc Co; Emory wrd/o A W Downing con; P A Goodridge wit; W E Brickhouse as to Arthur's age; m 8 Dec 1852 by J A Weed.

WYATT James W to Virginia Fitchett 30 May 1845; d/o William Fitchett Sr dec'd; Calvin H Savage sec & as to ages; m 30 May 1845 by G C Wescoat.

WYATT John R to Miss Elizabeth Jane Kellam 21 Dec 1846; d/o Stewart Kellam dec'd; John B Smith sec & as to ages m 21 Dec 1846 by G C Wescoat.

WYATT William to Margaret Smith Tankard 4 Nov 1811; William of Acc Co; d/o John Tankard con; Ischar Lewis sec. (At the end of his con Jno Tankard speaks of the illness which few have escaped in the county and asks, "Does the Comet or Democracy bring this evil upon us?")

WYATT Wm to Sally Sturgis 18 Sep 1827; wid/o Wm Sturgis; Edward A Joynes sec & as to Wm's age; m 1827 by G C Wescoat.

Y

YATMAN John to Elizabeth Ayres 18 Oct 1803; Stuart Saunders sec; m (1803) by J Elliott.

YERBY Dr George T to Charlotte H Jacob 5 Apr 1824; Peter S Bowdoin gdn/o Charlotte sec; m 7 Apr 1824 by S Wilmer.

YERBY Wm to Mary Satchell 23 Nov 1782; Laban Johnson sec.

YOUNG Ezekiel to Sally Luker 3 Jan 1822; wid/o Walter Luker; James Young sec.

YOUNG George H to Nancy Ward 10 Feb 1809; d/o Littleton Ward con; Golding Ward sec.

YOUNG John to Suky Johnson 22 May 1794; d/o Obedience Johnson con; Major Pettit sec; m May 1794 by C Simkins.

YOUNG Littleton W to Elizabeth P Savage 24 Jun 1831; wid/o Wm

T Savage; James Young sec & as to Littleton's age; m 24 Jun 1831 by G Wescoat.

YOUNG Littleton W to Tabitha Scarborough 27 Nov 1838. HunParReg:35.

YOUNG Richard to Patsey Abdell 26 Oct 1797; Westerhouse Widgen sec; m (1797) by E Baker.

YOUNG Thomas to Elizabeth Trower 13 Aug 1810; d/o John Trower Sr con; Wm Costin sec; Thos Goffigon wit; m (1810) by J Elliott.

YOUNG Dr Thomas W to Margaret S Downing 24* May 1842; d/o Dr Edmund W P Downing; George Brickhouse sec & as to Margaret's age; m 22* May 1842 by G C Wescoat. *discrepancy

YOUNG William to Mary Darby 21 Jan 1748; d/o John Darby con; Peter Hog sec; Benja Darby & Jonah Jackson Jr wits.

MINISTERS

Fifty-one ministers submitted marriage returns to the Clerk of Northampton County from 1786-1854. A list of the ministers follows. It may also be of interest to note the number from each denomination. (This enumeration does not include the several Episcopal rectors of Hungars Parish 1660-1662.)

Baptist	14
Episcopal	8
Methodist	24
Universalist	1
Not identified	4

The Episcopal Church was struggling to survive the disestablishment of the state-supported Church of England after the American Revolution. The Baptist Church began to grow rapidly while the Methodist congregations were increasing by leaps and bounds. The list of ministers who submitted returns from 1786 on clearly reflects this situation. With the addition of some few denominations, a similar pattern of religious persuasion holds true to the present day on Virginia's Eastern Shore.

Ministers (who submitted to the Clerk of the Northampton County Court lists of the marriages which they had performed, 1786-1854):

Allen, John	Methodist
Ames, Shadrack T	Methodist
Baker, Elijah	Baptist
Bonwell, Charles	Methodist
Boston, S. C.	Baptist
Bradford	Baptist
Bratten, Isaac	Baptist
Burton, Joshua	Methodist
Chase, Moses B.	Episcopal (St. Geo. Parish-1824-26)
Costin, William	Baptist
Cunningham, James	Methodist
Curtis, John D.	Methodist
Dalby, Hezekiah	Methodist, South
Davis, Thomas	Episcopal (1809-15)
Dix, Levin	Baptist
Dix, William A.	Baptist
Elliott, John	Baptist
Elliott, Thomas A.	Methodist
Exall, George G.	Methodist
Fisher, Caleb	Baptist
Foster, Archibald	Methodist

Gunter, Stephen Selby	Episcopal (1824-1835)
Hazzarol, John T.	Methodist
Henry, John	??
Hill, Charles	Methodist, North
Jackson, William G.	Episcopal (1835-1841)
Johnson, B. H.	(Methodist?)
Laws, William	Baptist (Upper Acc. Co.)
Lewis, Jefferson	Methodist
Lumsden, George L.	Universalist (Belle Haven, Va.)
Maddux, John B.	Methodist
Milvin, Avery	Methodist
Moorman, Samuel T.	Methodist, South
Newell, M. B.	(Methodist?)
Oldham, Montcalm	Methodist, South
Rawson, James	Episcopal (1850-1854)
Simkins, Coventon	Methodist
Snead, William B.	Methodist
Sorin, M.	??
Stevenson, Edward	Methodist
Symes, Robert S.	??
Ufford, John	Episcopal (1843-1850)
Walker, Joseph	Baptist
Warren, Patrick, Jr.	Baptist
Weed, J. Ambler	Episcopal (1850-1853)
Wescoat, George C.	Methodist
Williams, Peter, Jr.	Methodist
Wilmer, Simon	Episcopal (1819-1824)
Wilshire, George	Methodist
Windsor, Robert C.	Baptist
Woolford, Stevens W.	Baptist

CLERKS OF COURT

Northampton County Clerks 1632-1854*

The Clerks of the Court were appointed by the Justices and among other duties were charged to issue and record marriage bonds and licenses.

1632	Henry Bagwell	1705	Robert Howson
1638	George Dawe	1720	James Locker
1641	Thomas Cooke	1721	Hillary Stringer
1642	Edwin Conway	1722	Godfrey Pole
1648	Edmond Matthews	1729	Thomas Cable
1658	John Boys	1743	Griffin Stith
1659	Robert Hutchinson	1783	William Stith
1665	William Melling	1791	Thomas L. Savage
1670	Daniel Neech	1813	Caleb B. Upshur
1671	John Culpepper	1821	Nathaniel J. Winder
1674	Daniel Neech	1844	Lewis O. Rogers
1703	Hancock Custis	1852	La Fayette Harmanson

* Whitelaw: 255

FREE NEGRO SURNAMES

To facilitate research in African-American studies. Free Negro, Mulatto or Slave has been indicated on the marriage entry when it could be ascertained. Many clerks and ministers were especially diligent in recording the race of the individuals to be married. If not so recorded, race can often be determined, especially for witnesses, since in the case of slaves and free blacks, they "had first to be charged as the law directs". (See Raleigh Thompson entry-1835). The record of free blacks who married slaves frequently gives interesting details supplied by the slaves' owners. (See Arthur Becket and Edward Wickes entries, both 1839).

A very helpful indicator, of course, is the knowledge of family surnames. Most of the names listed below are predominantly those of free black families. Those marked by an asterisk in many instances are shared by both races. The list, of course has been drawn only from the marriage entries and is by no means inclusive of all the African-American families living on the Eastern Shore in the period covered.

*Ames	Drighouse	Mingo	Scisco
Anthony	Drigus	Morris	*Simkins
Becket	Francis	Moses	Stephens
Bevans	*Giddens	Nedab	Thompson
Bingham	*Harmon	Pool	Toyer
*Brickhouse	Jeffery	Press	Webb
*Carter	Jubilee	*Read	Weeks
Church	Lang	Rozelle	Wiecks
*Collins	Liverpool	Sample	
Cottrell	*Major	Satchell	

STATISTICS

For those with a mind for figures, a few statistics which may be of interest concerning this compilation have been assembled.

Total Marriage Entries	3285
Marriage License Bonds	3180
Original bonds (recorded by S. Nottingham in 1929) now missing	13
Marriages abstracted from Bible Records	25
Bible entries from which data was used	120
Total Minister Returns	2070
Minister Returns submitted prior to 1791	135
Returns by Jno Laurence, Clerk of Hungars Parish 1660-1662	62
Returns to the Court (Licenses) made during the 1722-1740	18

More than 62% of the Marriage Entries bear minister verification.

REFERENCES

BOOKS AND COMPILATIONS

Billings, Warren M., Editor. *The Papers of Francis Howard, Baron Howard of Effingham 1643-1695*. Virginia State Library and Archives, Richmond, Virginia. 1989.

Mariner, Kirk. *Revival's Children, A Religious History of Virginia's Eastern Shore*. Peninsula Press, Salisbury, Maryland. 1979.

McDonald, Cecil D., Jr. *Some Virginia Marriages. 1700-1825*. Privately printed. 1319 N 169th Street, Seattle, Washington, 98133. 1974. (Virginia State Library, Richmond)

Mihalyka, Jean M., compiler. *Bible Records. Accomack and Northampton Counties, Virginia*. 10 volumes. Unpublished compilation. Copies deposited in Northampton Co., Va. Clerk's Office; Eastern Shore of Virginia Public Library, Accomac, Va.; Virginia State Library, Richmond, Va.; Sargeant Room, Norfolk Public Library; DAR Library, Washington, D.C.

Mihalyka, Jean M., compiler. *Church Records. Northampton County, Virginia*. Unpublished compilation. Copies in various repositories. (See above entry.)

Nottingham, Stratton. *The Marriage License Bonds of Northampton County, Virginia from 1706 to 1854*. Onancock, Virginia, 1929. Genealogical Publishing Co., Baltimore, Md. 1974. Reprint.

Turman, Nora Miller. *St. James Church and St. George Parish 1763-1990. Accomack County, Virginia*. Eastern Shore Printers, Onancock, Va. 1990.

Whitelaw, Ralph T. *Virginia's Eastern Shore*. Virginia Historical Society, Richmond, Virginia. 1951. 2 v.

DOCUMENTS (printed and manuscript)

The Acts of the General Assembly of Virginia... Samuel Shepherd, Printer to the Commonwealth. Richmond, 1845.

The Code of Virginia. Printed by Wm F. Ritchie, Public Printer. Richmond, 1849.

Hening, William Waller, ed. *The Statutes at Large; Being a Collection of all the Laws of Virginia...1619-1792.* R & W & G Bartow. New York. 1809-1823. 13 vol. Reprint 1969.

Hungars Parish Register, Northampton County, Virginia 1836-1895. Copy of original manuscript in Rector's Office, Eastville, Virginia.

Marriage License Bonds, Northampton County, Virginia 1706-1854. Original manuscripts - Clerk's Office, Eastville, Va.

Marriage Licenses, Northampton County, Virginia 1722-1727; 1735-1740; 1850-1860. Original manuscripts. Clerk's Office, Eastville, Va.

Minister's Returns, Northampton County, Virginia 1786-1854. Original manuscripts. Clerk's Office, Eastville, Va.

Northampton County, Virginia - Order, Will and Deed Book IX (#7) 1657-1666. Original manuscript - Clerk's Office, Eastville, Va.

Register of Free Negroes, Northampton County, Virginia (1853-1861). Original manuscript - Clerk's Office, Eastville, Va.

UNPUBLISHED RESEARCH MATERIAL

Selected data from the research files of:
    John B. Bell, Williamsburg, Virginia
    Clarence E. Doughty, Mays Landing, New Jersey
    Kirk Mariner, DM., Arlington, Virginia
    David Scott, MD., Marionville, Virginia
    Ruth E. Williams, Chesapeake, Virginia
    E. Spencer Wise, Virginia Beach, Virginia

INDEX

----, Ann 44 ANN 6 Ervin 63
MARGARET A C 111 Martha 105
MARY 27 Peggy 106 Thomas 55
ABBOT, MARGARET 39
ABDEEL, Abel 28 Elisha 11 Jacob
49 53 KESIAH 90 Major 46
MARY 32 NANCY 12 53 Wm 1 72
97
ABDEL, ESTHER 118 MARGARET
54
ABDELL, Abel 41 ADAH 115
BECKAH 87 BETSEY 7 111
Bowdoin 10 ELIZABETH 15 Geo
25 85 Jacob 87 KESIAH 41 LEAH
57 MARGARET 88 MARY 87
NANCY 53 PATSEY 128 Peggy 68
RACHEL 14 ROSEY 68 Sarah
114 Shepherd 24
ABDIL, ESTHER 112 John 112
Preeson 51
ABDILL, POLLY 15
ABELL, PEGGY 10
ADAMS, Jno 10 John 3 31 36 50 96
Obed 13
ADDISON, ANN E S 67 Edw'd V 54
89 Edw'd W 87 Edwd U 111
HARRIET 76 J 23 JANE O 5 Jno
98 John 23 36 49 110 Kendall 10
51 87 114 Kendall F 105 Littleton
89 108 LOUISA W 49
MARGARET 11 53 MARGRET W
23 MARY 108 NANCY S 93
NANCY 104 PEGGY 12 97
PRISCILLAH 10 ROSANNA 89
ROSEY 60 ROSY W 92 SALLIE
35 Thomas 12 104 Thomas E 23
80 Thos 10 47 108 Thos E 49 54
92 William 76 Wm 67
AILWORTH, James J 126
AIMES, Edmund 82 NANCY 70 Wm
19

AITCHISON, Sam'l 43 Samuel 46
ALLEGOOD, John 58 SARAH 58
AMES, ANN 84 CATHARINE C 13
CATHERINE 57 ESKEY 58 James
84 Jenny 72 John 40 Levin 60
Levin S 108 MARGARET 13
MARY P 17 MATILDA ANN 108
Nath'l 41 84 Peggy 72 Rachel 13
Samuel 108 SARAH S 27
Shadrack T 27 Thomas 13 114
ANDERSON, ANNE 96 BETSEY 20 C
F 4 21 68 83 F 2 Matthew 96
MOLLY 48 P W 87 Wm B 2
ANDRESS, Andrew 24 John 75
SARAH 24
ANDREW, Francis 88 101 Maddox
93
ANDREWS, ADAH 28 38 68 ANNE
116 DRUSILLA 101 ELIZA 86
ELIZABETH ANN 126
ELIZABETH 54 73 ESTHER 97
HANNAH 57 HARRIET S 31 Isaac
10 31 49 62 87 92-93 97 JULIET
J 62 LAVENIA 85 Littleton 59 70
Maddox 33 45 Major 27 68 104
RACHEL 26 59 ROSANNA 114
ROSEY J 115 SALLY 103 SARAH
40 67 103 Shephard 85
Shepherd 31 68 115 126 Southey
28 103 SUSANNA 89 125 Wm 29
77 116 125 Wm W 19
ANNIS, MARY 89
ANNO, MARY 49
ANTHONY, Abel 81 Mary 91 NANCY
81 PEGGY 91
ARBUCKLE, James 3
ARMISTEAD, ELIZABETH 51
ARNOLD, ANNE 99
ASH, ANNE 88
ASHBY, Albert G 91 CATY 48 Geo
14 Jacob R 37 JULIA 87 POLLY

ASHBY (cont)
  60 Robert 14 60 Sam'l 4
ASHLIN, Lee 13
ASHLY, Washpon 117
ATCHISON, Samuel 65
AVERY, Isaac 79 Isaac W 66
AVORY, MARY 27
AYRES, ELIZABETH 127 Elligood 21
  Richard J 27
BADGER, Elizabeth P 6 Ezekiel 42
  LETTITIA R 111 MARGARET G
  30 Mary 66 111 MARY ANN 66
  Nath'l 66 111 Thomas W 6 30 50
  Thos W 8 18 97 116
BAGWELL, ADAH 78 Elizabeth 78
  Heley D 92 MARGARET 85 Thos
  78 Thos H 20 113
BAIKE, MARY 122
BAILEY, Edw'd 18 ESTHER 42 Isaac
  42 Susan 67
BAIN, ELIZABETH 118 Wm 28 50
  85 95 103 107
BAKER, Elijah 34 84 97 105 109
  120 Hugh 108 IBBY 95 Isaiah
  126 Isaiah W 16 94 JANE 66
  MARY 82 106 ROSEY 81
  SUSANNA 21 Thomas 81-82 106
BALL, David B 44 DELIA 89 James
  S 15 Luther 55 84
BAPTIST, MARIA S 59
BARCRAFT, ELIZABETH 1 Wm 1
BARCROFT, CATHARINE 53 Jas 68
BARECRAFT, BETSEY 37 Wm Jr 94
BARLOW, ELIZABETH 17 26 67
  Henry 22 66 MARY 22 56 SALLY
  67 SUSANNA 110 Thomas 26
BARNARD, John 17 25
BARNES, ANNE 98 MARGARET 122
  Preeson 98
BARRAUD, Daniel 104 SARAH 104
BARRET, AMY 34 David 66 MOLLY
  66
BARRETT, NANCY 113 SALLY 90
  Wm 90
BATSON, BARBARA 112 BRIDGET
  127 Jacob 112 Ralph 127 SARAH
  127
BAYATON, MARY 114
BAYLY, ANNE U 95 Egbert G 4 60
  Richard D 95 126 Sarah D 126
  SARAH UPSHUR 126
BAYTON, Ann 55 122
BEACH, Levin 2 69 79 95 97 Sally 2

BEACH (cont)
  William 88 Wm 83-84
BEARCRAFT, ELIZABETH 43 MARY
  74 SALLY 34
BEAVANS, COMFORT 19 KESIAH
  89 Mary 110 Molly 51 NANCY 20
  89 Nath'l 110 RACHEL 51
  Samuel 19 29 56 99 119
BEAVENS, NANCY ANN 115
BECKET, DIANA 72 Isaac 27 72
  Joshua 95 Juliet 119 JULIET 67
  KESIAH 64 LEAH 95 Maria 119
  MARIA 96 Mark 72 MARY 72
  NANCY 116 PRISCILLIA 83
  ROSEY 9 ROSY ANN 98 SALLY
  119 Sarah 83 SUKEY 20
BEDELL, ELIZABETH C 63 James
  63
BELL, ABIGAIL 26 ADAH 41 ANN
  SINIOR 55 ANN 88 ANNE 111
  Anthony 6 20 47 88 111-112
  BETSEY 75 BRIDGET 47
  CATHERINE 86 CHARLOTTE 87
  Edmund 10-11 47 88 ELIZA J 84
  ELIZABETH JANE 35
  ELIZABETH 20 59 120 ESTHER
  34 69 Ezekiel 103 Geo 35 41
  George 30 65 104 HANNAH 65
  Isaac 25 80 93 112 Jesse 35 86
  98 Jno F 98 Joab 41 John 47
  115 Jos E 70 116 Joseph E 6 8
  15 20 30 66 76 KEZIAH 47
  LOUISA 115 LUCRETIA 46
  MARGARET JANE 87
  MARGARET 88 Mary Jarvis 74
  MARY SUSAN 87 MARY 14 28 46
  54 67 95 MOLLY 76 NANCY 42
  54 Nath'l 110 Polly 20 POLLY 41
  88 109 REBECCA 84 Richard 73
  109 Rob't 32 74 Robert 14 43 65
  SALLY 10 64 SARAH JARVIS 74
  SARAH 30 90 Smith 47 88
  SUKEY 31 SUSAN 46 SUSEY 6
  Tabitha 87 TABITHA M 112
  Thomas 30 46-47 55 90 Thos 54
  95 Tinney 87 Wm 6 Wm H 36 68
  87 111
BELOAT, NANCY 15 SUSANNA 23
BELOATE, Geo 64 John Tankard
  101
BELOTE, Abbot 118 ANNE 18
  Benjamin 60 Betsy 48 DELITHA
  107 Edw'd 91 Edward 12 ELIZ 60

BELOTE (cont)
 ELIZABETH 48 57 ESTHER A 33
 ESTHER 85 Geo T 35 George 127
 George Jr 3 George T 66 117
 John 1 32 80 91 Kendal 30
 Kendall 21 54 80 119 Laban 33
 45 85 Levin 48 52 MARGARET 2
 63 127 MARY 12 NERVILLA 54
 RACHEL 91 SALLY 80 SARAH 28
 Smith 33 45 87 100 Susan 57
 SUSANNA 84 102 TABITHA S 45
 TABITHA 91 Walter 113 Wm 1 28
 111
BENIAN, JANE 43
BENNETT, Chas 66 Covington 17
BENSON, ANN 43 CATHARINE 77
 Edmund 24 James 111 Kealy W
 91 Nath'l 102 RACHEL 24
BENSTON, ANN 31 Betsey 24
 BETSEY BENSON 8 SALLY 29
BENTHALL, Azel 40 51 69 Dan'l 64
 73 Daniel 43 ELISHABA 42
 FRANCES 51 121 LEAH 40
 MARY 63 Mathew 88 Nathaniel
 77 PATIENCE 18 RACHEL 114
 SINAH 30 Wm 17 63 121
BEVANS, ADAH 19 BETSEY 6
 EMILY 29 John 4 82 MARY 4
 Molly 19 Sam'l Sr 82 Samuel 5
 115 SUKEY 5 Tom 29
BIBBINS, MARY 77 Nanny 77
BIGELOW, Geo 88
BIGGS, ALICHIA 103 ANNE 109
 Christopher 103 119-120
 ELISHA 104 ELIZABETH 73 Jno
 46 John 76 109 John W 65 73 76
 MARGARET 27 Nancy 76 109
 SALLY 120 SUKEY 76 SUSAN
 ANN 65 SUSAN 76 Tabitha 11 16
 33 TINNEY 119
BINGHAM, ANN 29 BETSEY 4
 CHARLOTTE 17 ELIZABETH 29
 EMELINE 68 JENNEY 45
 Lucretia 68 LUREY 72
 MARGARET 39 Moses 9 POLLY
 56 Robert J 17 TAMAR 20
 TINSEY 39-40
BIRCH, Jno R 17 115 John 6
 LIVINIA 24
BIRD, John 54 69 POLLY 9 SALLY
 54 SUSAN 40
BISHOP, Ann 109 CAROLINE 68
 Edward 46 FANNY 127 GRACY

BISHOP (cont)
 25 JANE 63 John 4 25 125 Nath'l
 19 72 POLLY 56 SARAH 51 Wm
 68 117
BLACKS, ADAH 100
BLAIKLEY, Cath 113 Catherine 31
BLAIR, Jno 69 120 John 56 KASIAH
 17
BLOODSWORTH, BETSY 67 Pitt
 Price 67
BLOXOM, John 116 Nicholas 1
 POLLY B 57 POLLY 18 SALLY
 116 Wm 27 70
BOGGS, George 27 John 3 39 92
BOISNARD, Edw'd R 105 Edward R
 59 John 88
BONEWELL, John K 17 MARGARET
 S 17 MARGARET 110
BONNEWILL, Geo 14 24
BONWELL, Charles 23 32 71 MARY
 ANN 71
BOOK, Ezekiel 100
BOOL, ADELINE 16 David 20 27
 Edward 7 34 Elizabeth 42 Geo 65
 George 40 71 George N 53 85
 James M 10 John 51 KEZIAH 14
 LEANA 40 Major 51 MARGARET
 ANN 7 Michael 16 Nicholas 27
 PRISCILLA 114 RITTA 92 SARAH
 ANN 72 Spencer 72 83 97 SUSAN
 100
BOOLL, NANCY 91 PATSEY 2
 PEGGY 19 VIOLETTA 68
BOOTH, Geo G 95 John 101 SALLY
 101
BOSWELL, ELIZABETH 12
BOWDOIN, Adm 61 ELIZABETH U
 98 ELIZABETH 61 64 FANNY B
 105 Grace 82 Jno 101 John 82
 102 John R 33 LOUISA 32
 MARGARET 126 MARGARETTA
 82 MARY 49 127 Peter 18 32 49
 61 66 98-99 102 105 124-126
 Peter S 3 127 SARAH 90 Severn
 E 75 William J 62 Wm J 5 32 46
BOWEN, ANN 9
BOWKER, Abraham 81 112
BOWLE, John 66
BOYD, Alex 16 Alexander 33 SARAH
 114
BRADFORD, Abel 48 61 ELIZABETH
 61 Ezra 15 JENNY 81 NANCY 48
 Nath'l J 80 91 ROSEY 113

BRADFORD (cont)
SUSANNA 80
BRAISER, ZILLAH 87
BRATTEN, Isaac 28 74 MARY 28
BRICKHOUS, Elam L 12 Elizabeth 12
BRICKHOUSE, Albert 70 ANGELINE B 72 ANNE H 125 BETTY JENNEY 19 C 39 Chas 100 Eadith S 49 EDITH S 23 Elam L 22-23 73 ELIZABETH S 22 ELIZABETH 114 Esther 19 Frances D 72 FRANCES D 107 G A 89 Geo 18 30 46 73 George 5 86 108 128 George Sr 112 Hezekiah 15 James M 77 115 JANE 112 115 Jas M 22 John 9 88 95 John Jr 65 114 John N 2 22 49 John Sr 37 LUCY 118 Major 10 59 86 MARGARET S 70 MARGARET 73 108 MARGT D 58 MARY S 82 MARY 37 NAOMI D 117 PEGEY 108 PEGGY 2 POLLY N 30 POLLY 103 RACHEL 59 Rob't 34 72 104 Robert 12 S S 69 SALLY A S 5 SALLY JOYNES 73 SALLY W 107 Smith 22 Smith L 12 58 Smith N 16 SUSAN T W 49 SUSAN 95 Thomas E 4 Thomas S 22 29 47 58 72 82 85 107 125 Thos 74 Thos S 88 105 URSULA B 85 W E 127 Wm E 121
BRIGGS, ANN S 97
BRITTINGHAM, Elijah 15 21-22 68 79 Elijah Jr 54 122 Elijah Sr 2 G W 123 Geo W 29 36 81 George W 83 Joseph B 80 MARGARET 2 MARY A H 15
BROOKE, Wm 31
BROUGHTON, ELIZABETH D 105 Isaac 105 SALLY 86
BROUNLEY, Wm R 119
BROWN, Allen 61 84 99 109 ELIZA ANN 61 Elizabeth 109 HANNAH 79 MARY ANN 99 Nathaniel 79 Samuel W 23
BRUFF, Joseph 13
BRYAN, ANNE 52 ESTHER 104 Henry 31 49-50 52 62 80 Levin 31 MARY 31 NANCY 31 Nathaniel 76 SUSANNA 50
BRYANT, Henry 31
BRYON, Nath'l 75

BUCNER, Abner 45
BULL, Elizabeth 107 HARRIOT 88 Isaac 47 John 19 49 118 MARGARET 82 MARY 35 Michael 56 Nancy 91 Richard 35 SALLY 56 SARAH 25 SUSAN ANN 91
BULLICK, Thos 33
BULLOCK, ELIZ 41 MARY 81 NANCY 75 SARAH 56 Thomas 87 Thos 51 56 73
BUNTIN, James 100
BUNTING, ANN 93 ANNE 14 DELITHA 26 ELIZABETH 115 Francis A 91 Holloway 14 43 James S 115 JENNEY 24 John S 20 93 Jonathan 93 MARY 52 Nancy 115 Samuel 20 41 Solomon 14 91 96 Wm 115
BURK, Thos 65
BURKE, SALLY 125
BURNHAM, ANN 95
BURRAS, Wm L 94
BURRIS, ARINTHIA S G 43 MARY ANN 74 N G 27 42 PEGGY 123 SALLY 88 Wm S 14
BURRON, ELIZABETH B 104 Jno B 104 Sarah B 104
BURTON, Elizabeth M 60 ESTHER 79 84 John 5 26 45 79 99 Joshua 114 MARGARET 91 MARY 10 SCARBROUGH 100 SUSANNA 45 Wm 10 82 91
BYRD, ELIZABETH 96 MAHALA 43 Peggy 43 Sally 54 Thos 43 Wm 43 54
CABLE, Eleanor 63 Elisabeth 81 106-107 ESTHER 82 Marg't 48 Margaret 79 Sarah 107 SARAH 79 Thomas 63 82 Thos 23 48 61-62 87 105-106 Wm 64
CAMPBELL, ELIZABETH 90 MARGARET 77 MOLLY 80 Nicholas 112 ROSE MARY 112 William J 77 Wm J 25 106 Wm T 58
CAPLE, ANN 24 BETSEY 113 Catharine 58 ELIZABETH 58 John 58 Mager 58 Major 15 Peggy 24 POLLY 41 SALLY 58 SUSANNA 99
CAREY, Purnall B 119
CARMINE, Wm 40 Wm T 109
CARPENTER, ABIGAIL 87 ADAH 3

CARPENTER (cont)
72 111 Ann 17 ANNE 6 Charles
51 120 Charles Jr 112
ELIZABETH G 110 ELIZABETH
ISABELLA 88 ELIZABETH 22
ESTHER 68 James S 26 28 37
111 115 Jno 50 John 3 41 48-49
68 115-116 John Sr 22 88 LEAH
F 75 LUCY ANN 77 LUCY 30
MARY 48-49 NANCY 98 Patrick
102 SALLY 28 Sam'l G 77
Samuel G 61 75 87 SARAH 59
Stephen 6 59 SUSANNA 51 120
Wm 32 73 98 104
CARSON, Jno 4
CARTER, Benjamin 16 Edw'd 15 30
105 Ezekiel 106 HANNAH 58
Isaiah 20 89 James 115 Jas 83
MARGARET 106 MARY ANN 5
CARY, MOLLY 47 Obed 30 50 67 90
Obid 27 SUSEY 117
CASEY, EMORY 71 ESTHER 6 Jno
42 John 22 MARY ANN 22
CAUL, Daniel 58 SUSANNA 58
CHANCE, NANCY 48 SALLY 94
SARAH 37 SUSAN 48 TINNEY 7
William 7 Wm 1
CHANDLER, REBECCA 127
Zorobabel 98
CHARLETON, BRIDGET 38
CHARNICK, Jno T 40
CHARNOCK, George 79 James 12
82
CHAUNCEY, Elihu 93 Henrietta T
93 SARAH 93
CHRISTIAN, Elizabeth M 12
ELIZABETH 54 70 ESTHER 23
George 90 George E 28 M 76
MARGARET 35 69 MATILDA 2
Mich'l 63 98 102 Michael 3 35 49
79 NANCY 49 ROSE 35 95 98
ROSETTA 98 SALLY 2 SUSANNA
3 William 35 Wm 42 49 69-70
Wm A 2 13 84 Wm S 28
CHURCH, Abel 70 Isaac 70 MARY B
30 RACHEL 81 SUKEY 70 Thos
Sr 127 Wm 17-18
CHURN, BETSEY 94 John 61
KETURAH 125 KITURAH 61
MARGARET S 5 MARGARET 4
NANCY 37 SALLY 29 61 SARAH
37 Severn 4 SUSANNA 37 Tamor
4 William 5 61 104 Wm W 18

CLARK, MARY 2 Piner 85 Piner W
73 97 ROSEY 41 Thos 14 William
17 Wm 2 93
CLARKE, ELIZABETH 41 Piner W
119 Wm 50
CLAY, Benoni 34 ELIZA 16
ELIZABETH 36 James 36 NANCY
38 123 Sally 38 SUSAN C 122
Wm 35
CLAYTON, SINAH 81
CLEGG, ADAH 55 AGNES 69 ANNE
19 Clark 110 ELIZABETH 39
ESTHER 110 FANNEY 113
Hillary 19 90 Isaac 54-55 93
LOVEY 85 MAHALA 126 Major
67 126 MARGARET 58 Peggy 60
PEGGY 124 Peter 18 85 Peter M
49 ROSANNA 30 ROSEY 7 67
SALLY 90-91 SUKEY 122
SUSANNAH 90
CLERKE, Thos 24
COBB, Arthur 8 24 28 48 69 79
ELIZABETH 126 Nathan F 37 68
Southey 126 Southy 23 Stratton
1
COLEBURN, CATHERINE 48 Geo 48
HENRIETTA 68 John A 68
Richard 2 68 Thomas A 60 Thos
A 40 92
COLLEVER, MARY 46
COLLINS, ADAH 16 70 96 ANN 86
108 BETSEY 51 82 CHRYSANNA
38 ELISHE 121 ELIZ 100 ELIZA
17 86 Elizabeth 10 ELIZABETH
100 ESTHER 9 FANNY 6 JENNY
101 Jno 119 John 44 71 116
John T 7 Little Peggy 106
LOUISA 99 LOVEY 60 LURANY
55 Mac 5 Mack 55 MAHALA 116
Maria 60 Mary 86 MARY 6
MOLLY 115 NANCY 55 71 82
Nathaniel 46 86 PATSY 46 Peggy
55 82 PEGGY 17 106 POLLY 44
Rafe 9 Ralph 9 83 Ritta 17 100
RITTER 9 ROSEY 2 79 Samuel R
26 Short John 118 Southy 77
Victor 108
COLLONNA, Major 6
COLONNA, Major D 60 MARGARET
W 6
COMMINES, John 20
COOK, ANN 38 ELIZABETH 1
MARGARET 40 NANCY 112

COPES, FANNY 71 Levin 71 Thos 116 Wm P 3 33
CORE, Caleb 30 Charles 10 ELIZABETH 78 ESTHER 69 JANE 87 John 18 87 98 106 KESIAH 10 MARY 25 NANCY 41 SALLEY 106 Wm H 91
CORMICK, Jno 25
CORNAGH, HELLEN 69
COSTIN, A 111 Abraham 15 25 43 89 Abram 21 33 51 61 73 76 81-82 107 118 121 ANN 74 ANNE 122 BETSEY 111 Bowdoin 107 CHARLOTTE 27 Coventon R 46 Elijah 21 ELISHE 124 ELIZABETH ANN 65 ELIZABETH 60 65 82 89 107 Frances 15 120 FRANCES S 98 Francis 76 79 GRACE 19 Henry 32 107 Jacob 39 James 46 60 James H 80 John 27 32 LEAH 35 LOUISA 24 Lucretia 25 Margaret 50 MARGARET ANN 46 MARGARET 39 MARIA 27 MARY 79 Mathew 22 Matthew 25 107 NANCY 44 84 120 NELLEY 25 NELLY 108 PATEY 76 Patrick F 65 120 PATSEY 76 PEGGY 32 46 127 POLLY 55 REBEKAH 107 ROSALINE 7 ROSE 60 Rosey L 54 Rosey S 122 SALLY 33 43-44 Samuel 64 71 124 SUKEY 25 64 96 SUKY 122 SUSANNA 79 Thos 97 VIRGINIA T 80 William 35 57 Wm 25 44 60 80 84 111 128 Wm G 71 98 Wm Sr 55 65 122
COTTERIL, HARRIET 27 John 27
COTTINGHAM, E D 112 Elisha D 33 ELIZABETH W 21 Henry 21 124 MARY S 124 Wm H 72
COTTMAN, Joseph 114
COULSTON, CHARITY 13
COURSER, FRANCES 86 NICEY 9
COWARD, LEAH 70 Samuel 70 116
COWDEY, Joshua 113
COWDREE, Savage 89
COWDREY, Savage 70 102
COWDRY, ESTHER 11 117 FRANCES 34 Josias 34 SARAH 42 Thos 14 42 Wm 11
COWLES, Rachel 40
COX, James 126 MARY 103 NANCY 64 PATSEY 3 Sam'l 89 SUSANNA

COX (cont) 75
CRAICK, SALLY 66
CRAIK, ANN 54 POLLY A 80 Wm 54
CREEKMORE, Wm W 19
CREW, ELIZABETH 50
CRIPPEN, BETSEY 65
CROCKET, Thomas 113 ZIPPOROH 113
CULLIN, POLLY 71
CURRIE, POLLY 84
CURTIS, MARY 25
CUSTIS, Abram 41 ANN 80 106 ANNE 50 CATH 120 Edm'd R 98 Edmund 50 120 Edmund R 60 103 ELIZABETH L 126 ELIZABETH 44-45 Henry 46 John 11 25 63 114 125 John 4th 106 LAURA E 33 Mary 25 MARY 38 80 NANCY 3 PEGGY 125 PRISCILLIA 83 Robertson 20 Robinson 23 35 80 98 SALLY 41 Sarah 23 Thomas B 5 Thos V 62 Wm P 105
CUTLAR, NANCY 81
CUTLER, ANNA M 34 ELIZABETH 81 PEGGY J 12 Rich'd 108 Richard 73 ROSEY 23 SARAH 8 SUSAN ANN 74 TABITHA R 53 W W 113 William W 34 74 Wm W 15
DALBY, ANN S 22 ANN 42 Benj J 55 Benja 55 Benja J 22 67 Benjamin J 2 7 69 Branson 56 75 101 Bridget 14 BRIDGET 47 CASSEY 127 CATHERINE E 75 CATHERINE 62 ELIZABETH 96 ELLEN 71 FERIBA 57 Henry 90 Hezekiah 7-8 22 67 75 96 James 14 24 47 67-68 96 114 Jas B 77 Jno L 78 John 18 31 42 63-64 97 103-104 Joseph 89 117 JOSINA J 47 KESIAH 84 KEZIAH 1 MARGARET S 104 MARGARET 103 Mary Ann 55 MARY 66 MILLY 86 Nath'l 126 Nathaniel 56 71 Peggy 71 PEGGY 31 86 RACHEL 90 SALLY 90 Samuel 24 SARAH 1 104 Severn 84 SUSAN 56 62 SUSANNA 103 Thomas 14 24 31 49 Thos 15 VIRGINIA ADAMS 55 Waterfield 1 Wm L 75
DAN, Silas 5

DANFORD, ELIZ 107
DANN, BETSEY 5 Silas 5
DARBY, ANN 8 Benja 128 Benjamin
  10 56 Esther Christian 78
  Francis 97 HARRIET B 78 Jno 56
  John 78 113 128 MARY 10 79
  128 NANCY 113 Nath'l 12 50-51
  79 Nathaniel 78 RACHEL 56
  SARAH 66 Shadrack 8
DARCY, BRIDGET 43
DASHIEL, Rob't 103
DAVIS, ANN 94 ANNA 22 HARRIET
  88 JANE 13 JENNY 13 POLLY
  104 Thos 78 89 96 102 116 125
DAWSON, LOUISA 50 PEGGY 46
  Thos 112
DEALE, SARAH 117
DEARE, ARADY 127 Wm 127
DELASTATIOUS, Ezekiel 70
DENHAM, Rob't 46
DENIS, Lucy 14 MARY 14 Sukey 14
DENNIS, ADAH 3 ANNE 16
  Archibald 16 24 31 101 114
  BETSEY 24 ELIZABETH 80
  Hezekiah 24 James 17 22 26-27
  52 112 JENNY 17 JINNY 114
  John 4 45 58 120 John G 118
  Joseph 49 Littleton 64 125 Major
  114 MARY 24 Michael 16 31
  NANCY 12 114 PATSY 49
  PATTSEY 114 POLLY 49 RACHEL
  49 101 Reubin 49 ROSEY 31
  ROSY 31 SALLY 24 63 Sam'l 11
  68 William 88 Wm 49 57 Wm Jr
  98
DENWOOD, MARY 127
DEWEY, ELIZABETH 81 MARY 101
  Nancy 81 Thos 101
DILLION, ANNE 48 Charles 13 48
  61 99 103 111 123 126 Jno 32
  MARY 123 NANNY 13
DILLON, Charles 32 71 126 NANCY
  126 Thomas 13
DIX, ANNE 113 ELIZABETH A 125
  Isaac 78 113 Jno S 7 30 73 98
  John S 44 Levin 25 112 SABRA
  M 112 Wm A 125
DIXON, ANN FITCHETT 127 ANN 28
  ANNE MARY 112 ANNE 9 Bridget
  4 Christopher 72 96 CLEAR 46
  ELISHE 123 Elizabeth 22
  ELIZABETH 44 100 105 ESTHER
  W 51 Jno W 28 John 4 18 32 41

DIXON (cont)
  46 67 100 112 Lucie A 94
  LUCRETIA 22 LUCY ANN 46
  MARGARET 50 MARTHA E 94
  MARY 11 41 Michael 88 90 97
  NANCY 1 NELLY 32 PEGGY 23
  72 97 POLLY 36 43 74 Ralph 9
  36 71 SALLY 4 62 SANTICA 72
  SARAH 67 SOPHIA 74 SUKEY 36
  123 SUSANNA 18 T W 28
  Thomas 83 122 Thos 97 Thos Jr
  47 Tilney 1 97 W W 46 94
  William 33 Wm 9 21 43-44 65 92
  107 Wm Jr 88
DIXSON, Benja 18 97 John 106
  SUSANNA 97
DODD, ELIZABETH 41
DOLBY, Benja 86 Benja J 2 BETTY
  21 BRIDGET 89 CATHERINE 98
  ESTHER 8 54 Isaac 79 James 8
  43 69 74 84 John 3 15 23-24 29
  37 64 89 98 John Jr 3 41 John
  Sr 8 MARY SMITH 116 PEGGY
  84 95 SALLY 81 SUSAN 8 Thos
  79 Wm 25
DONJEUX, EULALIE 65
DORMAN, PEGGY 60 Wm 102
DORSEY, ELIZABETH B 61
DOUGLAS, Geo 47
DOUTY, James 88 James P 30
DOWNES, CHARLOTTE 118 Daniel
  118 ELIZA 56 MARGARET E 32
  Thomas 74 Wm 21 50 71
DOWNING, A W 127 ARINTHIA B 30
  Arthur 23 Arthur S Sr 103
  BETTY 23 Caleb Jr 9 COMFORT
  37 Edm'd W P 31 Edmund 60
  Edmund W P 88 128 Edw'd W P
  30 ELIZABETH 34 60 105
  EMORY V 127 John 21 John Jr
  23 MARGARET S 128
  MARGARET 69 SALLIE E 121
  Wm 34 88 Zero 116 Zerobabel 69
  116 Zerobable 34 Zillah TURNER
  103
DOWNS, ADAH 85 BETSEY 71
  ESTHER 65 Nancy 71 Thomas 90
  123 Wm 113
DOWTY, Addison 56 Archabald 58
  Archibald 18 37 CATHERINE 33
  DRUSILLA 97 ELEANOR 116
  Elisha 53 ELIZA ANN 117
  ELIZABETH 8 82 104 ELLEN A

DOWTY (cont)
68 Ely 16 68 Hezekiah 56 86 109
James 31 91 117 John 3 103
John W 19 Josiah 91 LUCY 58
Major 27 37 68 86 MARGARET 3
Michael 42 Nancy 3 NANCY 13
PEGGY 79 Peter 9 POLLY 56 116
RACHEL 70 ROSEY 54 91
Rowland 105 116 SALLY T 91
SALLY 19 48 SEYMOUR 80
SUSANNA 49 86 TABBY 39
Thomas 33 114 123 Thos 1 104
123 Wm 3 8 Zob 3
DRAITON, ANN 49
DRIGGUS, ANNE 81
DRIGHOUSE, BETSEY 16 BETSY 15
CATHARINE 81 115 Dilly 89
DILLY 72 ELISHE 64 LEAR 20
Nathan 4 15 55 108 SALLY 89
108 SUKEY 89 Wm 116
DRIGUS, Wm 20
DRUMMOND, James 43 Rob't 29
Wm 30
DRYSDALE, MARY ANN 41
DUMUS, MARGARET 21
DUNCAN, John H 38 Thomas 4 Wm
T 15 109
DUNN, Thos 35
DUNTON, ADAH 51 61 67 ADELINE
11 ANN C 105 ANN JACOB 124
ANN 90 ANNE K J 103 ANNE 96
108 Ben 100 Benja 108 123
Benja F 13 Benjamin 66 85 91
Benjamin F 4 28 121 BETSEY
125 127 Betty 96 BETTY 25
BRIDGET 49 Carvy 93
CATHERINE SABRA 105 David A
77 105 Dicke 40 Dickie 18 26 29
83 90 Edw'd M 45 Elias 13 45 49
73 124 Elias Jr 114 Elias Sr 29
96 Eliz H 118 ELIZABETH S 53
ELIZABETH 15 55 84 90 120
EMMA S 39 ESTHER 46
FRANCES 43 Geo B 115 Geo W
76 Hancock 53 92 124
HENRIETTA 104 Henry G 9 13
Isaac 54 114 Jacob 25 65 116
James 39 JANE 56 JENNEY 70
Jno R 89 JOANNA 116 John 14
43 60 97 101 John R 126 KESSY
103 KITURAH G 121 LAVINIA A
W 122 LAVINIA 123 LEAH 26
Levin 43 123 MARGARET 14 60

DUNTON (cont)
Mary 105 MARY ANN 34 MARY C
6 MARY W 35 MARY 4 66 114
Mat H 13 Matthew 53 Matthew H
34 115 Mich'l Jr 111 Michael 4 8
16 26 51 63 79 114-115 Michael
Sr 125 NANCY JACOB 124
NANCY 13 52 NANNY 29 Nathin
H 61 PEGGY G 13 PEGGY 27 96
127 POLLY 115 Rich'd Jr 93
Rich'd T 68 83 Richard 21 114
Richards 3 Richards Jr 40
Rickard 11 Rickard Jr 7 Rickards
15 28 89 110 119 Rickards Jr 45
54-55 Rickets 39 ROSE 82
ROSINA B 124 Sally 64 SALLY 11
28 64 83 96 107 Sam'l W 6
Samuel W 105 120 SARAH A 28
SARAH 40 65 123 SMART 124
SOPHIA E 105 Stephen 61 104
SUKEY 4 87 SUSAN 66
SUSANNA G 13 SUSANNA 4
Thomas 4 23 80 120 122 Thomas
K 36 46 63 106-107 Thooms K
35 Thos 10 33 Thos K 52 74 W M
77 William 96 105 Wm 13 38 46
50 55-56 Wm M 10 16 66 60 Wm
Sr 111
DUSTIN, PEGGY 80
EDMONDS, Ann 8 ELIZABETH 29
Thomas 29
EDMUNDS, Ann 4 BETSEY 112
BRIDGET 69 David 28 69 110
NANCY 28 PEGGY 18 Sarah 48
SARAH ANN 4 SINAH 28 TAMAR
48 Thos 4 48
EDWARDS, MARG'T 99
ELLEGOOD, ELENOR 44 ESTHER
119 Jno 112 John 44
MARGARET 124 P Norly 49 61
117
ELLIET, ELIZABETH 120
ELLIGOOD, ELIZABETH 36 MARY
18 SUSANNA 56
ELLIOT, ANNE 47 BETTY 85 ELIZA
63 James 47 Jno 46 SUSANNA
21 Thomas 85 Thos 21
ELLIOTT, 5 ANN W 96 ANN 107
BRIDGET 43 GRACE 49 James
63 Jeremiah 79 Jerimiah 22 Jno
9 John 49 121 John T 68 81
John W 46 84 112 Nehimiah 61
POLLY 70 76 PRISCILA 22

ELLIOTT (cont)
    Rachel 79 ROSY ANN 79 ROSY W 121 SALLY 50 SUSAN 79 Thomas 50 Wm 43 Wm W 33 70
ELLIS, Maria 21 Ves 16 31 56
EMMERSON, ANN 110
ENHOLM, Laurance 21 Laurence 108 Lawrence 55
ERRISTALL, JANE 49
ESHON, ANNE 50 Daniel 13 25 32 42 ELIZABETH 118 George 32 41 89 NANCY 7 Nath'l 23 SARAH 27 SUSANNA 63 116 Thomas 41
EVANS, ANN 40 ANNE K 127 Arthur 18 41 75 89 93 BETSEY 41 CAROLINE 6 CATHERINE 120 Edward 92 ELIZ A 20 ELIZABETH 75 104 ESTHER 46 Isaac S 21 Jno 121 John 21 32 40-41 94 107 120 John K 27 127 LEAH 98 LOUISA 52 Lucinda 20 MARGARET 43 84 MARY A 60 MARY 75 Nancy 6 NANCY 21 PEGGY T 78 PEGGY 96 113 POLLY 104 Richard 9 104 SALLY P 118 SARAH ANN 84 SUSAN 32 SUSANNA 109-110 Thomas 71 Thomas E 72 Thomas S 44 118 Thos 46 Thos E 78 122 Thos L 52 Thos S 21-22 Wm 84 96 Wm S 36 50 107 113
EVENS, John 64
EWELL, ESTHER A 45 John 8 35 45
EWING, BETSY 56 David 7 POLLY 48
EYRE, ELIZABETH 15 EMILY ANN 105 Grace 105 John 64 73 90 101 103 105 127 Littleton 11 25 62 78 MARGARET 78 Neech 95 SARAH 11 64 Severn 11 78 Wm 16 29 76 92 105 Wm L 68
FAIRFAX, ELIZABETH 23 Jas 23
FATHERLY, Elizabeth R 8 John 113 MARGARET 113 Wm J 73
FATHERY, ADAH 121 Jacob 41
FIITZHUGH, ELIZ 70
FINNEY, Louis C H 88 Wm R 56
FISHER, ANN W 51 BRIDGET 26 Daniel 101 E J 77 EDITH E 49 Edwin J 74 77 FRANCES ELLEN 45 Fred B 60 115 Geo 3 51 89 George 85 James 58 92 Jno R 2 John R 45 66 113 118 KESIAH

FISHER (cont)
    101 M W 17 Maddox 23 81 MARGARET 56 MARY B 75 MARY W 83 MARY 127 Miers W 5 7 111 NANCY 25 ROSE 23 ROSEY ANN 92 ROSEY 50 Sally Y 75 SALLY 72 Sam'l P 93 Samuel P 72 SUSAN B 93 SUSANNA 63 Thomas B 83 Thos 56 Thos B 76 91 W R 72 Wm 48 Wm R 49 83
FISHERMAN, MOLLY 82
FITCHET, James N 104 PEGGY 76 Wm J 104
FITCHETT, Charles 12 25 Chas 123 Christofer D 63 Christopher 27 82 99 106 Christopher D 44 Damiel 33 Daniel 14 32 38 46 99 120-121 124 Edw'd C 46 ELIZA 83 ELIZABETH A 86 ELIZABETH P 12 ELIZABETH S 107-108 ELIZABETH 21 61 107 EMILINE 31 FRANCES 8 George P 75 102 Gracy 59 GRACY 9 HARRIET 66 James 53 83 Jas 66 Jno R 95 Joshua 18 21 31 60 82 Joshua Sr 33 Leah 108 LEAH 106 Lucy Ann 105 MARGARET S 95 MARGT 116 Martha 25 31 MARY ANN 121 MARY P 25 NANCEY 120 NANCY 18 33 Nath'l P 83 Nehemiah 37 53 70 114 Patrick H 124 Patsey 82 POLLY 124 RACHEL 114 Rob't 86 Robert 71 77 122-123 Rosa 31 SABRA P 59 SARAH 95 121 SUKEY 81 Susan 83 SUSAN 30 57 SUSANNA 70 Thomas 61 Thomas D 85 Thos 12 95 VIRGINIA U 124 VIRGINIA 127 W T 26 William 95 William Sr 127 Wm 30 Wm J 7-8 67-68 83-84 115 Wm P C 86 Wm Sr 57 Wm T 1 32 55 65 109 123
FITCHEW, ANNE 63 Henry 15 SALLY 57 Vussy 63
FITZGERALD, RACHEL 41
FITZHUGH, Henry 68
FLETCHER, BETSEY 22 CATHARINE 18 Charles 19 Edmund 4 ESTHER 19 FANNY 25 Jas 16 MAHALA 9 Nathan R 56 95 NELLY 16 PEGGY 79 SALLY 16 69 Samuel 16 Thomas

147

FLETCHER (cont)
   22 Wm 16 18
FLOOD, ELIZABETH 36 John 9 17
   22 36 53 113 SUKEY JARVIS 80
FLOYAD, Mathew 16
FLOYD, ADAH 16 AILSIE T 106 ANN
   ELIZABETH 78 ANN 113 Anne S
   78 ANNE 68 119 Benj 103 Betsey
   11 CATHARINE S 58 CATHARINE
   9 CATHERINE S 58 Charles 52
   59 63 69 DRUSILLA 3
   ELEANORE S 15 Elijah 13 40
   106 ELIZABETH S S 125
   ELIZABETH 11 17 52 ELLEN S
   75 ESTHER 31 88 116 Jacob 45
   James 9 21 104 121 Jas 76 Jas
   G 1 45 Jno 97 Jno K 103 John
   16 40 42 49 81 102 109 126
   John K 53 58 77 108 John R 99
   Lavenia A 15 LAVENIA C 54
   Lavinia 58 LETTY 42 Major 9
   MARGARET 40 79 97 125 MARY
   42 49 63 81 Mathew 119
   Matthew 6 36 122 126 NANCY 28
   76 PEGGY 16 59 POLLY 112
   Sally 4 17 112 SALLY 42 Sam'l G
   9 Sam'l L 35 Samuel L 23 SARAH
   J W 13 Shepherd 28 58
   Shepherd B 68 93 106 109 120
   125 Shepperd B 16 SUKEY
   JARVIS 80 SUKEY 59 Wm 31 50
   79 99 105 Wm H 80 104 Wm S
   14 56 71 73 113
FLYBRASS, ANNE 48
FORSE, James 21 65 82 92
   MARGARET 31
FOX, ELIZABETH 98
FRANCIS, COMFORT 20 John 41
   MARY 99 SALLY 41 Wm 82 Wm
   Jr 20 119
FRAZER, John 33-34
FREEMAN, ELIZABETH 51
FRESHWATER, ELISHE 66 Mark 73
   106 MRS 101 NANCY 9 71 101
   126 Nath'l 33 POLLY 55 SALLY
   18 110 124 SARAH 73 SUSAN 38
   Thos 97 Wm 18
FROST, Jacob 106 John 64 124
   MARY 44 PEGGY 76 POLLY 126
   RACHEL 34 Reuben 38 SALLY 35
   William 44 Wm 34
FULWELL, ELIZABETH 39 J L 109
   Jno Lewis 51 67 90 John Lewis 1

FULWELL (cont)
   63 John Lewis 97 L 33
   MARGARET 63
GADD, MARY J 72
GALE, Levin 125 LUCY 86 MARY 19
GALT, Dickie 40 106
GANNETT, Unital 52
GARDINER, MARY STEAD
   PINCKNEY 75 SARAH S 2
   TINSEY 115 Walter C 2 Wm C 75
GARDNER, Benja 17 EMMA E 98
GARRET, Amos 117 MARGARET
   117
GARRETT, A C 92 ELIZABETH 20
   MARY EDNA 69 Unital 52
GARRIS, ELIZABETH 104 SARAH
   21 Thomas 21 Thos 104 Wm 1
   10
GARRISON, Abel 51 ANN D 25
   James R 13 Joshua 9 39 44 50
   104 108 SARAH 29
GARROTT, Thos 104
GASCOIGNE, ANNE 57 Wm 57
GASCOYNE, Henry 103 Henry Sr 7
   PEGGY 103 RACHEL 105 SALLY
   B 109 SARAH 7
GAULT, ANNE M 78 Dicky 16
   FANNY 40 FRANCES 40 LEAH 54
   LUCY 16
GAYLE, Christopher 10 41 John 75
   John S 8
GEORGE, CATHARINE 90
GIBB, Sarah 112 Zerababel 72
   Zerobabel 22 Zorobabel 38
GIBBONS, Thomas 53
GIBSON, Jas 62
GIDDENS, Benjamin 41 ELIZABETH
   56 FANNY 36 Henry 21 87 107
   John 101 MOLLY 101 SALLY 87
GIDINGS, Henry 85
GIFFITH, RACHEL 50
GILDEN, Charles 53 81 ELIZABETH
   34 81 MARY 53 Wm 34
GILDING, Charles 67
GILDON, AGATHA 57 Charles 57
   Elizabeth R 8 George 12 Jno 14
   John 12 MARY A 8 SUSAN 12
GILLET, Wm 111 116
GLADSTON, MARY 64 Wm 64
GLANVILLE, Edm'd 26 Edmund 4
   11 15 22 49 54 62 75-76 95 103
   110 117 MARGARET 123
GLEESON, John 50 112

GLEGG, Wm 122
GLISAN, John 74 120
GODFERRY, MARY 29
GODMIN, Sarah 11
GODWIN, ANN 56 Archibald 97 103
  Devorax 10 47 53 56-57 87
  Edmund 12 Edmund S 84 Edwin
  54 120 ELISHE 57 ELIZA 101
  EMILY 28 Esau 116 FRANCES
  109 Griffin 28 Jos P 45 Joseph
  63 Kendall 127 Laban 51 78
  LETITIA M 58 Littleton 58
  Littleton K 41 MARGARET ANN
  59 67 Mary 11 MARY 91 103
  SALLY ANN 54 SALLY 30 89
  Sarah 11 Susanna 87 SUSANNA
  66 87 121 Wm 18
GOFFIGON, AMELIA 98 ANN 61
  ANNE 14 BETSEY 120 BRIDGET
  75 Edwin 34 40 95 99 ELIZ 33
  96 ELIZABETH 9 57 ESTHER W
  95 FANNY 55 FRANCES D 14 95
  FRANCES 52 55 James 27 57
  72-73 93 95 Jas 108 120 Jno 14
  55 57 64 Jno Jr 37 John 14 31
  59 75 124 John Sr 17 LEAR 124
  MARGARET 123 MARIA 73
  MARTHA 60 MARY ANN 93
  MARY E 59 NANCY 51 Nath'l 9
  43 51 64 84 123 Nath'l L 14
  Nathaniel 52 Nathaniel S 55 99
  Nathl L 94 Obadiah 73 90 Obed 4
  44 Obediah 60 Peter 9 11 14 16
  ROSY 73 SALLY F 55 SALLY 118
  SARAH 72 124 Southey 14 27 34
  52 64 94 122 Southy 55 57 72
  SUSAN ANN 60 TABITHA 9 16
  Thos 9 128 William 16 Wm 50-51
  60 73 75 83 107
GOFFINGON, MARY 21 SALLY 11
GOODAY, LEVICY 1 Reuben 14
  Rhuben 45
GOODRIDGE, P A 127
GOODY, Rubin 108 Wm T 34
GOOLDSBURRY, ELIZABETH 40
GORE, Daniel 110 ELIZABETH 110
GOTHING, JANE 24
GRAVES, AGNES 70 ELISHE 124
  ELIZABETH 9 George 9 Jno Jr 44
  John 21 John Sr 2 70 MOLLY 20
  Peter 124 RACHEL 88 Thos 52
  107 Wm 9 30 117
GRAY, A 89 George 9 23

GREEN, ANNE 49 ELIZABETH 90
  ESTHER 52 George 52
  MARGARET 90 SARAH 88 Wm
  88
GREENAWAY, Mary 66 Rob't 24 66
GREENWAY, Robert 39 44
GRICE, ABAGAIL 7 AGNESS 31
  Thomas 7
GRIFFETH, ANGELINE 71 ANN 102
  B 118 Benja 122 Benjamin 118
  CATY 99 Daniel 96 ELIZABETH
  122 FRANCES 74 Jeremiah 70
  98 John 118 MARGT 20 MARY
  96 Moses 77 99 NANCY 65
  Nathan 32 77 NELLY 120 Sally
  102 122 Smith 67 Thomas 77
  Thomas L 122 Thos 74 120
GRIFFIN, BETSY 26 PEGGY 30
  SALLY 86
GRIFFITH, ANNE 26 B 21 107 Benja
  5 49 51 126 Benjamine 122
  Charles 102 ELIZABETH A 36
  ELIZABETH 22 36 Hezekiah 120
  John 21 96 John H 36 111 LILLY
  77 LOUISA 21 MARY E 111
  MARY 80 Moses 82 Nathan 120
  RACHEL 120 SALLY 58-59
  SARAH ANN 74 Sary 58 Thomas
  74 Thos 24 Wm 36 74 98
GRISE, SUSANNAH 63
GROTEN, DRUSILLA 72 James G 72
  Kendall 125 NANCY 94 Thomas
  72 94
GROVES, ANNE 58 ELISHE 124
  John 15 MARGARET 58 Peter 45
  58
GUNTER, ANN W 23 CATHARINE P
  8 John W F 4 91 Jos S M 100
  MARGARET A J 8 MARY ANN
  100 S S 23 Stephen S 8 59
GUY, AILSEY 77 ELIZABETH 81
  ESTHER 102 George 115 Henry
  51 62 John 46 84 102 105
  LUCRETIA 62 Mary 77 MARY 49
  121 Matthew 48 102 SUSANNA
  46
HACK, ELIZABETH 53
HADLOCK, HARRIET P 67 Robert 67
HAEY, MARIAM 63
HAGGAMAN, NANCY 108
HAGGOMAN, BETTY 53 65 ELISHE
  57 John 53 MARY 62 POLLY 42
  Robert 42 64 SALLY 84 SARAH

HAGGOMAN (cont)
123 Silvanus 57
HALE, PATTY 24
HALET, Robert 66
HALEY, Benj 98 ELIZABETH 34
FANNY 98 NANCY 70 Rob't 70
Wm J 70
HALL, ANN 13 ATHALIAH 3 Dan'l
Roles 102 E 5 Elisha 25-26
ESTHER 5 HARRIET 30 John 3
66 Margaret ANN 25-26 NANCY
66 Robert 13 Thomas 25 30 Thos
27
HALLET, FRANCES 38 John 38 Wm
74
HALLETT, DIANNA 27 ELIZABETH
D 66 John 66 97 John T 32 46
108 MARGARET A 66 MARY F 1
Michael 66 Thomas 20 27 107
Thos 44
HAMBY, John 28 POLLY 98 SUSAN
94 Thomas 98 Wm 30
HAMILTON, Andrew 72 114 Jno 49
MARY 72 Nancy 87
HAMPLETON, James 22 86 MOLLY
90 NANCY 69 William 90
HANAFORD, SARAH 82
HANBY, BETSEY 70 ELISHE 101 Go
Jr 5 John 105 Joseph 6 28 31 57
97 PEGGY 31 Polly 6 31 Wm 12
37 57 71 74 100 103 121
HARDEN, PATSEY 116
HARGISS, Hessey Virginia 115
HARISON, James 116
HARLOW, David 57 80
HARMAN, ARINTHIA J 4 HETTY 43
120 Kely 4 SALLY 14 TABITHA 6
HARMANSON, Patrick 18 ADAH 45
ALICIA 102 ANNE 40 Argall 102
BRIDGET 34 CAROLINE E 29
CATHARINE 26 ELISHE 61 Eliza
84 Elizabeth 61 ELIZABETH
SABRA 94 ELIZABETH 62 91 105
121 ESTHER 23 Geo 15 20 34
102 123 George 105 Gertrude 34
105 GRACE 82 HANNAH 63
Henry 1 7 34 62 84 95 121
ISABELL 34 ISABELLA 38 Jno 23
37 59 127 Jno H 35 John 26 33
45 50 62 66 80 87 101-102 John
H 7 John S 91 John Staughton
38 JULIET B 35 Kendall 91 L 50
93 Lafayette 21 109 116

HARMANSON (cont)
LUCRETIA 7 MARGARET J 117
MARGARET MAPP 102
MARGARET 45 MARIA A 77
Mathew 57 Mathew Sr 62
Matthew 30 40 45 Matthews 26
Patrick 45 59 PEGGY 95 ROSE
47 114 SARAH 53 87 SOPHIA 30
84 105 Susanna 87 SUSANNA 50
SUSANNAH 62 VIRGINIA S 63
Wm 23 39 53 57 63 98 102 104-
105 114 Wm P 1 64
HARMON, CATHARINE 2-3 Geo 121
HARMONSON, Isabell 87
HARRISON, Abel 16 80 104 ANN
126 ANNE 75 BETSEY 41
CHARLOTTE 30 ELIZA ANN 116
ELIZA 60 ELIZABETH 112
ESTHER 37 Isma 126 Jane W 36
Jas S 16 John 1 MARY 16 78
NANCY 104 122 Newton 12 39
111 122 POLLY 66 RACHEL 86
Robert H 30 86 Salathiel 31 66
75 112 SARAH 86 SUSAN 39
SUSANNA 113 Wm 75 90 114
HART, Stephen 94 SUSANNA 94
HARVARD, Wm 106
HARVEY, Jonathan 27
HARWOOD, John 44 117
HAVARD, RACHELL 44 William 71
HAWKINS, James 79
HAYLEY, ANNE 52 Robert 52
HAYS, SUSANNA 101 Wm 117
HAYWARD, Wm 125
HAZE, John 26 MARGARET 26
HEATH, ADAH 25 58 Augustus C E
4 BETSEY 102 Bridget 58
BRIDGET 3 DELITHA 43 EDITH
4 ELIZABETH 94 George 25 Isme
102 James 111 Jno S 72 Joanna
2 John S 18 31 65 94 Josiah 119
JULIET E 97 Louis D 10 Luke 1
55 MAHALA 114 MARY 55
MELINDA D 35 NANCY 117
Patience 43 PEGGY 111 POLLY
106 PRISCILLA 119 Rufus 62
SARAH ANN 65 SEYMOUR 28
SUSAN W 62 William 3 Wm 28
HELLETT, Thomas 113
HENDERSON, BETSEY 89 EDNA 35
EDNEY 35 ELIZA E 113 Jacob 21
John M 5 John T 89 92
MARGARET 92 PEGGY 54 SALLY

HENDERSON (cont)
  A 2 SALLY C 83 SUSANNA 21
  Thos 3 79 Wm 83 113
HENRY, SUSANNA 102
HERBERT, POLLY 107
HERITAGE, ANNE 35
HEWES, MARY 88
HEWITT, Robert 4 SARAH 17
HICKMAN, ADAH 112 BETSEY 28
  Betsy 9 DAMIA 21 Eliz 123
  ELIZABETH 18 George 28 Laban
  31 MOLLY 64 Nath'l 123
  Nathaniel 32 70 Nathaniel B 59
  PATSEY 73 POLLY 123 Selby 9
  SUSEY 21
HIGGINS, Michael N 112
HILL, Rachel 32
HITCHEN, Wm 77
HITCHENS, George 77 MARGARET 51
HITCHINS, NANCY 123
HOG, Peter 34 84 128
HOLBROOK, Jane 79 MARGARET 52 Samuel 5 52
HOLBROOKE, JANE 33 66 John 66
HOLBROOKS, Edward 59
HOLCROFT, MARTHA ANN ELIZA 107
HOLDCROFT, Wm 107
HOLDEN, Geo 48 79
HOLLAND, ANNE 10 Edw'd 121
  Edward 94 ELIZABETH 79 96
  HARRIET G 105 Jacob 81 John
  79 JULIET B 48 MARIA S 19
  NANCY 13 Nat'l 30 Nath'l 10 13
  19 60 105 111 116 121
  Nathaniel 48 Susanna B 10
  SUSANNA 49
HOLMES, ELIZABETH 25 SALLY 94
HOLT, Abel 50 Albert G 75 Anne 42
  ANNE 80 89 Edward 112 Eldred
  R 47 49 ESTHER W 103 Geo 15
  17 62 113-114 George 42 90 93
  96 118 George Jr 125-126
  George Sr 103 Margaret 42
  MARGARET E 93 Martin M M
  103 Mary 62 Stuart 8 21 72
  SUSANNA 8
HOMES, Edw'd 71 ELIZABETH 79
HOPKINS, ANN W 84 ANN 33
  Ellison A 122 Maxamilian 81
  Maximilian 95 SUSAN F 68 Wm
  W 33

HORNER, CATHERINE 85 Moses
  119 NANCY 70 Susan 70
HORNSBY, Wm 111
HORTON, RACHEL P 37
HOSHIER, EMMY J 40
HOSIER, BETSEY 46 Emanuel 17
  Mahala 40
HOSIR, Manuel 24
HOUGHTON, Jacob 87
HOWELL, EMELINE 20 LAVINIA
  118 MARGARET 52 MARGRET 1
  Mary 20 NANCY 115 SALLY 60
  Sukey 118 Wm 1 60
HOWSON, Rob't 11 29
HUBBARD, SALLY 75
HUBBERD, Edmund 64
HUDSON, BARBARY 3
HUGHES, BETSEY 101 MARY 98
  NANCY 123
HULINGS, David W 122-123 Maria
  H P 122-123 MARIA PATTON 123
  MARY R 122
HUNT, ANN 2 ANNE 83 Azariah 55
  102 114 126 BETSEY 94 DELITHA
  120 ELISHE 102 FANNY 55
  Gawton 15 91 94 116 Hillary 55
  Hillery 123 MARGARET 120 Mary
  E 105 NANCY 114 Obadiah 120
  Obed 76 Obediah 42 51 56 120
  ROSE 56 SALLY 36 SARAH 3 55
  120 SUKEY 64 94 Thomas 83
  120 Thomas O 109 Thos C 49
  VIRGINIA A 105
HURST, Thos 104
HUTCHESON, PEGGY 114
HUTSON, BRIDGET 116 NANCY 89
  PEGGY 86
HYSLOP, CHARLOTTE 107 Custis
  43 79 NANCY 79 SUSAN 76
  Susana 107 Susanna 76 Walter
  25 41 43 47 50 52-53 59 73 80
  88 92 103 116
INNIS, FRANCES 82
IREVANE, NORA 31
IRONMONGER, Edward 56
ISDALE, MARGARET 115
ISDELL, Edward 1 James 16 24 112
  LAVINIA 70 MARIA 7 MARY 112
  Matthew 7 Nancy 61 NANCY 24
  SARAH 111 Wm 61
JACKSON, DESDEMONA 65 JENNY
  124 Jonah Jr 128 Jonas 124
  MARGARET 68 MOLLY 24 Wm

JACKSON (cont)
98 Wm G 90
JACOB, Abraham 18 93 117 ANN
25 30 114 ANNE S 87 ANNE 29
74 117 BETTY 45 CHARLOTTE H
127 DREUSILLA 14 ELINOR 31
ELISHE 11 28 ELIZA 46
Elizabeth 27 ELIZABETH B 27
ELIZABETH 5 91 Emeline 100
EMILY 13 Esau 5 11 22 40 42 45
54 57 64 97 ESTHER 18 Eyre 45
Hancock 29 32 45 54 59 83 117
119 Hancock Sr 29 HENRIETTA
P 73 Isaac 102 James 82 127 Jas
55 Jno C 30 73 John 1 25 52 56
63 75 102 John C 13 John Sr 44
KESSEY 54 MARGARET D 83
MARGARET 11 33 42 56 93
MARTHA 28 MARY POLLY 93
MARY 44 75 79 116 NANCY 50
104 PEGGY 40 117 Philip 6 28
116 POLLY 38 RACHEL 118
Rich'd 40 Richard 71 Rob't 27
Rob't C 26 Robert 33 87 Robert C
119 Robert Clark 114 SALLY
ANN 122 SALLY H 36 SALLY 40-
41 65 102 Sarah 40-41 SARAH
ANN 119 SARAH 22 SINAH 110
SUSAN M 11 SUSANNA 26 97
Teackle 42 120 Teackle W 23 49
70 93 Teagle 25 Thoas 39
Thomas 28 73 75 83 91 103 Thos
60 104 119 Thos Jr 30 Tinsey 55
VIANNA GRAY 42 W E 27 50 W
W 85 Wm 16 28 30 55 118 122
Wm W 83
JAMES, Andrew 1 14 28 94 ANN
ELIZA 49 ANN 53 ANNE 101
ANSLEY 24 Bridget 47
CAROLINE 82 CASSANDRA 65
ELIZABETH 33 45 47 Hez P 34
118 Hezekiah 75 95 101
Hezekiah P 8 John 81 John S
108 MALANA 92 MARGARET 91
MARIA 94 NANCY 74 POLLY 47
Rob't 33 Robert 81 91 ROSANNA
56 ROSEY 1 SALLY A 108 SALLY
95 SUSANNA 28 91 Thomas 40
82 96 101 Thos 45 124 William
67 Wm 3 89 Wm D 1 91
JARVIS, Elizabeth U 99 ELIZABETH
W 61 ELIZABETH 101
HENRIETTA SARAH 93 Jesse N 2

JARVIS (cont)
22 94 LAURA 95 Marg't 93
Margaret 98 MARGARET A 98
MARGARET 10 MARIA ANN 99
MARY E 79 MARY 7 SALLY 95
Thomas 19 76 Thomas R 36 95
Thos 14 43 Thos B 91 Thos W B
119 William 7 William B 79 Wm
10 43 55 63 93 95 101 122-123
Wm Jr 24 122 Wm Sr 61 95
JEFFEREY, BETHANY 108
JEFFERSON, POLLY 65 Silas 21 24
44 60 65 80 94
JEFFERY, Littleton 6 NANCY 6
JEFFERYS, Wm 41
JEFFRIES, BETSEY 19 LEAH 52
SOPHIA 16
JEFFRY, POLLY 29
JEFRES, Wm 35
JENKINS, CHARLOTTE 11 George
11
JENNE, ELIZABETH 90 Wm 57
JENNEY, ESTHER 92
JESTER, Joseph 126
JOFFLIF, ECKAY 114
JOHNSON, Amos 88 122 ANN 111
ANNA 111 ANNE 17 51 65 75
116 Benja 97 Benjamin 51 114
BETSY 68 Butifiler 17 CASSA 3
ELENOR 114 ELISHE 90 ELIZA
100 Elizabeth 113 ELIZABETH A
55 ELIZABETH M 4 ELIZABETH
S 3 ELIZABETH 14 97 112 121
Emeline 100 EMELINE 53 68
FANNY 84 FRANCES L 69 George
F 3 Guhu 28 HARRIOT A 107
HENRIETTA 122 Isaac 97 Ismay
61 James 53 82 86 97 100 107
116 JANE 77 Jas 11 122 Jeheu
69 Jehugh 87 Jeptha 25 37 54-
55 91 113 Jno T 92 Johannes 18
24 37 41 106 116-117 Johannis
12 47 66 89 John 32 67-68 91
113 122 John P 2 111 John T 40
107 John Y 30 Kelly 17 L S 88
Laban 127 Laban S 87 LOUISA B
45 Luke 110 MARGARET ANN 83
MARGARET E S 37 Margaret R
45 MARGARET S 27 40
MARGARET 67 91 122 MARY
ANN 115 MARY 10 88 MATILDAH
17 Moses 14 88 NANCY 79
Obadiah 17 Obed 90 Obed R 45

JOHNSON (cont)
  Obediah 97 111 117 Obedience
  12 62 65 127 Obedience R 20 42
  92 PEGGY 12 76 Polly 107 Powell
  35 Priscilla 111 RACHEL 2
  RACHELL 1 Rich'd 91 115
  Richard 40 116 Robinson 10
  ROSE 32 113 Rosey 87 ROSEY
  34 ROSY M 91 SALLY 5 35 82
  Samuel 83 SARAH A 45 SARAH
  94 96-97 SUKEY 42 SUKY 127
  SUSAN 42 SUSANNA 97 111
  Thomas 27 94 Thomas Jr 69 75
  111 115 Thos 40 101 Thos Jr 3
  William P 3 Wm 76 Wm G 23 93
  Wm P 45 80 98 Wm Sr 119
JOINS, Rachel 21
JONES, BETSEY 41 BETSY 113
  CATH S 115 CATHARINE F 70
  Catharine S 70 CHARLOTTE 99
  David 24 34 56 72 ELIZABETH
  125 EMELINE 118 GRACE 65
  Isaac 82 James H 46 Jno 106
  John 80 LETITIA M 80 LISHA 46
  Littleton 85 99 124 LUCRETIA 46
  Nathaniel 46 120-121 124 NELLY
  121 PEGGY 28 Richard 118 125
  SALLY 76 SUSAN 119 124
  SUSANNA 82 Teackle 76 Thomas
  98 Wm 120 Zerobabel 60
  Zorobabel 28 49 102
JORDAN, DOROTHY 91
JOYNE, Edmund 1 49 71 ELISHE
  58 ESTHER 71 HENRIETTA 49
  MARGARET 2 53 Nan 121
  SARAH 113 TABITHA 1 Thos 1
  Watkins 81 Wm 2
JOYNES, BICEY 111 CAROLINE 48
  Edmond 92 Edmund 64 103 107
  Edw'd 86 Edward 38 104 108
  113 Edward A 127 Edward J 126
  Elisha 65 ELIZABETH 7 John 88
  Margaret 104 Margaret Ann 92
  MARGARET ANN 108
  MARGARET 29 38 MARY 21 99
  NANCY 69 97 121 PEGGY 61
  POLLY 89 101 R A 104
  REBECCA M 107 Robert A 5 7 43
  67 92 117 Robt A 101 S A 111
  SALLY S 65 SARAH 31 Shepherd
  A 13 SUSANNA 34 SUSEY 92
  TABITHA WYATT 111 Thomas 48
  Thos R 82 Tully A T 62 Watkins

JOYNES (cont)
  88 Wm 70
JUSTICE, NANCY 51
KECHINE, DEBORA 104
KEE, POLLY 1
KELLAM, PEGGY 22 ADAH 112 ANN
  E 1 CATHERINE 112 Charles 112
  117 Custis 104 Edmond 89
  Edmund 82 Edw'd 93 Edward 54
  94 ELIZABETH J 66 ELIZABETH
  JANE 127 ELIZABETH W 89
  ELIZABETH 31 ESTHER M 82
  FRANCES E 1 George 43 J H 119
  James 65 James L 68 Jno H 119
  MARGARET S 4 MARGARET 126
  ROSEY 50 S E D 85 Sam'l 3
  SARAH ANN 97 Stewart 127
  SUSAN 117 Thomas 26 Thomas
  H 1
KELLUM, Benja 71 Custis 11
  Edward 62 LAURANNA 59
  LURANAR 59 MARGT 65 NANCY
  T 93 NANCY 51 ROSE 52 SABRA
  52 Severn 1 Smith 59 Stephen 52
  Thos 72 Wm 126
KELLY, Ann 44 Betsey 51 Charles
  27 32 ELIZABETH 1 8 35 Jesse
  11 MARGARET ELIZABETH 11
  MARY ANN 27 44 Obed 35
  PATSEY 51 RACHEL 81 Sylvester
  1 22 Sylvester M 33 115
KEMP, ADAH 32 Alex 31 John 32
  SARAH 93
KENDAL, Margt 48
KENDALL, Ann 93 ANNE 23
  BETSEY 43 Catharine H G 60
  Custis 11 23 37 86 110 Dr John
  25 ELISHE 48 ELIZABETH B 48
  ELIZABETH C 122 ELIZABETH H
  38 Elizabeth W 122 ELIZABETH
  84 88 ESTHER 25 38 Geo 9 59
  82 95 George 71 88 106 George
  Mason 75 Henry B 30 40 84 107
  119 125 Jno 20 John 6 24-25 38
  49 53 79 88 93 102 106 John Jr
  45 82 John W 7 Littleton 30 74
  Littleton Sr 76 102 LOUISA 60
  Lucretia 48 Margaret 1
  MARGARET 102 MARY ANN 25
  MARY 74 MASON 114 NANCY 10
  59 94 Peggy 23 PEGGY 93 SALLY
  63 SARAH 1 88 Sorrowful
  Margaret 16 SORROWFUL

KENDALL (cont)
  MARGARET 15 SUKEY 38
  SUSAN ANN 17 SUSAN 7
  SUSANNA 27 Thomas 38 102
  Thomas L 115 Thos L 94 110 Wm
  3 9 15 63 79 91 Wm H 70 Wm Jr
  64 94 Wm Sr 114
KENNARD, SALLY S 74 Wm 72 74
KER, Jno 4 John 35 54 74-75 77
  112 SALLY 5
KERBY, Rob't 81
KETCHAM, Oliver 87 SARAH M 87
KEY, POLLY 1
KILMAN, BETSY 12
KITSON, Martha Willoughby 104
  NANCY 104 Thos 104
KITTERIDGE, William Sargant 65
KNIGHT, ADAH 125 ANNE 124
  BETSEY 39 92 CLARA 89
  ELIZABETH S 108 John 89 109
  121 John Jr 119 MARG 40 MARY
  A 57 MOLLY 119 PEGGY 18
  REBECCA 94 SALLY 109
  Susanna 35 SUSANNA 119
  Thomas 96 99 108 Thos 35 Wm
  9 18 57 108 125 Wm K 66
LAMBERTSON, RHODA 38
LANG, Abraham 6 20 29 38-39 81
  89 100 115 PEGGY 29
LANGDON, Michael 95 Nancy 95
LANKFORD, Killiam 53
LARRE, KATHARINE 15
LAURENCE, Joseph 88
LAWRENCE, Levin 105 PATIENCE
  64
LAWSON, MARY ANN 103
LEATHERBURY, ELIZABETH J 85
  ELIZABETH 26 J W 24 James M
  26 Jno W 14 23 56 95 108 John
  W 12 57 60 63 66-67 70 85 89
  98 Margaret C 66 Virginia L 75
  Wm J 85 Wm T 72
LECATO, John 59-60
LEWES, Isachar 69
LEWIS, ADAH 79 Ben 100 BETSY
  65 Fielding 106 Geo 74 George
  56 91 Ischar 127 Issacher 45
  KITTY 48 LETTA 83 Levin 60
  Margaretta 25 MARY J 93
  MOLLY 25 NANCY 1 PEGGY 100
  Thomas 70 106 Thos 20 85 122
  William 5 83 Wm 3 61 93
LINGO, CATHERINE 64 Margaret 64

LINGO (cont)
  SUKEY 8
LINGOE, ELIZ 29
LITTLETON, ESTHER 92
LIVERPOOL, Josiah 6 37 SALLY 37
  Sarah 6
LONG, LEANNE 2
LONGO, MARY 43
LUCAR, George 42
LUCOR, Thos 57
LUCRE, DELITHA 51
LUDDINGTON, HANNA 12
LUKE, ANNE 15 63 BETSEY 52
  Daniel 8 26 83 89 97 117 EDITH
  117 JANE 26 JENNEY 21 John
  46 127 MOLLY 37 PEGGY 83 89
  SALLY 104
LUKER, CAROLINE S F 74
  ELIZABETH N 13 John 58 John
  W 13 SALLY A 123 SALLY 127
  SUSANNA 84 Thos 65 Walter 74
  94 113 123 127
LUNE, MARTHA 113
LURTON, Jacob 95
LYON, James 92 105 MARGARET A
  105
MACDANIEL, MARY 45
MACGAWAN, John 30 90
MACGOWAN, John 127
MACINTOSH, Margaret 109
MACKY, Wilcock 59
MADDOX, John 114
MADDUX, John B 50 REBECCA 54
  Thos 54
MAJOR, AMIE 78 ELIZABETH 85
  JANE 34 John 81 85 90 Littleton
  116 MARGARET 55 MARY 50
  NANCY 81 114 Peggy 35 PEGGY
  18 Wm 18 53 57 78 Wm Jr 35
MALEY, MARGARET 51
MANARRELL, ANNE 103
MANLOW, MARY 41
MAPP, ADAH 51 ADRIANA 53
  BETSEY 91 ELIZABETH 64
  ESTHER 13 58 Ether 16 Francis
  B 49 Howsen 64 Howson 45 51
  60 103 117 JANE 5 Jno 16 52
  John 10 82 90 John C 56 106
  118 LEAH 60 117 Margaret 86
  MARGARET C 48 MARGARET 48
  MARY 16 Peggy 108 Rich'd 15
  Richard 72 Robins 5 15 41 53
  75-76 85 116 Samuel 10 53

MAPP (cont)
  SARAH 10 86 SUSANNA 58
  Victor 48 Wm 58
MAPPS, Rich'd 2
MARRINER, ELIZABETH 112
MARSHALL, ELIZABETH 62-63
  Jacob 54 Jno 24 John 61 66
  SARAH 59 106 Thomas 59
MARTHA, BOOL 27
MARTIN, ELIZABETH A 73 James R
  B 9 MARY 16 NELLY 116 Peter
  73 SALLY 4 Wm 49 80
MARTYNE, J J 89
MASLIN, SUSAN E 69
MASON, Arroda 95 HENNY 95 Wm
  H 46
MASSEY, Anne 2 ELIZABETH 2
MATHEW, ANSLEY 77
MATHEWS, CATHARINE 40 Custis
  26 101 ELIZABETH 15 John 95
  John Custis 15 26 30 54 KESIAH
  78 Levin 25 80 MARGARET 66
  Mary 51 Michael 51-52 98 108
  110 NANCY 51 PEGGY 1 26
  ROSEY 30 Sally 67 Sam'l H 67
  Samuel H 78 SUSAN 67 SUSEY
  122 William 118 Wm 51 108
MATTHEW, Custis 127 Lewis M 93
  Lewis N 64
MATTHEWS, DAMARIS 5-6 ELIZA J
  104 ELIZABETH 41 62 ESTHER
  16 HARRIET P 106 John 62 John
  Custis 16 Levin 59 104 Lewis N
  68 Lewis R 106 Margaret 104
  MARGARET ANN 59 MARGARET
  S 92 MARGARET 33 Mary 6
  MARY 115 Michael R 67 Samuel
  H 78 SUSAN 34 TEACKLE 41
  William 33 Wm 34 Wm K 63
MATTOCKS, ELIZABETH 11
MAYO, LOUISA M 92 P 56 P P 34
  Peter P 107 110
MAZELINE, MARY J 69
MAZLIN, LUCY 104
MCCOWAN, BETSY 99 CATY 103
  John 46 103 NANCY 122
MCCOWN, John 32
MCCRADY, MOLLY 64 NANCY 58
  SALLY 80
MCCREADY, CATHARINE 112
MCCROSKEY, Sam'l Smith 82
MCDANIEL, POLLY 33
MCDONALD, Hugh 51 MARY 51

MCDONALD (cont)
  Wm Gibb 112
MCGREGOR, NANCY 80
MCINTOSH, MARGARET B 122
MCLANACHAN, Elijah 112
MCLAUGHLIN, Alexander 56
MCMETH, JENNEY 23
MCMULLEN, ---- 30
MEAR, Wm 61
MEARS, ADAH S 83 Alex W F 10 60-
  62 121 Alexander W F 2 57
  CATHARINE 26 ELIZ A 4
  ELIZABETH J M 92 ELIZABETH
  W 18 ELIZABETH 28 97 ESTHER
  37 Frances L 27 George 83
  James 37 Jamima 42 John 26 28
  111 Littleton 35 Lorenzo D 6
  LOVEY 52 MAHALA F 61
  MALINDA 111 MARGARET F 18
  MARGARET S 12 MARY J 60
  MARY M 91 MARY 13 Reubin 13
  Richard 18 40 60-61 ROSY P 42
  SALLY B 87 SUSAN S 40 SUSAN
  78 Thomas C 12 27 87 Thos C
  119 William 13 97 Wm 4 87
MEARSE, William 13
MEGRIGER, NANCY 80 Sally 80
MEHOLLOMES, LURANA 9 NANCY
  18 Thomas 15 59 Wm W 20 101
MEHOLLOMS, George 115 MARY 14
  PEGGY 9 Thos 59
MELBORNE, ARINTHIA C 71 John
  71
MELHOLLOMES, Geo 34 50 SUSAN
  T 42 Thomas 42
MELHOLLOMS, Geo 56 NANCY 97
  SARAH 98 TAMAR 18
MELVIL, AGNES 112
METCALF, SARAH 41
MICHAEL, ANNE 111 COMFORT 92
  Jno 35 53 Joachim 11 17 32 35
  40 45 51 58 114 117 John 70
  John Jr 59 MARGARET 45 110
  MARY BLAIKLEY 97 PATIENCE
  17 PEGGY 59 SARAH 64 Tilney
  63-64 88 Wm 110 Wm
  Wainhouse 88
MIERS, Alex W F 83
MIFFLIN, ANN 34 ANNE 86 Edw'd
  92
MILBOURN, ANN 118 John C 98
  MARY H 98 SALLY 33 Thomas 33
  90 Thos 40 118

MILBOURNE, MARY 33 Thomas 33
MILBY, Adiel 2 John 57 59 82 86 92
  Leah 80 NANCY 2 ROSANNA 18
  SALLY 59 SUSANNA 82 TABITHA
  28
MILES, ANN 115 POLLY 48 Richard
  11 Wm 6 79
MILHAS, Joseph 82
MILLER, LILLY 44 MARY 126
  PEGGY 87
MILLS, Agnes 33 BETSEY 101
  Elizabeth 123 Jacob 34 123 127
  JEACA 22 NANCY 39 46 SUKEY
  30 SUSAN 33 SUSANNA 99 Wm
  22
MINSON, John G 7 100 Samuel 108
MISTER, ELIZABETH 68 EMILY 112
  Gilbert 112 123 MARGARET E
  119 Wm 68 119
MITCHELL, Wm D 19
MOOR, ESTHER 66 Isaac Jr 117
  Jacob 11 58 John 63 Levi 5 69
  Mathew 66 75 Matthew 54
  Matthew D 77 85 MILLY 41
  SARAH 5
MOORE, Abram 78 99 119 126
  ADELIA 47 ANGELINE 113
  Arcadia 51 BETSEY 9 78 Betsy
  119 CATHARINE 109
  ELIZABETH ANN 67 Ellen C 101
  EMILY S 124 Geo 8-9 Isaac 9
  ISABELL 101 Jacob 24-25 Jno
  78 John 22 46 95 122 124
  Joseph 10 LUCEY 25 LUCRETIA
  124 Mack 99 MARGARET S 64
  MARY 111 118 Mathew D 86
  Matt D 126 Matthew D 64 67
  NANCY 122 126 Peter 122 POLLY
  99 SALLY 37 SANTEKEY 33
  SOPHIA 33 SUSANNA 51 Thomas
  36 Thos 21 Tubman L 13 Wm D
  113
MORE, Mathew 44 SALLY 44
MORGAN, Griffith 39
MORRIS, BRIDGET 69 Henry 106
  Jacob 100 Levin 65 72 LOUISA
  65 MARY 5 NANNY 115 Revel 5
  SALLY 89 SARAH 45 SOPHIA 81
  SUKEY 106
MOSES, BETSEY 64 BETSY 115
  Frederick 20 Jenny 115
MUNES, JOAN 32
MURRY, MARY 43

NAGLE, MOLLY 77
NEALE, CATHARINE T 110
  Elizabeth T 110 Hamilton 28 109
NEDAB, Stephen 72
NEHULIAN, ELICE 24
NELSON, ANN 28 Charles 12 ELIZ
  25 ELIZABETH W 16 ELIZABETH
  51 Jno Sr 55 John 9 39 96 John
  G 104 John Jr 28 34 109 John
  Sr 63 LEAH 63 MARGARET B 52
  MARGARET JANE 7 MARIA J
  109 MARY 39 POLLY S 109
  SALLY B 12 Sally T 16 SARAH E
  109 SARAH 57 Southey 109
  Southy 51-52 109 119 Wm 90 99
NEWMAN, MATILDA 38
NICHOLSON, Elizabeth B 112
  HARRIET S 22 Jas M 115 Jno 60
  Jno W 33 John W 100 Levin H 22
  112
NIGHELL, Elizabeth 62
NOEL, Edward 72
NOLEN, Lewis 92 POLLY 32 Thos L
  38
NORTRIP, NANCY 60
NOTINGHAM, Susan B 36
NOTTIGNHAM, ESTHER 16
NOTTINGHAM, A J 19 Abel 81 94
  Adderson 7 31-32 45 50 122
  Addison 67 Andrew J 14 35 Ann
  24 Ann Jacob 119 ANNE S 124
  ANNE 22 25 30 BELL SARAH 29
  Benja 3 78 81 99 Benjamin 17 70
  99 CASSEY 36-37 EDEY 28
  EDITH 123 Edw'd W 93 95 108
  112 Edward W 54 Elisha 99
  Elizabeth 11 ELIZABETH ANN 89
  Elizabeth Upshur 110
  ELIZABETH W 13 ELIZABETH 9
  27 35 99 Ellison S 71 EMILY 53
  ESTHER 120 FANNEY 29
  Frances 106 Geo Upshur 110
  HARRIET 110 Harrison 20 26
  Isaac 33 36 46 52 57 61 117
  Jacob 7 12 29 35-36 81 84 94
  Jacob E 42 Jacob Jr 63 102 109
  Jacob Sr 106 James 42 James B
  27 44 Jno 14 86 John 12 24 35-
  36 93 John E 32 62 110 122-124
  John R 54 John Sr 15 Jos 120
  Jos Walter 119 Joseph 91 125
  Joseph D 89 112 119 Joshua 44
  53 89 109 L B 4 7 10 69 96 98

NOTTINGHAM (cont)
121 LAVINIA 37 Leah U 91
Leon'd B 77 Leonard B 4-5 51 83
94 97 106-107 118 124 Leonard
J 94 Levin 37 64 120 LUCY ANN
36 Luther 19 65 119 124 Major
Smith 13 MARGARET M 51-52
MARGARET 50 62 64 81 99 103
116 123 MARGT 92 MARIA B
119 MARIA SUSAN 36 MARIA 90
MARY ANN 94 MARY B 42 MARY
E 42 51 MARY P 81 MARY S 103
MARY SUSAN 119 MARY 5 7 67
124 Michael 23 MOLLY 81
NANCY 12 21 24 26 48 PATSY F
121 PEGGY 81 POLLY 125 Rich'd
12 49 66 78 80-81 124 126
Richard 3 9 26 Rob't 47 Rob't B
53 Rob't J 125 Robert 112 Robert
B 95 119 ROSEY 69 S 34 S S 3
27 Sally 25 Sally R 13 SALLY 60
93 SARAH 13 57 Severn 37 39 41
69 117 123 127 Severn E 44 60
Smith 4 13 30 52-53 55 57 103
105 109 122 125 Smith L 79
Smith S 6 12 20 33 69 81 100
124 SUKEY 107 SUSANNA 12 49
Thomas 29 49 62-63 65 94 123
Thomas J 63 121 Thomas Sr 123
Thomas W 5 Thos 21 64 110 124
Thos H 71 125 Thos J 19 96
Thos Jr 41 123 Thos Sr 12 124
Victor A 22 36 39 48 77 85 121
VIRGINIA A J 94 VIRGINIA S 13
William P 5 Wm 4 21 49-50 52-
53 60 124 Wm B 22 Wm C 71
Wm E 37 50 92 116 Wm J 6 12
35-36 58 111 Wm Jr 25 110 Wm
P 15 29 37 53 70 Wm T 1 14-15
26 32 54 86 102 104 118
NUTTS, BRIDGET 100 SABRA 100
O'DEAR, AGNES 71 BETSEY 117
ESTHER 90 George 17 36 44
Joseph 71 78 Laban 79
MALINDA 16-17 PATSEY 36
PEGGY 9 SALLY 107 SUKEY 47
William 17
O'DIER, Mary 96
O'HARA, John 2
OAG, ESTHER 1 Robert 32
ODEAR, ESTHER 15 SUSANNA 89
Wm 15
OGG, SUSAN 29

OLDHAM, Leroi 126 Leroy 91 101
125 Montcalm 24 51 95 126
OLIVER, Wm W 2
ONLY, PATIENCE 53 PHILLIS 72
Wm 8
OUTIN, Timothy 26
OUTTEN, BETSEY 103 George F 25-
26 George T 60 Jacob 77
OWENS, SARAH A 106
PAKE, Elisabeth 5 SALLEY 5
PALKER, BETSEY 108
PALMER, Sam'l 46 62 114 Sarah 34
PARKER, Alfred 6 11 60 110 Anne
Stratton 105 110 ANNE 105
ARINTHIA DARBY 73 BETSEY
108 ELIZABETH 93 Geo Jr 110
Jacob G 95 102 105 110 112 125
Jas 45 Jno W H 69 John S 75 96
106 115 JULIET J 2 MARY 66
PEGGY E 110 POLLY 18 S E 54
SALLY B 102 SARAH ANDREWS
110 SARAH 62 Severn E 10 64
110 Thos 3 98 Wm A 2 Wm H 61
PARKERSON, ELIZABETH 44 Geo
37 George 74 Levin 26
MARGARET 74 MARY 37 SARAH
58 Wm 6
PARKINSON, Eliz 101 George 8 Wm
23
PARKS, Chas 62 JANE 62
PARLKER, BETSEY 108
PARRAMORE, HARRIET B D 61
HENRIETTA 54 MARGARET A 78
ROSEY 50 SARAH 21 Thos 8 54
Thos Sr 126 Wm 7 77
PARROTT, Geo 27 George 107
PARSON, Samuel H 36
PARSONS, Ann 102 ANN 23
ELCANA B 36 ELIZABETH 50
121 ESTHER 96 102 112 FANNY
97 Jno G 104 John 59 John C
112 John G 50 Marriot 43
Marriott 4 112 121 MARY 59
NANCY 52 62 96 Polly S 3 Rosey
102 Sally 4 36 SALLY 83 Sam'l
50 Samuel H 20 SUSAN 20 77 98
Thos 102 Wm 50 83 96-97 118
Wm Jr 98 Wm S 84 97 Wm Sr 3
PARVIN, MARIA 15 Zacheus 15
PAULIN, Jos W 85
PEAK, Robert 79 Siller 19
PEAKE, BETSEY 19
PEARSON, Adah 45 ADAH 101

PEARSON (cont)
  ELIZABETH S 85-86 Jos 91
  Joseph J 11 MARY 60 NANCY 67
  Patrick 102 TAMAR 45 Thomas
  45 67 Thos 45 102 Wm 86
PEATON, NANCY 94
PECK, SALLY 5
PEED, Thomas 39 60 104
PERKESON, Elisabeth 9
PERKINS, Adah 19 George 96
PETERKIN, James 56 58 69 86 Jas
  101 111
PETTIT, ADAH 89 ELIZABETH 10
  Jacob 111 Maj 32 Major 40 77 80
  86 90 127 Steward 26 Stewart 87
  SUSAN 35 Thomas 94 W M 50
  Wm M 35
PETTITT, AMY 1 ANNE 90 Major
  124 MARY 71 120 RACHEL 103
  Thomas 90 Wm 103 120
PHABEN, ANNE 15 ESTHER 77 Paul
  15 Wm 15 77
PHABIN, Wm 66
PIGOT, 5 ANNE 15 ELIZABETH 64
  67 John 67 Salem 15
PIPER, AGNES 18
PITS, Hezekiah 108
PITT, Jacob 51
PITTS, ANNE 97 ELIZABETH R 116
  ELIZABETH 117 Geo 12 George
  117 Hez 10 35 Hezekiah 5 18 51
  56 93 Jacob 120 Jno 108 John
  80 97 LEAH 80 Major 53 108 116
  Major S 5 116 MARGARET 51
  MARY ANNE 33 MARY 116 Mr
  116 NANCY 5 POLLY 14 RACHEL
  120 Rob't 57 SALLEY 108 SARAH
  D 20 TAMAR 43 VIANER GRAY
  53 Wm G 21 93 115
POLE, Geo 114 Godfrey 42 81 102
POLK, Josiah T 119 Rob't 17 41 57
  Robert 116
POOL, ABSEL 45 ADAH 59 72
  BETSEY 100 Charles 16 19 78
  100 George 59 106 Hessey 100
  Joseph 81 KESIAH 100 MARY
  110 PEGGY 2 78 SALLY 100
  SARAH 72 SUSAN 19 Warren H
  90
PORTER, Jonathan 53
POTT, ELIZABETH 43
POTTER, J R 44
POULSON, ANNE B 14 HESSY 110

POULSON (cont)
  James 100 James B 78 Jas 48
  LUCY 24 R J 48
POWEL, Jno 87 Susanna Godwin 87
POWELL, Abel 31-32 83 86 ANN N
  68 ANN 42 ANNE W 95 BARBARY
  73 BETSY 23 ELIZABETH 31 63
  123 Geo 123 George 3 35 46 57
  68 85 HANNAH BELL 3 HANNAH
  36 96 Jackson B 11 122 James
  18 25 Jas 39 Jesse 23 John 17
  John H 19 39 88 LAURETTA 118
  MARGARET L 83 MARIAH S 109
  MARY A 11 MARY ANN 14
  NANNY 31 Nath'l 57 66 71
  Nathaniel 3 PAMELA E J 5
  PEGGY 35 123 R W 69 RACHEL
  86 Robert 116 ROSE 17 SALLY
  18 85 94 Sarah 17 SARAH 32 57
  Seth 16 48 66 111 Thomas 18 35
  38 44 63 74 123 Wm 94
PRATT, ADAH 126 ANNE 19 Elishe
  84 James 11 John 44 MARY 21
  MOLLY 43 NANCY 19 52 ROSEY
  84 Salley 19 SALLY 49 Sarah 52
  SUSEY 71
PREESON, ANN 46 Elizabeth 11
  Esther 48 81 ESTHER 3
  MARGARET 63 SUSANNA 11 42
  Thomas 23 Thos 3 11 48 62 79
  82 Zerub 15 Zerubable 63
PRESS, CAROLINE 100 Edm'd 19
  Edmund 6 38 51 MOLLY 6
  SUSANNA 51 TABBY 38
PURNAL, BETSEY 59
RAFIELD, HANNAH 112 John 64
  101
RALIEGH, Walter 52 83
RASCO, Peter 24 SARAH 90 Wm 55
RASCOE, ELIZABETH 5 MARY 69
  Wm 43
RASIN, SUSANNA 104
RAYFIELD, Dennard 126 Edward 60
  ELIZABETH 10 Harrison 56 101
  Harrison T 15 115 John 126
  John H 4 16 LAVENIA 15 MARY
  W 126 Thos W 47
READ, Adah 6 20 ANN MARIA 20
  ANN 6 Betsey 6 Calvin 123
  Calvin H 47 54 83 CHILAMETHIA
  72 CORINTHIA V J 123 Edmund
  91 ELIZABETH JANE 91 EMILY
  91 Isaac 68 JUNO 72 L H 81

READ (cont)
LEAH 99 Luther H 25 73 95
Margaret L 91 123 MARGARET S
83 PENDA 68 Reubin 29 Rich'd H
17 66 Richard H 106 Richard T
123 Rickard P 36 SALLY 70
SARAH 111
REED, Reuben 82 115
REEVE, MARY 24
REGUS, Louis P 13
REID, Reuben 69
RESPASS, LUCY 97 Sophia 97
RESPESS, ESTHER 1 Jno 62 John
1 47 88 LUCRETIA 47 Thos 48
REW, Southey 28 Southy 17 47
REYNOLDS, ELIZABETH 97
HARRIOT 92 SUSANNA 83
RICHARDSON, Charles A 74 Chas A
50 ELIZA 70 ELIZABETH 8
FANNY 39 Geo 7 111 Kendall 7
88 KESSY 98 Levi 14 64 86 Levin
93 Major 17 Major F 40
MARGARET 29 NANCY 7 86
PAMELA 68 POLLY 15 104
RACHAEL 8 SALLY 14 Smith 13
Solomon 1 80 SUKEY 66
SUSANNA 66 Wm 7 31 68
RIDLEY, ANN P 33 ELIZABETH 44
ESTHER P 12 ESTHER 12
ROSENA T 109 Seldon 7 Seldon
S 66 Wm 92 Wm P 12 116 Wm W
12 33 41 92 109
RILEY, ELLIN G 26 Frances 26 Geo
26
RIPPEN, ANNE 82 David 120
ELIZABETH 117 124 John 117
SUSANNA 43 Thos 124 Wm 20
47 82 117
RIPPIN, ESTHER 39 FANNY 17
MARGARET 27 MOLLY 47 POLLY
23 Thomas 27 William 39 Wm 19
RO, ANN 25
ROBBINS, Jno E 87
ROBERTS, AGNES 63 AMELIA 74
Archibald 50 ARINTHIA 42
Arthur 25 29 65 67-68 88 97 111
114 Arthur E 5 61 Arthur Jr 59
Arthur T 68 123 CATY 32
DIMARARA 18 Edm'd 94 100 107
111 Edmund 112 Edw'd P 29 40
Edward P 94 112 Elias 15 46 71
79 122 ELIZA 11 Elizabeth 11
ELIZABETH A 121 ELIZABETH

ROBERTS (cont)
61 Emery L 54 Esther W 121
ESTHER 84 123 Francis 11 34
Frank 88 Jacob 38 59 69 104
125 Jno 24 JOANNA 89
JOANNAH 15 John 10 15 78 84
92 Joshua K 18 68 82 100
Legustus 35 47 LOVY 67 Luther
W 50 MARGARET 34 66 88
MARY E 112 Moses 1 74 84-85
NANCY 22 30 Peggy 71 PEGGY 1
38 85 POLLY 17 22 RACHEL 48
ROSY 123 Sally 42 121 Sally A
75 SALLY 8 64 89 SARAH ANN
88 SARAH 98 102 Shepherd 124
SUSAN 102 Teackle 8 29-30 41
47 116 123 127 Thomas N B 61
Thomas Sr 22 Thos Jr 79 Thos N
B 40 VIRGINIA S W 75 William
32 Wm 8 26 38 46 52 84 86 89
Wm Jr 16 26 49 96 Zorobabel 46
ROBERTSON, PHEBE 66
ROBINS, Arthur 29 111 Arthur Jr
10 BETSEY 4 BRIDGET 119
BRIDGIT 93 CATHERINE 48
Edw'd Jr 100 Edward 10 66 82
110 Edward T 47 ELIZABETH U
55 ELIZABETH 5 47 ESTHER 10
82 FRANCES 64 Jno 47 68 82
Jno Jr 114 Jno S 16 John 5 10-
11 37 55 57 60 62 92 JULIET 23
Lettice 4 Mack 71 MARGARET 29
114 MARIA 62 Mark 71 Mary 28
MARY 4 10 24 111 PEGGY 71
POLLY 40 118 ROSEY 110
SARAH 37 47 SUSANNA 62
Teackle 38 70 Temple N 17
Thomas Sr 23 Thos 4 91 Tillar 10
Wm 46
ROBINSON, Levin 87 MARY 27
SALLY 17 Wm 27 Wm G 113
RODGERS, ANN 84 Arthur 59
ELIZABETH WISE 110 Jackson
51 KEZIAH 21 PALMER 1
ROGERS, Arthur 110 Elizabeth 105
ESLAND 58 James W 116 JANE
94 JENNEY 94 John 35 Levin
105 Louis P 12 MARY 28
PRISCILLA 26 Rachel 105 Rob't
12 Robert 81 SUSANNA 35 104
ROLLY, HARRIET A 32 William 32
ROOKS, Arthur 4 EMILY S 71
HARRIOT 53 ISETTA 5 John 53

ROOKS (cont)
71 MARY 73 NANCY 104 Patrick
7 112 Sally 5 William Sr 101 Wm
38 90 112 Wm Sr 5 25 117
ROSE, Isaac 64 Jacob 101 ROSEY
89
ROSS, Ann 7 David 67 Jesse 89 Jno
111 John 17 35 49 54 John B 70
MARGARET ANN 111
MARGARET 7 MARY M 35 SALLY
49
ROWAND, D 2
ROWE, Thos B 70
RUSH, ELIZABETH 79 Thomas 79
RUSSEL, PEGGY 119 SUSANNA 85
SUSEY 84
RUSSELL, SALLY 39
RUTHERFORD, NANCY 102
RUTTER, CAROLINE T 62
SABERS, NANNY 19
SABRAH, MARY 106
SALTS, ELIZABETH 119 JANE 114
John 119 PEGGY 94
SALUSBURY, Wm 123
SAMPLE, John 115 MOLLY 20
SINAH 115 Wm 119
SAMPSON, PEGGY 24 Stephen 51
SANDERS, Richard 122 SARAH 122
Stuart 18 58
SANDFORD, NANCY 108
SANFORD, ANN 12 EMILENE 70
James 12 28 65 117-118 James
H 70 Jas 111 Robert 13 70 110
SARAH L 118
SARRELL, SARA 5
SATCHEL, Chas 115
SATCHELL, ADAH 98 BETTY 30 C
98 Charles 72 95 Charles Jr 63
Charles S 30 Chas 49 80 Chas S
96 JOANNA 48 John 25
MARGARET 95 Maria S 4 MARY
83 127 PARMER 66 Sarah 28
SARAH 62 95 Southey 30 Southy
29 62 SUSANNA 72 Thomas S 90
Thos 56 Thos S 63 Wm 30 62 97
114 120 Wm Jr 1 21 28 55 98
115 Wm Sr 98
SATCHILL, Wm 92
SAUNDERS, ESTHER 33 James 13
20-22 33 37 46 74-75 120-121
John 44 MARGARET S 20 MARY
A 26 MARY ANN 44 RACHAEL 21
SALLY 21 Samuel 20 SARAH E

SAUNDERS (cont)
121 Stuart 4-5 21 39 110 113
127 SUSAN 78 Tibitha 21 Wm 13
SAV-AGE, Wm Jr 126
SAVAGE, Abel 65 101 122 ANN
RITTER 88 ANNA GLOWINA 64
ANNE 53 ANSLY 56 Arthur 14 25
Arthur R 13 34 54 BETSEY 122
Caleb 61 65 Caleb R 73 Calvin H
60 127 CATY 104 Delither 111
DOROTHY 103 Edward C 116
ELIZ ANN 68 ELIZABETH ANN 50
68 ELIZABETH P 127
ELIZABETH 85 EMELINE 118
Esther 20 ESTHER 57 97
FARABEE 82 Geo 62 Geo G 45
Geo J 118 Geo S 53 George 3 58
George L 115 HANNAH 72 James
M 84 109 Jno 49 Jno Jr 48 John
51 53 61 113 John M 7 27 68
125 LAURA M 86 LAURA S 65
LEAH L 125 LEAH 47 108 Litt 96
110 Littleton 35 80-81 Mahala 86
117 MAHALA ANN 117 Major 68
MALANA 65 Margaret 54-55
MARGARET ANN 61 Margaret
Teackle 125 MARGARET 11 14
20 81 100 MARIA C 8 MARIA
TEACKLE 78 Mary 61 MARY ANN
125 MARY BURTON 34 MARY 20
23 56 65 Michael 23 78 Michael
R 111 115 Michael Sr 37 MOLLY
B 37 MOLLY 29 NANCY 9 108
Nath'l 2 39 102-103 Nath'l Lytt
83 Nathaniel 88 PEGGY T 52
PEGGY 2 49 111 Peter B 8 83
Preson 33 56 100 Preson Jr 85
Richard 119 Robert B 57 Rosey
M 52 ROSEY W 2 ROSEY 61 115
SALLY T 3 SALLY 52-53 Samuel
71 Sarah 25 Severn 36 66
SOPHIA 21 61 Susan 74 SUSAN
E 125 SUSAN 78 115 TAMAR A 2
Thomas 11 72 Thomas Jr 65
Thos 82 Thos Jr 20 42 Thos L 74
125 Thos Lyt 37 78 Thos Lytt 78
Thos M 108 Thos Sr 20 William F
8 Wm 2 29 61 80 83 114 Wm B 2
78 95 110 Wm Jr 14 76-77 Wm
K 118 Wm Lytt 127 Wm M 61
108 Wm S 47 Wm Sr 2 12 Wm T
127-128
SCARBOROUGH, Edmund 31

SCARBOROUGH (cont)
 ESTHER 86 Henry 56 81 JULIET
 J 78 SUSAN 31 TABITHA 128
 Thos 60 Wm M 83
SCARBROUGH, Thos 103
SCARBURG, Edmond 93
SCARBURGH, Geo P 11 George P 37
SCHERER, Sam'l 19
SCHYN, WINNIFRED 111
SCISCO, Betty 118 JULIET ANN 16
 LUCY 118 Major 99 Maria 95
 Rachel 118 RACHEL ANN 119
 Samuel 41
SCOTT, ANN 98 126 ANNE 51 117
 Barthemy 103 Benj 92 Benja 31
 Benja N 14 37 Benjamin N 14
 Daniel 19 103 ELISHE 71 ELIZA
 ANN 66 ELIZABETH ANN 113
 ELIZABETH N 64 ELIZABETH S
 25 ELIZABETH SUSAN 39
 ELIZABETH 6 18 ESTHER 7 45
 FANNY 16 Geo 45 96 117 Geo T
 85 HANNAH E 66 HANNAH 100
 Henry 105 Hillery 88 Jno N 90
 John 16 19 37 39 43 58 67 119
 124 John N 99 108 John Sr 5
 KEZIAH 105 LEAH 43 Levin 32
 MARGARET E A 116 MARGARET
 37 41 MARIA 88 MARY ANN 14
 MARY JULIET 19 MARY 59 90 97
 NANCY 10 126 Obediah 19 39
 PEGGY 101 121 RACHEL 49
 REBECCA 127 ROSEY 17 47
 Salley 19 Sally H 113 SALLY S
 108 Sarah 23 SARAH ANN 100
 SARAH 103 116 Solomon 105
 SOPHIA 69 SUKEY 104
 SUSANNA 67 Thomas 97-98 104
 106 Thomas G 100 Thomas W 96
 Thos 113 Thos G 43 94 126 Wm
 18 23 39 84-85 100-101 116 121
 Wm J 46 Wm Jr 120 Wm Sr 9
 100 Wm W 25 65 117 Zerobabel
 41 Zorobabel 126
SEATON, ELIZABETH 100 Jenny
 100 PEGGY 117 Thos 13
SEGAR, DIANA D 43 John 13 43 95
 111
SEYMOUR, Digby 79 ROSEY D 84
 Sarah 22 SARAH 79
SHEA, Wm 93
SHEERWOOD, MARY 23
SHEPHARD, ELIZABETH 38 IBBY

SHEPHARD (cont)
 38
SHEPHERD, BETSEY 20
SHEPPARD, Jos 31
SHORES, ROSE 56
SICKLES, REBECCA 96
SIMKINS, Ann 15 Arthur 36 39 55
 64 Coventon 4 12 15 18 23 39 45
 70 100 114 Dilly 51 118 ELISA
 58 ELIZABETH 39 ELMIRA 96
 FANNIE O 35 Geo 81 George 98
 Jesse 52 Jesse J 35 75 82 118
 Jno 2 Jno A 86 John 4 20 39 45-
 46 48 55-58 62 64 79 83 92 98
 127 John A 35 Margaret 114
 Mary 83 Peggy 33 Sabra 25 Sally
 62 SUKEY 118 SUSAN 30
 Thomas 96 Thos 20 Wm 33 39
 58 Wm Jr 25
SIMPKINS, Arthur 16 Coventon 37
SMAW, ANNA 56 Daniel G 76 Danil
 59 ELISHE 9 ELIZABETH G 84
 Henry 32 36 43 54 56 71 94 117
 120 Jno G 74 John 9 36 84 114
SMITH, ANN T 38 ANN WALTER 84
 ANN 3 12 91 ANNA TEACKLE 27
 BETSEY FLOYD 60 BETSEY 25
 Caleb 90 CATHARINE 40
 CATHERINE 124 ELISHE 79
 Elizabeth 78 ELIZABETH F 87
 ELIZABETH G 22 ELIZABETH T
 110 ELIZABETH 77 90 Esau 80
 FRANCES 24 108 Geo 79 George
 3 77 84 120 Hannah 32 Hugh G
 87 Isaac 27 29 38 57 78 88-89
 110 Isaac Sr 41 James 50 72 118
 Jno 87 John 10 56 John B 127
 John C 10 86 Jonathan 111
 LUCY JANE 10 LYDIA 79
 MARGARET A S 86 MARIA 88
 Mary 87 MARY ANNE 29 NANCY
 13 32 50 PEGGY 8 47 Peter B 62
 POLLY 106 Rich'd 25 31 67 112
 Richard 25 41 107 ROSY 75 Sally
 WILSON 48 SALLY 98 116
 SARAH A 86 SARAH 3 107
 SUCKY 118 SUKEY 55 111
 SUSAN 28 111 120 SUSANNA 28
 92 101 Thomas 28 47 68 73
 Thomas Jr 7-8 42 58 78 82 85-
 86 94 116 Thomas Sr 75
 Thorowgood 5 56 Thos 25 Thos
 Jr 33 53 68 117 124 Thos Sr 86

SMITH (cont)
  Wm 8 48 65 85 124 Wm A 46
  Wm G 51 107 Wm S 32 69
SNAIL, SALLY 44
SNAILS, OLIVE 86
SNALE, KEZIAH 117
SNEAD, Adah 32 ADAH 102 ANNE
  120 CATHARINE 45 116
  ELIZABETH 76 116 MARY B 32
  SALLY C 126 Thomas 116
  Thomas B 11 Wm 6 102
SOALS, ELIZABETH 117
SOBERS, Nancy 19
SOMERS, George 79
SPADY, Abraham 126 ANN 10 74
  ARINTHIA S 27 BETSEY 24
  BETSY 33 CATHERINE 72 E J 98
  ELIZABETH S 95 ELIZABETH
  119 EMILY S 122 HARRIET 73
  Jacob 10-11 28 56 86 118 Jno
  44 Jno Jr 79 John 17 108 110
  126-127 John H 80 John Jr 36
  122 124 John S 50 107 John Sr
  21 73 85 LAVENIA 71 LEAH 17
  44 LOUISA C 42 LUCRETIA 118
  MARGARET E 102 MARGARET
  21 78 MARY 120 MOLLY 126
  PEGGY 104 109 ROSEY E 72
  ROSY S 21 SARAH 94 Southey
  35 Southy 21 39 74 95 120
  SUKEY 26 125 T F 55 Thomas 33
  Thomas F 27 Thomas S 119 Thos
  F 46 79 Westerhouse 71-72 102
  Wm 26 76 94 102
SPEAKMAN, ANNE 122 BETSEY
  109 ELIZABETH SPADY 18
  ELIZABETH 4 Henry 24 Jno 47
  John 17 LAVENIA ANN 52
  MARGARET 121 MARY 102
  Shepherd 32 SUSAN ANN 32
  Thomas 9 17 102 Thos 4 65
  TINNY 9 Wm 113 Wm S 18 52
  112
SPIRES, ELIZABETH 7
STAKES, MARY 37 POLLY 80
STEAPHENS, MARY ANN 40
STEELE, Wm 49
STEPHENS, ABIGAIL 45 Adah 19-20
  Amy 95 CATY 99 Cudjo 53 81
  Dilly 99 ELIZABETH 22 Ephram
  118 Horace 72 101 Isaac 40 70
  119 LEAH 95 LILLY 106 Lucy
  115 MATILDA 6 PATIENCE 81

STEPHENS (cont)
  PEGGY 115 RACHEL 22 SABRA
  19 Severn 99-100 Susan 22
  William 70 Wm 72
STEPNEY, York 45 72
STERLING, John 45
STEVENS, ABIGAIL 6 AMEY 106
  ANN 40 ARINTHIA 17 BETSEY 19
  BETTY 83 George 67 Horace 17
  Littleton 19 MARY 72 PEGGY 81
  SALLY 6 Samuel 39 TAMAR 106
  Wm 19
STEVENSON, Chas 106 JUDITH 4
  Nath'l 51
STEWART, Andrew 89 ANN S 29
  ELIZABETH 73 James 29 73
  James H 42 59 Joshua G 3 15 29
STITH, Drury 2 ELIZ BUCKNER 103
  Elizabeth 89 ELIZABETH 78
  Griffin 22 45 69 78 96 103 105
  Griffin Jr 3 5 23 64 113 Griffin Sr
  56 Jno 58 Jno B 116 Jno
  Buckner 69 116 John 121 Mary
  17 90 MARY BLAIKLEY 69 Mary
  ELIZABETH 110 SARAH 91
  SUSANNA 56 Wm 22 26 31 52
  72-73 81 89 110 113 122
STIVENS, LEAH 106
STOAKLEY, Wm 11
STOCKLEY, ANNE 110 119 C B 126
  Charles B 38 69 John 69 87
  MARGARET 69 MARY 51 SARAH
  ANN 38 SMART 120 Thos 98 Wm
  119-120 Woodman 120
STOCKLY, Alexr 110 Charles B 56
  John 46 Thos G 95
STOIT, Benjamin 109 ELIZABETH
  109 John 85 NANCY 85
STOKELEY, Abel 81
STOKELY, Wm 38 44 123
STOKES, Wm 110
STOKLEY, Eyrs 37 96
STOTT, ADAH 69 ANNE 5 Bennet 5
  BETSEY 56 79 BRIDGIT 3
  CHARLOTTE 11 Coventon 40 85
  ELIZABETH 8 57 88 HENRIETTA
  61 HETTY 1 JANETTE H 83
  JOANNA 34 83 Johathan 34
  John 125 John S 24 Jonathan 5
  11 45 69 83 Keley 10 18 110
  Laban 8 40 48 50 83 86 97
  Laban Sr 10 117 Luther 10
  MAHALA 10 NANCY 85 97 125

STOTT (cont)
  NICEY H 97 Peggy Waterfield 117
  PEGGY 50 Rachall 26 ROSEY
  107 SALLY 60 Sam'l S 75 94
  Samuel 101 SARAH 40 SUSANNA
  50 111 Thos 125 Wm 3
STOYTE, John 127 SALLY 18 Wm
  45
STRATTON, ADAH 100 AGNES 82
  121 ANN GERTRUDE 78 ANNE
  W 62 ANNE 100 Benja 10 100
  Benjamin 3 BETSEY 3 Jno Jr 46
  Jno N 91 104 Jno Sr 110 John
  13 34 53 69-71 73 78 91 121
  125 John Jr 30 103 John N 50
  Nath'l 51 121 SALLY 125 SARAH
  73 SUSANNA 120 Thomas 120
  Thos 53 Upshur L 105 Wm 3 60
STRINGER, Eleshe 62 Elicia 105
  ELISHE 75 ELIZABETH 90
  GRACE 11 Hillary 3 10-11
  HILLARY 34 ISABELL 24 Jacob
  30 75 John 36 John Sr 90
  MARGARET 3 10 RACHEL 36
  SUSANNA 114
STRIPE, ELIZABETH 9 25 56 KESSY
  125 Moses 9 NANCY 58 Peter 125
  SALLY 71 Whittenton 49
STRIPS, ELISHA 23
STUARD, Elibet W 56 Matilder 56
STURGES, James 50
STURGIS, Jacob 97 John 84 87
  MAHALA 102 MARIA 49 MARTHA
  104 PEGGY 97 SALLY 127
  SUSANNA 26 Wm 104 127 Wm T
  66
SUMERS, George 122
SUTTIE, Thos 33
TANKARD, ---- 59 ELIZABETH 37
  Geo L E 101 George L E 29 80
  GEORGIANNA 37 HANNAH 64
  Jno 127 John 1 8 29 37 40 45 59
  64 80 127 John W 106
  MARGARET SMITH 127
  MARGARET 59 MARY T S 29
  NANCY 114 PATIENCE 49
  SARAH FRANCES COOPER 80
  SARAH 1 8 SUSAN P 40
TATEM, James 88 ROSEY 88
TATIM, Polly 101 SARAH 101
TATUM, James 7 MARY 7
TAXEWELL, Wm 48
TAYLOR, ANN 3 Bartholomew 13

TAYLOR (cont)
  BETSEY 7 Betsy 119 BETSY 70
  74 ELIZABETH 61 George 47 61
  99 Grace DUMCOMBE 34 James
  95 John 7 22 61 119 John B 78
  LEAH 47 Major 74 113
  MARGARET L 34 MARY 21 61
  NANCY 55 108 POLLY 12 SARAH
  86 SUKEY 47 SUSAN W 103
  SUSAN 119 Susanna 92 Thos
  Teackle 74 Wm 82
TAZEWELL, GERTRUDE 102 Henry
  62 Wm 34 47 Wm Jr 20
TEACKLE, ANN STOACKLEY 37
  ANN 41 96 Caleb 103 CATEY 96
  CATHERINE S 73 CATHERINE
  96 ELIZABETH 103 John 96
  John Jr 92 LEAR 11 MARGARET
  92 Thomas 37 Thos U 57
TEAGNER, BETSY 87
TEAGUE, ELIZA 19 RACHEL 72
TERRIER, CHARLOTTE 56 John C
  70 LAVINIA 40
THOM, Wm Alex 74
THOMAS, Benja 85 Benjamin 116
  BRIDGET 25 Edward C 67 Geo J
  35 Harrison 4 Jno B 104 John 25
  103 116 John B 29 34 John W
  105 Joseph W 42 Leavin J 65
  Levin J 103 MARGARET S 34
  MARY M 88 NANCY 83 PEGGY
  114 SALLY 52 SUSANNA 52 Wm
  73 83 102 112 114 125
THOMPSON, ABIGAIL 115 ADAH
  100 BETSEY 100 BETSY 20
  ELISHE 50 Isaac 27 59 Jacob 6
  72 LOUISA 17 LUCY 27 MARY 10
  Peter 16 POLLY 117 Rolla 67
  SARAH 6 TABITHA J 10 THAMAR
  116 Wm 10 17 20
THURMUR, ANNA KATHARINA 41
THURSTON, Abner 112 Azariah 52
  66 BETSY 46 ELIZABETH 22
  Leah 66
THURTIN, Abner 38
TIGNER, BETSY 87
TIGNOR, MARGARET 87
TILGHMAN, NANCY 125
TILNEY, SARAH 54
TIMMONS, ELIZABETH 123 LOVEY
  119
TOLEMAN, ANN 33 ELIZ 30 SALLY
  113 SUSANNA 10 Wm 47

TOLLMAN, Ebenezer 114 Jos 82
TOLMAN, Wm 10
TOMLINSON, Henry 45 55 102
TOMPKINS, Ann Custis 125 Jno 79
   John 77 Peggy CUSTIS 126 T 110
   126
TOMPSON, MARY 109 Rob't 109
TOMSON, Lilly 17 RACHEL 100
TOPPING, ANN S 29 David 27 29 40
   58 87 108 114 125
TOWNSEND, Angelo A 10 28 33
   Littleton 3 32 122 N B 48 Nath'l
   B 63
TOYER, George 6 LOUISA 6 Peter 16
TRADER, TINNEY 111
TRAVIS, ANNE W 38 ARINTHIA 124
   Dennard 32 44 125 ELIZABETH
   113 Elliott 38 44 James 33 53 64
   70 76 87 108 115 123 127
   LOUISA 32 MARY 52 PEGGY 113
   SALLY 44 Shadrack 113
TREHEARN, Curtis 96
TREHEARNE, Custis 98
TROWER, ANNE 22 BETSEY 92 123
   CHARLOTT 21 Delitha 90
   Douglas 119 Douglass 86 123
   ELISHE 15 ELIZA 63 Elizabeth 9
   120 ELIZABETH 24 128
   EMELINE 90 ESTHER 127
   JENNY S 9 Jno R 72 John 19 43
   46 63 90 94 122 John Jr 87
   John Sr 54 128 LOUISIANA W 57
   MARGARET 54 MARY 43 NANCY
   99 121 Nelley 46 PEGGY 87
   Robert 22 80 90 99 ROSA 99
   ROSANNA 99 Sally 122 SALLY M
   123 SALLY 46 SUKEY 82 SUSAN
   80 TAMAR 46 Wm 22 80 96 114
   Wm H 72
TURNER, ANN 99 Edw'd 2 70
   Edward 89 Edward R 13 48 97
   105 ELIZABETH S 105
   ELIZABETH 71 ESTHER 77 Geo
   29 53 Geo Nicholas 114 George
   35 89 JENNET S 111 Jno 11 Jno
   Furbush 116 John 2 11 49 65
   104 116 John Furbush 14 77 92
   John G 42 116 John T 65
   Joshua B 3 68 94 KEZIAH 32
   MARGARET A T 3 MARGARET 76
   MARY 111 116 Moses 123 125
   NANCY 92 PATIENCE 11 PEGGY
   41 53 76 POLLY 89 PRISCILLA

TURNER (cont)
   14 SALLY 49 Sam'l James 66
   SARAH 35 70 SUSANNA 28
   Teackle 11 67 90 Teackle J 7
   Teackle J 12 85 100 113 117
   Teagle J 3 ZILLAH 27
TURPIN, ELIZABETH 7 64 Jno S 95
   John 61 John D 84 John S 3 6
   61 100 SARAH 61 Thomas H 55
TWIFORD, DIRECTOR 114
   ELIZABETH 71 JOICE 64 Obed
   34 71
TYE, Wm 116
TYLER, Benj 102 Benja 106 113
   Benjamin 60 85 John 106 112
   MARY L 60 SARAH E 85 Thos 99
TYLOR, AMEY 127 BETSEY 99
   MARY 78 SALLY 7
TYSON, FANNY 55 John 18 42 84
   101 119 125 MARGARET 101
   MARY 125 NANCY 36 Nath'l 36
   Samuel 55 SUSAN ANN 108
   Thomas 93 101 108 119 125
   VIRGINIA S 93 Wm 94
UNDERHILL, Amos 94 Amos Jr 2
   Athaliah 14 BETSEY 85 Edmund
   W 5 James 91 MARIA 42 MARY
   ANN 91 Michael 42 RACHEL 65
   Thos 14 31 33 57 85 VIANNA 60
   William 60
UPSHUR, A P 68 Abel 30 67 85 Abel
   P 33 78 Ann B 11 ANN 33 ANNE
   E 68 ANNE 105 Arthur B 116 C
   B 1 118 126 Caleb B 7 32 125
   ELIZABETH P 74 ELIZABETH 24
   105 Geo P 39 George 17 George L
   73 George P 85 125 James 5 24
   Jno 116 Job 116 John 5 24 26
   81 105 John D 91 John Jr 21 45
   58 109 John L 68 John Sr 47
   124 Judge A P 85 JULIET S 33
   JULIET 32 L 83 L Sr 32 LAURA A
   11 LEAH C 68 Litt 96 Littleton 33
   38 67-68 74 Margaret 5
   MARGARET M 77 MARY JANE
   19 MARY W 91 MARY 58
   RACHEL 5 SALLY T B 47 SALLY
   45 SARAH DOWNING 5 SARAH
   40 Susan 19 SUSAN P B 85
   SUSAN 67 Thomas Jr 7 Thomas
   Sr 109 Thos 7 40 45 69 Thos W
   100 W B 17 William M 77 Wm B
   97 111 Wm M 91

VANDEGROT, MARTHA 116
VAUGHN, CATHERINE B 69
VERMILLON, NANCY 78
VICCUS, ESTHER 113 POLLY 21
VICHUS, Thos 109
WADDELOW, ANN 38
WADDEY, Edw'd R 19 26 Edward P
   28 Edward R 54 78 EMELINE 74
   John R 31 62 73 90 MARY
   JACOB 62
WADDY, E R 123 Edw'd R 17 54
   John R 40 NANCY 98 Wm E 6
WAGGOMAN, MARY 62
WAINHOUSE, Francis Jr 54 ROSE
   69
WAISTECOATE, Stephen 51
WALKER, ELENOR 39 Henry 109
   John 39 MARY 86 Robert 55
WALSTONE, Wm 108
WALTER, ANNE 101 John 64 76
   101 LEAH 76 MARY 64 PEGGY
   SMITH COOPER 59 Sally Bunker
   59 SARAH 16 Solomon 59
   SUSANNA 88
WALTHAM, Jno 10 MARGARET 2
   SALLY 12 SUSANNA 15-16 Wm 2
   26 30 54 125
WAPLES, ELIZABETH 57
WARD, ADAH 18 Albert D 87 105
   Alex W 50 100 109 Alexander W
   2 14 30 89 ANN A 31 42 ANN 16
   CINTHIA ANN 100 EDNA 50
   ELIZA E 87 ELIZABETH 52
   Golding 50 71 127 James 18 112
   JANE 48 Letitia R 87 Littleton 31
   112 127 MARGARET ANN 10
   MARGARET 117 MARY ANN 105
   MARY W 36 NANCY B 83 NANCY
   127 RACHEL 84 Samuel B 16
   Stephen 52 66 97 111 Susan 16
   Tully S 10 36 48 50 Wm 31 Wm
   Jr 112 Wm Sr 112
WARE, ANN 96
WARREN, Adah 92 ADAH 9
   Angeline B 124 ANN 9 BETSEY
   122 Calvin L 18 Devorax 47 62
   87 Devorix 10 ELIZ 58
   ELIZABETH H 105 ELIZABETH
   18 27 ESTHER 8 10 27 93
   FANNY 21 FRANCES 37 Geo 122
   HANNAH 101 Henry 1 126 Hillery
   93 James 4 121 John 42 73 89
   John Jr 105 John P 80 John Sr 6

WARREN (cont)
   Jos 113 Joseph 27 33 79 98 107
   123 Leonard 107 MAHALA 92
   MARY 107 Mathew 37 Matthew
   108 MOLLY 73 NANCY 80 P Jr
   30 Patrick 21 117 Patrick Jr 6 12
   PEGGY 43 Peter 19 58 66 SALLY
   J 6 SALLY 36 79 Seth 8 59
   Solomon 120 SUKEY 43 Wm 95
   102 109 122
WARRINGTON, George 4 93 John 58
   MARGARET 4 118 SUSAN 93
WATCH, PEGGY 26
WATERFEILD, MARY 25
WATERFIELD, Elias 101
   ELIZABETH 93 ELLENOR 39
   ESTHER 29 58 Geo 8 92 Jacob
   31 101 112 Jno 30 39 Jno Jr 117
   John 18 29 51 John Jr 29
   MAHALA 51 56 MARGARET 83
   117 Mary 117 Meshack 51 68
   NANCY 13 75 PEGGY 102 POLLY
   101 Richard 13 SALLY 3 SMART
   58 SUSANNA 31 Thomas 83 Thos
   18 117 Wm 5 24 29 61 67 88
WATERFORD, FANNY 96
WATERS, Thos 65 Wm 10 46
WATERSON, COMFORT 69 Eliz 69
   Eliza 127 Elizabeth 5 Jno 57 127
   John 5 69 MARY 73 SARAH 71
WATSON, BETSEY 69 Edmund 7 18
   Elijah 113 ELIZA 106
   ELIZABETH 77 Jacob 76 KEZIAH
   57 Littleton 26 LOVELY 18
   NANCY 26 Rachel 88 Reavil 43
   48 Revil 56 Samuel 17 SARAH
   101 Wm 80 126 Wm C 50
WATT, James 46
WATTS, FRANCES 125 Thomas 117
   125
WATTSON, Robert 126 SARAH 126
WEBB, James S 37 98 LISHE 47
   SALLY 37 Southey 48 Southy 7
   Thos 121
WEDGEON, Thos N 88
WEEKS, BETSEY 96 CHRISTIANA
   89 COMFORT 81 James 81 115
   John 81 LUSEY 111 MARGARET
   81 Tinsey 72
WEICKS, Gabe 19 Jenny 19
   MARGARET 19 SUSAN 19
WEIR, Jas 67
WEISINGER, Catharine S 70

WELCH, ESTHER 99 John 90
William 99 Wm 71
WELCHE, MARY A 89 Wm 89
WELSH, William 70
WESCOAT, Wm 10 Ann P 91 108
Edmund 7 30 47 ELIZABETH 47
FRANCES 57 Geo 14 Geo C 15
18 68 74 George 69 George C 20
H P 50 91 Hez P 7 67 Hezekiah P
Sr 50 J P 12 80 JEMIMA 69 John
91 103 108-109 111 John B 1
John Jr 23-24 79 Joshua 29
Joshua P 45 52 55 57 88 108
122 Major 41 MARY ANNE 47
MOLLY 7 Patty 92 PATTY 111
PEGGY 7 POLLY 92 Rosey 108-
109 ROSEY G 74 SALLY 59
SUSAN S 50 Thomas J 85
VIANNA 30 103 Wm 57 Wm H 23
WESCOT, VIENNA 68
WESCOTE, Littleton 116
WEST, ANN CUSTIS 14 BETSY 41
CATHARINE 9 CATHERINE 61
Charles 1 14 48 56 63 76
Charles J D 115 Chas 76 CLARA
J 50 ELIZABETH 1 34 John 15-
16 104 John C 118 John T 119
124 Jos 116 LOUISA Y 9 NANCY
5 Nath'l 7 14 57 Nathaniel 9 108
124 POLLY 39 SALLY C 63
SALLY 114 Sam'l S 7 Samuel S
11 89 SARAH ANN P 124 SUSAN
7 TABITHA S 76 Tamer 114
Thomas 57 Wm 6 Wm W 77 117
WESTCOAT, MARY 110
WESTCOT, NANCY 8 PEGGY 114
WESTERHOUSE, ADAH 119 Ann
125 ANNA CATHARINE 106
ANNE 97 Bridget 22 BRIDGET 65
95 KEZIAH 26 Reubin 8
SUSANNA 24 Thos 119 Wm 65
80 95 106
WESTWOOD, Jas 73
WHALEY, Joshua 117 PATSEY 77
WHEATLY, ELIZA 107
WHEELER, ANNE 113 BETSY 67
BETTY 67 EDY 122 ESTHER 4
John 3 125 John Jr 18 John Sr
99 MARGARET 21 MARY 99
NAOMI 23 PEGGY 57 SALLY 89
SARAH 105 Thomas A 21
WHEELOR, ANN SUSAN 29 BETSEY
63 68 ELIZABETH 32 JENNEY

WHEELOR (cont)
77 John 3 24 NANCY 125 PEGGY
46 Thomas 29
WHITE, BARBARA 101 BETTY 94
CAMILLA 15 ELIZABETH 51 54
110 124 Geo D 10 George D 31
89 103 HANNAH 30 110 Jas A 17
Jno 40 John 15 Levin 124
MARGARET 117 MARY 34
NANCY 14 89 Obedience 14 90
PEGGY 1 73 SALLY 14 54
Susannah 73 TAMARZENE 12
Teackle S 12 Thos 22 Wm 23 30
34 54 86 94 100 111 Wm Jr 12
90 104 Wm Sr 91
WHITEHEAD, CHARLOTTE 107 Jno
24 John 52 67 75 96 125 John
Sr 107 MARY T 22 NANCY 23 52
94 SALLY 58 Stephen 107
SUSAN 107 SUSANNA 24
Thomas 22 Thos 126 Wm 77 94
107
WHITTINGTON, ELIZA 99
WICKES, Sally 96 Severn 39
WID-GEON, Westerhouse 124
WIDGEN, ANN 35 John Jr 40
Joseph 80 Leaven 83 Nancy 35
Severn 124 Walter W 96 116
Westerhouse 18 98 128
WIDGEON, ADAH 33 124 Ann 109
ANN 4 BRIDGET 25 E 87 ELISHE
82 ELIZABETH 59 ESTHER 112
FRANCES WILKINS 36 FRANCES
50 Jno Sr 120 John 8 38 84 86
109 John Sr 18 Jonah 33 Jos S
60 Jos W 83 Levin 24 MARY 109
MOLLY 20 NANCY 109 Nath'l 3
63 75 82 96 109 121 Nathaniel
74 PATSY S 96 PEGGY 53
PRISCILLA 38 SALLY 32 120
Severn 74 124 SUKEY 8 SUSAN
109 SUSANNA 24 Thomas 59
Thos 22 25 113 119 Thos N 6
Walter W 34 46 86 96 124
Westerhouse 3 20 76 96 103
WIGEON, Severn 109
WIGGON, Rob't 112
WILIAMS, ELIZA C 19
WILKERSON, ELIZA 19
WILKIMS, W W 102
WILKINS, ADAH 107 AGNES 117
ANN 117 ANNE 62 85 Argyl 126
ARINTHIA S 1 Benja 33 Benjamin

WILKINS (cont)
22 BETSEY 39 DELITHA A 23
Elizabeth 55 ELIZABETH ANN 54
ELIZABETH S 76 ELIZABETH W
93 ELIZABETH 22 38 71 75 99
EMILY 42 ESTHER 31 Geo F 17
28 38-39 66 87 94 George F 13
28 48 53 66-67 97-98 100
Harriet 70 Henry 9 Hetty 42 J W
75 101 James 19 James C 95
JANE 4 JENNEY 73 Jno 39 46 62
Jno B 98 Jno S 48 51 Jno T 18
100 Jno W 99 Joachim Michael
71 JOANNA 80 John 31 47 50 60
75 93 100 102 125 John Jr 23
117 John M 23 47 John Sr 4 70
107 109 John T 86 John W 104
Jonathan 31 102 JUDA 112
JUDITH 109 LEAR 73 Leonard T
1 Littleton 33 Major 49 85
MARGARET ANN 65 MARGARET
S 53 95 MARGARET 47 50 MARY
5 NANCY 26 55 103 Nath'l 117
Nath'l Jr 31 72 114 Patrick 5
PEGGY 71 85 102 114 Peter 65
75 92 POLLY 125 RACHEL 102
SARAH 60 Severn 27 39 65 90
SMART 126 Southey S 13 42
Susan 117 SUSAN 17 SUSANNA
31 46 67 Thomas M 74 Thos 38
Thos M 76 Watkins 75 William Sr
93 Wm 27 55 114 119 Wm E 1
54 99 Wm J 42 Wm S 32 Wm Sr
21 35 111 Wm W 87
WILKINSON, E C 60 Stephen 11 39
112 123 Stephon 99
WILKISON, DOROTHY 106
WILLET, Douglas 51 ELIZ 109 LEAR
109 NANCY 109
WILLETT, Douglas 71 ELIZ 73
Elizabeth 23 Thomas 73 Wm 101
WILLIAM, Peter 4
WILLIAMS, Ann J 36 77 ANN S 77
ANN 88 ANNE 27 Azariah 8 25
34-35 38 44 47 96 126 Benja 36
Benja S 36 BETSEY 113 BETSY
106 Christopher 26 120-121
Curtis F 3 EDITH ESTHER 35
Edward 86 89 ELISHA 70-71 Eliz
106 ELIZABETH ANN 36
ELIZABETH P 81 ELIZABETH 26
99 EMILY S 94 FRANCES 8 73
HARRIET 17 Jacob 37 James 41

WILLIAMS (cont)
55 63 78 86 James D 36 James
Sr 125 Jas 98 Jno 13 JOANNA
47 John 10 12 47 50 John D 74
John Jr 75 John W 65 94
LAVINIA 4 LEAH 98 Margaret 35
81 99 120 MARGARET B 120
MARGARET S 77 MARGARET
SUSAN 121 MARGARET 47 55
85 MARY ANN 96 106 MARY G
46 MARY S 35 MARY 12 70
NANCY 38 44 82 P 11-12 PEGGY
39 Peter 6 19 22 47 70 85 96 106
113 122 Peter Jr 16 21 38 Peter
Sr 17 73 POLLY 120-121
RACHEL 13 Rob't F 44 Robert 8
Robert F 77 SALLY 41 44 75
Saml S 106 Samuel 36 38 43 73
Samuel S 106 Samuel W 63
SARAH GREEN 99 SARAH 37 64
SUKEY 108 SUSAN A 106
SUSAN 36 SUSEY 77 Thomas 13
Thomas B 9 29 Thomas Jr 51
Thomas N 42 W 94 Wm 75 Wm A
15
WILLIG, CECELIA 62
WILLIS, ANN 16 COMFORT 70 126
Custis 61 ELISHE 59 ELISHEY
120 ELIZA 71 ELIZABETH
CUSTIS 29 ELIZABETH 86 113
EMILY S 61 FRANCES 103 Geo
101 George 52 70 James 17 71
John 71 76 Josiah 8 44 102 119
123 Josias 70 120 123 Josias Jr
103 Littleton 29 LUCRETIA 10
Mariot 117 Marriot 103 Marriott
16 Marrot 59 85 103 126 Mary A
29 NANCY 37 Parker 22 PEGGY
44 98 POLLY 8 77 RACHEL 119
123 SARAH 12 SUSANNA 85 102
Thomas 98 Wm 36 71 121
WILSON, Anne 20 76 ANNE S 110
ANNE 45 Arthur A 55 122
BETSEY 36 44 117 Chas 14
Edw'd H C 5 52 ELISHE 78
ELIZABETH 42 64 86 GRACE 90
H L 108 Harold L 89 James 126
James B 72 86 107 James M 40
James S 9 109 John L 77 John S
121 John T 67 Levin 125
Littleton 53 80 Margaret S 76
Margret S 5 Mary Ann F 102
MARY 80 Moses 53 58 NANCY 34

WILSON (cont)
    38 Naney 45 NICE 126 PEGGY
    20 43-44 POLLY 53 126
    RACHELL 9 SALLEY 20 SALLIE E
    72 SMARTA 39 Stoakley W 94
    Stoakly 20 SUSAN ANN 55
    SUSANNA 119 Thomas 42 Thos
    37 66 124 Wm 6 18 43 71 99
    109 119 Wm B 14 94 Wm W 5 12
    44 114
WINDER, CHARLOTTE L 77 Comfort
    Gore 92 Jno H 92 John 44 103
    John E 26 30 John H 40 77 123
    LAURETTA A 92 Levin 82 Levin Y
    40 N 102 N J 125 Nath'l 14 38
    Nath'l J 19 Nathaniel J 48
    SARAH C 62 Sarah U 62 SUSAN
    C 40
WINDOW, James 101 LEAH 24
WINDSOR, R 14 Rob't 38
WINGATE, CAROLINE 32 Daniel 39
    ELISHE PARKS 76 EMILY 39
    Hickson 32 James 63 NANCY 14
    119 ROSY ANN 63 SALLY 77-78
    125 Sarah Ann 13 SARAH ANN
    39 Severn 99 Southy 102 119
    Wm 24 76 78
WISE, ANNE 79 ELEANOR D 23
    FRANCES 39 Jno Jr 2 Jno R 23

WISE (cont)
    Johannes 67 87-88 John 28 79
    101 LEAH 59 MARGT H 101
    MARY R 38 MARY 32 Peter 101
    SARAH 101 Thos P 18 Tully R 17
    38 Zachariah 21 29
WOOD, Jas 66 MARGARET 72
    REBECKA 33 SALLY 112 Wm 33
    42 56 72 93
WOODHOUSE, SUSAN BISHOP 77
WOODWARD, WELTHA 34
WOOSER, Jacob 16
WRIGHT, SALLY 68
WYATT, ELIZABETH S 63 John 63
    PATSEY 108 SALLY 84 Susan 84
    Wm 91 Wm Jr 10 69 103
YARDLY, ROSE 84
YERBY, ANNIE E 62 Geo T 2 8 28
    127 George T 42
YERLY, Geo T 92
YETMAN, ELIZABETH 31 John 31
YOUNG, ELIZABETH B 67
    ELIZABETH P 93 ELIZABETH W
    15 Ezekiel 74 103 George H 2
    James 3 41 57 104 Jno 81 Jno T
    74 John 15 MARY A T 57 Rich'd
    8 80-81 Richard 67 101 SARAH
    A H 2 Thomas 34 40 63 74 93
    Thos 31

www.ingramcontent.com/pod-product-compliance
Lightning Source LLC
Chambersburg PA
CBHW071423160426
43195CB00013B/1786